THE RISE OF
ANDREW JACKSON

THE RISE OF
ANDREW
JACKSON

MYTH, MANIPULATION, AND THE MAKING OF MODERN POLITICS

DAVID S. HEIDLER
AND JEANNE T. HEIDLER

BASIC BOOKS
New York

Basic Books
Hachette Book Group
1290 Avenue of the Americas, New York, NY 10104
www.basicbooks.com

Printed in the United States of America

First Edition: October 2018

Published by Basic Books, an imprint of Perseus Books, LLC, a subsidiary of Hachette Book Group, Inc. The Basic Books name and logo is a trademark of the Hachette Book Group.

The Hachette Speakers Bureau provides a wide range of authors for speaking events. To find out more, go to www.hachettespeakersbureau.com or call (866) 376-6591.

The publisher is not responsible for websites (or their content) that are not owned by the publisher.

PRINT BOOK INTERIOR DESIGN BY JEFF WILLIAMS.

Names: Heidler, David Stephen, 1955- author. | Heidler, Jeanne T., author.
Title: The rise of Andrew Jackson : myth, manipulation, and the making of modern politics / David S. Heidler and Jeanne T. Heidler.
Description: New York : Basic Books, 2018.
Identifiers: LCCN 2018015938| ISBN 9780465097562 (hardcover) | ISBN 9780465097579 (ebook)
Subjects: LCSH: Jackson, Andrew, 1767-1845. | Presidents--United States--Election--1828. | Political campaigns--United States--History--19th century. | Political parties—United States--History--19th century. | Political culture--United States--History--19th century. | United States--History--1815-1861. | Presidents--United States--Biography. | United States--Politics and government--1829-1837.

Classification: LCC E381 .H45 2018 | DDC 973.5/6092 [B] —dc23

LC record available at https://lccn.loc.gov/2018015938]

ISBNs: 978-0-465-09756-2 (hardcover), 978-0-465-09757-9 (ebook)

LSC-C

10 9 8 7 6 5 4 3 2 1

To our brothers

Clare D. Heidler III

John A. Heidler

Michael A. Twiggs

"Friends given by nature"

CONTENTS

ILLUSTRATIONS

EDITORIAL NOTE

We have not corrected most spelling and punctuation errors in quotations from correspondence, diaries, and newspapers. Such errors were frequent in the early nineteenth century and to indicate them as accurately transcribed with the insertion of *sic* seemed to heckle the writer more than inform the reader. Only in cases when confusion might result have we used *sic*. Otherwise, imaginative spellers and eccentric grammarians have been allowed to speak in the pages that follow free from a pedant's pen.

During the 1828 campaign, the famous engraver James Longacre copied a Ralph Earl portrait of Andrew Jackson that was sold to raise money for the campaign. The practice would be expanded in all future presidential campaigns. (Library of Congress)

INTRODUCTION

T HE COMMON PEOPLE OF AMERICA ADORED ANDREW JACKSON. No matter how far he traveled from his humble origins or how high he climbed above them, they always viewed him as a reflection of themselves. His first world was the frontier of the remote Carolina Upcountry, and the self-reliant folk of places like that could judge his angular face, calloused hands, and sinewed limbs as familiar features of a makeshift and hardscrabble life. Like him, many Americans ended the Revolutionary War with empty chairs by hearths reminding them of the highest toll of all in the quest for liberty. Like him, they endured deprivation with courage and loss with resilience. These plain folk intuitively admired a man who settled disputes quickly and whose horizons were not cluttered by doubt and anxiety, a man with a sense of self so unshakeable and stubborn that it could make him seem right against all comers even when he was wrong—especially when he was wrong.

As a rising man, Jackson entered an honorable profession (the law), attached himself to important people, acquired property, married well (though under strange circumstances), and rose to lead the Tennessee militia. He became a public man—for public men were the dominant people of the American scene—and entered politics though he possessed little political skill and a poor temperament for political life. His militia career provided him with

I

a constituency, and his military exploits, though brief and limited, were so gaudy that they made him a hero. He first appeared to the public at a time of seeming decline and possible revival. In the early decades of the nineteenth century, most Americans no longer lived on the frontier, and according to some, they were getting soft and losing the pluck that had made them hardy colonizers and happy warriors.

A vague fear arose that the great accomplishments of the American Revolution were fading away because a delicate people, corrupted by comfort and cynical about government, could not remember the cost of liberty. Andrew Jackson's image as the man who could reverse this disturbing drift began with his stunning victory over the British at New Orleans in January 1815. Nine years later, his first attempt to win the presidency saw his supporters insisting that he could renew the nation, and by 1828, most voters agreed that Jackson was crucial to securing America's future, in that he would draw on the best of its humble but energetic past.

In this setting and from these events, the remarkable rise of Andrew Jackson seemed to happen spontaneously, but there was much more to it than that. As early as 1816, a small group of people began working on a grand political project. Jackson's reputation as a peerless military hero fueled their enthusiasm and formed the foundation for his ascendant political career. Jackson's promoters harnessed a previously inchoate political movement spurred by broad discontent. People fumed over government corruption. They blamed the country's central bank for its wrecked economy. They chafed at the disdainful elitism of their "betters," who expected the deference of olden days to survive the passing fancy of democratic politics. Yeomen, mechanics, tradesmen, and small merchants were unembarrassed by the charge that democracy was the cudgel of the mob. They seemed to be yearning for an unshakeable and self-aware man ready to do right against all comers, even if he was wrong.

These ordinary, disaffected Americans voiced their resentment and rancor, but their utterances were so varied as to be discordant, and they were seemingly fated to remain so until the gaunt, cantankerous man appeared. He was nothing if not unshakeable and self-aware, but the growing mass of his followers at the start were neither, despite their veneer of purpose. Nevertheless, Andrew Jackson's boundless appeal for voters from starkly different social and economic backgrounds energized a broad and diverse population among whom quarrels were unavoidable.

People with different hopes and disparate dreams supported Andrew Jackson not only because of who he had been but also for what he seemed to be. A manufacturer in Pennsylvania who wanted protectionism saw Andrew Jackson as favoring stiff tariffs. A South Carolina planter who wanted free trade envisioned Jackson culling collectors and opening ports to the commerce of the world. Disgruntled Old Republicans nostalgic for Jeffersonian purity saw Jackson as a man intent on limiting the growing government and trimming its expansive Treasury. Federalists marginalized by the War of 1812 and vanishing under the relentless political march of their foes found a man ready to reject the quasi-religious tests of party and faction to allow them again to participate in the public commons and national government. A masterful politician with a scheme to make patronage and influence the bond of an invincible party perceived in Jackson a man who valued loyalty and would embrace ways to encourage it. A purist who believed patronage debased public service and promoted corruption saw a virtuous hero ready to quash special interests and stop their raids on the public till.

As people with opposite views on national issues found themselves in the same political movement, the men organizing it were able to diminish the importance of those differences and control a rambunctious movement while creating the impression that the man they were promoting was its founder. In the beginning, Andrew

Jackson's closest friend in Nashville, John Overton, led a group of managers and handlers whose varied backgrounds brought to their task an assortment of valuable skills. The wise and measured Overton first saw the possibilities Jackson's popularity presented in a political setting, and it was Overton who assembled the first team to promote Jackson's candidacy. This group, called the Nashville Junto, was a committee of talents. Among them was John Eaton, a scribe who wrote a laudatory biography and who later became a senator to protect Jackson's reputation in Washington. Editor George Wilson made his Nashville *Gazette* the first Jackson newspaper with a flair for disguising propaganda as hard news. Sam Houston was the young lieutenant in Jackson's army who had proven his mettle by surviving wounds that would have killed another man but that only spurred Houston to greater exertion. William B. Lewis, disdained by others for his obsequious manner and oily charm, could listen for gossip and quash it, forge deals without seeming to, and make promises as profitable as they were provisional.

Even with real talent supporting Jackson for high political office, the effort could have foundered on divisions caused by conflicting purposes and differing philosophies. The variety of views, in fact, would only multiply as the movement around the man grew and broadened. Many of the men who worked tirelessly to see Andrew Jackson elected were not what later generations would call Jacksonians. Some wanted to eliminate all property qualifications for the vote, which was a fundamental part of Jacksonian Democracy, but in the 1820s, just as many supporters thought too many people already voted. Men who wanted unimpeded territorial expansion, which became another tenet of Jacksonianism, labored and propagandized alongside men who feared that opening the West would diminish the political influence of the East. For every strict constructionist, there was a man eager to make the federal government less limited and more active. Some Jacksonians masked their artful use of patronage with the euphemism "rotation in office"—one would slip by calling it the "spoils system"—but trading government posts for political support was anathema to other Jackson loyalists in the 1820s. Men who figured prominently in Jackson's bids for the presidency sat on the boards of banks and lobbied for the establishment of Bank of the United States branches in their hometowns, while others would later denounce banks for what they called the manipulation of currency and credit to cheat ordinary people.

Because of these inconsistencies among the men who joined Andrew Jackson's campaigns and those who would govern after his victory, and because of the contradictions within the great mass of people who elected him, we have chosen to call his supporters in the 1820s Jacksonites rather than Jacksonians. Jacksonians supported universal white manhood suffrage, territorial expansion, and the elimination of the Second Bank of the United States; Jacksonites were those willing to use Jackson's popularity to achieve political power. Jacksonites had in common the quest to make Jackson president and to rise to powerful positions in their own right as a result of his victory. Some Jacksonites did not agree with Jackson on any issues but were willing to promote his fortunes to achieve theirs.

Jacksonites could be Jacksonians, and some would become Jacksonians, but the difference between the two, whether slight or wide, had to do with the difference between politics and philosophy. Jacksonians were true believers who knew in their bones that broader democracy benefited the country, that the government in Washington was corrupt, and that the Bank of the United States was unconstitutional. They believed that limiting the power of the national government would go far to cure the nation's ills and that state and local governments were the bulwarks of the people's freedom. Jacksonites believed in winning elections—and in arguments pitting philosophy against practicality, they had a point. Without their most basic impulse to dislodge the traditional ways of politics, the Jacksonian moment might never have happened.

Jacksonites faced a task larger than that of dismantling traditional politics and erecting something in its place. All the talk of promoting the interests of the common people, restoring honest government, expanding democracy, enhancing economic freedom, protecting Indians by relocating them, and curbing the moneyed interests could not completely mask the fact that the man at the center of the political project had a nasty temper, a violent streak, and a past littered with appalling lapses in judgment. Yet scores of operatives, handlers, editors, and politicians would deftly manage their unlikely project, which would eventually include a political genius in Martin Van Buren. Over the course of fifteen years, they changed American politics by creating an irresistible force out of a man whose sole claim on the public's affections derived from a thirty-minute battle on the banks of the Mississippi River in early 1815. They did this by launching the first modern presidential campaign in American history, the first instance of deliberate image building and mythmaking and of skillful manipulation of public perception and popular opinion.

American politics had from the beginning featured candidates mixing with the people and even holding social events. "Swilling the planters with bumbo" was the custom of plying voters with a rum-based punch, but the scope of such behavior was limited by the small number of men who had the right to vote. Even the largest instance of widespread activity before the 1820s was on a fairly small scale. John Beckley, the first clerk of the House of Representatives, did work in Pennsylvania for Thomas Jefferson during the elections of 1796 and 1800 that foreshadowed Jacksonite practices of the 1820s. Beckley enlisted local leaders to write letters and blanketed the countryside with ballots of Republican electors to

establish name recognition for Jefferson's ticket. But Beckley anticipated Jacksonite innovations primarily in his willingness to enter
the fray of partisan politics, which the Founding generation spurned
as unseemly. To be sure, the gentry rule that the presidential office
should seek the man rather than the other way around was not always strictly adhered to. But appearing to obey it prevented the use
of practices associated with a national campaign.[1]

The broader acceptance of outright politicking in the 1820s disclosed a major shift in attitudes about the proper methods of winning
elections. The men who achieved Andrew Jackson's transformation
into a political force saw nothing unseemly about the way they went
about it. They groomed him, protected him, and belled the cat of
his temper. They published quaint stories of his kindness and heroic
tales of his courage. They contrived ways to make him seem measured and statesmanlike. They made him the friend of debtors (he
dismissed them as deadbeats), the advocate for low tariffs or high
ones (he had no opinion on the matter), and the enemy of grasping
bankers (who were some of his best friends). He was made an icon
in the tradition of George Washington, though he had been among
those most critical of Washington at the end of his presidency. Jackson was made the ideological heir of Thomas Jefferson, though he
had openly opposed President Jefferson, and the Sage of Monticello
himself was openly dismayed by Jackson's rising popularity.

Such obstacles were minor inconveniences for clever men with
supple scruples. At first, armed with little more than intuition and
flinty resolve, Jackson's promoters linked him with the spirit of discontent that emerged after 1815. From those initial efforts, a gradual
blurring of the movement and the man proceeded until he ceased
to be the beneficiary of a popular program and instead became the
personification of it. By then, the little group of intuitive and resolute men had become legion, and they were being organized by Van

Buren, a mastermind with a national vision and the ability to make all things seem local. By then, Andrew Jackson had become wildly and irresistibly popular. He was meant to be.

The Jacksonites also innovated within existing political practices. Newspapers had been a part of politics in colonial times, though libel laws discouraged direct attacks on opponents, a restriction that vanished by the 1790s when Thomas Jefferson and Alexander Hamilton used rival newspapers to promote their views and attack opponents. The Jackson campaign pioneered uses for newspapers during the 1824 campaign. After Jackson lost that election in the House of Representatives to John Quincy Adams, Jacksonites increased their efforts to spend money as no campaign had ever done before. They financed editors to encourage attacks on the Adams administration, and where no papers friendly to Jackson existed, they founded them. Their newspaper network's highly disciplined message appeared in stories and opinion pieces pulled from subscription services and reprinted in local sheets in ways that prefigured the tactics of a modern press syndicate.

This was only one hallmark of a finely tuned and an always improving organization. Starting with the Nashville Junto, Jacksonites became adept at coordinating local activities on a national level. During the 1828 campaign, they set up committees at important hubs and staffed them with influential community leaders who were, in turn, directed and controlled by central committees in Washington and Nashville. These forerunners of Republican and Democratic National Committees instructed localities to hold Jackson rallies and parades, raise (Old) Hickory Poles, and distribute inexpensive likenesses of Jackson along with gimcracks lauding him and denouncing his dwindling number of critics. They organized straw polls after prudently determining favorable results, and they held mass public meetings to pass resolutions the local committee carefully drafted to ensure acceptance. The dutiful Jackson press

covered everything with a consistent message rendered in sufficiently different language to create the appearance that support for
the Hero was not only massive but spontaneous and diverse.

At a time when political parties were still considered soiled creatures of faction and parasitic entities that divided the nation, Adams men discovered too late that the tight organization of dissimilar
coalitions had become the key to victory. Though Jackson's supporters did not constitute a distinct party—everyone called himself a
Republican during those years—they began behaving like one, and
their opponents gradually realized that disdaining the new methods
of politics was a sure path to defeat. They watched helplessly as
Jacksonites learned from their loss in 1824 and proved amazingly
agile and able to attract talented people to their cause.

Though historians have looked at the elections of 1824 and 1828
as culturally, politically, and socially transformative, no one has provided a thorough telling of how Jackson and his managers created a
candidate and sold him to the American people. Unabashed admirers of Andrew Jackson are fewer now than in times past, but their
work still dominates the historical landscape by its sheer volume.
Nowadays critics eager to denounce Jackson grow in number because they condemn him as a racist whose attitude toward Indians
alone merits his banishment from the American pantheon as well as
American folding money. The admirers have a tendency to lionize
Jacksonites as Jacksonians with talk of common men rising and ordinary people gaining political clout. The critics hold in contempt
the people who supported Andrew Jackson as racists themselves, as
people spitting, scratching, and cussing while skinning their knuck-
les on the dirt floors of their jerry-built shacks. For our part, we have
labored in these pages to move beyond or, better yet, before caricature. Our aim is to understand Andrew Jackson, to comprehend the
supporters who shaped his candidacy, and to hear the voters who
made him president.

Because there were no formal political parties and factions supported a variety of favorite sons, it is easy to conclude that the campaigns of the 1820s were popularity contests devoid of issues. But doing so misses the point. The cunning men behind Jackson's candidacy convinced a plurality of the American people in 1824 that Andrew Jackson was on their side, whatever side it was. They made the people believe he shared their concerns, whether they planted cotton in the red clay of Georgia, worked a lathe in a mote-shot Philadelphia shop, or scored the earth for DeWitt Clinton's Erie Canal. When the numbers those people represented were insufficient for victory in 1824, Jacksonites and the man at their head redoubled their efforts at the methods that had worked, such as mass meetings, partisan coordination of the press, and lionization of their champion as a man of action forged by martial challenges. And after the failure of 1824 seemed to provide irrefutable evidence of corruption, they amplified their earlier calls to flush the sewer of national politics as practiced by the denizens of Washington, DC. They described the men there as having elevated the business of government over the people's interests, confusing the meanings of self-interest and public service. Doubtless, many of them believed this, but others realized that it was enough to act as if they did, which could pass for a reasonable definition of politics in its modern form.

IN THE SUMMER of 1845, a young portrait painter named George Healy arrived at Henry Clay's home outside Lexington, Kentucky, to paint the great man's likeness. Healy had just come from Andrew Jackson's Hermitage, where his portrait of Jackson would be the last of the old man from life. Withered and ailing, Jackson died shortly after the work was finished, but Healy had seen the younger champion of a political movement who gave his name to an age, and that is who he painted. This was by then an image of Jackson as imaginary as the one the men who made him president had created decades earlier, and both would prove enduring. Clay, curious about Healy's opinion of a lifelong enemy, asked whether Jackson was a "sincere" man, in the sense of frankness, candor, and authenticity.

"If General Jackson was not sincere," Healy said curtly, with the irritation of an admirer having to defend his idol, "then I do not know the meaning of the word."

Henry Clay nodded with weary resignation over the young man's apparent esteem for Jackson. He sighed. "I see that you, like all who approached that man, were fascinated by him."[2]

An entire generation of Americans would have said, *Just so.* As we will see, they had their reasons.

PROLOGUE

J OHN OVERTON READ THE LETTER. IT WAS A HURTFUL DOCU-
ment. That it denied his modest request for a small patronage
post might have wounded his pride, but worse was the letter's
author. Overton had tried to secure the position delicately by avoiding a direct request of his friend Andrew Jackson. Instead, he had
contacted William B. Lewis, his friend's toady. Overton did not need
the post for money, though he had a prudent man's mild anxiety that
there was never enough money for a possible emergency. Nor did
he want it for influence, about which he was uniquely indifferent.
Since helping to make Andrew Jackson the president of the United
States, Overton had visited him in the presidential residence only
one time. In that, he resembled quiet, retiring John Coffee, both of
them fierce in their attachment to Jackson but casual about what it
could do for them. Good men defined friendship that way. Overton
thought of himself as a good man.

He did not think William Berkeley Lewis was. During the years
of the long political quest, Lewis had been universally disliked in
Jackson's inner circle and was loathed by some who chafed at his
tattling, always served up sadly, and his unctuous manner, always
perfectly adjusted to fit Jackson's moods. The tone of Lewis's letter to
Overton was grating, a strange mélange of haughtiness and simpering. The post that Overton wanted, Lewis said, was not significant

enough for a man of his standing. It also carried duties that would be too taxing for Overton's health. Then Lewis went on for too long, as he was inclined to do, explaining some political realities. It would not be a good idea for Overton to have the post because he lived in Nashville—"a small place" in Lewis's words—"and it might be considered, by the citizens of other states, as bestowing too many favors on it."[1]

It was more than galling—the master engineer at the beginning of Jackson's campaign for the presidency being lectured to about politics and patronage by the likes of William Lewis. Overton could almost hear Lewis speaking the words he had written in his hushed and mildly urgent way, with his face a concerned frown and eyes insincerely sympathetic, a tone and an expression everyone had seen hundreds of times during the hard work of tamping down scandals and cultivating support. Lewis had been good at both, at least. Even John Eaton conceded that much to the bootlicker, even though Eaton was one who did not merely dislike but loathed Lewis.

John Overton folded the letter to file it away. Perhaps he would read it again, but probably not. Filing pieces of paper was a long-held habit that reflected his passion for order, but it had become less about keeping a careful chronicle and more a sign of his eccentricities, such as covering his bald pate with a handkerchief and mindlessly working his toothless gums like a forest ruminant. The filing habit had produced an enormous archive of paper, including a thick bundle of letters from Jackson, which formed a substantial portion of it. Overton had carefully ordered them over the years, and they spanned a half century. It was all there: the social ascent, the legal career, the violence to kill the gossip over the girl, the shady association with the alleged traitor, the military exploits, the political quest. Overton had been thinking about these letters from Andrew Jackson for months now, particularly about what to do with them. It weighed more on his mind of late, topping a list of worries that made for troubled days and wakeful nights. John Overton was fairly sure he was dying.

He and Jackson had known each other ever since Jackson first showed up on the western frontier. Overton was of Scottish ancestry and of Virginia stock, a family that moved from the Tidewater to the western part of the colony where John was born in 1766. After the American Revolution, the migrations continued. John and several siblings moved to Kentucky, and finally John shifted to the Mero District of North Carolina on the Cumberland River, the place that would become Tennessee. In those days, it was beyond the edge of civilization. The little settlement called Nashville was merely a collection of blockhouses inhabited by intrepid pioneers living in a wilderness of dangers.

The widow Rachel Donelson took in boarders, and Overton settled into a homestead where he shared a room and a bed with fellow lodger Andrew Jackson. Though only a year separated them in age, Jackson seemed coltish while Overton always seemed old. He instantly became the best friend of Jackson, full of sass and vinegar at twenty-two. More, Overton became Jackson's confidant as the tall raw-boned redhead fell in love with the widow Donelson's daughter, a slip of a (married) girl also named Rachel. None of these three could have suspected that their budding relations—both the friendly one between single men on a remote frontier and the romantic one between an impetuous lad and a fetching girl—would have profound consequences for their country.

So many years ago, a lifetime, in fact, from there to the vantage of old John Overton, who at sixty-six had finally grown into his age. He was a small man who had always seemed frail, but in younger days his face showed breeding and refinement. He began to lose his hair early and tried to hide it with bangs over his high forehead, but his eyes remained expressive into old age. His toothless mouth looked as if he had "swallowed his lips" and made his firm chin jut

Andrew Jackson's oldest friend in Nashville, Judge John Overton had the vision of making Jackson president and organized
the first campaign that almost made it happen. Through the
groups known as the Nashville Junto and the Nashville Central Committee, he contributed to Jackson's ultimate victory in
1828. (In S. G. Heiskell, *Andrew Jackson and Early Tennessee History* [Nashville, TN: American
Printing, 1920], 2:122.)

upward almost to touch a nose once Roman, now a beak. When
he had formed plans to make Jackson president, Overton's broad
mouth often held the hint of a smile, and his measured voice gave
soothing assurance that here stood a man who knew what he was
talking about when he chose to talk about something. Overton was
prudent by nature and guarded from experience. These qualities

alone made him an invaluable ally of a man who was temperamentally impetuous with a reputation for volatility.

Also, Overton was rich. Some said he was so beyond measure. Like Jackson, he was a lawyer and had become a judge, but land speculation was his business. His mastery of the tedious details of questionable titles and illegitimate claims enabled him to buy and sell acreage shrewdly and profitably. He and Jackson often were partners in land ventures, including the purchase of a coveted expanse at Chickasaw Bluffs. At first, the land was of seemingly little value because of its Indian inhabitants, but after Jackson cleared them away with one of the treaties he described as negotiated agreements, the site became Memphis.

Overton had no political ambitions for himself. Rather, he became a wise counselor who was always sensitive to the best possible option among an array of difficult choices. In 1814, shortly after Jackson was regionally celebrated for his initial military exploits, Overton assessed the chances for Jackson's political career. He thought the Tennessee gubernatorial race would be a good start, but after Jackson's victory at New Orleans in 1815, the best possible option was no longer to become the procurator of a provincial outpost. Andrew Jackson should be president. The small group that became known as the Nashville Junto formed in Overton's mind years before it fell into place one evening in a bustling town on the Cumberland. It happened amid clouds of cigar smoke and hearty laughter, the kind of gathering where men begin to see the main chance, the right champion, and slowly close their hands around the possible to shape it into a certainty. The man with the sure voice sat at their head that night, and for several thousand nights thereafter, and nobody, not even old General Jackson himself, thought to question his intuition, let alone his judgment.

It made the letter from Lewis all the more galling. But Overton would only file it away, another thing of this earth that was of fading importance, like dipping snuff with Margaret Eaton or listening to Emily Donelson play the pianoforte. He was never one for grudges, in any case, just as he had never been particularly pious, and neither trait was going to change now as he contemplated a rendezvous with his Maker. At most, he filed away galling letters and bowed to the sensibilities of religious companions, especially Rachel's, by tempering his habit of registering exasperation by saying, "By Jupiter!" rather than "By God!"—though he could comically forget and turn the exclamation into "By G—Jupiter!" It made him an entertaining companion, even as he approached the end with stoicism and resignation.[2]

Beneath that characteristic calm, though, was a concern. His archive of paper included sheaf after sheaf with broad strokes scrawled in anger and solicitude and all the emotions between, with secrets and plans, and always ending with the large name of the large man, his friend, now president. There was too much in those letters about everything, but especially about the series of calculated risks that had won the prize. Overton made his decision.

CHAPTER 1

HICKORY

THE WAR OF 1812 ENDED WITH A VICTORY SO RESOUNDING that most Americans forgot that, for the most part, the conflict with Britain had been incompetently prosecuted and rife with catastrophes. Its first two years were a chronicle of military ineffectiveness on the Canadian border, political impotence in Washington, and dissent bordering on treason in New England. Even pride over the stirring victories of United States frigates on the high seas was short-lived, because the British navy quickly reestablished its dominance, blockading American ships in port. Then Napoleon Bonaparte's defeat in the spring of 1814 freed thousands of British regulars to descend on North America and smash the pesky Americans whose little fit of temper had been an annoying distraction while Britain fought France for its life. The British government always saw the American war as an affront. To them, it made the United States an undeclared ally of Napoleon. British resentment ran deep, and the government relished the chance to give the Yanks a good thrashing, one richly deserved.

It looked as if that would happen just as the British planned. In the summer of 1814, a massive offensive thundered down from

Canada into New York, with redcoats thick on the ground and Royal Navy vessels straining their masts on Lake Champlain. A squadron of enormous ships under clouds of sail roamed Chesapeake Bay and landed a British army to march on Washington. That army scattered Maryland militiamen and then staged a festival of arson and vandalism in the American capital. Congress and President James Madison fled. Jaunty British officers held a mock banquet in the presidential residence before setting it on fire. They burned the Capitol and other public buildings too.

Even though American forces turned back the invasion of New York and foiled the British occupation of Baltimore, the country's mood was grim as the government limped back to Washington and surveyed the smoldering ruins. Meanwhile, reports of a vanguard contacting Indians in Spanish Florida pointed to a troubling shift in British plans. America's underpopulated South featured rivers as ready-made avenues of invasion to the interior. Angry Indians could become British allies. New Orleans was a plum target—"beauty and booty," as the British thought of the city.

Britain's coiling southern campaign proceeded at a leisurely pace. As ships and gunboats gathered in Jamaican waters and the army that had burned Washington assembled at Negril Bay, there was no sense of urgency; victory was inevitable. It was sure to happen when the Duke of Wellington's veterans routed the southern version of the Maryland militia, the "dirty shirts," as the British derisively called them. There was plenty of time to choose the place and pick the fight they were sure to win.

Yet an unexpected variable altered Britain's fate in North America. The irresistible power of Britain's assembled forces had not reckoned on meeting an immovable object. He was not much to look at, to be sure. Standing some six-foot-one and weighing less than 150 pounds, the immovable object resembled a clothed skeleton. If necessary, he could live off acorns. Plenty of men believed he could chew nails. His followers were confident he would kill anything that crossed him without pausing to weigh the costs or ponder the consequences. He brooked no disobedience, loathed disloyalty, and, like a skilled predator, could smell the stink of fear on a man as well as he could on a varmint. His long, angular face was comically equine, but his eyes, the transparent blue of a robin's egg, warned against laughter.

The Indians the British counted on as allies called him "Sharp Knife." The Americans the British counted on to break and run knew him too. They feared him and loved him, sometimes at the same time. They saw an unbending and unbreakable will in the set of his jaw, the eruptions of his brittle temper, a raw courage to kill anything that crossed him. He would not be humbled or hewed. It was the reason they called him "Old Hickory."

The British eventually learned that their Indian allies had second thoughts about fighting Sharp Knife again. Even worse for the British, the dirty shirts who loved and feared Old Hickory would rather die than risk his ire by running. And when it was over, and the bodies of Wellington's veterans littered the Chalmette Plain, Americans everywhere settled yet another name on Andrew Jackson. "Hero" might have seemed the ultimate accolade, but it was merely the prelude for a better one, the best one of all.

———

Most of these events almost never happened because Jackson's war got off to a disastrous start. By 1812, Andrew Jackson had served as the major general of the Tennessee militia, Second Division, for ten years without commanding men in the field, let alone fighting a battle. When war with Britain seemed certain, Jackson offered his two thousand men to help invade Canada, but President James Madison's administration merely acknowledged the offer and otherwise ignored it.

Madison had his reasons. Six years earlier, Jackson had in some way participated in Aaron Burr's mysterious plans that the United States government eventually deemed a conspiracy. Burr was arrested and tried for treason. Jackson's participation was slight, and he wasn't alone in judging Burr innocent—a jury in Richmond refused to convict Burr—but the affair left Jackson with a trail of enemies, many of them influential. He had railed against President Thomas Jefferson, Madison's great friend and political soul mate, for arresting the wrong man, and he had made no secret that he thought General James Wilkinson was the real culprit in whatever evil plans were afoot. Jackson was so fixated on the perceived injustices riddling the Burr affair that he supported a challenger against James Madison's presidential candidacy in 1808. "I'll tell you why they don't employ Jackson," Burr at the time told a young New York politician named Martin Van Buren: "it's because he's a friend of mine."[1]

In 1812, Jefferson was in retirement at Monticello, and Madison was the president. James Wilkinson was still a senior general in the United States Army, just as he had been during the Burr affair when, in some people's estimation, Jackson had slandered him. And so it was on October 21 of that year, almost four months to the day from the declaration of war on Great Britain, that Secretary of War William Eustis sent a request to Tennessee governor Willie Blount with a notable omission. The War Department wanted Blount to raise fifteen hundred volunteers for federal service to help James Wilkinson defend New Orleans. The snub was subtle but clear: Eustis did not mention Andrew Jackson—the government wanted any Tennessean but him.

Blount knew that putting the state's men in service without the popular Andrew Jackson was politically impossible, especially if those men were to serve under the universally disliked James Wilkinson. It took him a while to decide, but Blount finally chose to defy the implicit wish of the Madison administration. Pulling one of the blank commissions from the stack the War Department had sent to Nashville, Governor Blount scratched in Jackson's name as a major general of the United States Volunteers. When he informed Jackson of Madison's call for soldiers, he spoke plainly: "You will command them." Blount refrained from telling Jackson that the federal government hadn't wanted him.[2]

Jackson didn't like the idea of serving under Wilkinson, but he was willing to swallow the "bitter pill" to serve the country. He assembled officers and men for the journey to Louisiana, but bad luck plagued the undertaking from its start. Brutal cold froze the Cumberland River and prevented the delivery of supplies, including weapons. Problems with pay had men grumbling as they shivered week after week in a makeshift camp with little to do but nurse their grievances. By the end of December, his army still in Nashville, Jackson sensed "the seeds of mutiny."[3]

Blount had wanted to follow the traditional militia procedure of allowing the rank and file to elect field officers, but Jackson insisted on picking his deputies, so Blount reluctantly agreed. The result was a group Jackson knew and trusted. The topmost were not all tough men, but they were at least competent: Tom Benton and William Hall in charge of his infantry, John Coffee in command of his cavalry, Billy Carroll as his brigade inspector, neighbor William Berkeley Lewis as his quartermaster, earnest John Reid as his aide.

Coffee was one of the tough ones. He had been a surveyor before a soldier, and until recently a clerk before a colonel, but he approached new jobs with a laconic confidence, and he seemed to have been born on horseback. Actually, he was born in Virginia, but some would say that was the same thing. Coffee grew up in North Carolina before moving to Nashville in 1798; when he was elevated to cavalry commander, he and Jackson had known each other for fifteen years, and fondly from the first. Coffee was remarkable in never having quarreled with Jackson during all the years they were business partners, close friends, and finally family. Coffee wed Mary Donelson, Rachel Jackson's niece, in 1809. Mary, called Polly, was a favorite with everyone, including Uncle Jackson, so the match especially pleased him. Coffee might have been surprised when after the wedding ceremony, Andrew Jackson wordlessly handed him a sheaf of papers neatly tied. Coffee recognized them. They were his IOUs for loans from Jackson, now forgiven, a wedding present. Surely Coffee thanked him, but he would have more or less mumbled it, which was his way.

Three years later, Polly and John Coffee still acted like newlyweds. She was pretty with dark Donelson eyes and a mouth whose full lips suggested a bit of a pout, and he was gallant. His tender letters revealed a perpetual suitor, a hidden side of a man shy with the rest of the world. But bashfulness also masked a man good to have around when a fight was brewing. Large and lumbering, Coffee was slow to speak and slower to anger, but that made every single word he uttered sound important or ominous, depending on his mood. He was a lamb with his Polly, but his anger, once raised, made him dangerous beyond belief.[4]

The volunteers milling around Nashville with time on their hands liked their hard liquor and raucous carousing. They wanted their government pay for both and could get feisty if denied one or prohibited from the other, and if the money went missing. Colonel Coffee could calm things down just by showing up. Swaggering men stopped still, went silent, and studied their shoes. Everyone had heard about Coffee's anger. Nobody wanted to see it.[5]

By the start of 1813, after the soldiers finally received pay, Jackson believed he could begin the journey to New Orleans. He had to cover the expedition's expenses with a personal loan of $1,650, but his high spirits more than compensated for the imposition. He wrote to acting secretary of war James Monroe (Eustis was fired after the war's early military disasters) that his force numbered 2,070 men. His pride that it exceeded the War Department's request was evident. Nor was this all. Everyone, said Jackson, was primed to answer "the call of their country to execute the will of the Government; who have no constitutional scruples; and if the Government orders, will rejoice at the opportunity of placing the American Eagle on the ramparts of Mobile, Pensacola, and Fort St. Augustine. And effectually banishing from the southern coasts all British influence. At New-Orleans I shall anxiously await the orders of the Government."[6]

Monroe was fortunate not to be in the War Department when Jackson's letter arrived because John Armstrong had taken over the position on January 5. Even so, he might have winced over the bluster and the remark about men willing to act without the restraint of "constitutional scruples." The official explanation about defending New Orleans was supposed to mask the government's real plans, which involved offensive operations against Spanish Florida. Jackson's way of announcing things best left unsaid was one of the many reasons the government was wary of him.

Jackson started out from Nashville on January 10, but the bad portents continued. At Natchez, several letters from Wilkinson were waiting for him. The first was overly cordial, almost syrupy, but the others were strangely evasive and defensive. All of them emphasized that Jackson was not to come to New Orleans. Among other impediments, Wilkinson said, he had no place in New Orleans to lodge a couple thousand Tennesseans. Another letter told Jackson to be ready for hot work near Mobile or Pensacola and repeated the order to stay put in Natchez. These were troubling communications. Wilkinson had promised shelter and provisions, but days became weeks and Jackson remained almost two hundred miles north of New Orleans with his men exposed to the elements and forced to forage for food. Finally, in mid-March, Jackson received a short note from Secretary of War Armstrong telling him, in so many words, to go home. His men were no longer needed and were consequently dismissed from the service. He was to turn over to Wilkinson all federal property, especially weapons, and return to Tennessee.[7]

It was a stunning blow, and Jackson had difficulty understanding it. At first, he thought it might be a mistake. He muttered that Armstrong "must have been drunk when he wrote" the dismissal order. But then he began to believe something worse. He did not know that the War Department's decision to dismiss the Tennessee Volunteers was a result of Congress's refusal to fund a West Florida invasion, so he immediately suspected a hidden purpose behind the entire episode. Until Jackson had objected, Wilkinson had been trying to enlist the Tennessee Volunteers in the regular army. Jackson was convinced that a conspiracy against him was under way. He believed that the order to turn over weapons was meant to make his men helpless as they marched through potentially hostile Indian country. The choice of being scalped or joining the regular army made recruiting all the easier for Wilkinson. Jackson became irate as he thought about it, and there soon followed one of his explosions.[8]

He fulminated with a purpose. He had more than two thousand men more than eight hundred miles from home with no money, no food, and no transportation. Jackson barked that his men would, by the eternal, keep their weapons. He would not see them stranded, hungry, and helpless, and he would not see them scooped up by Wilkinson like so many wastrels at a back-alley saloon. He would take everyone home. He shamed Wilkinson into providing enough rations for three weeks. With a loan of $1,000, he purchased and rented eleven wagons to convey the increasing numbers of sick. Marching toward Tennessee, the volunteers faced dense woods, hostile Indians, and high-running creeks. As more men became ill, the wagons could not hold them, and they fell out from the march. Jackson slid off his saddle and lifted one of them onto his horse. His officers wordlessly followed the example. Mile after mile and day after day passed. The rations would not last, so he stopped eating. The men noticed, of course. At first, they had called him "Hickory" in tribute to his toughness, but because they were mostly boys, and everyone looked "old" to them, he soon became "Old Hickory." Andrew Jackson was forty-six.[9]

When he brought them to Nashville at the end of April 1813, he looked a hundred. The government didn't want him, and the entire expedition had been a wasteful embarrassment. But the volunteers wept when they saw the town and cheered when he spurred his horse toward the Hermitage and Mrs. Jackson, his Rachel.

The War of 1812, such as it was, was over for him, it seemed. And yet, his decision to defy his government and keep the weapons was fateful. His resolve to bring his men home was pivotal for everything that followed. The upcoming Creek campaign would be a test, and his miraculous victory at New Orleans would be spectacular.

But that April day in Nashville when weak men found the strength to fill the air with loud noise, that was something more. They were amazed by their deliverance and by the author of it. Andrew Jackson had turned the sobering humiliation into his finest hour.

＝＝＝

THE GOVERNMENT WAS apparently intent on excluding Jackson from the war with Britain, but another conflict would pluck him from obscurity. In 1812, the Creek Indian nation in the Mississippi Territory went to war with itself. It was a civil war, an internal affair coincidental to America's war with Britain, but inevitably the two struggles merged, in part because Jackson, like many Americans, believed all Indians were British pawns. Nothing the British had done sparked the grim fight in the river-laced land that would become Alabama. Creeks called Red Sticks sneered at their brethren for adopting the white farming practices of an American acculturation program. Red Sticks believed Americans were causing Creek cultural disintegration and societal decline. Fueled by a nativist religious resurgence, they went to war on those Creeks they believed to be traitors.[10]

The violence soon spilled over. The government man in charge of the acculturation program was a strong-willed but mild-mannered North Carolina gentleman named Benjamin Hawkins. His long service as an Indian agent dated from 1796. After almost two decades, Hawkins glumly watched his life's work collapse. As the Creek civil war intensified, local whites succumbed to panic and ambushed Red Sticks at Burnt Corn Creek, less than fifty miles north of the Florida line. That was on July 27, 1813, and a month later, on August 30, Red Sticks retaliated at Fort Mims with horrific ferocity. When done, they had killed almost all of the stockade's four hundred inhabitants, whether armed fighting men or women with babes in their arms. Ghastly descriptions of the slaughter quickly spread. White faces turned stony when they heard that the killing had featured methodical mutilation and people burned alive in blockhouse infernos.[11]

The massacre at Fort Mims reanimated Andrew Jackson. At the time, he was ill in bed, his shoulder shattered by a bullet and his left arm useless, the result of a quarrel, Tennessee style. Hearing the news, he came to life. The crisis down south made mere physical impairment a miserable excuse for refusing to do a man's work. He was determined to take the field. As terror and anger gripped the Mississippi Territory and along the borders of Tennessee and Georgia, the federal government called up state and territorial militias. Blount informed Jackson of this new call to service, but Old Hickory was already preparing to summon the men from the Natchez expedition. "We must hasten to the frontier," he told them, "or we will find it drenched in the blood of our fellow-citizens." He sent Coffee ahead with the cavalry and followed with his infantry several days later. By mid-October, they were all racing deep into the heart of Creek country.[12]

"The health of your general is restored," he proclaimed to the Tennessee Volunteers, but that was not true by any measure. Jackson was gravely ill when he left Nashville. His left arm was in a sling, and a spiking fever brought on sweats that soaked his clothes on frosty mornings. The demands of the campaign only made it worse. During the coming winter, the multiple challenges he faced nearly broke him. He would fight Red Sticks, rage at supply contractors, argue with superiors and brother officers, and cope with the diminishing loyalty of starving soldiers, but most of all he would endure the agonies of his broken body, with its ruined innards. Constipation locked him up for days at a time, and then dysentery doubled him over in his saddle or, if he was lucky, at a more convenient location, such as his camp desk. Another bullet from another, older quarrel remained lodged in his lung, and when the coughing started, it sometimes brought up blood. Rheumatism sent sharp pains radiating through his right arm when he reached too eagerly or turned too quickly. His skin was the color of parchment and the texture of leather, and his face was pitted from smallpox that had nearly killed him when he was a mere boy. A white welt on his forehead stood out in relief, a relic of the American Revolution during his time as a prisoner when a British officer had split open Jackson's scalp with a saber for his impertinence in refusing to polish the man's boots.[13]

Early in the new expedition, Jackson's resolve was tested. The infantry took less than a week to reach the Coosa River over mountainous terrain Jackson called "the american alps," but his men felled trees for a stockade there on empty stomachs. Civilian contractors were supposed to supply Jackson's fast-moving column, but they could not travel through the trackless country. The men huddled hungry at the little bastion on the Coosa they named Fort Strother. Jackson knew what hunger could do to men in ordinary times; in trying ones, it could change loyal soldiers into mutineers. He feared famine more than Red Sticks, but he vowed to "push forward if I [must] live upon acorns." Others eyed the horses.[14]

━━━

JACKSON'S FIRST TARGET was the Red Stick town called Tallushatchee, which John Coffee attacked on November 3. Jackson could take care of himself, but Coffee could kill Indians better than anyone Jackson had ever seen. Tallushatchee offered proof of Coffee's thoroughness. The counting of bodies after the battle revealed a grim tale. One dead woman had been trying to escape with a baby. The child was alive. He was bawling, and his hands flailed the air to push away and then reach for the soldiers who took him among their prisoners. Almost one hundred Red Stick women and children had been captured, and the baby was offered to them. The women turned away. The child's family had all been killed, they said, and now there was no one to care for him. They said he should die too.

An interpreter took the child to Old Hickory, and at his headquarters the general spooned some nourishment into the baby, frowned over him during the night, and by the following day had made a decision. Jackson wrote to his childless wife that he was sending her a baby. The boy was perhaps eleven months old, certainly old enough to have had a name, but as a foundling, he would never hear it again, that name having died on the bloody ground at Tallushatchee with his parents. Eager to resume his campaign without distractions, Jackson sent the child to Huntsville, where a local family briefly cared for him; they probably gave the child his new name. When he arrived in Nashville, he was already being called Lyncoya. Rachel Jackson was jubilant. In 1808, she and her husband had taken in an infant belonging to Rachel's brother Severn Donelson and his wife, adopting him as Andrew Jackson Jr., but Rachel brimmed with affection for all children. There was always room under her roof for another niece or nephew or, in this case, war orphan. Jackson wrote to Rachel that the little fellow was to be "well taken care of, he may have been given to me for some Valuable purpose—in fact when I reflect he as to his relations is so much like myself I feel an unusual sympathy for him—tell my dear little Andrew to treat him well."[15]

Was Andrew Jackson's gesture at Tallushatchee evidence that he had some hidden affection for Indians? Certainly, the act of taking an Indian child into his home could be interpreted as compassionate, a contrast to the callous image of Old Hickory as an inveterate Indian hater. Perhaps the cruelties of the Creek War, Tallushatchee among them, were compelled by hard necessities and were not a reflection of Jackson's prejudice against Indians. Whatever his reasons or his hatreds, Jackson saved Lyncoya from death by abandonment, and the child did live with the Jackson family at the Hermitage, where everyone treated him with kindness. After all, the little boy was by all accounts pleasant and affable, and as Rachel realized, he was truly an orphan of the storm. As Jackson mused to her, Lyncoya's situation resembled her husband's own troubled youth.

Still, Jackson, like many frontier Americans, would never shake the idea that Indians were a class of disagreeable humanity, a culturally backward group rather than variously formed individuals. Jackson occasionally expressed benevolent though condescending views of Indians, suggesting an ambivalence about them that is nicely captured by the Lyncoya story as well as the fact that Cherokee and Creek allies fought on the American side during the Creek War.

His actions, though, were seldom ambivalent. Though doubtlessly sincere in his empathy for Lyncoya's plight, Jackson never expressed a word of remorse about the death of the child's family. In fact, the two events—killing the boy's parents and folding the boy into the bosom of Jackson's own family—seemed utterly unrelated in Jackson's mind. Possibly they had to be. If Jackson had linked his killing of Lyncoya's family with an obligation to save the orphan it created, guilt rather than compassion might have led to his decision to take the child into his home. Because Jackson did not wear guilt gladly, he never wore it at all.

The frontier of Jackson's childhood was remarkably free of Indians, at least in his immediate environs near the border between North and South Carolina. A residual animosity against Indians persisted nonetheless. Old folks entertained youngsters with stories of the settlement's early days when Indian conflicts were frequent and violent. In the mid-1770s, during the American Revolution, southwest South Carolina suffered horrific destruction in the Cherokee War, and Jackson no doubt heard about the conflict's brutality from his family and neighbors. He may have even talked to white refugees from the war. Knowledge of Indians came to him secondhand, though, and no personal experience from Jackson's youth could have instilled in him a pathological hatred for Indians. Not until he traveled to Tennessee in 1788 was he exposed to Indians in significant numbers, and he readily adopted the attitude of most Tennesseans regarding them and how to deal with them.

When Jackson crossed the Appalachian Mountains in 1788 and settled at Nashville, the place was not even Tennessee but a part of North Carolina's western wilderness. Nashville's muddy streets boasted only a few businesses and cabins, with most people living outside of town on farms. Out there in the countryside, families huddled in blockhouses fortified against Indian attacks, a defensive tactic typical of the American frontier, whether in the valley of the Ohio or that of the Cumberland. Jackson took lodgings and meals at just such a place owned by the widow Rachel Stockley Donelson. Someone had killed her husband in 1786; some said it was Indians, others were not so sure. In any case, Mrs. Donelson was grateful to have Andrew Jackson arrive—another man, which meant another gun, in case there was trouble with the Indians.

Jackson consequently walked into a place where warfare against Indians was the natural state of affairs, and he rapidly adopted what his new white neighbors regarded as the correct attitude about the matter. His education, in fact, began even before his arrival. On the journey west, he narrowly avoided a violent encounter with a roving band of Indian raiders. As he settled into his new community and sought public acclaim through a political career, Jackson condemned Indian treaties as a waste of time while demanding that Indians who violated those agreements be punished.[16]

There would have been some reason behind such a belief—it was, after all, a rational response to a pressing problem—but other motives also prompted it. As later events would show, even peaceful Indians fully intent upon embracing acculturation and accommodating white customs were not welcome neighbors as long as they occupied land that whites wanted. In the 1790s, violence on the frontier provided a reason to attack Indians, but those attacks were also a convenient way to accomplish another less defensive and defensible objective. The mere presence of Indians limited settlement, and weak demand for a plentiful supply of land suppressed its price. If the land, the region's principal article of trade, were thus made worthless, the region's economy would collapse. Jackson intended to make his fortune in Tennessee, and like other prominent citizens, to do so he speculated in land, including land not yet relinquished by Indians. Jackson and his fellow speculators would not allow the land to sink into worthlessness.

However, describing Jackson and westerners like him as ruthless capitalists eager to exploit the land by shoving Indians off it reduces a complex situation to a simplistic caricature in which all Indians were noble victims, and all whites were wicked exploiters. The truth lay somewhere in between. Each side committed horrific acts that left grieving widows and orphans in Indian villages and white frontier cabins alike. Jackson was neither blind to this suffering nor bloodthirsty in condoning it. He wanted peace with the Indians, and he and other frontier leaders denounced random attacks by settlers on Indian towns because such raids almost always provoked retaliation.

Even so, for thirty years both his rhetoric about and his behavior toward Indians were remarkably consistent. Some would say they were static. To his thinking, the consistency was warranted. In Jackson's world, Fort Mims was not merely an incident of exceptional violence. It was the natural order of things in a place where people fought to the death for access to limited resources. Fort Mims was a victory for Indians in that larger fight, as was Tallushatchee a victory for him, and after that, Talladega and Emuckfau Creek and Enotochopco and finally Tohopeka, the place of the great Horseshoe Bend on the Tallapoosa. The euphony of the names belies the horrors of their destruction by Coffee and his colleagues, ordered by Old Hickory, the man who spooned sugared water into an Indian baby before sending the boy to the safety of his home. There, his wife would love Lyncoya even more because he was a foundling, would love him no less because he was not white, and would believe his heaven no less grand because he was red.[17]

<hr />

AFTER DESTROYING TALLUSHATCHEE, Jackson plunged thirty miles deeper into Creek country to do the same to Talladega on November 9. That was the last action of 1813 because Jackson ran out of food and had to return to Fort Strother. He implored Governor Blount and railed at contractors, but no supplies came, and after a time his men laid plans to leave. He had two brigades of United States Volunteers—these were the men of the Natchez expedition—and one brigade of militia, for a total of about two thousand. Jackson skillfully

played the volunteers and the militia against each other by appealing
to their respective pride, but he finally had to promise to take everyone home if food did not arrive in forty-eight hours. He stretched the
wait to four days but knew that the army would dissolve if he waited
any longer. He led the men out of Fort Strother north for Tennessee.
He wrote explaining to Governor Blount that "a turbulent & mutinous disposition has manifested itself in my Camp."[18]

Within hours of leaving the Coosa River, the retreating cara-
van ran into a small supply train heading the other way. Wagons of
flour meant biscuits and some 150 cattle meant charred meat, and
after a few hours of feasting everyone was satisfied and happy. Oddly
enough, though, that was when the real trouble began. Grumbling
over the prospect of returning to Fort Strother, the army decided it
would instead continue its trek to Tennessee. Jackson galloped his
horse to block the way, a musket in the crook of his good right arm.
The men paused. Coffee quietly ambled to Jackson's side and stood
expressionless. John Reid, a handsome lad everyone liked, stood at
his other side. The tableau was imposing. The affable kid on one
side, the quietly menacing giant on the other, and in the middle,
the man on horseback with a look that by itself could kill. It would
have had to. Jackson later discovered that the musket was broken.

For the time being, he was able to face down the mutiny and
take everyone back to the Coosa, but the men were sullen, and
the want of supplies encouraged continued discontent. Throughout December no food came, and a listless brigade made ready to
sneak away in the night. It was a spontaneous act of survival, little
more. Jackson wheeled two field pieces to block the trail home and
made certain the potential deserters knew the primed cannons had
matches poised above touchholes. The men decided to chance star-
vation. It was at least a slower way to die.

With his campaign at an endless pause, Jackson admitted that he
was "wearied with dating letters at this place," but more dispiriting

developments were pending. Stopping desertion became impossible when much of Jackson's army insisted that their enlistments had expired. As they left for home, they left Jackson nonplussed. In addition to starving armies to death, state and federal governments had created inconsistent and conflicting regulations that made it impossible to figure out the span of a soldier's service. Unsure that he had the right to make them stay, Jackson had to let them go. In the midst of this depressing confusion, a letter arrived from Governor Blount suggesting that Jackson should come home too.[19]

Jackson exploded over Tennessee's "fireside Patriots" whose short memories and lack of resolve threatened to leave Fort Mims unavenged. He said he would not leave Fort Strother if but a handful of men remained with him, and he almost had to make good on that pledge. Jackson's determination steeled Blount, and reinforcements and rations to feed them arrived in early 1814. Jackson did not tarry. He knew now that enlistments could unexpectedly expire and food could run out rapidly. He later wrote Billy Carroll, his brigade inspector, that "the disorder that prevailed amongst officers & men in our late excursion, was a striking example, and a sufficient warning never to enter the country of our enemy with troops not reduced to some kind of obedience & order." That was putting it mildly. When affection for him was not enough to see the campaign continue, he was prepared to mete out harsh discipline. It was the reason that, of all the forces that had entered the fight the previous fall, Jackson's would be the only one to end it that spring.[20]

He pressed on with all speed toward Red Stick strongholds south of the Coosa. His three thousand men covered seventy miles to win a sharply fought engagement at Emuckfau Creek on January 22, but Coffee took a bullet in his side. Jackson could ill afford to lose him, but he also had the uneasy feeling of being surrounded by superior numbers, so he cautiously withdrew north. Coffee's absence partly accounted for the army's muddled performance at Enotochopco two days later, and the near defeat there convinced Jackson that he must return to Fort Strother, disappointing as that was. New troops continued to arrive on the Coosa to swell his numbers. Creek and Cherokee allies not only increased Jackson's strength but also brought a knowledge of the terrain. Most heartening, though, was the arrival of the Thirty-Ninth United States Infantry, regular troops whose discipline promised to keep order in his camp as well as give him the ability to launch a formidable offensive. John Coffee was even up and moving around.

By March Jackson was ready. He descended the Coosa to veer west toward Tohopeka, the Horseshoe Bend of the Tallapoosa River. The Horseshoe formed a peninsula on the river's northern bank, a wide expanse of land on which an enormous number of Red Sticks had gathered, including at least eight hundred warriors. They believed that the river at their backs would shield their rear from attack. Accordingly, the Red Sticks had constructed a formidable series of angled breastworks across the entire peninsula, anchoring both flanks on the Tallapoosa. Jackson and his officers took the measure of this imposing defensive position and saw right away that the Red Sticks had not reckoned on facing artillery. Worse, they had not realized that the Tallapoosa could be something other than a protective barrier. It was also a cordon blocking their escape.

On the morning of March 27, Coffee left with his cavalry and Indian allies to take up positions on the other side of the Tallapoosa. There they could both gain the Red Stick rear and block Red Stick flight. Meanwhile, Jackson trained his two field pieces on the defenses. For two hours, his artillery tore holes in the elaborate breastworks while his men's muskets peppered their defenders. With Coffee finally in position, Jackson ordered the frontal assault, leading with the Thirty-Ninth Infantry. Coffee brought part of his command across the Tallapoosa and mounted an attack from the rear. His Cherokees stole Red Stick canoes, forcing those who tried to flee to swim and become easy targets for Coffee's marksmen. The fight lasted for several hours, descending into hand-to-hand combat when Jackson's men finally broke through the fortifications. The killing continued until nightfall. It was a scene of horrific carnage that left more than five hundred warriors dead on the ground and at least a couple hundred bobbing in the Tallapoosa, black patches of blood staining the river's yellow water. Possibly a hundred Red Sticks escaped that night, but they were no longer fighters but fugitives. The Creek War was over.[21]

Americans had not had good news about any war since the previous fall, and they responded to Jackson's victory against the Creeks with celebrations and praise. The news raced through the West and within weeks was being reported from Washington, Kentucky, to Washington, DC, and beyond. "Victory entwines the fairest wreaths for the brows of the gallant Jackson and of his intrepid followers," glowed one newspaper. Major General Thomas Pinckney of the United States Army, who had ostensibly been in charge of the Creek War but who had scored few successes during it, lauded "the military talents and enterprise of Gen. Jackson." If Pinckney sounded subdued, those who knew of the government's earlier attitude toward Old Hickory might have marveled over the difference that time and victory could make. Two weeks after Horseshoe Bend, Jackson was appointed a brigadier general in the regular army, and two weeks after that, when the resignation of William Henry Harrison made the slot available, he became a major general. He was now Thomas Pinckney's colleague.[22]

The man the government had abandoned in Natchez had in the span of a single year become the country's darling. He made apparent that he did not intend to rest on his laurels. In the weeks after his victory at Horseshoe Bend, he scoured the countryside for Red Stick refugees. He hurried to their sacred site at the Hickory Ground expecting another battle and was disappointed to find it deserted, but he need not have been. After he established Fort Jackson at the fork of the Coosa and the Tallapoosa Rivers, starving Red Sticks began showing up to surrender in exchange for something to eat. Armed with his newly minted authority as a major general in the regular army, Jackson replaced Thomas Pinckney as a negotiator to bring about a formal end to the Creek War. The old Creek agent Benjamin Hawkins was supposed to participate, but he seemed in a daze as Jackson dictated terms, secured the Treaty of Fort Jackson, and then gathered his army to vanish southward. Afterward Hawkins was troubled that Jackson's treaty treated Creek allies as harshly as Red Stick enemies. He wrote to the War Department to relate particulars that were at odds with the laudatory stories in the press and among the public. His was the first smidgen of news to escape the grasp of Jackson's immediate circle that conveyed all was not quite as it seemed to be.

Hawkins would find that his words did not matter, and worse, that he did not matter. The government was as eager for victories as the people were, and how those victories happened was of little concern to either of them. Courtly old Benjamin Hawkins would not be the first man to find out that he was no longer significant in the coming order of things according to Jackson. In due course, the letters he wrote vanished from the War Department's archives, just as the man who wrote them vanished from American memory.[23]

CHAPTER 2

HERO

A FTER SIGNING THE TREATY OF FORT JACKSON, ANDREW Jackson had reason to hurry. News of British ships in the Gulf of Mexico alarmed him, especially because he believed the arrival of the British could revive the hope of victory for those Red Sticks who had fled to Spanish West Florida. Jackson also did not believe Spain's claims of neutrality regarding the Anglo-American war. He demanded that Governor Don Mateo González Manrique explain his relations with the British and insisted that he turn over two mixed-ancestry Red Sticks, Peter McQueen and Josiah Francis, prominent figures in the Creek War known to be sheltering in Pensacola. Manrique indignantly refused on both counts. When Jackson arrived with his men in Mobile, his disquiet only increased. The British had established a base on the Apalachicola River and were in Pensacola behaving more like owners than guests. And when a hundred Royal Marines with several hundred Red Sticks sallied forth from Pensacola in September to attack Fort Bowyer at the entrance of Mobile Bay, they confirmed Old Hickory's worst suspicions. It was little consolation that the British failed at Bowyer. He knew that this was only the tip of the British spear. Sooner or later, a much larger army would come into the Gulf.[1]

Jackson had already asked the War Department for permission to take Pensacola, but he believed these rapid developments compelled him to move without orders. The British had tried to bolster the town's defenses, but Jackson easily took it on November 7 and shooed the British back to the Apalachicola. He destroyed Pensacola's fortifications to make it useless as a base for future British operations and turned it back over to a fuming Manrique before returning with his army to Mobile. He did not receive Secretary of War James Monroe's instructions not to take Pensacola until weeks later.[2]

At Mobile, Jackson paused. He brooded over the evolving strategic situation. Pensacola had been worth taking for no other reason than to learn more about British plans. They were chilling. From the West Indies would come a mighty host borne by warships of the Royal Navy. This time Fort Bowyer would not stand a chance, and Mobile would fall, not as a prize but to become a base for the march on the real target, New Orleans. As Jackson readied Mobile for the attack, he discerned almost too late that British plans had changed. They were not coming to Mobile. They were going to move directly on the Crescent City.[3]

Jackson inexplicably remained in Mobile. For the first time in the year-long campaign, he seemed to falter, and nobody has ever been able to explain why. Rather than racing to New Orleans, he tarried in Mobile for a full week. He did send Coffee's brigade to Baton Rouge, presumably to be in place for a British landing at any point on the Mississippi. But that was all he did. There was no rapid forced march of the type he had employed so successfully in 1812 and 1813. Possibly he was ill. His stomach had troubled him since Pensacola, and perhaps his chronic ailments had finally bested his indomitable will. But it is more likely that Jackson could not let go of the idea that Mobile was still the British target. He was obsessing over the town's defenses when he finally departed for New Orleans. For whatever reason and from whatever cause, Jackson was nearly late to his own party. Had the British taken advantage of his lapse, everything afterward would have been different.[4]

The more than seven days it took him to move his two thousand men to New Orleans must have seemed an eternity. It certainly appeared that way to the citizens of the city, an edgy and angry lot riddled with conflicting loyalties and prone to suspect all outsiders. Creoles of French and Spanish descent were the majority, but Americans controlled the government, and Creole resentment over that was only slightly outweighed by their apprehension over being pillaged by the British. Jackson had known the Americans who now wielded influence and authority in New Orleans for almost twenty years. He had met Governor William C. C. Claiborne and the lawyer Edward Livingston when they all served together in Congress in the late 1790s, and the memories from their youth endured. Claiborne had always liked the rangy Tennessean, and seeing him ride into New Orleans that chilly December day was cause for relief. Jackson's arrival lifted an onerous burden from the governor's sloping shoulders. As for Livingston, he soon became Jackson's chief adviser about the cultural politics of the city. Jackson needed the advice. He never warmed to the French or the Spanish in New Orleans, nor they to him. Creoles still chafed at the United States acquisition of Louisiana a decade earlier, and at first sight, Jackson did not impress them in 1814 any more than the modest flag-raising ceremony had in 1804.

Jackson forlornly surveyed the local militia while hastily cobbling together a defensive force and inspecting the city's environs. He enlisted whoever would serve, including Free Men of Color, Creoles, resident Americans, Choctaw Indians from Mississippi, and even Baratarian pirates commanded by the dashing buccaneers Jean and Pierre Lafitte and Dominique You. This motley collection joined Jackson's regulars and militia, but he still judged his strength to be inadequate. He expected reinforcements from Kentucky and anxiously watched the river for Tennessee militia being brought down by Billy Carroll, but New Orleans felt very lonely and naked as the December days passed. He had not heard from the federal government in two months and could only guess that Washington was preoccupied by the war elsewhere. With fewer than five thousand men, Old Hickory would have to defend a half dozen potential points of attack. Many believed New Orleans was indefensible, and whispers of surrender were in the air. Jackson declared martial law.

The British were among those who believed New Orleans was indefensible. They appeared off Lakes Borgne and Pontchartrain on December 12 and in short order overwhelmed the small squadron of United States Navy gunboats stationed there. All the various routes to New Orleans lay open to British plans after that, and they went about preparing for their attack with unnerving deliberation. Major General John Keane seemed blissfully indifferent to the dirty shirts and their backwoods commander upriver, even when reports told of a brigade coming from Baton Rouge to reinforce Jackson. They were Coffee's men. He had driven them at an astonishing pace—even for cavalrymen, because it was densely wooded terrain—that amounted to more than forty miles a day to reach New Orleans in time. Right behind him was Billy Carroll by river with three thousand Tennesseans he relentlessly trained on the flatboats during their journey.

These arrivals gave Jackson the strength to think about harassing the British, if only to counter their arrogance. Keane captured the plantation belonging to Gabriel Villeré less than ten miles south of the city and set up his headquarters there. On the night of December 23, Jackson staged an audacious strike on the British, and though the gesture was more symbolic than meaningful—the British remained in place after the battle—it bolstered American morale and gave Creoles reason to mute talk of surrender. Two

American ships on the Mississippi commanded by Commander Daniel Todd Patterson bombarded the British now and then, disconcerting rather than endangering them, but the unexpected pugnacity of surprise raids and shelling from ships caused Keane to hesitate. Not only were parts of the British army still en route but also the expedition's commander in chief, Lieutenant General Sir Edward Pakenham, a veteran of Britain's Peninsular War against Napoleon and brother-in-law of the Duke of Wellington. Pakenham was within days of arriving with some of Wellington's veterans and heavy artillery. Keane was confident that Pakenham would be irresistible in the attack and invincible in finishing it, so the British waited. The man, the men, and the guns arrived on Christmas Day.

Pakenham doubtless did not like what he saw when he surveyed the British position. Jackson had spent the extra time afforded by Keane's delay strengthening a line along the Rodriguez Canal, a natural barrier before the flat Chalmette Plain. An impassable swamp anchored Jackson's left flank on its east, while the Mississippi River did the same for his right, where Patterson's ships provided additional cover. A battery manned by Kentuckians on the Mississippi's far bank could command the plain from the west. Pakenham tested this line with probing attacks on December 29 and January 1, and both times he was disappointed that it did not break and run as he had been told American forces were likely to do. As Keane had done, Pakenham took a step back to consider his next move. He brought up more artillery, and as Jackson had done during Keane's period of inaction, he dug in further and placed his artillery more effectively.

On January 2, the Kentuckians Jackson had been expecting arrived, two thousand strong, but many without weapons, which made them mouths to feed rather than help in the coming fight. Jackson scrounged for every gun he could find while Pakenham took several days to bring up two thousand more men, a clear sign of his impending main assault. Pakenham noticed how the American battery across the river could, if in his hands, fire along the length of Jackson's line before the onslaught of Wellington's veterans would complete its demolition. He sent a sizable party across the river on the night of January 7 to take the battery in advance of his frontal assault the next morning. Pakenham also ordered a constant fire of Congreve rockets toward the Rodriguez line. They were regularly used by the British during the war—Francis Scott Key had noted their "red glare" at Baltimore when he wrote "The Star-Spangled Banner"—but they were more frightening than destructive. They did, at the very least, deprive the Americans of sleep.

Through that night and the following day, the gaunt man with the hawk face, his thick gray hair seeming to stand on end, trotted his horse the length of the line to bark encouragement and mock the rockets as harmless toys. Out of his saddle, he helped sight a field piece or gnawed bacon with wide-eyed boys. He kept them calm the next morning before dawn when they heard the distant cadence of drums mixed with the whine of bagpipes. It was dim as the sun broke the eastern horizon because a dense fog had settled on the Chalmette Plain. The drums and pipes came closer. The men they heralded were the victors of a European war in which enormous armies had clashed under storied generals and field marshals. The temptation to run before the remorseless advance of an invincible army was almost overwhelming. But Andrew Jackson stood fast, and his men did, too, straining their eyes into the fog.

Jackson's artillery fired toward the sound of pipes, and then as the fog began to lift, his guns took aim at Pakenham's army. His men opened fire as well. Redcoats in orderly lines stretched back across the plain as far as anyone could see. Their bayonets and buttons caught the patchy sunlight, and soon enough they were good targets. Jackson's artillery, not Pakenham's, tore holes in the enemy's lines. Jackson's veterans of Tohopeka stood their ground to cut down Wellington's from Salamanca and Toulouse. Jackson's dirty

A CORRECT VIEW of the BATTLE Near the City of NEW ORLEANS, on the Eighth of January 1815, Under the Command of Gen! And? Jackson, Over 10,000 British Troops, in which 3 of their most distinguished Generals were killed,& several wounded and upwards of 3,000 of their choicest Soldiers were killed,wounded, and made Prisoners, &c

This contemporary engraving of the Battle of New Orleans was published within a few years of the battle to publicize Andrew Jackson's heroic deeds in defending the nation from the British. (Library of Congress.)

shirts staggered and then stalled Pakenham's assault, and finally, they killed Pakenham himself as he desperately tried to rally his flagging effort. It took less than thirty minutes for Jackson's men to kill or wound more than 1,500 of Pakenham's 8,000 men and, in the aftermath, capture 500 more, a British loss of 25 percent of their force in Louisiana, a lethal blow to their morale as well as their manpower. With Pakenham dead and Keane wounded, command devolved on General John Lambert, and he ignored Pakenham's final order to commit British reserves. Lambert stopped the battle and withdrew. Jackson took stock on his side: his men had beaten the British at the cost of 6 killed and 7 wounded.

A few more Americans had been killed on the other side of the river, where the British had finally taken the battery from the

Kentuckians, but that small British victory was too little and too late to be of any use to their dead comrades on the ground before the Rodriguez Canal. It was only one of the crucial points of Pakenham's plan that had gone awry. In fact, almost nothing had happened as he had envisioned. Ladders and bundled sugarcane for crossing canals and scaling Jackson's breastworks went missing when they were most needed. The main part of the British assault fell on the American left, which was Jackson's strongest position, and the fog that the British had counted on for cover also prevented officers from assessing their disintegrating situation. And then the fog had lifted at the worst possible moment to expose them to withering fire. In sum, it made for one of the worst disasters ever to befall a British army. For Jackson, it was a victory so lightly won, costing him only a fraction of the people he had lost at Villeré Plantation, that he saw in it the hand of God.[5]

To the day they died, the dirty shirts of the Rodriguez Canal would remember the eighth of January in the year 1815. And because so many of them did not die that day, they spread news of the event across the entire nation, and quickly. In New Orleans, pictures on the walls of the Cabildo trembled when three thousand people crammed into the Place d'Armes to shout themselves hoarse at the sight of Andrew Jackson. Children in song mingled their piping voices with pealing church bells as priests in Saint Louis Cathedral intoned *Te Deum* at a high mass of thanksgiving. Creoles smiled as widely and danced as fervently as did exuberant Americans, and Jackson in return had nothing but praise for the patriotism and courage of every citizen. "Even the softer sex encouraged their husbands and brothers to remain at the post of danger and duty," he declared, and he thanked Jean Lafitte for countless occasions of vital service. The two had struck a bargain in December—Lafitte's help in exchange for Jackson's pardon—but victory in January had made the formerly reviled pirate Jackson's bosom friend. Rachel came down from Nashville and was awestruck by the pageantry, particularly at the Washington Birthday Ball that February. She soon confessed to tiring "of the Disipation of this place, so much amusement Ball Concerts Plays theaters, etc."[6]

In London, the curmudgeonly British writer William Cobbett heard about Jackson's victory and praised him for serving out of a sense of duty rather than for material gain, which Cobbett felt was the main motivation for British officers. To be sure, the British, who had been much looking forward to the dissipation of Le Vieux Carré, were quite bitter about being denied their "booty and beauty" by the American hick and his rowdy gaggle of squirrel hunters and 'possum chasers. But the people of New Orleans, and soon the people of America, thought the hick and the men called dirty shirts were mighty fine. The Place d'Armes would change its name. It is still called Jackson Square.[7]

EVEN THOUGH THE Treaty of Ghent had been signed in Europe almost two weeks before the Battle of New Orleans, Andrew Jackson's victory on the Rodriguez Canal gave the impression that the War of 1812 ended with an American victory. As a consequence, his achievement quickly became something greater than the stunning martial triumph it, in fact, was. Old Hickory at New Orleans planted the idea that the United States had won the war and that God, through His instrument Andrew Jackson, was directly responsible for the happy conclusion. Speeches in Congress strained for superlatives in describing a man who eighteen months earlier had been beneath the notice of anyone outside Tennessee. Indeed, when government leaders had noticed Jackson at all, they dismissed him as a hothead and a crank. After New Orleans, though, he became the new George Washington, an American Cincinnatus who had left his plow to save his country. Newspapers caromed between panegyrics and poetry. "I to the listening world do now proclaim," versifier Francis Hopkins told the readers of Washington's *National Intelligencer*, "JACKSON'S brave deeds, his never-dying fame." In addition to copperplate engravings in books and framed prints for parlors both elegant and plain, artists and illustrators used any medium that could hold an image, from planks of wood to bolts of cloth, to depict the general and his men standing firm on the Rodriguez Canal, Andrew Jackson most conspicuous of all.[8]

In the nation's capital, the *National Intelligencer* became a clearinghouse of information from all over the country reporting on Jackson's mood and charting his travels. "None but a man of the first rate talents and undaunted courage could have overcome such a crowd of impediments," the paper gushed about Jackson's defense of New Orleans before tracing his journey back to Nashville that spring. That trip resembled a royal progress, with banquets at frequent stops where local dignitaries spouted speeches of praise and blushing maidens warbled sentimental songs. At one such event at Washington in the Mississippi Territory, two boys gained a small measure of local fame by reading Jackson an admiring tribute, the sentiments if not the exact words of which he had heard dozens of times and would hear dozens more before reaching the Cumberland; it must have been growing tedious. Jackson usually responded by stating his admiration for the boys for admiring him.[9]

The country could not hear enough about Jackson, and rumors of his bad health or serious mishaps were breathlessly reported. In 1815, the first summer of his fame, news came from Philadelphia through New Orleans that Jackson "had been killed in an affray with a gentleman of Tennessee," a story incredible for both its provenance and particulars. The *National Intelligencer* reassured its readers that it was not true, noting that "the momentary belief" that Jackson was dead had "excited so much horror." That was because the public was enthralled with stories that an uprising of Indians in the Northwest would soon cause Jackson "to take the field himself, and when he takes it he will take it with such a force as will decide the Indian War in a very short time, and so decide it as to prevent its renewal."[10]

Newspapers scrambled for bits of information about his life. They garbled the facts they could find and filled in the rest with pure fiction. One account had Jackson "born in the northern part of Scotland." The inventive biographer was so eager to get to press that he missed the absurdity in saying that Jackson's "father died while he was an infant." Jackson's father had died at age twenty-nine, two years after bringing his family to America from County Antrim in the north of Ireland, and two weeks before his son Andrew was born. Yet, this account had Jackson's widowed mother bringing the infant Andrew to North Carolina in the company of a (completely invented) distant relation. She was depicted as too poor to school him in anything but "the rudiments of our language," but at age ten, Jackson's prospects improved when "a gentleman of fortune" became his patron and saw to his excellent education. None of this was true. The biographer had Jackson leaving school at age nineteen (his formal education ended when he was thirteen) to read law under an accomplished attorney and gain admittance to the bar (which did not happen until Jackson had moved to Salisbury, North Carolina, after the American Revolution). He had Jackson moving to Tennessee (which did not exist when Jackson migrated to the region) and quickly becoming "a famous lawyer" (he was the district attorney for the Western District of North Carolina) and then a major in the Tennessee militia (he was a captain as judge advocate for the Davidson County militia). Rising from his fictional rank of major, Jackson became a fictional colonel before moving to western Tennessee to become a fictional brigadier general. (Jackson lived in what became western Tennessee from the time of his arrival in 1788, and it was in 1802 that he won election as major general of the Tennessee militia.) Jackson's men adored him, the biographer claimed, and he could summon a legion with a single word, which was possibly the only unalloyed bit of truth in the entire piece, although the men's love for him had not always been apparent during the Creek War. Readers were to know, however, that he was "passionately fond . . . of the fairer sex" and that the "foible has occasioned him some trouble" because Jackson was "unmarried." Jackson was "moderately" wealthy, and as to appearance, he was "very tall and thin—and very ugly," which was why "his men uniformly call him 'Hickory Face.'"[11]

Being told Jackson was "very ugly" must have jarred readers eager for an accurate image of their hero. A better description, presumably written by John Coffee for the *Richmond Enquirer*, was more appropriate for the savior of the country. Jackson was "tall, thin, and spare, but muscular and hardy, with an eye quick, & penetrating." He was "a man of Iron" but as saintly as he was severe: "To the poor, he is liberal, to the unfortunate charitable, to the humblest private he is mild and tender, to the base and disaffected to this country stern and unbending, yet just." A somewhat more truthful literary portrait, however, did not help people in need of a real likeness. Secretary Alexander Dallas at the War Department found himself in that predicament after Congress voted for the minting of a gold medal to commemorate the victory at New Orleans. One side would be Jackson's profile. Neither Dallas nor any artist he sought to employ knew what Andrew Jackson looked like. Thus the door was opened for portrait painter Ralph Eleasar Whiteside Earl, who came to Nashville in 1817 to paint Andrew Jackson and his chief lieutenants from the Battle of New Orleans. Earl planned to crown his efforts with an epic treatment of the battle itself.[12]

Earl was a New England native whose father had been an artist of some note, and the younger Earl had studied under John Trumbull and Benjamin West in London and gazed on beautiful masterpieces

This picture of Jackson was distributed shortly after the Battle of New Orleans when the public was eager for his image. It is a good example of how inaccurate most of these early likenesses of him could be. (Library of Congress.)

from previous centuries at the Louvre. But none of that could make a marginally competent technician into a luminous talent. His persistence was a good substitute for ability, though, and something about him appealed to Old Hickory from the start. Earl produced portraits of Jackson, John Coffee, and Billy Carroll, but he never got around to the Battle of New Orleans. Instead, he became one of those people who having met their destiny never foolishly strays from it. In Earl's case, his destiny was to marry one of Rachel Jackson's nieces, become an intimate friend of Old Hickory, and establish himself as a noted portrait artist among an appreciative, undiscriminating Nashville clientele. But mostly he would paint portraits of Andrew Jackson. In 1819 the Corporation of the City of New York commissioned John Vanderlyn to produce a portrait of Jackson. Friends referred Vanderlyn to Earl, and Old Hickory's friend readily supplied a character study of Old Hickory's face, for Ralph Earl was a pleasant and accommodating man. But only Vanderlyn's superb talent could overcome Earl's chronic deficiencies, which never produced more than a primitive simplicity. On those occasions when Earl grew ambitious, the results were often flat and sometimes absurd. John James Audubon passed through Nashville early in Earl's career and was not impressed. "I Never Saw," Audubon wrote in his journal, "a Worst painted sign in the Street of Paris."[13]

But Earl wasn't painting signs in Paris. He was painting Andrew Jackson, who liked what he saw, and Earl was doing it for the American people, who saw what they liked. The imperfections of Earl's many canvases could not mar Jackson's real image for Americans any more than the imperfections of Andrew Jackson himself could diminish his status as the nation's peerless hero. It was only a matter of time before such unyielding adulation made thoughtful men consider its possibilities. As the nation was shouting, "*Hero*," a few thoughtful men began whispering, "*President*."

———

As EARLY AS 1814, John Overton was gauging Andrew Jackson's political prospects in Tennessee, specifically the chance of his being voted governor. Old Hickory's success in the Creek War was one prompt, but another was the constituency Jackson commanded in the most literal sense as a major general of the Tennessee militia.

Also, the venerable political organization called the Blount faction, named after William, would be at Jackson's disposal. Blount had been a master politician and peerless land speculator in Tennessee's earliest days, when he served as the state's first governor and then as one of its first United States senators. From those lofty perches, he had established an elaborate network of patronage for a growing cadre of protégés, Andrew Jackson and John Overton among them. This was in the 1790s, when Jackson and Overton were young lawyers in a lawless land as well as land speculators in a place careless with land titles, especially if they were held by Indians. Blount's land schemes eventually became too disreputable for the Senate, leading to his expulsion in 1797, but neither disgrace nor his death two years later could slow the well-oiled machine he had created. Half-brother Willie Blount took its helm and through the first decade of the 1800s found an able partner in Overton. So able was the latter that the organization was increasingly called the Blount-Overton faction.[14]

Though intricate in reach and broad in membership, the faction's functions were simple, for it was essentially a political party in a nation where parties weren't supposed to exist. By the end of the eighteenth century, the British Parliament's party system appeared to Americans as designed exclusively to trample liberty while enriching politicians, patrons, and clients. After the Revolution, Americans continued to disdain parties as nests of self-interested corruption, but as they sought to govern themselves, they discovered that implementing policies required coherent political organizations. Thus did factions spring up to win elections and frame policy. Political machines in various forms had already existed in the colonies, and they persisted in the states during and after the Revolution. Politicians on the national level were slower to admit this reality, and Thomas Jefferson in his 1801 inaugural address was still clinging to the fiction that everyone was a Federalist and everyone was a Republican, but everyone was in fact perfectly aware that this was not the case.

In Tennessee, the Blounts had always known the rules of the game better than most in that they understood that everything started with family. A faction's political leaders had appointive offices in their gift, so a post for a wastrel brother-in-law or a tippling uncle sealed a bond of immense political potential by extending its influence among a beneficiary's kith and kin. Everyone fretted over the day when an unfortunate event at the polls would remove the brother-in-law or uncle from favor and, in turn, employment, so real incentives encouraged everyone to work for victory in elections. A strong faction put the right people in office, who were then disciplined by self-interest to set policy according to the faction's leadership. The trick was to employ the benefits of a faction without wearing too flagrantly the taint of self-interest and corruption those benefits imparted.

The most common way to avoid the appearance of self-interest was to foreswear ambition and deny aspiration, and not only for public office but for public acclaim. Andrew Jackson had done this repeatedly ever since he first joined the Blount faction in the 1790s. Early on, for instance, he made everyone aware that he only reluctantly attended the Tennessee constitutional convention in 1796 and that he only grudgingly served in the House of Representatives and the Senate afterward. He resigned from both bodies before the expiration of his terms and returned to Nashville to make very public announcements about his permanent retirement from public life. When he became a major general in the Tennessee militia, it was not depicted as one of those political plums that fell from Governor Archibald Roane's tree, and it had nothing to do with Roane being a Blount man, like Jackson, with whom he was also friends. No, it was Jackson's sacrifice compelled by the frontier menace of hostile Indians or, in the absence of that, of Spaniards pushing up to the border while plotting America's commercial ruin. Through it all, Jackson insisted that he wanted only to retire to the Hermitage—the name of his home was the perfect badge for a man claiming to desire only solitude and repose—and live out his remaining years with his family as a careful squire and loving husband. Whether Overton's ideas about his becoming governor enticed him, they were set aside by Jackson when he chose to remain a major general in the United States Army. In any case, men were soon whispering something a bit grander than "governor," and they had Old Hickory's ear.

In October 1815, Jackson received a letter from Billy Carroll telling about his travels in Kentucky, Ohio, and his native state of Pennsylvania. He had talked with "leading characters of the states" and had been assured that "most . . . are solicitous that you should become a candidate for the next President." One of Carroll's contacts was Henry Baldwin of Pittsburgh, a rising industrialist and politician who was quite keen for a Jackson candidacy. It was promising that Baldwin owned and edited a newspaper. Carroll's note was soon followed by others. Colonel Andrew Hynes had been in Kentucky where John Adair was optimistic about Jackson's prospects. "He had little doubt," Hynes told Jackson, "with the proper management of your friends that you might be elevated to the" presidency. Then came an encouraging missive from Anthony Butler about the sentiments of influential people in Virginia and Pennsylvania, including current members of Congress, who were stroking chins and murmuring "Jackson" and "president" over cigars and brandy. Butler knew that Jackson planned to visit Washington on military matters that fall and suggested that he should begin conversations about his promising political future. The nation needed a strong leader, Butler stressed, and "every man in the U.S. looks to you as this individual." Butler ended with the magic words: it was Jackson's *duty* to accept.[15]

Jackson met these communications with silence. Years later, William B. Lewis would claim that Old Hickory had dismissed the flattering suggestions as preposterous. But Lewis was never the most reliable witness, and even if Jackson had scoffed, he was doubtless pleased, but not commenting, especially when the talk did not stop. Rather, it periodically appeared in the press, which gave it more weight than after-dinner musings in smoky Washington parlors.[16]

Jackson's trip to the nation's capital seemed sensible because the government had appointed him commander of the US Army's Southern Department. Personal consultation with his superiors about the challenges facing the region was in order. The journey from Nashville became another series of banquets at towns and hamlets intent on glorifying the Hero of New Orleans, and the press provided detailed descriptions of the festivities. In that respect, the trip gave Jackson the chance to cultivate popular support beyond Tennessee without seeming to. At Lynchburg, Virginia, the town fathers managed to lure Thomas Jefferson from Monticello for a three-hundred-person dinner in Jackson's honor. Though still fairly vigorous at seventy-two, Jefferson rarely traveled, and the seventy-mile trip was as taxing as it was exceptional for him. He had not seen Andrew Jackson in seventeen years, not since Jackson briefly held William Blount's vacated Senate seat and Jefferson as vice president presided over the Senate. The young Tennessean had not impressed Jefferson then, nor had subsequent reports of Jackson's behavior altered his opinion, particularly Jackson's alleged connection to Aaron Burr and his opposition to James Madison in 1808. Yet victory at New Orleans had made all the difference for Jefferson, as with other Americans, and at Lynchburg, he was uncharacteristically ready with a toast. Jefferson was bashful about speaking in public, but his voice though soft was firm: "Honor and gratitude," he said, "to those who have filled the measure of their country's honor." Jackson immediately gained the floor and raised his glass. "James

Monroe," he said, "late Secretary of War." It was an extraordinary exchange that at least one later Jackson biographer interpreted as Old Hickory's effort to discourage talk about his political prospects. The press at the time was a bit more skeptical. "This was kind in Gen. Jackson," observed one newspaper. "[For] we have no doubt that Mr. Jefferson intended that Gen. Jackson should suppose that he had his eyes on him, when he gave the toast."[17]

Astute observers might have noticed Old Hickory's traveling companion, a pleasant and handsome young man, thirty-one years old, who had been Jackson's chief aide during the war. By the fall of 1815, everyone knew that John Reid was writing Andrew Jackson's biography because he had weeks before published an advertisement seeking advanced purchases of it. Reid said the book would be a fine production, an octavo volume of about four hundred pages, "neatly bound and lettered, with accurate drawings . . . and a correct likeness of the General." He planned to complete it by the end of the year for delivery in the spring. Priced at four dollars—about seventy dollars today—the book was pricey, but Reid and his backers were counting on the presentation and the subject making it marketable, especially because he had testimonials from Carroll, Coffee, and others about his qualifications and knowledge. Jackson chimed in with his own testimonial that Reid had been a witness to many of the events the book would describe, but he was also careful to say that the idea for the biography had been entirely Reid's.[18]

Only the part about John Reid's firsthand experience alongside Jackson was true, for the biography was not Reid's idea; nor was he even the original person chosen to write it. The author was supposed to have been the accomplished historian David Ramsay of Charleston, South Carolina. Ramsay had started his career as a physician, but his flair for illuminating epic events on the page made him famous and wealthy, both because his books were good reads and were secured by copyrights. As the War of 1812 was coming

to a close, Ramsay was in his mid-sixties but hale, and he was putting the finishing touches on a three-volume history of the United
States, which meant he would be ready to begin a new project. His
friend Robert Y. Hayne suggested that he write about Andrew Jackson. Why Hayne brought him the idea can only be surmised. It is
likely that Hayne got the idea from his brother Arthur, who was a
colonel in the army. Where Arthur P. Hayne got the idea is easier to
deduce: he was a colonel in Andrew Jackson's army.

David Ramsay enthusiastically embraced the project. It promised to be extremely lucrative. Jackson's popularity and Ramsay's
reputation suggested an almost limitless market for the book. Reid's
role at this point was to supply Ramsay with material from Andrew
Jackson's letters and official documents, which Reid was already in-
dexing and archiving. Reid had Old Hickory's permission, Ramsay,
his blessing, and by the spring of 1815, everything was in place for
an outstanding work by a proven author with a talent for speedy
composition. Then on the morning of May 6, as David Ramsay
strode down the sidewalk of Charleston's Broad Street, a deranged
tailor passed him, wheeled, and slid a handkerchief off a horse pistol
loaded with buckshot. William Linnen shot Ramsay in the back.
The wounds were mortal.[19]

Ramsay's death stopped the Jackson biography before it began.
Jackson's reaction to the setback, especially his urgency in finding
a replacement for Ramsay, reveals his significant involvement in
a project that clearly meant more to him than was evident at the
time. Arthur Hayne's hope that it could be published before the end
of the congressional session in 1817 indicated a purpose aimed more
at Jackson's political advancement than his place in posterity.[20]

The wish for the book's hasty completion caused Jackson to settle for John Reid. There was much to recommend him, especially
his familiarity with the events and with the documentary evidence

of the same. Nevertheless, Reid lacked Ramsay's reputation, and that seems to have made it necessary for an underwriter to cover costs. References to the benefactor never provide a name, but someone came up with the enormous sum of $30,000, more than a half million dollars today.[21]

Everyone in Jackson's circle pitched in. Robert Y. Hayne assisted Reid in attracting subscribers and gave him practical advice about publishers and press runs. Because Hayne was David Ramsay's executor and had access to his papers, he could send Reid book proposals that Ramsey had used to place his history of the United States. Thomas Cooper took on the role of Reid's informal agent and soon had publishers in northeastern cities competing for the proposed manuscript. Mathew Carey in Philadelphia was selected. Jackson contacted him to solicit his "patronage" and to urge an active advertising campaign.[22]

As Jackson wished, Reid worked hard and wrote quickly to produce at least four chapters by the time they traveled to Washington in November 1815, but the progress made unlikely the spring delivery that the advertisements had promised and that Jackson wanted. It made Reid more eager to return to the work when they left the capital at the end of December. He stopped for a brief visit at his family's home near New London, Virginia, while Jackson continued to Nashville. Reid tarried because his sister Maria was dying from tuberculosis. Her death and funeral extended Reid's stay to mid-January.[23]

As bad roads and worse weather impeded Jackson's progress toward home, he prodded the budding author with letters. "I need not say to you my anxiety for your success in your book," he said. "There are many weighty reasons, that create this anxiety." By the time this letter arrived in Virginia, John Reid himself was dead. On January 17, he came down with typhoid and developed a severe case of pneumonia that killed him in less than a day. Jackson received this news from Reid's father on February 2 and could scarcely believe it. And while his condolence letter to Nathan Reid Jr. expressed profound grief over Reid's death, it also touched on Reid's project, an inappropriate matter considering the circumstances, but Jackson did partly cloak his intent by stating that the biography would become a philanthropic exercise for Reid's widow and orphaned children.[24]

Jackson scrambled to secure the documents Reid had been using, some of which had been with him in Virginia. The suggestion from Abram Maury, Reid's father-in-law, that proceeds from the sale of those documents could help his daughter Elizabeth and her children sent Jackson into a mild panic. His response was immediate and brisk: the originals were to be carefully packed and returned to the Hermitage, by Elizabeth Reid herself if possible, but by the safest conveyance in any case. Maury assured Jackson that his son Daniel would personally see to it.[25]

With the documents accounted for, a search commenced for Reid's successor. At this point, Ramsay's murder and Reid's untimely death would have given a superstitious author pause. A half dozen candidates were considered, scrutinized, and evaluated by Jackson and his friends, who wanted to bring aboard a man from the western regions who would more readily understand events and Jackson's significant role in them. In a few months, Jackson selected John Henry Eaton. He was a western man only by transplant, having grown up in North Carolina, where he was educated at the state university and began practicing law; he had moved to Tennessee in time to serve in the Creek War as a private in the Tennessee militia. More important, he became family of a sort by marrying Andrew Jackson's ward, Myra Lewis, and he joined Jackson's political circle by throwing in with the Blount-Overton faction. Both connections landed him a seat in the Tennessee legislature. His work on

Jackson's biography drew him even closer to Andrew Jackson, especially when Eaton discovered that Reid had not been as far along in the project as everyone had thought.[26]

The delay in publication frustrated Jackson and his friends. Some of those friends, like the Hayne brothers, were already weighing his potential for high political office, and the biography was clearly a step in that direction. Each disappointment and every setback only made them more determined to have the book in the hands of the public while the iron of Jackson's popularity was still hot. True to custom, Jackson habitually disclaimed any desire for office and publicly made gestures to discourage speculation. But privately he became so thoroughly involved with shaping his exploits that it would be easy to conclude that he was secretly spinning ambitious plans in concert with like-minded friends.

For Jackson, however, there was something else behind his desire for positive publicity. A hint was nestled in one of his last letters to John Reid, the one urging him to complete the work, in which Jackson had said, "You like myself have your enemies." Had Reid been alive to read that observation, part of it would have puzzled him, for he was too young to have too many enemies. As for Andrew Jackson, the nation's adored Hero, Reid had just seen the man take Washington by storm. In countless parlors, countless admirers had hung on his every word, men had jostled to be noticed and to receive a bow, and invitations to dinners at the Monroe home or with the president and the effervescent Dolley had been waiting for Old Hickory. Jackson's sliver of doubt about the durability of his acclaim revealed his suspiciousness. Reid at least knew something about its origin, for he understood why he was writing the book, just as John Eaton would learn as he thumbed through the mass of papers to decide what to put in and, more importantly, what to leave out. The story of Andrew Jackson, hero, had many sides, as the Creek agent

Benjamin Hawkins and others would have told. Jackson wanted his side told first, lest, like Pakenham lifeless on the Chalmette Plain, he himself would be late to battle with all his plans awry. Eaton would learn what Reid had known and what Ramsay had not lived long enough to find out.[27]

= CHAPTER 3 =

IMAGE

ROM ONE PERSPECTIVE, THE TASK OF BOTH JOHN REID AND John Eaton as biographers was easy. They simply had to tell the exciting story of a man already wearing the laurels of a grateful nation. Andrew Jackson had won acclaim with spectacular victories over rampaging Indians and remorseless redcoats, and Americans everywhere were hungry for the details about those events and the man responsible for them. It would have been hard for even a hack to botch the job, given such an eager audience. And both Reid and Eaton had talent.[1]

After Eaton took over, his talent and skill would be tested. He had to tell Jackson's story without revealing too much of Jackson's history, some of which was unsavory. Eaton focused on Jackson's military exploits in the Creek War and the War of 1812, and left years of Jackson's life in Tennessee largely blank, as though nothing of any importance at all happened to him between 1804 and 1812. Vague references to domestic bliss at Jackson's modest Hermitage on the Cumberland River ignored some memorable episodes, such as the muddled origins of his marriage to Rachel Donelson Robards. Eaton's only remark about Rachel Jackson in the final book did not mention her by name but merely described her as "an amiable and affectionate consort."[2]

The absence of Rachel Jackson in the biography was obviously a conscious omission, one dictated by her desire for privacy and by her husband's hypersensitivity about his marriage. In the 1817 edition of the biography, those mere five words about Jackson's "consort" allowed some accounts of Jackson's life to describe him as a bachelor and something of a rake. Neither in the 1817 nor any subsequent edition of the biography would Rachel appear as a significant figure. And there were reasons for this beyond her privacy and his touchiness.

Rachel's family was of good stock, her father a Donelson and one of the founders of the little settlement on the Cumberland named Nashville. That fact alone made the Donelsons prominent in the community. Yet Rachel's life was etched by the frontier. She spoke with the thick twang of the backwoods, and in a vocabulary rich with regionalisms that would have struck eastern ears as unrefined, even uncouth, especially when she regularly mixed up subjects and verbs. She liked tobacco, later preferred a pipe to smoke it, and never learned her letters beyond the rudiments. The infrequent correspondence she scrawled over the years gives the impression of her gripping a pencil while biting her tongue. She was a spirited girl, though, pretty and pleasant and acquainted with the toll of the wilderness. When she was eighteen, someone—Indians or white robbers, depending on whom one asked—killed her father, leaving her mother a forlorn widow in a remote blockhouse and in need of protectors. The widow Donelson took in boarders.

Her first was a bookish lawyer named John Overton, a Virginia transplant by way of Kentucky, whose owl-like eyes made him seem older than his twenty-three years, but whose soft voice and slight frame didn't promise much in the way of protection. That situation improved when the gangly redhead with the long face and commanding presence came along. Andy Jackson wasn't built much better than Overton, but his height and carriage made him seem formidable, and his pockmarked face with the strange welt on his brow suggested a man who had seen something of life, though he was barely past twenty. He and Overton hit it off immediately, which made the household pleasant.

It was the girl, however, who made it glow, even though she wasn't supposed to be there. By the time Overton and Jackson showed up in Nashville, Rachel Donelson was married to a dashing Kentuckian name Lewis Robards and had been living far away from her girlhood home. Possibly it had started out as a love match. Rachel was fetching, and Robards came from a good Virginia family that pronounced its name "Roberts" and had the habit of marrying well. But even if loveless and arranged, the union seemed likely to be prosperous if not palatable. Sadly, it became neither quickly. Robards was proud of his wife, but he bristled when other men noticed why. Soon he was flying into jealous rages if Rachel traded a routine pleasantry with anyone male over fifteen and under fifty. He was verbally abusive and, encouraged by strong drink, he could use an open hand to drive home his point. It all drove Rachel Robards to go home to her mother. She was there when the solemn Overton arrived, and so she was there when the tall, blue-eyed stranger from North Carolina came looking for bed and board.

Both of the young men were captivated from the beginning. Overton was bashful by nature, and Rachel possibly flirted a bit even though married—after all, she was unhappily married. For whatever reason, Overton tended to be wistful when she took up a bucket to carry water or pushed her hair away from her face when sweating over a chore. Rachel moved with an easy grace, smiles coming naturally to her and with something like the aroma of earth about her, the sort of thing that made men pause to stare and stammer—the very thing that made Lewis Robards crazy with jealousy.

Rachel liked John Overton, but she fell in love with Andrew Jackson, most likely within days of meeting him. There was probably flirtation in play, but there did not need to be. Andrew Jackson was enchanted the moment he laid eyes on Rachel Robards. He had known women of a type before, mostly prostitutes he encountered in South Carolina's Low Country, where the blades of Charleston could shed genteel habits to rollick at gaming tables and retire to low-lit bedchambers. When Jackson lived in North Carolina reading law, he scandalized a respectable social get-together by inviting two local whores to attend as his guests. They were a novelty act of a mother and her daughter, the latter learning the family trade. That part of his past Jackson would not have talked about in Nashville or, later on, have included in Eaton's biography, but knowing a bit about women and their hardships made him sympathetic to the plight of the dark-haired girl at the widow Donelson's.

It soon became plain that the two were more than friends. When Robards showed up to reconcile with his wife, he found a young woman changed and distant. He was accustomed to imagining her supposed assignations with other men, and even if she and Jackson had been on their most reticent behavior, it would not have mattered. Lewis Robards suspected the worst, threw one of his tantrums, and decamped for Kentucky.

Later, speculation had Jackson, after this episode, intent on shielding Rachel from her abusive husband by taking her to Natchez in the summer of 1791. The place, at some remove from Nashville, was in Spanish territory, and Jackson had business interests there ranging from slave trading to land speculation. Such activities had required him to swear allegiance to the king of Spain, which was unappealing but had the advantage of giving him access to Spanish legal authority. According to the stories, he was ready to use that access as soon as he heard that Robards had divorced Rachel. By then, Jackson had left her with friends in Natchez and returned to

Nashville, but he raced back with the glad tidings and, it was said, married Rachel under Spanish law.[3]

It is unlikely that any of this happened in this way. No document records a marriage in Natchez, but there is one that indicates the two were living as man and wife as early as January 1791, months before they presumably traveled there and months before Jackson could have heard that Lewis Robards had obtained a divorce. In short, the Natchez marriage is almost surely a fiction, but none of their neighbors cared that they were not formally married. On a frontier where the wilderness could swallow up a spouse without a trace, marriage as a state of mind was not that rare, and it could carry as much weight as officially sanctioned matrimony. If anyone chuckled over the Jacksons, it would have been with good-natured references to rising sap and buzzing bees, and it would have been kept quiet in any case. Everyone knew about the husband's reaction to jokes of a particular type. Moreover, nobody would want to wound the smiling girl they liked and were glad to see at last happy.[4]

Two uneventful years later, though, the fact that they were not married suddenly became a problem, and the scandal of their situation forever scarred her heart and set him to cocking his ear for gossip and cocking his pistols to stop it. John Overton brought them unsettling news. Lewis Robards had only petitioned the Virginia legislature (then with jurisdiction over Kentucky) for permission to seek a divorce. He had not obtained a final decree dissolving the marriage. At the time, people in the region were eager to shed their backwoods past and enter more fashionable society, and their previous indifference to Jackson and Rachel's quasi-marriage disappeared. It was in this atmosphere that Andrew and Rachel discovered not only that they were not legally married but also that Rachel was legally a bigamist, with the sin of adultery thrown in for shameful measure.

Overton also reported that Robards had finally obtained his divorce, but the development itself troubled the owlish lawyer more than its tardiness. Overton could feel the rough winds of change blowing across the Cumberland regarding matters of love and legality. It was on his advice that his friends quietly married in the traditional way of listening to a parson tell them what they already knew about sickness, health, and putting things asunder. But that was not the end of it, because the circumstances of her divorce were humiliating. The Kentucky court in granting Lewis Robards his divorce did so because Rachel had abandoned him to live in sin with another man. It branded her in the documentary record as a fallen woman. When the community's casual indifference became something less forgiving, Rachel's eyes became sad and haunted. Over the years, she buried herself in her Bible for solace, puzzling out the words with fierce resolve, becoming pious as she became portly.

Andrew Jackson loved her more than life and never minded the rough grammar, the rounding figure, or even the pipe. He cherished the simple niceness of a good person who was devoted to him with the same fierce resolve she gave to her devotionals. It is unlikely that Rachel knew Shakespeare's dictum about Caesar's wife and suspicion, but it was her curse that she was fated to learn it.

═══════

LOVING RACHEL BROUGHT out the best in Andrew Jackson. No anecdotes, no written accounts, no recollections of either friends or enemies ever told of anything but his utter devotion, unswerving loyalty, and absolute fidelity to the woman who always remained for him the pretty, smiling girl who stunned him that autumn on the Cumberland. He was supernaturally indifferent to time or tide when it came to her, and for him, the passing years never sagged her face or form. His love ran so deep and strong that Andrew Jackson was willing to do more than die for Rachel. He was willing to kill for her.

That willingness stemmed from a fury that resided deep within him and that could be easily provoked. Jackson was always more or less angry about something. As a boy, he clenched fists over harmless jokes and unintentional slights. Orphaned by the Revolutionary War, he could not live with his few remaining relatives because his temper caused scenes and disturbed guests. As a cub attorney with more sass than sense, he challenged an elderly lawyer to a duel merely for pointing out his inexperience. Everyone liked and respected Waightstill Avery, and friends stopped Jackson's encounter with him before either resorted to gunplay, but nobody could cure Jackson's habit of taking offense when none was meant. For a man like him, protecting his wife's reputation could mean something other than outrage over loose talk. It could be an excuse to settle scores under the cloak of righteous indignation. Loving Rachel brought out the worst in Andrew Jackson.

That too was reason enough for John Eaton to limit to five words his reference to the otherwise heartwarming reality of Jackson's marriage. There would be no mention of Jackson's nearly fighting a duel with Governor John Sevier in 1803 because Sevier had spoken contemptuously of the marriage in public. Missing from Eaton's account was how Jackson still carried a bullet near his lungs from an 1806 duel in which he killed Charles Dickinson, a prominent young Nashville attorney who had spoken ill of Rachel. Also omitted in the manuscript were events that revealed a pattern of troubling anger. His violent reactions over Rachel, no matter how unseemly, had the merit of being understandable. When it became necessary to explain them, they could be correctly depicted as a loving husband defending his wife's reputation. Other events in Jackson's past did not have the same justification. They were simply unseemly, especially as the excuse of youth faded with Jackson's age, which grayed his hair without curing his temperament. He was forty-six years old when he went looking for a fight on the streets of Nashville that exploded into a vicious brawl that nearly killed him. The fight almost kept him from the Creek War.

The incident serves as an illustrative example rather than an exception. After the canceled Natchez expedition, a quarrel broke out between young Billy Carroll, Jackson's inspector general, and Jesse Benton, brother of Thomas Hart Benton, one of Jackson's colonels in Tennessee's United States Volunteers. The Bentons were a study in contrasts, with Tom eager for a career in the regular army and Jesse something of a hothead with a wicked pen. It did not take long for Jesse to raise a minor argument to a question of honor, and by early June 1813, he had managed to goad Carroll into a duel. Carroll asked Jackson to serve as his second, and to his credit, Jackson refused. He pointed out that not only his age but his position in the community required that he not participate in such an event. He might have had in mind the consequences of his killing Dickinson seven years earlier, a deed illegal in Tennessee and socially catastrophic for Jackson because Dickinson had been prominent in the East and popular in Nashville's finer parlors. As Jackson tried to patch things up between Jesse and Billy, however, he heard talk hinting that Carroll was a coward, and good sense ceased to guide any of his decisions afterward. Convinced that ruffians with Jesse Benton's encouragement were slandering Carroll, Jackson told Billy he would make arrangements for the duel.

What resulted was a farce. Jesse and Billy agreed to begin the duel paces apart and facing away from each other. On the order to fire, they were to wheel and shoot. Benton, however, planned what he considered a clever if ungainly tactic by turning and assuming a sideways crouch. Carroll squinted at the comic posture of Benton in profile, while Benton shot Carroll in the thumb. Carroll's shot hit Benton in his buttocks. And having satisfied the requirements of "honor" by way of such wounds, they quit the field and commenced to mend. It could have ended there, but when the duel took place, Thomas Hart Benton was in Washington securing reimbursement for Andrew Jackson's expenses during the Natchez expedition. He returned after successfully arguing Jackson's case and was furious to find that Jackson had taken Carroll's part against his brother.

Soon enough, Tom Benton made the mistake of saying that Jackson had acted dishonorably. Jackson pledged to horsewhip him for that remark. The young officer let it be known that he was anything but frightened, and there the matter lay until September 4, when Jackson heard that the Benton brothers had come into Nashville. He, John Coffee, Rachel's nephew Stockley Hays, and a few other friends prowled the town, looking for trouble. They found it at the hotel where the Bentons had taken rooms. In one hand Jackson carried a whip, but he had a pistol in the other. And thus armed, he charged toward Tom Benton, who was standing on the porch of the hotel. Jesse Benton, seeing Jackson trotting at his brother with a pistol, drew his weapon and fired. The bullet tore into Jackson's left shoulder. Jackson fired too, but in the excitement he didn't hit anyone, and neither did Tom as pistol reports flurried. All missed their marks, though one gun was discharged close enough to Tom Benton's clothing to singe his sleeve. Coffee shot at him but missed, and as the muzzle-loaded firearms were spent with no time for reloading, Jackson's companions went into action. They jumped the Bentons and slashed them with knives. Jesse remembered that he had double-primed his pistol, so he rammed its barrel against Stockley Hays's chest and pulled the trigger. The gun misfired. Pinned to the ground, Jesse felt someone kicking his head while Hays worked on him with a knife.

The discovery that Jackson was bleeding to death ended the fracas. As doctors across town stanched Jackson's wound and tried to repair his arm, Thomas Hart Benton surveyed the scene of the mayhem and marveled that the attack on him and his brother had been carried out in the same hotel where district judge Bennet Searcy was lodging. "So little are the laws and its ministers respected!" Benton would exclaim. Jackson had given Captain Billy Carroll permission to stay away, and lest there was any question about cowardice, Old Hickory scrawled out a "certificate" declaring Billy wasn't one. Benton could not say whether such a document reflected "less honor upon the General or the Captain."[5]

Jesse Benton recovered from the stab wounds that had mainly gashed his arms, and Thomas Hart Benton achieved his wish to receive a regular commission as a lieutenant colonel in the Thirty-Ninth Infantry. He fought in the Creek War that Jackson almost missed because of the shattered arm, but the experience left Lieutenant Colonel Benton embittered. He acidly noted how "the puppies of the Genl [Jackson] receive all the honor." Jesse never forgave, but Tom moved to Missouri after the war and in time became sufficiently important to contemplate the vagaries of fame and the peculiarities of politics. In contrast to his unforgiving brother, Thomas Hart Benton would one day see the wisdom in rolling over, on command.[6]

═══

EATON OVERLOOKED THE brawl with the Bentons as his sanitized story rolled on, just as he ignored that Jackson routinely speculated in land, often successfully but at least once so recklessly as to incur nearly ruinous debt. Eaton did not include Jackson's meetings with Aaron Burr to discuss Burr's mysterious plans for flatboats carrying armed men down the Mississippi, their purposes possibly sinister, certainly illegal. Jackson's pastime of racing fast horses for large wagers and laying odds on spurred roosters at boisterous cockfights did not make the manuscript, either.

Instead, in Jackson's story, according to Eaton, the hero is staid, humble, and self-effacing. His time as a judge on Tennessee's Superior Court lasted only "a short time," even though Jackson had served on the bench for six years. The biography described Jackson's appealing humility, which was devoid of self-flattery and pretensions to honors and distinction. The biography treated his election as major general of the Tennessee militia in the same way. He had not known he was being considered for the post, said Reid/Eaton, which was one of their deliberate misrepresentations. In fact, Jackson had challenged John Sevier for the militia post and won only because his friend Archibald Roane, as Tennessee's governor, broke a tie by casting the deciding vote. Emphasizing the theme of humility, the biography noted that when the war broke out in 1812, Jackson's "proud and inflexible mind . . . could not venture to solicit an appointment in the army." This too was deliberately presented, though it went beyond misrepresentation.[7]

Evasions, half-truths, and even some outright fabrications were understandable, for John Eaton would not have been doing his job had he told the complete, unvarnished truth. The book was meant to focus on Jackson's military campaigns and thereby to launch his budding political career. When Eaton was truthful, as in his discussion of the barbarities of the Creek War, he knew it could not hurt Jackson—on the contrary, many Americans were not troubled by brutality toward Indians. Contemplating the Red Sticks after Horseshoe Bend, a Boston newspaper crowed that "one more victory will probably complete their extermination, and finish the proof that we are better than the English in India."[8]

Indeed, Indian warfare was a pitiless business, and people who waged it were angered when judged by critics invoking refined rules with lofty references to the laws of nations. In a war marked by massacre and blood vengeance, military men had to do things—or, at least, felt they had to do things—that were unthinkable to contemplative souls in the sedate cities of the East. Most of the public could understand a plain telling of the horrors at Tallushatchee, Talladega, Emuckfau, and Enotochopco, because angry and frightened men with Fort Mims fresh on their minds were not likely to cut corners when it came to killing. John Coffee was an example of that, a quiet and gentle bear of a man who made war like a merciless khan, slaughtering by day and sleeping untroubled at night.

But if Eaton was truthful about Jackson's military career, he did not give the entire truth of it. Calculated barbarities committed in cold blood were omitted. The clash at Horseshoe Bend on the Tallapoosa was a fierce fight to the death, but the killing continued long after the battle was over. While daylight lasted, Jackson's men systematically executed wounded Creek warriors by leisurely wandering the field and shooting the fallen at point-blank range. At first light the following day, they continued the coldblooded chore. Jackson wanted an accurate number of the Red Stick dead, and he got it by literally counting noses: he ordered the tip of each warrior's nose clipped and tallied. The biography did not mention this. Instead, it addressed why some 350 survivors were only women and children by explaining that Indians rarely surrendered. "Faithless themselves," Eaton mused, "they place no faith in the faith of others." In reality, their enemy's actions after Horseshoe Bend gave Red Sticks reason not to place faith in anything but their feet as a means of survival. Possibly a hundred of them managed to get away in the dark, but some did not get far enough. It was later said that when Jackson learned of warriors taking refuge in a hollow of the Tallapoosa's steep bank, he ordered poles hammered into the ground to collapse it and bury them alive.[9]

Eaton did not tell about these incidents. Rather he described why Jackson found it necessary to deprive his own dead of decent burials. Old Hickory had weighted the corpses, forty-nine in number, to sink in the Tallapoosa because Creeks easily discovered graves. Jackson was not worried about his men's bodies being desecrated. Rather, he wanted to prevent white scalps from being displayed in Creek villages. Trophies like that encouraged a mistaken belief in Red Stick victory that would embolden them to continue the fight. The point Eaton intended to convey was clear. Jackson understood how to end the war and was almost alone in his willingness to do it.[10]

Nor did Eaton tell the truth about Old Hickory at Fort Jackson. The Creeks allied with Jackson thought they understood him, as did his foes, but they were perplexed by the staggering example of bad faith at Fort Jackson. They were not alone; the events there had profoundly troubled Benjamin Hawkins as well. Jackson shoved him aside and became the sole negotiator at Fort Jackson, except that the event he staged did not resemble negotiations in any sense of the word. To a solemn gathering of Creeks on August 1, 1814, he flatly stated his terms: he intended to impose a land cession that did more than compensate the United States for the cost of the Creek War. It would be large enough to separate all southeastern Indians from meddling Europeans on the Gulf Coast. Jackson reminded the stone-faced Creek headmen that they had listened to "bad men," and he explained that only the surrender of an enormous quantity of land would prove Creek friendship and guarantee the security of the United States.

The Creeks were expressionless in the presence of Americans but flabbergasted in private as they contemplated the expanse of land Jackson planned to take. At twenty-two million acres, it was enormous. More than a third of it belonged to Creeks who had fought at Jackson's side. They tried to persuade him of the unfairness of the arrangement, but they could not divert him from a punitive peace visited upon all southeastern Indians, especially Creeks, friends as well as foes. It was all the more exasperating that those foes were all but absent at Fort Jackson. Only one Creek in the assemblage was a Red Stick.

Benjamin Hawkins grumbled, but his government liked the Treaty of Fort Jackson's national security rationale, and Jackson was crafty in pointing to a benefit for the old Civilization Program cherished by Hawkins. Constricting Creek hunting grounds would force them to adopt agriculture and husbandry. The supposed benefits to the Indians themselves made it into Eaton's book. "It is a happy consideration," he wrote about the Treaty of Fort Jackson, "that whilst these advantages were obtained, no material injury was done those vanquished people." It was a statement made implausible by Jackson's candid one to his friends. He boasted to John Overton that he had scarfed up "the cream of Creek country," but Jackson was being modest. He had done even more than that. He had prepared a way to take significant tracts of land from other southeastern Indians as well. Cherokees who were at Fort Jackson had an inkling that this might be their future, but their objections went unheeded.[11]

It was normal for an Indian treaty to lack precision concerning land. Such treaties recognized no clear boundaries separating the underpopulated land of one tribe from that of another because such boundaries didn't exist. Hunting parties freely crossed such terrain and understood that it was under a neighbor's sphere of influence rather than plainly possessed under a deed or title. It was only when government surveyors began determining what belonged to whom that the fluid borders described in treaties became hard lines of demarcation. The enormity of the Fort Jackson cession put the placement of a thousand-mile perimeter at the discretion of men lugging transits, chains, poles, and plumb bobs through a trackless wilderness. An imaginative surveyor fearless about confronting Indians could go a long way in carving out a large bit of land that was not part of the already vast cession. That was the reason Andrew Jackson wanted a fearless, creative surveyor on the commission that Congress created in March 1815 to ascertain and mark off the Fort Jackson cession. John Coffee came to mind.[12]

Jackson couldn't simply plant Coffee on the commission, which already had its full complement of three members. Instead, Old Hickory finagled a provisional appointment for his trusted lieutenant under the guise of making him a substitute, if necessary, for Benjamin Hawkins, whom he described to the government as in bad health. Despite his nebulous status, Coffee acted as if he were a fully authorized member of the commission. He immediately traveled to the Coosa River in December 1815 and struck out with his equipment and a menacing manner. More than his attitude, the direction of Coffee's work troubled the Cherokees. He began rapidly running a line north, which made no sense if the primary reason for the treaty was to separate the Creeks from Spaniards to the south. Instead, Coffee was establishing as a fact that about fifty miles of land north of the Coosa belonged to the Creeks (which made it part of the cession) rather than to the Cherokees (who stood to lose it). The Cherokees pointed out the error, but they also knew enough to be afraid of John Coffee. They sent a delegation to Washington. Coffee continued to run the line.[13]

The Cherokees were right in thinking it all very curious. The War Department instructed the commissioners to postpone any work on the northern part of the cession until the government could sort out what the Cherokee delegation was so agitated about. Meanwhile, Coffee ignored everybody but Andrew Jackson, who urged him to hasten his work; Jackson was in Washington when the protesting Cherokees arrived and knew exactly why they were upset. It would be of little comfort to them that John Coffee was in the process of also stealing land from Chickasaws and Choctaws. In its seeming endless reach, the Treaty of Fort Jackson was more than a way to separate Indians from interlopers, more even than a way to separate them from their hunting grounds to force them to become farmers. The treaty was part of a larger plan, which was why it became politically necessary in a few years to revise descriptions of how it came about using admiring pamphlets and newspaper articles. No matter how it was represented, though, in August 1814 Andrew Jackson had taken the first step toward finally getting rid of the people his treaty victimized. Jackson revealed the future by parting a veil at Fort Jackson. The future was Indian removal.

AFTER THE VICTORY at Horseshoe Bend, people took only slight notice of an incident that had preceded it. Poor discipline was a problem for Jackson's army from the time it entered Creek country, and Jackson's efforts to quell discontent ranged freely between the carrot and the stick, but ultimately, he resorted to a firing squad. In March 1814 he planned his march to the Tallapoosa under the shadow of reports that men who had left the army—the ones who used the vague enlistment terms to their advantage—were denigrating him as a feckless incompetent. His friends assured him that nobody listened to this sort of talk, but the prospect of his reputation being tarnished in Tennessee set his nerves on edge and rubbed his patience raw. As he prepared to plunge deeper into the wilderness with a group of men prone to disorder over the smallest grievance, he was in no mood to brook the slightest hint of disobedience. This likely had much to do with how he handled the incident involving a Tennessee militia private named John Wood.[14]

Almost nothing is known about Wood, and confused, contradictory accounts cloud what he did to get into trouble. He was a Bedford County native and part of James Harris's company, but he was also so inconspicuous that, after he was executed, official accounts routinely confused his name as "Woods." It was the last of the many misunderstandings that plagued this young man during his brief and otherwise uneventful service, for he had not been in the army long enough to see a battle. Moreover, he had not been on earth long enough to be in the army, at least legally. John Wood was seventeen.

But he was willing and, as it turned out, foolhardy. The lad was on early-morning guard duty when a sympathetic officer gave him permission to leave his post and eat breakfast. Wood did not tarry over his meal, but he finished later than others, and another officer assumed he was an idler. He ordered Wood to clean up the mess area. Private Wood told the man that he had to return to his guard post. Possibly there was something in the boy's manner that suggested impertinence, for the officer chose to interpret Wood's explanation as insubordinate. When he barked at John Wood, the boy barked back. The officer made to take away Wood's rifle, but Wood leveled it with a terse promise to shoot him or anyone else who tried to take it. By then the exchange was becoming a disturbance. Having gained an audience, the officer could not let the matter go. Having resolved that he was right, John Wood would not back down. Accounts independent of one another tell of General Jackson emerging from his tent bellowing, "Shoot the damned rascal!" He descended on the scene, and the boy was easily disarmed by someone, by Jackson himself in some accounts. In any case, John Wood finally gave up his weapon without complaint. Jackson had Wood arrested. In a blur, he was court-martialed for mutiny, found guilty, and sentenced to death. Some later described his court martial as perfunctory, and many thought it irregular. It seems to have mystified John Wood, especially when he heard his sentence.

Wood's friends tried to prevent his execution with personal appeals to Jackson bolstered by petitions pleading for clemency and signed by many. So it was said. But it was also remembered that Jackson was inflexible. His general order for John Wood's execution described a chronic mutineer. He noted how Wood had committed previous and similar offenses, which Old Hickory had unwisely forgiven. This latest transgression was dangerously injurious to morale. As one newspaper later noted, John Wood had to die because he had tried "to canker the heart of an army—to paralyze the efforts of the government." It was quite an ambition for a boy not yet eighteen. And, of course, it wasn't true.[15]

At noon on March 14, before the assembled army, a guard selected from the recently arrived Thirty-Ninth Infantry escorted John Wood out of camp and placed him "in a proper situation" to hear a recitation of General Jackson's order. The chaplain read a brief devotional, and after only the slightest pause, the left section of the guard took a step forward, presented arms, and on the order to take aim and fire, shot John Wood dead. He slumped lifelessly "without the least emotion."[16]

"The execution of a private, John Woods [*sic*] . . . produced, at this time, the most salutary effects," John Eaton wrote for Jackson's biography. It laid to rest, said Eaton, the idea that militia could behave differently from real soldiers with impunity. Nevertheless, Eaton carefully noted that the harsh verdict was "painful" to "the feelings of General Jackson" but that he had no choice. The press at the time of the event shared the sentiment. Editorial comments decried the "blackest mutiny" pervading the army before Wood's death and celebrated the "considerable harmony" in the camp after it.[17]

But an alternative account, in which the whole episode was the product of misunderstandings, not mutiny and necessity, would appear years later. In fact, John Wood's fit of temper that March day was his first violation of good order, not a repeat of previous offenses. He had joined the army in January 1814, weeks after the December troubles that Jackson linked him to in his general order. Some men who witnessed these events were later willing to point this out. But at the time, victory at Horseshoe Bend was enough to outshine the pain as well as the particulars of Wood's death. He was of a type, and certainly one that Andrew Jackson knew better than most. Even as boys, this type was hard-bitten, touchy, fiercely independent, and prone to impetuous reactions when crossed or cornered. The way John Wood behaved that chilly March morning at Fort Strother should not have surprised anybody, least of all Andrew Jackson. When Old Hickory saw that boy's gun snatched away, when he put the boy before the guns of his guards, he might as well have been looking at himself at seventeen, had he met someone unforgiving.

In his first edition of Jackson's life, Eaton stuck to the Wood story as Jackson, and the nation's newspapers, told it. The document justifying Wood's death became a matter of record, though, and it would need explaining in later editions, taxing Eaton's powers of invention. A similar event, however, Eaton would simply leave out altogether.

After the victory at New Orleans, reports of a mutiny near Mobile came to Jackson's headquarters. Militiamen at Fort Jackson had insisted that their term of enlistment had expired. They planned to go home. Their commander Col. Philip Pipkin disagreed, as did Brig. Gen. James Winchester, commanding at Mobile. Nevertheless, the impatient militiamen felt emboldened by the clear signs that the war was all but over. They not only brazenly left camp but also raided the fort's supply larder to provision their trip home. Their number was not insignificant—about two hundred headed north for Tennessee—but after their capture, it was the six ringleaders who faced the charge of mutiny. By the strictest definition of the term, they were guilty, but postwar leniency was not without precedent. Also, the old and persistent problem of confused enlistment schedules provided an excuse to mitigate both the charge and the sentence. Yet a court martial sentenced them to die. When the verdict and sentence landed on Jackson's desk for final approval, he did not hesitate to give it on January 22, 1815. The execution was only delayed by the lingering threat the British supposedly posed against Mobile, but when that ended, so did the reprieve. The men were shot on February 21. It would later seem outrageous to some that the doomed six were executed after the British were gone.

John Eaton did not mention it in the biography, yet the executions, like other things, would one day be difficult to explain. They seemed unnecessary, and worse. Nobody bothered to remember those men in 1815. In due course, their names, along with that of John Wood, would become household words.

IN EATON'S BIOGRAPHY, sharp readers could discern Jackson's biggest concerns by the trouble Eaton took to explain them. A third of the book attempted to explain Jackson's attack on Pensacola and his later heavy hand in New Orleans after the January 8 victory. In 1817, more and more people were coming to believe that Jackson regarded himself as above the law. Rather, it appeared that he thought he was a law unto himself. This unbecoming stance was possibly the reason Eaton glossed over his legal career, especially the part he spent as a judge of Tennessee's Superior Court. It was certainly the reason for the extensive explanation about New Orleans.

In late March 1815, the usually laudatory *National Intelligencer* casually observed that Jackson's recent restriction of the press in New Orleans "appears to have excited some dissatisfaction." That was putting it mildly. Jackson had done considerably more than check the press. Over the course of the first two months of 1815, he had locked up a member of the Louisiana legislature and arrested a federal district court judge.[18]

Jackson believed he had valid reasons to be cautious. Immediately after the battle, he had suspected that the British were not done with New Orleans, a suspicion others shared. "You know that they are as audacious as persevering," the French consul observed about the beaten redcoats, adding, "the fate of Louisiana is hanging by a thread." Adding to the apprehension was that the British remained at Villeré Plantation for a couple of weeks. They were preparing to evacuate, but Jackson did not know that. When the British finally departed, they headed to Mobile and took Fort Bowyer at the mouth of the bay as a preliminary to implementing their original plan of moving on New Orleans from there by way of Baton Rouge. Only after news about the Treaty of Ghent arrived at Mobile did the British quickly leave Fort Bowyer, sailing away for good.[19]

In the intervening two months, though, before formal notification of the peace, Jackson had no idea what the British planned to do next. He insisted on keeping the militia in place, including the local Louisiana units. When grumbling grew louder over continued service in the face of a diminishing threat, Jackson extended martial law. Men were eager to return to their businesses and plantations, but they faced new curfews and restrictions on their movements. The man who had been everyone's hero after January 8 became increasingly unpopular in the city he had defended. And as dissatisfaction with his stringent policies mounted, questions about him inevitably circulated. Jackson's performance during the previous winter's crisis came under scrutiny. He took too long to start for New Orleans, it was said, and after arriving, he remained ignorant of the region's geography. The result was an unimpeded British approach that surprised everyone and could have turned out differently if the British had not been so cautious. Finally, Jackson had tried to cover errors with "a little bombast" in his report of the battle.[20]

Such criticism was nothing compared to the anger over the continued imposition of martial law. Militiamen began to desert their posts, some to go home, others to sample the pleasures of New Orleans. In December 1814, when there had been talk of capitulation, Jackson had suspended the Louisiana legislature and placed guards at the doors of the capitol. After the victory, the legislature resumed its session and provided a glimpse of the growing dissatisfaction by passing a resolution expressing gratitude to the city's defenders that omitted any mention of Andrew Jackson. Angered by this and other little gestures of defiance, Jackson looked under bedsteads for dangerous ones. He was convinced that the Creoles of New Orleans were behind the complaints and were promoting sedition, so he sent the French consul Louis de Toussard and as many French speakers as he could round up out of the city. He moved to control information published by the city's newspapers. When an anonymous letter to the editor of the *Courier de la Louisiane* protested Jackson's treatment of the French population and his muzzling of the press, he deemed it as more than inflammatory. It was designed, he concluded, to incite mutiny in his army while divulging to British spies in New Orleans that the city was ripe for conquest. He browbeat the *Courier*'s editor into revealing the author of the piece, who turned out to be the naturalized Frenchman Louis Louallier. Jackson promptly jailed him.[21]

Louallier's detention was shocking for at least two reasons. First, he was universally admired for having raised considerable sums of money to clothe bedraggled militiamen as they arrived in New Orleans. Second, he had earnestly supported Jackson's defense of the city where it counted most, in the Louisiana legislature, of which he was a member. Alarmed by the continuation of martial law and outraged over the military imprisonment of a prominent political figure for exercising a right guaranteed by the Constitution, Federal District Judge Dominick A. Hall issued a writ of habeas corpus demanding Louallier's release. Jackson arrested Judge Hall. A US attorney then asked a state judge to issue a writ for Hall, but Jackson preemptively arrested both the attorney and the Louisiana jurist. Though he later changed his mind about imprisoning the last two men, he did deport Judge Hall to Baton Rouge.

News of the peace treaty with England didn't make any difference in Jackson's behavior. He stubbornly waited for official confirmation, which brought simmering complaints to a boil as New Orleans's citizens counted up innocent men thrown into jail and harmless people exiled from their homes. Finally, in mid-March when Jackson at last received official word that the war was over, he lifted martial law, released Louallier, and let the exiles return. Whether for good, as Jackson would insist, or for ill, as those wronged would claim, the damage to the lustrous reputation earned at the Rodriguez Canal mere weeks earlier was palpable. Dominick Hall, for one, was beyond fulmination when he was able to return to New Orleans. He demanded that Jackson appear in his court on March 24 to explain why he should not be held in contempt, and after several days of arguments and testimony, with Jackson represented by Edward Livingston and John Reid, Hall fined him a whopping $1,000. Much was later made out of Jackson's admirable submission to Hall's judicial authority. Not only did he pay the fine but stories spread of how he calmed citizens angry over the persecution of him, their hero. The two months under Old Hickory's iron rule, however, must have been hard to forget. And as newspapers noted, and not just those in and near New Orleans, George Washington would never have done what Andrew Jackson did. "That man, as good as he was great," said a New England print, "did at all times and in every pressing emergency, pay homage to the civil authority of his country."[22]

Hall's verdict was one thing, but unfavorable comparisons to George Washington called into question Jackson's temperament. As his political star began to rise, this question would lead to others about his judgment, maturity, and respect for the law. Jackson and his handlers knew the dangerous snares that he had set with his own hands. Even as he was leaving New Orleans, they began a project to impugn Louallier, discredit Hall, and paint Jackson as the only person in the affair with strategic prudence and an unshakeable sense of duty, the only man who could protect New Orleans from its careless citizenry.[23]

For a time after New Orleans, Andrew Jackson was apparently not as concerned about public opinion as he was about explaining things to the War Department. He drafted a report full of bombast, self-congratulation, and personal attacks on Dominick Hall. John Reid sharpened his pencil to soften the language and the meaning, especially regarding Judge Hall. But even with judicious editing, the account of martial law, citizens driven from their homes, and the locking up of officials from the federal bench and state legislature left acting Secretary of War Alexander Dallas troubled and President James Madison uneasy. At the same time, they gauged Jackson's immense and growing popularity. Dallas wearily took up his pen to address General Jackson in a way that others would also use when forced to confront Old Hickory's transgressions. He and the president were not entirely satisfied with the explanation of his behavior, Dallas said gingerly, but he quickly added that they were certain he had good reasons for it. That communication was a preface to Jackson's visit to the capital in December, the one when John Reid accompanied him as he breezed through social engagements and sat in official meetings tranquil and confident and vindicated. After all, the War Department had already offered Jackson a permanent position in the army as one of the country's two major generals.[24]

John Eaton's pages of explanation about New Orleans emphasized military necessity, mutinous militia, seditious citizens, and Dominick Hall acting "much more officious than duty required."[25] The Potomac was a Rubicon of sorts, as president and cabinet later discovered, but the republic had its citizens in need of the true story, per Andrew Jackson and properly related. Public opinion was a court less demanding than Judge Hall's but with the potential of being more unforgiving in the long run. Eaton had every right to feel a sense of accomplishment in having described the best parts of Jackson's past while obscuring or omitting the rest. As he had come to know the man, though, he should have understood as his book went to press that there would be the need for another one, and yet another one after that. Even as Mathew Carey's publishing house was crating and shipping leather-bound volumes in 1817, Andrew Jackson was embarking on another mottled adventure.

CHAPTER 4

CAESAR

A S MAJOR GENERAL OF THE UNITED STATES ARMY'S SOUTH-
ern Division, Andrew Jackson would cause controversy and
exasperate his civilian superiors, the definition of a querulous
but influential subordinate, the man few dared to correct and nobody
managed to control. In some measure, every secretary who headed
the War Department, whether they were regular appointees such as
John Armstrong or placeholders such as Alexander Dallas, had to
cope with Jackson's activities as well as his anger. All had a taste of
the Jackson Problem. William H. Crawford got a bellyful of it.

Nothing portended a rocky tenure for Crawford when James Madison appointed him secretary of war in the summer of 1815. Crawford had just returned from his wartime post as minister to France,
where his sagacity, wit, and intelligence had impressed his hosts and
pleased his government. Crawford was a Virginian by birth, a Georgian by choice, and universally popular in the political world he had
traversed for a quarter century, his principled stances leavened by
humor. A big man with a dominating presence despite a comical lack
of functional agility, he was prone to bump into furniture and turn
over flower vases with an absent-minded indifference that deceived

many into thinking him dense. But they soon knew better. William H. Crawford would shift in his chair and lean forward, elbow on his desk and chin cupped in his palm, and speak slowly, even sleepily. Soft southern cadences would give way to a melody hard or gentle, depending on the listener and the subject. If Crawford liked his audience, the words could be lyrical, which they usually were, because Crawford liked almost everyone.

Almost everyone liked Crawford back, Thomas Jefferson and James Madison affectionately so. In Georgia, where Crawford had enemies if only because politics requires them, his chief foe was crusty old Indian fighter John Clark, a man in the mold of Andrew Jackson with the same brittle temper and violent responses to minor slights. In his mellow moments, though, Clark chuckled over Crawford's japes and smiled over the fact that, putting aside his politics, Crawford was an easy man to like, in his way.

Crawford's career moved him from local office, the Georgia legislature, and the US Senate in a seemingly effortless upward arc boosted by his stint in Paris and by his quiet charisma. Many of his former colleagues in Congress traced the arc, measured the man, and concluded that Crawford should succeed James Madison as president in 1816. That sentiment was already emerging when Crawford settled into what he expected to be a quiet time at the War Department. The war with Britain had been over for six months, and nothing but Indian unrest on the frontiers loomed as a possible problem. Crawford had ideas about how to resolve those difficulties, but he soon discovered a related issue of an unexpected sort. When he first came to his new job, he didn't know that John Coffee was running the northern line, and when he found out about it, he was puzzled. Crawford met the delegation of angry Cherokees that had traveled to Washington to complain, and, after giving the matter some thought and doing a bit of detective work, he found their objections had merit. With unfeigned innocence, he believed that Coffee's survey embracing some three million acres of Cherokee land was simply a mistake on Coffee's part. Crawford disallowed that section of the treaty, confident that after every-one knew of the error, they would not mind, especially because he planned to acquire the land legitimately. He ordered Coffee to stop his work until the government could negotiate a purchase from the Cherokees.[1]

Andrew Jackson minded very much. He exploded over what he deemed unprecedented interference and railed at Crawford's igno-rant tampering with the treaty because of Indians whom Jackson described as untrustworthy and diabolical. "I cannot believe," he snarled at Crawford, "the doctrine advanced by you have been sanc-tioned by him [Madison], but is the offspring of your own mind." Another affront, in Jackson's mind, was the secretary's polite but firm countermanding of Old Hickory's policy to treat as enemies any Indians who loitered in the cession. Striving for fairness and open dealing with unoffending Indians seemed a sensible policy to Crawford. He did not know that in the process he was creating an instant and enduring enemy in Andrew Jackson.[2]

———

JULIUS CAESAR'S GAUL had consisted of three parts. Andrew Jack-son's was divided into two, which were East and West Florida. The British during their ownership from 1763 to 1783 had split the prov-ince to better manage Florida's large area and unevenly distributed population. The peninsula had few Europeans, and the panhandle more, though not an abundance. A bit more thickly peopled, West Florida exemplified Spain as a fading global power. Small garrisons at Saint Marks and the provincial capital of Pensacola were on the edge of His Most Catholic Majesty's fraying Imperium, which had suffered under Napoleon Bonaparte in Europe and from revolutions in Latin America. Too weak to police the province but too prideful to let it go, Spain's administrators clung to the Floridas, but only just barely. They could scarcely pretend to govern them.

In the 1810s, Spain's problems in Florida were increasingly of Andrew Jackson's making. During the War of 1812, he had openly advocated what the Madison administration secretly wanted, to extend American control east from the Louisiana Purchase's nebulous boundary to take as much of the Gulf Coast as could be had. The lack of money and the risks of attacking a neutral power while the nation was at war with Britain had stayed the government's hand. Jackson began the war champing at the West Florida bit, and after Horseshoe Bend, he kicked over the traces to take Pensacola without the slightest authority to do so. He gave it back when he feared for the safety of Mobile, and then for New Orleans. By that point, he had tangible proof from the War Department that the government had not wanted him to attack Pensacola, and more might have been made of the foray had his victory at New Orleans not followed it so closely.[3]

Jackson's government chose to overlook the Pensacola incident, but Spain had neither forgotten nor forgiven it. Meanwhile, Red Sticks who had escaped Horseshoe Bend for West Florida stewed over the Treaty of Fort Jackson, a grudge they shared with their former enemies, the Creeks being pushed off their lands by the cession, many of whom also ended up in Florida. The anger of the dispossessed Indians only increased when American squatters began rushing into the cession after the treaty. Americans thought all Indians living in Florida were Seminoles, which wasn't at all accurate, but whatever Florida Indians were called, they were angry when squatters raided from the north to steal their livestock and carry off runaway slaves who, like Red Stick fugitives, were seeking sanctuary in the slackly governed Spanish province. Seminoles called these runaways "maroons" and looked upon them as allies against a common enemy. Americans looked on Indians and fugitive slaves as a dangerous combination.[4]

Spaniards in Florida had their own fugitive slave problem. At Prospect Bluff on the Apalachicola River sat an abandoned British fort, a formidable eight-sided structure bristling with heavy artillery and abundant stores of small arms, gunpowder, and shot. In 1815, runaway slaves, along with some Indian allies, occupied the place soon called "Negro Fort." There they defied Spanish authority. Spain did not have the means to enforce its will at Negro Fort. Andrew Jackson did, but from Washington, William Crawford told him the decision to move against Negro Fort rested exclusively with the president. Nevertheless, Jackson contrived a way for the US Army and Navy to destroy the place on July 27, 1816. He assured Crawford that Spain would not object to American operations on their river. He also promised that the show of American force would awe the southern frontier into peace. In the former prediction, he would be proven correct; in the latter, he was quite wrong, presuming he ever meant to be right.[5]

Crawford was confused by Jackson's blithe insubordination and also frustrated by the inability to react in a timely way to developments on a remote frontier. The distance between Washington and Spanish Florida justified giving a military commander who had to respond to events on the ground a fair amount of autonomy, but Jackson's independence too often became defiance of civilian control of the military. So far, his success in the field had masked the dangers of his attitude while shielding him from its consequences, as Crawford discovered. Because Spain did not protest Jackson's interfering in its provincial affairs, and because the frontier didn't immediately boil over following the American attack on Negro Fort, Crawford adopted the passivity of his predecessors regarding his prickly commander of the Southern Division.

In any case, Crawford was distracted by more proximate matters. Growing skepticism about James Monroe's plans to become president saw a substantial part of the Republican congressional caucus leaning toward Crawford as Madison's successor. Crawford was flattered, and for a time, the possibility of becoming the Republican nominee seems to have preoccupied him. Ultimately, he stepped aside for Monroe in a selfless act that everyone planned to reward when Crawford's turn came. Monroe was assured the presidency.

Near the end of the Madison administration, Crawford moved from War to Treasury. The move made Crawford giddy, even if his new job meant coping with books bleeding red. Ledgers might not add up, but they didn't defy logic and disobey orders. At the department he left behind, Crawford's good fortune meant George Graham quickly became one of the most beleaguered men in Washington. Since 1814, Graham had been the chief clerk in the War Department, and for that reason alone he was capable of running it until President-elect Monroe could appoint a permanent secretary. Graham could have been a mere placeholder, and when he is remembered at all, that is usually how. But he was an imposing figure with a fine education, a lawyer by profession, and a soldier who had led troops in combat during the recent war. His clerkship at the War Department with its revolving door of temporary or failed secretaries superintending a war going wrong would have worn down a lesser man, but George Graham did not flinch from his duty. Crawford had packed hastily to move out of his office. Graham soon discovered why.

In mid-January 1817, a letter from Major General Jackson hit Graham's desk like a bomb. It was about Major Stephen Long. Jackson had discovered that Long was missing, and he concluded that without his knowledge, let alone his approval, Long had been transferred to the Northern Division. The action was inexcusable, fumed Jackson, who declared that all communications to officers in his department should—must—pass through him. Graham promptly sent

Jackson an explanation of what had happened with Long, which was not a reassignment but a grant of leave Long had requested. Graham assured Jackson that as soon as Long's furlough ended he would return to the Southern Division. Graham then closed the letter by gently broaching the ticklish subject of Jackson's prerogatives. He reminded the major general that the War Department could send any officer where it pleased, "at its discretion."[6]

Jackson dismissed Graham's explanation about Long and rejected the War Department's claim to superior authority. He said that Graham would "destroy the chain [of command]," and he added, without a trace of irony or self-awareness, that it would dismantle "every principle of subordination necessary for the existence of an army." Jackson then issued a remarkable division order stating that no transfers could take place from his command without his knowledge, a tacit claim that they also required his approval. As the disagreement stretched over weeks and then months, it made Graham's life miserable and even distracted the new president from his labors. Monroe was in his sixth month as president when he found himself still trying to soothe his petulant general with reassurances that under normal circumstances Jackson was correct but also reminding him that the president, not generals, had the ultimate authority over the army.[7]

Jackson would not let the matter go, and as it gradually emerged that other officers found his behavior appalling, he made new enemies. Jackson angrily questioned Brigadier General Winfield Scott about rumors that Scott was criticizing him anonymously in newspapers. Scott told Jackson he had written no articles, but he did believe that Jackson's division order was "mutinous in its character." The exchange began yet another feud, the list of them lengthening with every new controversy.[8]

Monroe's new secretary of war, John C. Calhoun, inherited the chain-of-command dispute from George Graham in early December

1817 and ended it as soon as he could. Calhoun consequently began his tenure at War by making peace with Andrew Jackson. He tried to do this by agreeing with him, up to a point. Under almost all circumstances, Calhoun conceded, orders would go through Jackson. Only when the rapid delivery of directives was necessary would the practice be modified, but in any case, copies of orders would be sent to Jackson as a matter of policy. Calhoun managed to describe essentially the same system that both George Graham and James Monroe had outlined, but he did so with a meekness that made all the difference. Jackson scrawled a note on Calhoun's letter. The new secretary, Jackson crowed, had seen the light.[9]

Nevertheless, Calhoun could have counted his settling matters with Jackson as his first signal achievement. He was not Monroe's first choice to head the War Department, particularly from a geographical perspective, because the South Carolinian Calhoun and the Georgian Crawford weighted the cabinet with southerners. But Monroe discovered that nobody wanted the War Department, and he had to settle for the intelligent and earnest young man with the dark eyes and fixed stare.

At thirty-five, Calhoun was not just young but the youngest of the cabinet secretaries. Secretary of State John Quincy Adams, like Jackson, was around fifty, and William H. Crawford was a robust but sage forty-five. Calhoun's youth also made him the most inexperienced on the national stage, though he had made the most of his years in the House of Representatives, where he began his career in 1811 as one of Henry Clay's "War Hawks," that group of angry young men intent on fighting Britain for American honor. Clay as Speaker had elevated Calhoun with key committee appointments, and Calhoun built on the opportunities with a tireless work ethic and a flair for cutting through complex problems. If there was a fault in the apparently flawless young man, it lay hidden beneath careful words and cautious alliances. Some saw in Calhoun something mildly troubling. He was handsome but with a humorless smile and a habit of mirthless laughter. Adams did not like him, but that meant less than Crawford's suspicions. Adams was misanthropic by nature, but Crawford tended to give everyone a chance. Calhoun seems to have irked Crawford from the start.

With John Calhoun, however, everyone was inclined occasionally to pause and gauge the possible unfairness of their judgments. He was plainly a patriot, whatever else they thought of him. He seemed as loyal to James Monroe as any of them. Doubtless he was ambitious, as both Adams and Crawford were, and that fact made him a rival in waiting, just as they were already rivals with each other in fact. And if they dared to concede it, what troubled Adams and Crawford most was their premonition that Calhoun was in a hurry and did not plan to wait. For his part, Crawford could at least sympathize with the young man whose new job came with a particularly heavy cross to bear. Crawford might have impishly mused that it was made of hickory. The thought would have put a twinkle in the Georgian's eyes.

By the time John C. Calhoun took over the War Department, the Florida border was in full turmoil. Raiding American settlers had given rise to increased Seminole and Red Stick retaliation, a situation that Jackson insisted made necessary an increased military presence. More soldiers, however, had further angered rather than awed the Indians. Jackson's subordinate in command of the region was General Edmund Pendleton Gaines, a career officer with a distinguished record, but whose judgment proved no better than his chief's—or, more accurately, whose attitudes about settlers, Indians, and Spanish Florida were in perfect harmony with Jackson's. Gaines had organized the destruction of Negro Fort, and when Indians ranging up from Florida butchered a family in a remote cabin, he was more than ready to respond with a hard and heavy hand. The Creeks in Fowltown defied his orders to come to him for talks, and Gaines made an example of them by burning down their village. They responded by ambushing army supply boats on the Apalachicola that were carrying sick civilians as well as soldiers. The Creeks killed forty-five of the approximately fifty people in the boats, including four children. They carried off one woman.[10]

Gaines wanted a war over this, and Jackson agreed. In Washington, Calhoun did too, though he was anxious about war's potential scope and likely consequences, a worry shared by President Monroe. Calhoun drafted orders authorizing Gaines to cross the Spanish border under the internationally recognized rule that allowed the pursuit of malefactors across borders. But Calhoun explicitly told Gaines to give Spanish towns and military garrisons a wide berth. Monroe and Calhoun then made a fateful decision by judging the situation sufficiently grave to warrant division command. They told Andrew Jackson to lead an expedition that would punish Seminoles and Red Sticks with such vigor as to end depredations once and for all.[11]

Monroe and Calhoun expected the restrictions placed on Gaines to govern Jackson, but fresh from his tenuous resolution of the chain-of-command dispute, Calhoun did not want to state that expressly to his prickly general. It was a grave mistake, Calhoun realized, not to repeat those orders as a direct command to Andrew Jackson, especially after Monroe received a troubling letter from him. In it, Jackson told Monroe that the punitive action against the Indians in Florida presented a chance to take the province from Spain by force. If Monroe wanted that to happen, said Jackson, he need only send word by way of Tennessee congressman John Rhea. To the end of his days, James Monroe insisted that he never talked to Rhea about Jackson's proposal and consequently never authorized anything more than chastising the Florida Indians. Considering Monroe's usual way of dealing with unpleasant or inconvenient matters—that is, through indecision and inaction—his denials ring true. Indeed, at the time Monroe found the letter disquieting and told Calhoun to make sure Jackson knew he was to stay away from Spaniards. Calhoun did not do this, another serious mistake. His noted attention to detail was strangely absent in this crucial instance.[12]

Jackson with a four-thousand-man force of regulars and militia crossed the Florida line into Spanish territory on March 15, 1818, his fifty-first birthday, and commenced a campaign that later would be misleadingly called the Seminole War. It lasted some eight weeks. In that short span of time, as the Monroe administration later discovered, Andrew Jackson fought precious few Seminoles and Red Sticks. Instead, he killed four prisoners he stumbled upon and attacked Spaniards wherever he could find them. Indians fled their towns upon Sharp Knife's approach, while the small Spanish garrison at Saint Marks surrendered without firing a shot. After ranging around the region to burn a few more deserted Indian villages, Jackson sent a report to Calhoun announcing the end of the campaign and his imminent departure for Tennessee. Jackson did not go home, however. He marched westward to Pensacola and demanded its surrender. When the Spanish governor showed more spine than the commander of the isolated outpost at Saint Marks, Jackson called his bluff and attacked. Pensacola surrendered.

Jackson bundled off the Spanish soldiers from the Apalachicola and Pensacola on a ship to Cuba. He then stationed an American garrison in Pensacola, at present the (former) capital of West Florida. He also established a customs house and raised the American flag over "the ramparts of Fort Carlos de Barrancas." His work done, he left West Florida still composing his report, which he sent to the War Department while en route.[13]

The messenger carrying the report was delayed and did not reach Washington for quite some time, but his tardiness was the least of the many issues surrounding the entire affair. Jackson did not merely exceed his instructions; he violated his orders in every particular with remarkable enthusiasm. On his sole authority, he invaded Spanish territory under the guise of immediate pursuit, which, it turned out, was simply an excuse to enter the province and seize it. In doing so, he outraged international opinion and violated the United States Constitution, which gives the exclusive authority to declare war to Congress. He had offended both diplomatic sensibilities and the fundamental domestic law.

But that was not all. Jackson in Florida had ordered the executions of four men under the flimsiest of pretexts. The day after he seized Saint Marks, the US Navy delivered to him two Red Sticks it had captured by luring them aboard a vessel flying a Union Jack. Jackson hanged the prophet Josiah Francis and the headman Homathlemico without ceremony, as a letter to Rachel—rather than to his government—matter-of-factly described. His army also captured two British subjects, one an elderly Scot who traded with Indians in the region. The other, nabbed separately, was a former British marine turned soldier of fortune who had been recruiting Seminoles and maroons to fight in Latin American revolutions. Alexander Arbuthnot had written a few letters for his clients, mostly protests sent to American officials over settlers stealing Seminole property. Jackson interpreted the correspondence as incitement of Indians to make war on the United States. He made the same judgment regarding Lieutenant Robert Chrystie Ambrister's activities. Jackson assembled a number of his officers as a drumhead court martial that found both guilty, as Jackson wished, but recommended a lesser sentence of lashes and hard labor for Ambrister, citing his youth. Yet Jackson executed both men, the soldier Ambrister by firing squad and Arbuthnot by hanging. The noose was tied to a yardarm of his trading schooner, a vessel ironically named *Chance*. The surrendered Spaniards on the ship sailing toward Havana might have considered themselves lucky.[14]

In early May, Monroe and his cabinet learned about Jackson taking Saint Marks, but after that, news was sparse until mid-June when reports about the executions of Arbuthnot and Ambrister and the taking of Pensacola reached the capital as rumors. Monroe immediately returned to Washington from an inspection tour of Chesapeake Bay fortifications. In a brief conversation with John Quincy Adams, the president showed the side of him that even his friends found maddening, a sort of dimwitted talent for grasping the obvious. If the news were true, Monroe solemnly mused, Jackson had certainly disobeyed his orders. After this insightful observation, the president left for his farm in Virginia.[15]

The president had the excuse of lacking information to cover the fact that he was running away, but as official dispatches began arriving in early July, his excuse evaporated, and he came back to Washington. The cabinet pored over what documents it had—including the December 1817 orders to Gaines and Jackson—and mulled the administration's options. The process could not have comforted the president. His secretaries offered either virtuous advice that was politically perilous or pragmatic counsel that was distasteful to consider. Worse, the cabinet could not come to an agreement. Calhoun's was the virtuous point of view. He fumed that the taking of Fort Saint Marks and Pensacola made plain Jackson's wanton disregard for executive authority and congressional prerogative. William H. Crawford watched his young colleague's performance with interest. It revealed a trace of vanity. Calhoun seemed as angered by the breach of his authority as much as the president's. And though Crawford was just as displeased as Calhoun, he was careful to hear everyone else before speaking. His rivals looking back on the frantic meetings in July would recall this reticence as shrewd rather than merely deliberative.

President Monroe was too unsettled to notice such nuances. Unconstitutional antics in West Florida could not be ignored, but

Jackson's titanic popularity confused the matter. No matter how much Old Hickory deserved it, an official reprimand of a man like that was to throw rocks at a hornets' nest. John Quincy Adams offered a way forward. Just as voluble as Calhoun, but on the other side of the debate, Adams had been trying to buy Florida from Spain for months and despised the pointless meetings with Spanish minister Don Luis de Onís, a wily negotiator who haggled sensibly one minute only to talk jabberwocky the next. In clipped phrases and likely with his finger tapping the table to emphasize his precisely enunciated words, Adams bluntly said that chastising Jackson would achieve only two ends, both of them bad. It would enrage the public and stiffen Spain's resolve to keep Florida. Monroe listened to Adams talk sense and later told Thomas Jefferson what they were all forlornly thinking. Punishing Old Hickory would "be the triumph of Spain, & confirm her in the disposition not to cede Florida."[16]

The Monroe administration decided to do nothing. It would neither condone nor condemn Jackson's campaign, and it would certainly not discipline Jackson. Calhoun was not happy, and both he and the president tried gentle persuasion in an effort to save some of the executive's dignity. Would Jackson at least say that he had misunderstood his orders? The response was an unequivocal no. And as if to put an exclamation mark on it, Jackson was preparing troops to march on Saint Augustine, the capital of Spanish East Florida. Calhoun did not waste a second pondering that news. He sent a direct order to Jackson forbidding any such campaign and tersely informing him that the United States intended to restore West Florida to Spain.[17]

John Quincy Adams then faced the challenge of explaining to Onís why Jackson was right (pursuit of perpetrators) and how Spain was wrong (failing to control the Indians) while highlighting American magnanimity in returning a pacified province—but, Adams added for good measure, only after Spain could demonstrate its ability to keep it that way. Luck seemed on the secretary's side. After Onís had registered the obligatory protests, he seemed more tractable about selling Florida. Adams's luck held when it became clear that Britain would disregard popular anger at home over Arbuthnot and Ambrister because London was wearied from fighting Bonaparte and tired of quarreling with Americans. They would not renew troubles over the fate of two adventurers in the Florida wilderness.[18]

So far, then, Monroe, his cabinet, and Andrew Jackson seemed likely, somehow, to avoid a diplomatic catastrophe. They were also lucky so far in that Congress had not been in session and would not convene until December, allowing everyone to handle one crisis at a time. Surveying the prospect of congressional displeasure, though, Jackson was not as sanguine as he had been about the executive branch. He devoted considerable energy to compiling justifications for his campaign in West Florida. Hirelings and henchmen, both in uniform and not, ranged across the region collecting affidavits to prove that the Spaniards in Saint Marks and Pensacola had been sheltering Indians hostile to the United States.[19]

It was a backward process. The justification for a war should come before it is waged, not afterward. Jackson's ex post facto evidence gathering was peculiar in this regard, though Andrew Jackson would make a habit of it. He was the man of action who, after the act, became uncharacteristically reflective. In particular, he would again resort to sworn testimony to counter critics. He would use the technique to defend everything from his business practices to his personal life. That he used it for the first time after the Florida campaign suggests it was someone else's idea, someone with the lawyerly habit of recording opinions, citing precedents, and amassing evidence. One can think of it as similar to Jackson settling on John Coffee as a good man to have on his side in a fight or to run a sketchy property line through Indian country. Dealing with smooth politicians and their oily arguments and oblique attacks required another kind of talent. Coffee could be crucial in a fight, but John Overton was indispensable in an argument.

━━━

JOHN OVERTON BEGAN countering criticism of Jackson's Florida invasion as soon as it was over. His first defenses appeared in newspapers such as the Nashville *Whig*, where Overton dismissed attacks from the paper's crosstown rival, the *Clarion*, as the shallow and self-interested maundering of its owner Andrew Erwin, a personal and political enemy of Jackson's. Overton's efforts followed a canny strategy of emphasizing Jackson's patriotism and selfless devotion to duty, even if duty endangered his person and reputation. It was designed to generate a level of public support that would make the government at least leave Jackson alone even if it could not positively endorse him. The administration did not worry Overton so much as Congress did. In the latter forum, the test would be constitutional as well as political, and much more public. Because Jackson had usurped Congress's exclusive authority to declare war, the constitutional issues were nettlesome, hence the plan to blunt their thorns with a flurry of supportive affidavits. The political side seemed easier because some in Congress were, like Monroe, already gauging Jackson's popularity against the perils of challenging it. As Congress prepared to gather in December, discrediting Erwin and others like him could go far in boosting Jackson's public standing while heightening the political consequences of disregarding it.

The publicity campaign had to be as swift and sure as Jackson's military one, because both were unprecedented. As more information became available, the potential enormity of how the Seminole War had begun and was prosecuted threw the press into confusion. Some papers refused to let hints of impropriety shake their belief in the Hero of New Orleans. For them Jackson remained "the able and successful supporter of his country's rights." Others were troubled. Similarly, Congress heard both sides and was left just as confused by the arguments. Jackson had done what was necessary to secure the border, said one side, while careful constitutionalists were outraged. Georgia senator Charles Tait could not have been happy to hear a respected friend say that "no man should be permitted in a free country to usurp the whole powers of the whole government and to treat with contempt all authority except that of his own will."[20]

That this was the correct response was obvious to many, but the intensity of Jackson's public support recommended a different approach, and that was essentially the choice facing Congress as it held lengthy congressional hearings in both houses in early 1819. Jackson could count more friends in the House, with its habit of bending to the popular will, but he had important ones in the aloof Senate, especially Tennessee's junior senator, fresh from his debut as a bestselling author. John Eaton was two years shy of the constitutionally mandated age of thirty for service in the US Senate, but the Tennessee legislature had not minded, and when Eaton arrived in Washington in 1818, his colleagues overlooked his youth. It was not only because of his connection to Jackson. Eaton's dashing good looks, ready smile, and sharp wit made him a good companion and an even better advocate, a worthy match for the state's senior senator, John Williams, who had fought under Jackson at Horseshoe Bend but who was having second and third thoughts about what his old commander had done in Florida.

In December 1818, as a clerk read James Monroe's Annual Message, every man in the House and Senate knew that their warmaking power had been usurped, and they saw Monroe's labored effort to place all blame for that on Spain's impotence as a clear misdirection likely to satisfy only Jackson partisans and those afraid of them. There was also the question of how many of the men in Congress were physically afraid of Jackson himself. As hearings loomed,

Eaton worried about Jackson coming to Washington and upsetting carefully laid plans to exonerate him with adulation. Eaton risked his patron's displeasure by expressing doubts about Jackson's self-control. Relishing the prospect of a furious Old Hickory tearing up the capital, Kentucky congressman Richard Johnson chuckled that "there will be a rattling among the dry Bones when he does come." That was precisely what kept John Eaton up nights.[21]

A Senate select committee began an investigation while the House's standing Military Affairs Committee worked quickly to bring in a report that spurred the longest debate the lower chamber had ever held. For twenty-seven days, representatives heard plaudits and attacks that covered every aspect of Jackson in Florida. Nothing, however, compared to the premier event in the process, the one most memorable for all observers and the one most consequential for the two men it forever made into bitter, vicious enemies. Speaker of the House Henry Clay stepped down from his chair and temporarily laid aside his authority as the presiding officer. He spoke on the floor for hours, but the essence of his speech emerged in its first minutes. Spectators packed the House galleries, and Clay's colleagues sat entranced at their desks, everyone in hushed awe. Henry Clay did many rare things in a performance that John Quincy Adams marveled was "one of the ablest speeches ever delivered in the House." It was the early afternoon of January 20, 1819, and nothing in Henry Clay's public life would ever be the same again.[22]

Andrew Jackson at last refused to view events in Washington from afar. He arrived in the capital three days after Clay's speech. He immediately heard what Clay had said about extralegal trials, killing Britons, murdering Indian prisoners, and violating the Constitution with an arrogant disregard for the people's tribunals in a manner that brought to mind the specter of history and the death of republics. Clay had not used the word, but others had, and it rang like a thudding knell in his warnings: *Caesar*. Jackson mobilized an attack on Clay with newspapers, but he also considered murdering Clay in a duel. Jackson moved darkly around the city, his face a thundercloud. He had an entourage of young officers with eyes darting to study faces and remember names, menacing men that one senator called Jackson's "brood of dragonnades."[23]

The sight of Jackson sharpening his sword made John Eaton more than uneasy. He began sharpening his pencil to begin work on a new edition of the biography. John Overton, John Coffee, and William B. Lewis would produce pamphlets and editorials, hoping that events would give them time to erase the name *Caesar* from *Jackson* and that the man would have enough restraint to help them all prove the charge wrong.

CHAPTER 5

TWO WASHINGTONS

Andrew Jackson's friends in the House of Representatives managed to blunt Clay's speech and check his influence. Jackson had protected the Georgia border just as he had New Orleans, they said, and for those willing to accept that ends justified means, that was a good enough reason to acquit him. One of Jackson's stoutest defenders was Kentuckian Richard M. Johnson, whose claim to killing the great Shawnee Tecumseh during the War of 1812 made him the House's premier authority on all things Indian, especially the slaying of them. Johnson's plea for Jackson was his first ingratiating step in emphasizing his allegiance to Old Hickory. More than a few representatives learned from Johnson's example.[1]

Jackson found backing in other corners of the government, too. He met separately with Secretary of War Calhoun and Secretary of State Adams. Both pleased him by voicing support for the Florida campaign. Calhoun sealed his reputation as an untrustworthy operator among those who knew about his positions during cabinet discussions, whereas Adams surprised everyone with his unexpected pragmatism. Calhoun just lied to Jackson's face, but Adams was at least sincere, because Jackson had in fact made dealing with Onís easier.

But the very thing Jackson's friends feared most could appear without warning. On February 3, 1819, during a meeting with Adams, Jackson lost his temper over a casual mention by Adams of William H. Crawford. Jackson listed in incredible detail Crawford's double-dealing with a shocking display of wrath that dismayed Adams. Jackson sputtered that Crawford and Henry Clay had formed a vile alliance to defeat President Monroe in the 1820 election. Adams did not know Jackson and did not know what to make of this unsettling performance. Meanwhile, an officer who had fought in Florida marveled over his chief's refraining from challenging critics to duels and expressed surprise at Old Hickory's self-control. The absence of gunplay was laudable, to be sure, but John Quincy Adams would have begged to differ about Jackson's self-control.[2]

In addition to Crawford and Clay, Jackson lashed out at the United States Senate, particularly its select committee under Pennsylvanian Abner Lacock. Already incensed by rumors that the committee would issue a highly critical report, Jackson exploded when John Wayles Eppes, who had openly disapproved of the Florida campaign, replaced a Jackson supporter on Lacock's committee. Old Hickory detected a conspiracy and apparently resolved to do something about the gaggle of sanctimonious senators. Conflicting accounts obscured at the time what happened, and in fact, there is some doubt that anything happened at all. In one telling, Jackson rushed to the Senate chamber "with two of his ruffians." Only Stephen Decatur's intervention, it was said, thwarted Jackson's plan to cut off John Wayles Eppes's ears. Commodore Decatur had a reputation for neither taking fright nor running away. Witnesses remembered him blocking Jackson's path outside the Senate chamber and saying in a hard voice that the general would have to go through him to get to Eppes. Andrew Jackson, it was said, muttered that it was "always safe in following the advice of a brave man." He turned from Decatur's steady stare and barked at his companions: "Let us retire."[3]

Regardless of the truth of this account, there was no doubt about the conclusions of the Senate Select Committee's report, which found Jackson's behavior indefensible from start to finish. His mustering of militia without congressional authority was illegal, his trial of Arbuthnot and Ambrister was irregular, his violation of standing orders by attacking Spanish posts was insubordinate, and his plan in August 1818 to take Saint Augustine on his sole authority was provocative toward Spain and in defiance of the Constitution. The report was persuasive enough to disconcert the Monroe administration and enrage Jackson's friends. Daniel Webster believed "a settled majority" in the Senate was ready to condemn Jackson.[4]

The Senate report could have tarnished Jackson's reputation, perhaps irreparably, if it had ever been endorsed by a vote. Two days before the Select Committee's findings were presented to the Senate, Secretary of State Adams signed a treaty with Onís that dazzled both the public and the politicians. It not only set terms for the purchase of East and West Florida but settled the border between the United States and Spanish territory from the heartland to the Pacific Coast, an achievement that prompted diplomatic historians to give it the grand name, the "Transcontinental Treaty." To Jackson's friends, it was a deliverance by immediately changing the terms of the debate. The House exonerated Jackson, forgetting Henry Clay's speech in the process, and the Senate ratified the Adams-Onís Treaty while tabling Lacock's report.

Yet Andrew Jackson had not forgotten Clay's attack and was angry when the Senate published the Select Committee's damning judgment in the *National Intelligencer*. Jackson wanted a rebuttal, and his friend Dr. James C. Bronaugh quickly collaborated with one of Jackson's "dragonnades," Captain Richard Keith Call, to produce it. Jackson reckoned it a fair start to the fight he was planning, an ear-biting, eye-gouging fracas if necessary, and not altogether in the figurative sense. He continued to rail against old and new enemies, especially Crawford and Clay because Jackson believed they were the secret authors of Lacock's report. Menacing talk from a man who had sliced off Indian noses and charged the Bentons with a whip and gun carried a bit more weight than the threats of the average backwoods blowhard. Some in Congress began slipping pistols in their pockets before leaving their lodgings, but the tough old rooster Abner Lacock scoffed at such precautions. He felt perfectly safe, he growled, tugging on a lobe with a chuckle to show that he had "passed his [Jackson's] lodgings every day and still" had his ears.[5]

Jackson departed Washington for home on March 9, 1819, carrying no ears as trophies and having fought no duels. His journey was full of banquets and tributes, which improved his mood. He grew exuberant when he reached Tennessee. He boasted how all of Knoxville had turned out to celebrate the "triumph over my enemies," by which he meant those in Washington, not Florida, and noted how all of the town's leading citizens, except for one, had joined the observance. The exception was Senator John Williams, who had criticized Jackson's campaign and was in no mood to pretend otherwise. He stayed home, which Jackson and his friends noticed.[6]

The American people squinted disapprovingly at Jackson's congressional critics, judging them to be a pretentious bunch partial to legalese and lawyerly tricks. Politicians talked, but Jackson achieved. President Monroe privately conceded that Jackson had won Florida for the United States, though he lamented how the feat made it impossible to discipline a man who had violated the law and flouted all authority. Contemplative men found Jackson, and even more, the adulation of him, troubling. Congratulatory feasts, teeming crowds filled with blushing maidens and admiring boys, town fathers reading platitudes of praise—it all indicated that something mildly disturbing was happening, that the "passions of the people" were being aroused. William Crawford heard from a friend uneasy that "General Jackson who is so respectable in most points of view . . . should for a moment lose sight of the true path of a republican citizen." Crawford might have closed his eyes after reading the next sentence: "I confess that I cannot see the least ground on which his conduct at Washington can be palliated." Like so many others, Crawford had pretended otherwise.[7]

Despite the public's approval, Jackson brooded over the specter of official censure, but his closest friend accurately gauged the mood of the country. John Overton envisioned a rising political force of incalculable power. He agreed to write a lengthy pamphlet defending the Florida campaign in part to humor Jackson but also because the approval of the American people confirmed his earlier conviction. In some ways, reactions to Jackson's feat in Florida were even more significant. That which should have tarnished his reputation burnished it. Overton realized before anyone else, even before Old Hickory himself, that a strange confluence of popular praise for a man who reminded people of George Washington and general dissatisfaction with established politicians was working an almost providential miracle. Andrew Jackson was going to become president because of two Washingtons: the man and the place. The trick was going to be how to help this miracle along. The greater trick was going to be staying out of its way.

Overton's pamphlet was titled "A Vindication of the Measures of the President and His Commanding Generals, in the Commencement and Termination of the Seminole War" and appeared under the signature "A Citizen of the State of Tennessee." In similar vindications published in newspapers, he wrote under the pseudonym "Aristides," after the statesman and general of ancient Athens noted for his integrity and passion for justice. These writings compensated for their lack of originality—Overton mainly echoed Monroe's Annual Message about Spanish impotence and Indian depredations requiring an effective response—with repetitions and relentlessly detailed arguments. Jackson wanted to join this chorus, but his enthusiasm for controversy made his inner circle anxious. Overton advised him to scrap the idea of a "Memorial" to show Senate critics the error of their ways and instead to adopt a studied indifference. Jackson refused. He sent his manuscript to Senator Eaton in Washington to solicit an opinion he likely expected would contradict that of his closest friend.[8]

Eaton called in reinforcements, not to persuade Old Hickory to leave the matter alone but to enlist help in editing Jackson's "Memorial" into acceptable shape. With Senators William Pinkney of Maryland and Rufus King of New York offering advice, Eaton removed as much of Jackson's self-serving bombast as he dared and then had King formally submit the relatively refined product to the Senate in February 1820, a full year after the congressional investigations of the Seminole War had concluded in a fashion mainly favorable for Jackson. Pinkney's and King's appearance in the affair's final scenes revealed that Jackson's political appeal had begun to transcend Tennessee loyalty as well as regional and party boundaries. King was a Federalist, and a stubborn one at that, who had watched with amused detachment while Republicans argued with Republicans over Jackson's Florida campaign. He mused that Jackson had possibly engineered the investigation of himself to keep his name before the public in advance of the coming presidential election. As they heard the New Yorker read Jackson's "Memorial" into the Senate record, it doubtless galled Republicans to see King lecture them about Andrew Jackson, but it should have worried them more.[9]

Eaton wrote Jackson that the Senate intended to print the "Memorial" in the hope that the news would finally convince him to end the matter. To nudge him to that conclusion, Eaton added that friends considered the Florida invasion a closed case. Eaton and other supporters had both tactics and public relations in mind. Further debate in the Senate could result in a vote on Lacock's committee report, and it was hard to predict how much of the old anti-Jackson sentiment the process would revive.[10]

Whether Jackson agreed or not, he was distracted by his plans for yet another military campaign. Spain stalled ratification of the Transcontinental Treaty as King Ferdinand VII gave away enormous amounts of Florida to royal favorites. Adams did not intend to take possession of a Florida fragmented by royal mischief, and he hinted that if the king did not sign the treaty selling Florida, the United States would simply take it. The threat rested on questionable legal ground, but Andrew Jackson was mobilizing his division on the Florida border even as Adams was lobbing ultimatums at the Spanish embassy. Monroe's attorney general was a thoughtful man named William Wirt, a Maryland resident who whiled away his spare time writing carefully researched biographies of the Founders. Wirt's response to the Florida affair was uncharacteristically flippant. Surveying the chance of Jackson invading Florida again and possibly Spanish lands beyond, Wirt laughed that "no one would enjoy the luxuriant frolic more than Jackson would, to be turned loose in Spanish Provinces, Cuba included." Wirt crowed, "Stand clear all you Arbuthnots and Ambristers."[11]

Ferdinand finally signed the treaty in the fall of 1820, which made another foray into Florida unnecessary, but the chance for one led by this increasingly popular man made thoughtful men say strange things. In a time of political drift and fluid loyalties in the United States government, the fate of Arbuthnot and Ambrister dwindled to something worse than insignificance. The old Scottish peddler and the young English officer had become little more than comic props for their executioner. William Wirt was a good man. In a calmer time and different place, remembering what he had written about men who had died hopeless and forlorn in the middle of nowhere could have made him close his eyes.

======

THE LENGTHY CONTROVERSY over the Seminole War and the acquisition of Florida occurred during the "Era of Good Feelings," a phrase
coined during the summer of 1817 in the *Columbian Centinel,* a Federalist newspaper in Boston. The label was a tolerable reference to
reality if one were willing to accept the absence of party strife as
proof of political harmony. The truth, as Henry Clay pointed out to
the Panglosses of his time, was that bickering had gone mute only
because the party system of the early republic was disintegrating.[12]

Rufus King was the Federalists' sacrificial lamb in the election
of 1816 and went to the slaughter meekly, gaining only 34 electoral
votes to James Monroe's 183, but he expected nothing more from
a fading organization clinging to majorities in only Massachusetts,
Connecticut, and tiny Delaware. The election made James Monroe
buoyant and magnanimous. He gloried in consensus, rang the knell
on confrontation, and spoke of the American people as a family
setting a place at the nation's dinner table for everybody, including
the dotty uncle of Hamiltonian Federalism. Even Andrew Jackson
joined the banquet, typically by trying to sit at the head of the table.
In 1816, he urged President-elect Monroe to appoint a Federalist to
the cabinet as an act of good faith toward a vanquished foe. Jackson
put this counsel in letters that would come to light later and prove
embarrassing when critics began scrutinizing Jackson's political loyalties. In retrospect, it would be clear that only naïfs could have
believed theirs was an era of durable congeniality. Henry Clay's confidence that the "era" would quickly close would seem prophetic.

The Seminole War controversy was an early warning sign, but
others came quickly on its heels to confirm Clay's prophecy. While
the argument over Florida was winding down, the quarrel over slavery came to the forefront when the Missouri Territory applied for
statehood. Quakers had made slavery an issue in the early days of
George Washington's presidency, but its capacity to unhinge political debate had chastened the political class into a prolonged silence.

When Missouri interrupted it in 1819, nearly twenty years of moral somnolence ended to almost everyone's dismay.

At the time, the Union was evenly divided between eleven slave and eleven free states, and not by chance. It was the result of an unspoken design to preserve southern political clout in the Senate as a bulwark against its diminishing presence in the population-based House of Representatives. Immigration and natural increase had given free states a 105–81 majority in the latter body, a gap that promised to worsen for southerners. When a few northerners moved to make the gradual elimination of slavery in Missouri a condition of its admission to the Union, southerners bristled over the breach of the sectional truce. After long and heated arguments, the resulting Missouri Compromise kept the balance, but it did so by ignoring the great moral quandary confronting the country, making the debate over Missouri about a scramble for political influence rather than the ethics of chattel bondage.

Missouri looms large in this nation's historical memory because of slavery, but the economic crash that happened in the same year was the major event for Americans at the time. A quarter century of war in Europe had profoundly dislocated regular economic activity across the globe, and peace in both Europe and North America gave rise to giddy optimism over the prospect of stable politics, cooperative diplomacy, and ocean commerce freed from embargoes and safe from privateers for the first time in a generation. Americans were more than giddy. In the years after 1815, not just banking practices but banking itself went haywire. In some states, anyone with a printing press could set up a bank by printing the certification charters on the same press that would produce their new bank's notes. Such establishments, routinely sanctioned by states, made imprudent loans, especially to land speculators confident that rising prices would float them free of debt. The feeling was contagious. Banks eased credit and printed more notes that passed for money, collectively flooding entire regions with currency whose volume devalued it more quickly than its ink dried. Behind it all lay the inescapable rule of all economic transactions, that no matter how simple or complex a system of finance, lenders will want their money returned with interest. The simplest explanation for the Panic of 1819 is that the rule finally asserted itself. When that happened, the system did not stop. It crashed.

As the Panic of 1819 became a full-blown depression, the search for someone or something to blame gained momentum. Banks became a prime target, and the biggest bank of all, the Second Bank of the United States, was the primary one. The first national bank was Alexander Hamilton's brainchild, and for that and other reasons it was an unpopular example of Federalist policies. In 1811, Congress refused to renew its twenty-year charter. The War of 1812, though, schooled politicians on the need for a central bank to control the currency and stabilize credit, so shortly after the return of peace, Congress passed legislation to establish a new bank. Called the BUS to distinguish it from its predecessor, its first three years were marred by mismanagement. The BUS did nothing to curb the bulging credit bubble. Rather, it embraced the boom while easing or restricting credit with no apparent design or plan. Finally, in 1818, the accountants at the BUS headquarters in Philadelphia coped with foreign demands for payments in specie by abruptly drawing down the currency supply, a deflationary policy that sent mildly troubling tremors across the country's financial landscape. The BUS came under new management in 1819, and when it further tightened credit, the tremor became a seismic event that coincided with the worldwide collapse of commodity prices. Former Treasury secretary Albert Gallatin darkly noted "the gloom spread on commerce . . . occasioned by the great fall in the price of our staples."[13]

The BUS called in loans from state banks that scrambled for the money by calling in loans on their own books, but the money represented in those arrangements did not exist. Depositors wanting to withdraw their money were turned away from empty vaults as banks closed their doors and pulled down their signs. Those that managed to survive did so by suspending specie payments, a practice they claimed was a temporary response to the crisis. A dwindling number of people believed them. Skilled artisans and common laborers stood idle, and hopelessly indebted farmers surveyed markets so depressed that yields would not cover the cost of production. The worst part of the nightmare was how quickly it happened and how widespread it was.[14]

Andrew Jackson knew the toll of ruinous debt from personal experience, and it informed his attitude about all aspects of the economic crisis, including its victims and its causes. In the 1790s, he had accepted promissory notes instead of cash in a land sale. It was a common practice, and Jackson believed his purchaser, fellow Tennessean David Allison, was reliable and trustworthy, but Allison went broke, making the notes Jackson held worthless. He had used those notes for large purchases that he was obligated to pay for with money he did not have. The liability nearly ruined him. It took him years to retire the debt, which also cost him countless sleepless nights of churning worry over the possibility of losing everything he owned. The episode soured Jackson on treating paper as money for the rest of his life, and he developed an abiding distrust of banks that issued it. "Society has been much demoralized by our paper banking system," Jackson declared with the certainty of a man who had narrowly escaped the perils of bad promissory notes. Having been a lonely debtor who met financial misfortune with fortitude, Jackson disdained those who got into trouble, whether by accident or from recklessness, particularly when they started bleating for help. Calls for legislative bailouts of institutions and individuals incensed him.[15]

In Tennessee, the economic panic brought about new political realignments and demolished old friendships. The state's two largest banks were the Nashville Bank, chartered in 1807, and the Bank of the State of Tennessee in Knoxville, which had been established by the legislature in 1811 to fill the void created by the lapsing Bank of the United States. Jackson's friends figured prominently in both banks. John Overton had interests in the Nashville Bank, where John Eaton was briefly on the board and William B. Lewis became one of its fixtures. Overton was also involved with Knoxville's Bank of Tennessee. Jackson's friend and Overton's brother-in-law Hugh Lawson White was its president, and chief cashier Luke Lea was the father of Overton's future son-in-law. Such interlocking relationships stemming from kin, marriage, and friendship made Tennessee banking a private preserve of the Blount-Overton faction, and many believed political influence and personal connections guided decisions about who received loans and who didn't. The faction led by Andrew Erwin chafed under the situation, but the merchants of Nashville grumbled as well. Billy Carroll, striving to introduce financial competitors, sat on the board of the town's Farmers and Mechanics' Bank that the legislature chartered in 1817 and joined others in trying to bring to Nashville a branch of the BUS. Nashville's most accomplished attorney, Felix Grundy, was part of the effort, and their plans were under way when the economy collapsed in 1819.[16]

Neither Carroll nor Grundy was part of the Erwin faction, but their initiatives put them at odds with the interests of the Blount-Overton group. Even before these developments, though, Andrew Jackson had taken a dislike to William Carroll. They had been close from the time Carroll, all of twenty-two but savvy and eager, showed up in Nashville as the emissary of Pittsburgh entrepreneurs who dispatched him to start a nail factory and run a hardware store. That was in 1810, and Billy's open and engaging manner first made Jackson his friend and then his mentor. Carroll was part of the fateful Natchez expedition, and Old Hickory took his side in the duel with Jesse Benton. At New Orleans, Carroll was among Jackson's most trusted lieutenants, a tireless recruiter and popular officer who kept men sharp with fair discipline and constant drill. His epic river journey to New Orleans was a storied part of the campaign, and Jackson had reason to remember fondly the day Carroll brought two thousand armed and able Tennessee boys to the Rodriguez Canal to bolster an army flagging under fear and fatigue. But idleness following the victory gave jealousies time to hatch, and vague incidents of backbiting by Carroll's brother officers seem to have occurred in the shadows. When an admirer bubbled that "Generals Jackson, Carroll, and Coffee are worth more than their weight in gold to the American government," Carroll's inclusion in that company made lesser men envious. Such men bending Old Hickory's ear began to bend his affections, and then reports reached the Hermitage that Carroll was among those alleging some of Jackson's land dealings associated with Indian treaties were tainted by fraud. Carroll's drift into the orbit of the Erwins merely completed his alienation from Jackson.[17]

Because the Blount-Overton faction controlled Tennessee banking, the economic crisis favored the fortunes of those opposing it, and the Erwins gathered support and momentum. Along with Newton Cannon, who represented a middle Tennessee district in Congress, the Williams brothers—John, who had criticized Jackson's Florida campaign in the United States Senate, and Thomas, in the state legislature—were the Erwin faction's most potent political members, but that changed. After the war, Carroll returned to his entrepreneurial roots by investing in the new-fangled steamship trade plying the Cumberland, but the panic destroyed the venture before it could be firmly established. The loss, however, paved Carroll's way for a career in politics. He became, with Felix Grundy, identified with measures to relieve the distress of debtors, which was strange because Carroll didn't support such proposals. It was Grundy who became a radical champion of debt relief in the Tennessee legislature, while Carroll made at most tepid statements about it in advance of his eventual run for governor. Andrew Jackson, never one for sub-tlety, merely saw a man he had grown to dislike cooperating with Felix Grundy, a man he mildly despised.

By the time of the panic, Felix Grundy had lived in Tennessee a little more than ten years, during which time he had mostly prac-ticed law, specializing in criminal defense cases. He first angered Andrew Jackson by embarrassing him on the witness stand in a murder trial. Grundy's skillful cross-examination had made Jackson lose his temper and appear foolish, which was more than enough reason to earn Jackson's lasting enmity. Nevertheless, Grundy found his place in Tennessee politics not so much by rising above factions as by standing apart from them. He won a seat in the House of Representatives in 1811 and lodged in the same boardinghouse as Clay and Calhoun, "War Hawks" all, as critics called them. Grundy and Clay never became friends, but they became friendly. Oppo-nents were seldom enemies for these men, a habit that made them jovial at parties and kept them calm in political contests. Grundy's self-control also made him dangerous in debates and irresistible in arguments. Felix Grundy, according to a judge, "could stand on a street corner and talk the cobblestones into life."[18]

Grundy had been out of public life for five years when the panic occurred, but the economic crisis made him a tireless advocate for democracy and a champion for radical economic populism. With popular sentiment behind him, he easily won a seat in the Tennes-see legislature and, that fall, stopped pro-bank legislation sponsored by a Blount-Overton man, Pleasant M. Miller. Moreover, Grundy secured measures to change the timetable and method for debt col-lection. In a special session of the legislature the following summer, he introduced a bill to create a government loan office, in essence a bank secured by the state's public credit. The Blount-Overton fac-tion bristled over the encroachment on its banking cartel, but it also raised credible objections about public money being used to pay off private debt. Grundy relished breaking the Blount-Overton grip on Tennessee finance and saw nothing wrong with using the state treasury to help his constituents. Naturally, his constituents saw nothing wrong with that either.

Andrew Jackson did. His conviction that an unhealthy reliance on credit had caused the panic was a valid judgment, but his readiness to define debtors as deadbeats and their advocates as demagogues did his cause little good. As Grundy was pushing the loan office, Jackson appeared in the state capital, then at Murfreesboro, to act on his righteous indignation. He presented a memorial to the legislature opposing the loan office legislation in particular and debt relief in general. Jackson's assertion that the loan office was unconstitutional led him to level wild charges of perjury against legislators he claimed had violated their oath of office. That was impolitic, but Jackson's repeating his critique of legislative incompetence and corruption in a local tavern made his friends cringe. The setting of this performance gave rise to rumors that strong spirits as much as strong convictions fueled his ire. "Such harshness, my dear General," William B. Lewis warned, "is calculated to do yourself an injury without producing the desired good." Jackson responded with a rant about banks violating both state and federal constitutions, but then grew uncharacteristically reflective in a rare moment of self-awareness. "I know I was warm at Murfreesborough," he conceded. "It is my foible on such Topics to get two warm & often I regret it." Jackson's enemies were "giving a high colouring" to his remarks, while Grundy, remaining calm, got his bill passed.[19]

To Overton, it was galling enough to have Erwin men crowing over the creation of Grundy's state-backed bank, but in 1821, something truly alarming occurred. William Carroll ran as the Erwin favorite for governor against the Blount-Overton candidate, Edward Ward. Never again to be "Billy," William Carroll crushed Ward by a vote of 31,290 to 7,294 to become Governor Carroll and mark a sea change in Tennessee politics. An Erwin man was governor, and the tight Blount-Overton hold on finance and politics was slipping.

Jackson was among those reciting jeremiads. Old Hickory condemned Carroll and his friends as rabble-rousers and bemoaned how "the wellfare and happiness of Tennessee as well as . . . its respectability" required Ward to win. Ward's loss made Jackson question if "there are a majority of honest men in Tennessee." He reflected a national consensus among established elites. A diplomat returning from abroad received a somber warning from a friend in New York: "You find us in many respects a people materially altered from what we were when you left us" and "strangely relaxed in our notions of political virtue and depravity."[20]

But there was more to it than that, as John Overton gradually realized. It was clear that self-interest accounted for part of the shift in Tennessee's politics in the wake of panic and depression. Farmers pleading for state intervention to prevent bank foreclosures had the numbers to make their champion Grundy influential in the state legislature. But the greater lesson was how they had made Carroll governor, despite the fact that he didn't agree with them. Carroll, like Jackson, thought the loan office was bad policy, and his first message to the legislature showed little sympathy for debtors. In recommending hard work and frugality as the best remedies for financial distress, Governor Carroll could have been reciting the jeremiad of Jackson. Yet the support for both Grundy and Carroll, despite their divergence on the issue of the moment, revealed something deeper: the population's doubts about the wisdom of gentry control over affairs. As Overton came to understand, Tennesseans were angry that entrenched and out-of-touch elites were harming them with harebrained schemes like the BUS. And they wanted change, even if that change did not align with their economic self-interest. Overton also came to understand that if properly managed and carefully organized, the mass of angry voters could crush what they opposed and make invincible what they favored. Discovering what the voters opposed was easy, and there lived in Tennessee a man already proven invincible, if he could calm down and keep quiet.[21]

———

JOHN OVERTON LEARNED to live with the fact that on any given day a newspaper report or a panicked letter would arrive about something Andrew Jackson had said or done that needed explaining and required repairs. He could be thankful that Jackson's views on Napoleon Bonaparte had not been circulated despite Old Hickory putting them in a letter to Edward Livingston, in which he rejoiced over Napoleon's return to France from exile in Elba. Jackson had enjoyed how Bonaparte sent Louis XVIII running to revive "the wonderfull revolution in France" that "fills every body and nation with astonishment." It was just the sort of talk that could have stoked the military chieftain charges into an uncontrollable blaze.[22]

But that was not all. Added to imprudent commentary on world events, the occasional brawl, and the threats of violence was Jackson's talent for making enemies. He managed to infuriate the state of Georgia during the Seminole War. He leveled charges of corruption and incompetence against former Georgia governor David B. Mitchell and then current governor William Rabun. Mitchell had the misfortune to be Benjamin Hawkins's successor as Creek agent, and because Jackson thought he had been slow to mobilize Creek warriors for the Florida invasion, he supported allegations that Mitchell was a slave smuggler. Jackson managed to destroy David Mitchell, but the man was not without friends, and those friends had long memories. Jackson's fight with Rabun was just as bad. Jackson ran afoul of the governor after Georgia militia attacked a friendly Creek village. Jackson ordered the militia captain arrested and put in federal custody by asserting that Rabun had no authority over his state's militia while Major General Andrew

Jackson was in the field. Rabun exclaimed that "wretched and con-temptible indeed must be our situation if this be the fact." The consequences of yet another incident in which Jackson forgot his place in the civil-military scheme of things loomed until the militia captain fled the country and Rabun died, thankfully of natural causes. Nevertheless, many Georgians would remember Jackson's imperious attitude toward civil authority. An odor of another sort hung over the incidents involving Mitchell and Rabun, too. Jackson's motives seemed mixed. Both men were political allies of William H. Crawford.[23]

The House of Representatives had exonerated Jackson for the Seminole War, and events had preempted any action by the Senate resulting from its damning official report, but men in both chambers remained troubled. Ultimately, they found a way to discipline Jackson. Major General Jacob Brown put it succinctly: Congress moved "to legislate Genl Jackson out of the service." The Panic of 1819 gave everyone cover for the deed. Crawford at Treasury cited the need to trim the budget in hard economic times, claiming that the army at its current size was an extravagance. As Congress moved to cut military spending, though, political intrigues that had nothing to do with Andrew Jackson framed their efforts. James Monroe had not begun his second term before Crawford, Adams, and Calhoun started maneuvering to become his successor in 1824. Each man's supporters sought to advance their favorite. Adams and Crawford men saw army reduction as a way to clip the upstart Calhoun's wings by slashing his department. Crawford's allies in Congress even revived the charges of Jackson's "Caesarism" to encourage reduction. In early 1821, Congress passed a bill cutting the army in half, eliminating the need for two major generals. Jackson was junior to Major General Brown and had to go.[24]

Monroe and Calhoun tried to soften the slap by offering Jackson a post that came with compensation, few burdens, and little chance for controversy. Early in his presidency, Monroe considered making Jackson a diplomat, perhaps to send him to Russia as the US minister. Thomas Jefferson soberly warned Monroe that it would take only weeks for Jackson to begin a feud with the czar. It occurred to the president in 1821 that he could avoid Jackson's clashing with a head of state by making Jackson one himself, as territorial governor of Florida.[25]

Andrew Jackson, however, did not want to be governor of Florida. He turned Monroe down. John Eaton and other friends in Washington urged him to reconsider, which suggests that Old Hickory's political planners saw an opportunity too good to let pass. John Coffee had moved to north Alabama by this time, and Jackson, missing his counsel as much as his camaraderie, kept a steady stream of letters open with his old friend. "My friends in Congress is determined to have me appointed whether I will accept or not," Jackson explained, clothing his pride in reluctance. He nevertheless inferred "there is some strong political reason operating with my friends."[26]

Jackson finally accepted the post, but he insisted that after establishing American government in Florida, he would resign. Neither Andrew nor Rachel Jackson wanted to live in Florida, and their doubts only grew when they encountered some difficulty in getting there. They had to travel by water to New Orleans and then to Blakely, Alabama, where they stopped to await official word from Spanish Governor José Callava in Pensacola that he was ready to transfer the province. The paperwork did not come, and its delay tested Jackson's patience. He even instructed American military forces in southern Alabama to move toward Pensacola, which was hardly a good start for the would-be proconsul. Soon enough, though, the last Spanish governor of West Florida completed his government's arrangements. Jackson took possession of the territory on July 17, 1821. It was the third time, of course, but at least this time it was legal.[27]

Jackson and his companions were never happy in Pensacola. The friends seeking to advance his political fortunes soon realized the appointment was a mistake. Rachel quickly became downright miserable. She could not shake her homesickness for the Hermitage, and the alien feel of the Panhandle made her uneasy. Andrew Jackson Donelson, serving as his uncle's aide, put a better face on everything. A recent graduate of the United States Military Academy, Donelson was adaptable by habit and changeable by nature. His commission was still shiny, but he was considering leaving the army to study law, which would have troubled the Jacksons had they not known him so well. Donelson grew up with them, more like their son than a nephew, coming to the Hermitage a wide-eyed and timid child after his father, Rachel's brother Samuel, died. Andrew was handsome and cheerful, but his ability to make Pensacola tolerable had limits. Nothing, as it turned out, could ease the administrative problems his uncle was to face.[28]

The tiff with Callava put Jackson on edge, but President Monroe's appointments to the government posts in Florida first surprised and then angered him. Monroe had not consulted him, which indicated the job was a sham and a mortifying one at that. Andrew Jackson Donelson knew "one motive for accepting the governorship was the promotion and assistance of his friends," and that the administration seemed not to know this irritated him. Jackson told Calhoun that running Florida's government would be hard without the help of people he trusted. It was a confidence disclosed with warm regard for the man Jackson believed had defended him during the Seminole controversy, so he felt free to criticize George Walton, whom Monroe had made territorial secretary. The man had ties to Crawford, Jackson growled. Not only that, but Eligius Fromentin, a former Catholic priest appointed as territorial judge, was a notorious womanizer.[29]

Jackson was in a foul mood almost every minute he was in Florida. He relished being ornery with Callava, whose sullen manner in transferring authority had annoyed him. Soon the former governor's obtuseness regarding a complicated legal matter gave Jackson a reason to be more than ornery. It concerned the estate of the late Don Nicholas Maria Vidal, whose heirs claimed they were being cheated. References to papers pertinent to the case and in Callava's possession prompted Jackson to order their surrender. When Callava refused, Jackson had him arrested.

A reprise of Jackson's actions at New Orleans and during the Seminole War seemed likely when Judge Fromentin, the alleged libertine, issued a writ of habeas corpus for Callava's release, but there, at least, matters took a different turn. Tossing federal magistrates into prison was bad for publicity and worse for the pocketbook. This time Jackson refrained from jailing the judge. He did browbeat him, though, and he disregarded his writ as impertinent and offensive. Jackson settled matters by presiding over his own court, convened for just this occasion, in which he ordered the heirs paid, closed the case, and, almost as an afterthought, liberated Callava. The former royal governor immediately marched on Washington, a one-man army whose principal weapon was a formal complaint against Andrew Jackson. Old Hickory did not care. He was leaving, too, a one-man army himself, but heading to winter quarters at the Hermitage, his principal weapon his new one of choice, a pouch full of sworn affidavits attesting to his proper conduct.[30]

Jackson never wanted to see Florida again. When he reached Nashville, he said as much to Monroe by announcing his resignation and recommending a replacement. Jackson's note was icy. He was out of temper with the president over the appointments— Monroe would ignore his suggestion about a replacement as well— but infuriated over Congress's plans to investigate his behavior as a territorial governor. There was talk of impeachment. Florida had not worked out at all.[31]

Congress's "Secrete combination to destroy" him would fail, he confidently predicted, and Jackson was correct in that nothing came of the congressional investigation, but he was furious that Monroe did not remove Judge Fromentin. Jackson demanded an explanation, even if he was unwilling to believe anything James Monroe said. An anonymous letter told him how Monroe had joined a plot to injure him. The Florida appointment had been intended to get him out of the way.[32]

Locking up the former Spanish governor had been a nice touch for a man in need of a reputation for calm deliberation. Former secretary of war George Eustis had to marvel. Andrew Jackson was "a man of such influence, of such fame, that he belongs only to his country—its character is in some degree identified with his." And yet, one could "only look upon the transactions of the General towards Col Callava, with regret" over "the passion, the violence, the want of reflection & dignity there exhibited."[33]

Eustis could think that Jackson was "too passionate—too self-willed ever to be entrusted with a power over the liberties of his fellow citizens," but Sam Overton, John's nephew, had been traveling in Pennsylvania with his ear to the ground and his eyes scanning taverns and hotel lobbies. Around cracker barrels and at crossroads, Sam Overton was hearing something different from Eustis's measured Washington talk. "The dominant party in Pennsylvania," he reported to his uncle's friend, "are determined to run you as a candidate for the next Presidency." The Keystone State could be key. And Virginia's eccentric congressman John Randolph was predicting Old Hickory's victory in 1824. The territorial governorship of Florida had been a mistake, but it had not hurt Jackson. Mistakes without consequences would become a trend for Old Hickory.[34]

ANDREW JACKSON FOR president? In the summer of 1822, the *Richmond Enquirer* was incredulous. "We never supposed," admitted editor Thomas Ritchie, that the idea would be taken "by anyone, seriously." The evidence was mounting "that he has some friends who are determined to push him." The observation was in response to something remarkable that had just happened in Tennessee. The state legislature had nominated Andrew Jackson for president.[35]

It was a significant achievement for people who just months before had been in disarray. Before William Carroll's election, the Overton faction had seemed unassailable. It had easily put John Eaton in the Senate in 1818 to replace another of its members, George Washington Campbell, when Monroe sent Campbell to Saint Petersburg as US minister to Russia. And the reach of its members was a study in influence built on the firm foundation of friendships and family ties, both by blood and by marriage. George Wilson ran the Nashville *Gazette*, which he moved from Knoxville the same year as Eaton's elevation. The paper gave Overton a forum to boost the faction's candidates, promote its interests, and defend Andrew Jackson.[36]

The Erwin faction had connections with Congressmen John Cocke and Newton Cannon, and Senator John Williams, and later would boast of national influence through the marriage of Andrew Erwin's son, James, to Henry Clay's daughter. Overton, however, had the same sort of valuable statewide ties, and he began strengthening them after the political reversals of 1821. Editor George Wilson was a Knoxville transplant with enduring links to the place, Overton's brother-in-law Hugh Lawson White was the son of Knoxville's founder, and Pleasant Miller had married the daughter of old William Blount himself.

Closing the twain of east and west in Tennessee was no small trick, but Jackson's people proved capable. Overton men did not all reside in Nashville, but they recognized it as the necessary hub for their efforts, and it was there that Overton formed a group to push

Jackson's presidential bid. These men—Overton, Wilson, Eaton, William B. Lewis, White, Miller, Sam Houston, Jackson's neighbor Alfred Balch, George Washington Campbell when he returned from Russia—formed the core of what became known as the Nashville Junto. It quickly grew in size and effectiveness. The Junto, for example, smoothed over Jackson's disputes with influential men, most notably with Felix Grundy, who ended his flirtation with the Erwins to become an early convert to the cause and a prominent jewel in the Junto's crown.[37]

The Junto also sent agents to potential supporters outside of Tennessee, sometimes to take advantage of interstate family ties. William B. Lewis, the most tireless of Jackson's advocates, was a masterful emissary, though his critics thought him more dog-like toward Jackson than dogged in his behalf. Like Balch, Lewis was Jackson's neighbor, but he was also family, in an extended sort of way, which was possibly one reason Jackson trusted him. Almost nobody else did. The very name William Berkeley Lewis announced his roots in the wealth and privilege of northern Virginia gentry, but he had a habit of self-effacement, strange given his station. He assumed the role of a menial with such oily ease he disgusted Jackson's other supporters. Lewis became a key figure in the Nashville Junto for his ability to defuse scandals and control damaging information, but his greatest asset as a political operative was his ability to gather gossip, which made some men resentful and others enraged. He had an irritating habit of repeating stories with little regard for their truth, and John Eaton could hardly abide him, despite being his brother-in-law.

John Eaton was married to Myra Lewis, and in 1813, William B. Lewis married her sister Margaret. Their common surname was a coincidence, for she was the daughter of Jackson's neighbor, the wealthy planter William T. Lewis, whose death had left Margaret as Jackson's ward. Lewis's marriage to her made him the master of Fairfield, an impressive estate situated some two miles south of

Nashville. It had long been a stopping place on the way to the Hermitage, and Jackson continued to be a frequent visitor, cementing an already solid bond from the war, when Lewis had served as Jackson's quartermaster and placed his fortune at Jackson's disposal to supply his army. Both Margaret and Myra were frail and would die young, Margaret only a year after her marriage, but her utility for her husband had served his purpose by then. He soon married again, this time to the daughter of North Carolinian Montfort Stokes. In the spring of 1822, Lewis traveled to North Carolina, ostensibly to visit his father-in-law, but that was merely an entrée for the more important errand Lewis was on, which Jackson himself had endorsed. Stokes was North Carolina's United States senator and had a great deal of influence in the state.[38]

Stokes and Jackson had been young lawyers in North Carolina before Jackson moved to Nashville. But Stokes believed Jackson's declarations about carefully avoiding the appearance of seeking acclaim, so he was inclined to dismiss rumors that his old friend was willing to be president. Lewis quietly set him right in his earnest way and directly asked whether Stokes would support Jackson for the presidency. Stokes was a Calhoun man, but he mused that if Calhoun's candidacy did not pan out, he would certainly consider Jackson. Lewis knew when to quit and did not press. The talk with Stokes was a start. There was plenty of time to snag Tarheels away from John C. Calhoun—particularly in view of the plans Jackson men were hatching in Pennsylvania, where Calhoun had his most ardent northern support.[39]

Like Stokes, most people did not take a Jackson candidacy seriously. South Carolina congressman and ardent Calhoun supporter George McDuffie scoffed that "the movements for Jackson have been made by the grog shop politicians of villages & the rabble of Philadelphia & Pittsburgh." It was a common refrain among Calhoun men who were counting on a strong showing in Pennsylvania to boost their man's chances. They dismissed rumors about Jackson as originating in the "dregs" of Pennsylvania's cities where insignificant people of the lowest class got drunk and talked rubbish about "the Hero," a man only marginally more literate than themselves. But, as Eaton realized in Washington, that kind of analysis was gravely misguided. In fact, by early 1822, several prominent Pennsylvania newspapers were encouraging a Jackson candidacy. Their support stemmed from a mixture of admiration for Old Hickory's military achievements and presumptions about his political positions. The military achievements reminded people of George Washington. The presumption about his politics seemed to pit him against Washington, DC.[40]

The citizens of Philadelphia who were inclined to support Jackson were not the human detritus Calhoun's men often believed them to be; they were Old Republicans, such as William Duane, who assumed that Jackson was against the tyranny of banks and opposed to a government guided by elites gathered in caucuses. Duane's protégé was the former banker Stephen Simpson, whose experience while working for the first Bank of the United States had turned him into a financial cynic with an acid pen. Simpson became a Jackson admirer while serving under him at New Orleans, and nothing had blunted his regard for the man in the seven years since. When Duane folded the *Aurora* in 1822, Simpson began hymning Jackson in the *Aurora*'s successor, the *Columbian Observer*, which Simpson founded to attack banks and promote Old Hickory.

Simpson believed he knew what had caused the Panic of 1819. The culprit was a rapidly expanding economy resting on the weak reeds of paper currency, reckless speculation, and easy credit. Only a return to Jeffersonian principles would put things right, and the outsider Jackson was just the man for the job. It didn't matter that Simpson's network of pro-Jackson men included such people as Pittsburgh's Henry Baldwin, who had been touting Old Hickory since 1815. Baldwin was a lawyer, but he had also branched out to iron mongering, and he presumed Old Hickory would support a tariff steep enough to protect American manufacturing from foreign competition. For a man like Baldwin, there were limits, after all, to the desire for limited government. For men such as Duane, Simpson, and Baldwin, vague presumptions about political positions were a comforting contrast to Washington's indifference and shadowy corruptions. John Eaton and William B. Lewis opened a line of communication with Simpson, whose *Columbian Observer* became a conduit to other newspapers for the material Eaton and Lewis supplied him, items nebulous enough to appeal to men who liked their government small and to others who liked it active.[41]

With things falling into place elsewhere, Jackson's friends moved to make his candidacy official by securing his nomination in the Tennessee legislature. There wasn't much risk in the initiative. Even though it was less than a year after the Overton faction's stunning loss to William Carroll, the appeal of a favorite son like Jackson was a safe bet. Jackson insisted that "the voice of the people" was responsible for the move, but he knew better, just as he knew the wisdom in using the refrain he would rely on for the next two years, which was always a variation of "I have long since determined to be perfectly silent—I never have been a candidate for office, I never will. The people have a right to call for any man's service in a republican government—and when they do, it is the duty of the individual, to yield his services to that call."[42]

Pleasant M. Miller made the motion in the House, using the opportunity to attack the congressional nominating caucus as undemocratic. It was the first effort in any state to make a nomination by a state legislature not just a legitimate way but a preferable one for designating a presidential candidate. The tradition of a meeting, or caucus, of congressional party members selecting their presidential candidate was already at odds with the growing spirit of democracy.

But it was more than a tradition; it was a mechanism for organizing campaigns and muscling the candidate to victory with coordinated purpose. It did not matter that the rules of the game were rigged against an outsider like Andrew Jackson. It mattered that they were the rules. To be a viable contender in this game, Jackson could not just break the rules. He had to change them. The first significant innovation was to introduce an alternative method for selecting a candidate. The voice of the people through their elected representatives in a state legislature had a nice sound to it, possibly one resonant enough to discredit the congressional nominating caucus.[43]

On July 20, 1822, the Tennessee House resolved that Andrew Jackson should become the next president of the United States. As the state Senate began considering the matter, Sam Houston watched the debate, his large frame impossible to ignore in the gallery. As a teenager, Houston had come to Tennessee with his mother and siblings and was only twenty-one when he suffered ghastly wounds at Horseshoe Bend. A barbed arrow pierced his thigh, but Houston continued fighting until an officer found him nearly collapsed and roughly pulled it out, taking a fair amount of muscle and flesh with it. Jackson saw Houston on the ground as a surgeon applied bandages that were quickly soaked in blood. It was curious how the young man's face was taut from the pain, but his eyes had only the slightest squint. It caused Andrew Jackson to look away before ordering Houston taken behind the lines and out of the fight. Jackson heard later that he had only just left when Sam Houston pushed away from the doctor, grabbed a weapon, and stumbled toward the sound of guns. By nightfall, he was nearly dead, the thigh still oozing, his arm and shoulder shattered by bullets that the doctor dug out by candlelight. The wound in the thigh never fully healed; the shoulder always ached when the weather was changing.

Sam Houston became Jackson's protégé, a Junto member, and, by the time he was watching the Senate discuss his hero's future, a new Tennessee congressman as part of the Overton faction's re-surgence. As soon as the Senate concurred with the House, Houston sped the news to Jackson. It was a grand day, Houston beamed, the beginning of the end of corruption in Washington. He insisted that Jackson had an obligation to accept the nomination and ride it like one of his Thoroughbreds to the Augean stables of the nation's capital. Houston's enthusiasm made him speak up and a bit out of turn. He dismissed Jackson's modestly stated preference for Adams or Calhoun, or even for Governor DeWitt Clinton of New York. No, said Sam Houston firmly and with purpose. All other candidates were part of the problem, were part of the entrenched elite in Washington. Only Jackson could save the country.[44]

Jackson was pleased by Houston's earnestness. And he had to admit that the nomination was gratifying proof of his popularity in Tennessee. Even better perhaps was how it would alarm those who "in their nightly dreams see the gosts of arbuthnot & Ambrister . . . and when these Demagogues see the Public Journals throughout the union their fears and alarms will doubly increase." One of those public journals, the *New Orleans Gazette*, was like Sam Houston and minced no words. With Jackson's name before the public, the editors expected everyone else to withdraw. The people would choose Jackson "by acclamation."[45]

That was the talk in a place that still remembered the distant sound of guns on that January morning in 1815. The talk, though, like the guns, reverberated beyond the region among Americans looking for another Washington, the general, who like Jackson had also won a seemingly hopeless war. The sound even reached the other Washington, the capital, where some men heard it as distant, muttering thunder, and others would not hear it at all—until it was too late.

CHAPTER 6

SOLON

OR MANY AMERICANS IN THE THIRD DECADE OF THE NINE-
teenth century, the nation's capital had become as alien as
the mountains of the moon. In one sense, this did not surprise. Concerns about establishing a federal district whose sole purpose was to host the capital were older than the government itself.
During the debates over drafting and ratifying the Constitution,
Virginia skeptic George Mason had predicted that such a locus of
power would "become the sanctuary of the blackest crimes."[1]

Foreigners found the place baffling, a village "only kept alive by
Congress." And for every admiring description—a Portuguese minister marveled over "the city of magnificent distances"—there was
a less flattering one about wallowing pigs, wandering dogs, and distances more peculiar than impressive. "The houses are here, there,
and no where," said a British actress, who noticed how the streets
were only "roads, crooked or straight, where buildings are *intended* to
be." There was a considerable amount of open space, such that "in
the midst of town, you can't help fancying you are in the country."[2]

Ordinary Americans, however, had begun to doubt that a bucolic
setting promoted wholesomeness. Washington's problem wasn't being

half-finished but the "congregation of government offices . . . where political characters, secretaries, clerks, placeholders, and place-seekers . . . congregate." Men on the make jostled at the public trough, some to dispense favors, others to receive them, in a dizzying whirl of intrigue and disregard for the public trust. For every quid, there was a winking quo. For every itching back, there was one hand to scratch it and another opening its palm for the grease of this piece of legislation or that bit of government largesse.[3]

In the midst of dubious dealings, social frivolity added to the impression that Washington's politicians were not competent to solve any problem larger than assembling a stylish guest list. The capital's denizens "lead a hard and troublesome life," lawyer, linguist, and bibliophile George Ticknor said with tongue in cheek. After all, President Monroe and his cabinet "entertain strangers . . . in a very laborious way." Ticknor spent four of his thirty-four years in Europe for seasoning, and the time had well prepared him to observe a place where "society is the business of life." He concluded that "people have nothing but one another to amuse themselves with; and as it is thus obviously for every man's interest to be agreeable, you may be sure very few fail." For many Americans, Ticknor could have been describing a European court with powdered ladies and mincing men.[4]

"So much bowing—so much simpering—so much smiling—so much grinning," muttered Attorney General William Wirt about New Year's festivities. "Such fawning, flattering, duplicity, hypocrisy." It made Wirt's head spin before it made his stomach turn. People in Washington took all the wrong things seriously, it seemed. Wirt introduced an officer from the War Department to Henry Clay and got the man's name wrong. "I'll be d[amne]d," Clay chuckled as the offended fellow strode away, "if you don't have a challenge [to a duel] in half an hour." Even those who had no stomach for simpering smiles seemed to avoid them out of snobbery, not refinement.

"There will be a drawing room [reception] this evening, for the first time this season," Massachusetts congressman Jonathan Russell sniffed, "but as it is *vulgar* to go [to] the first I shall of course stay at home." Russell's arch "of course" said it all.[5]

George Ticknor was a dazzled traveler who believed that "the only objection to society at Washington is, that there is too much of it." But much of the rest of the country seethed over the capital's gaiety while the burdens of just getting by weighed heavily on Americans unaware that attending a party at the wrong time was unsophisticated. The charitable explanation was Washington's incompetence. The sharper one was that the politicians didn't care. A visitor needed to watch Congress in action only briefly before making references to the capital as a "terrestrial paradise" where "the Capitol had its full complement of jackasses who are searching after *immortal glory*." Elaborate procedures, endless and digressive debates, points of order, yielding the floor to "my friend" (often actually a bitter enemy), and an abundance of tricks made it all appear vacuous. The government seemed intent on avoiding important business. "Such things cannot fail to make us very ridiculous abroad," an informed citizen reported, more in sadness than in anger. "They weaken the attachments that ought to prevail at home," he sighed. "The people at large are getting heartily tired of this abuse of the representative systems."[6]

Andrew Jackson's friends understood the general mood of the country about its elected officials, and they planned to portray him as an honest hero who would return the country to its virtuous roots. Other men were more prominent politically, but that also was an advantage for Jackson, because voter dissatisfaction focused on the very government these well-known men presided over. Jackson's military exploits had made him a national celebrity, but the nature of those exploits had also established him as a man of action. The Pennsylvania cowherd pulling udders a couple of hours before sunrise, the Alabama yeoman harnessing his plow by the pink light of dawn, the Louisiana boatman hauling his lines, the mechanic in Charleston, the laborer in New York—men like these all across the country did not know it was uncouth to go to the first party of the season, but they did know something about paying bills and keeping promises. Stephen Simpson, Sam Overton, Henry Baldwin, John Coffee, William B. Lewis, John Eaton saw these people and how their eyes lit up when they heard Andrew Jackson's name.[7]

At the same time, these ordinary Americans were gaining the means to become an irresistible partisan force. The American Revolution had planted the seeds for surging democracy, but the politics of deference had stunted them for decades. That situation began to change before the War of 1812 and continued through the early 1820s as citizen demands for more political participation became impossible to ignore and difficult to suppress. States responded by gradually extending voting rights to white adult males regardless of how much property they owned.

In tandem with these changes, many states modified the way they selected electors to the Electoral College. For years, the exclusive nature of public affairs had state legislatures designating electors, but after 1820, eighteen of the twenty-four states would choose electors by popular vote. Five of the eighteen states—Indiana, Illinois, Maine, Maryland, and Tennessee—split their popular vote into districts, which abandoned the winner-take-all system of the other thirteen states, to make decisions even more reflective of local will. The six remaining states—Delaware, Georgia, Louisiana, New York, South Carolina, and Vermont—still had legislatures choose electors, but the methods varied. New York, for instance, split electors based on proportional votes in the legislature rather than giving all to one candidate. In sum, these changes made popularity imperative for presidential candidates, which in turn made elections more complicated for them.[8]

For the right type of candidate, however, it made elections simpler. Expanding democracy meant the rejection of the politics of deference, the traditional system in which lower classes conceded governance to their social betters because of their supposedly superior wisdom. The financial Panic of 1819 increased this desire for social leveling. The common people disdained the idea that the only men qualified to run the government were those with the mysterious "talents" implied by membership in the ruling class. Whether occupying county, state, congressional, or even a presidential office, the high-born were judged as nothing more than highfalutin. Jackson could oppose government aid to victims of the panic all he wanted to, because what he believed was less important than what he was. Jackson's friends denounced Washington's elite as incompetent and uncaring. They condemned the congressional caucus choosing presidential candidates as undemocratic. In the process, they laid the foundation for a new political movement. A growing number of people were certain Andrew Jackson would go to a party if invited, no matter when it was held. His supporters planned to have the country throw him one.[9]

DANIEL WEBSTER WAS not exaggerating in 1822 when he quipped "that Presidential Candidates were springing up in all quarters." By some estimates, no fewer than sixteen men were eyeing the 1824 prize even before James Monroe finished reciting the inaugural oath of office in 1821. The scramble struck some as "disrespectful to the President," but they needn't have worried. The field narrowed as the months passed and support for this or that man dissipated or never materialized, as was the case for New York governor DeWitt Clinton. Nevertheless, the country still had an abundance of candidates as election year drew nigh. One reason was the disappearing Federalist Party, which made the Republican nomination a sure path to the presidency. Another was the absence of an incumbent seeking reelection or a designated successor to rally around. The opportunity was too golden to let pass, which meant every contender faced stiff competition.[10]

By the time the Tennessee legislature nominated Jackson in July 1822, the winnowing had left four other candidates. Unlike Jackson, they were all creatures of the capital and members of the professional political class, which seemed to ensure the ascendancy of one of them. It also caused them to dismiss Jackson's nomination as little more than a symbolic tribute that had something to do with the rift between Overton and Erwin factions in Tennessee. Treasury Secretary William Crawford knew that Old Hickory hated him, but Secretary of War John C. Calhoun and Secretary of State John Quincy Adams each persisted in the hope that Jackson would bow out and support them, one against the other. The fourth man, Henry Clay, had left the House of Representatives to repair his finances after the panic. Like Crawford, Clay knew how Jackson felt about him, but he couldn't see how that alone would motivate the candidacy of a political novice. Playing the game by its traditional rules, Clay returned to the House and resumed his Speakership in 1823, relatively close to the election. Even by then, the damage that identification with Washington politics could do to a man's chances wasn't clear.

The professionals' strengths blinded them to their weaknesses. Crawford's control of patronage at Treasury guaranteed a large and loyal following in every state of the Union. But it also opened him to allegations that he abused that patronage to boost his campaign. Adams had his family's name, the reputation of a brilliant and honorable man, and the support of most of New England, a section that felt marginalized in the growing nation and that consequently was eager for an Adams victory. But Adams's brilliance could make him arrogant, and his disagreeable manner did not bode well in a system that now rewarded popularity. Calhoun, also recognized as brilliant, had support outside of the South, especially in Pennsylvania, but his youth suggested he was overly ambitious, and acquaintances suspected he could lie with zeal. Colleagues familiar with the Seminole War controversy knew he could.

Henry Clay was a peerless orator whose considerable charm caused women to overlook his peculiar appearance and whose jovial manner made every man his friend, except for those who were committed enemies, such as Andrew Jackson. Clay was the "western" candidate, which was a strength, but the westerner Jackson emerged to challenge Clay, a threat the latter did not take seriously at first. His lack of perception was understandable. Governor William Carroll had endorsed Jackson after the legislature's nomination, but he privately assured Clay that if Jackson pulled out, Clay could win Tennessee. John Overton's nephew also told Clay that if Jackson did not run, Tennessee would be Clay's. Such messages pledged more than Tennessee's support. They implied Jackson would not actually seek the presidency.[11]

Supporters scattered across the country kept their favorites informed through regular correspondence, but campaigning by presidential candidates was viewed as unseemly grubbing for votes. John Eaton was quick to criticize Monroe's cabinet for its electioneering, claiming that rivalries threatened the security of the government. Traditional constraints reinforced by such sniping required the candidates to rely on supporters and surrogates to whip up support and denigrate opponents. These were far from organized campaigns in the modern sense. But down on the Cumberland, the Nashville Junto was greasing its axles and cinching its traces. Its bandwagon was makeshift at first, but it would do, at least if Old Hickory's handlers could keep him from careening out of control. Sam Houston reported to John Overton in December 1822 that Jackson was behaving. He had come to Nashville for a few days, but "all is quiet in the wigwam yet."[12]

The Junto's anxiety about Jackson's unpredictability persisted, though it helped that contacts could send him regular reports with generally good news about the presidential sweepstakes across the country. Houston told him that Alabama was drifting away from Crawford, which was an easy way to make Jackson cheerful. He enjoyed descriptions of the other candidates as nervous about the emerging will of the people, and John Eaton hoped that that would keep him calm. "It is incumbent on you," he wrote Jackson in January 1823, " . . . to act with the caution that belongs to you, when your own prudence shall suggest prudence to be necessary." Eaton implored Jackson to avoid writing anything provocative, to resist controversies, and to respond to questions about his plans with his usual, humble disclaimer about never seeking office but always answering the country's call.[13]

Eaton closed with the news that President Monroe that very day had asked his advice about sending Jackson to Mexico as the US minister. Jackson could have imagined the two sizing each other up, his trusted biographer facing the two-faced president smelling of ulterior motives. Monroe admitted that cynics might brand this move as merely a way to get Jackson out of the country, but it wasn't, he claimed unconvincingly. Eaton agreed that, yes, some people might think the offer of the appointment was rather coincidental, but the interview was cheering to Eaton. It raised the question of who were the amateurs at this game. Jackson had no intention of going to Mexico, but his refusal was measured and reasonable, a reassuring posture for the Junto. Mrs. Jackson refused to go, Jackson told Monroe, and he would not go without her, which was a good excuse. William Carroll sent another confidential letter to Henry Clay with the news: the government would not be able to send Jackson out of the country.[14]

By early 1823, several Pennsylvania county meetings had endorsed Jackson for the presidency, and he responded at first only in private letters, but finally one was clearly meant for publication. In it, Jackson repeated the theme of modest demurral qualified by his willingness to serve if called. Yet that spring, Jackson's involvement in his friends' efforts increased, and he began to pay more attention to the election. He started tracking in granular detail the activities of men who were seeking the presidency and, because of that, who had become his opponents. He fumed when Henry Clay had his friends try to secure a nomination from the Louisiana legislature and, worse, had the temerity to deploy his operatives in Tennessee. Jackson was increasingly confident that neither Clay nor Crawford had much chance outside their home turf, but he was tireless in expanding his reach and protecting his reputation. He told a friend in Alabama to correct a newspaper report criticizing the execution of Arbuthnot and Ambrister, and in the process to find out who dared write such slanders. Meanwhile, Jackson's friendly exchanges with John C. Calhoun showed another side of him. Jackson men knew that Calhoun was the primary rival in Pennsylvania, where they were incubating elaborate plans. Jackson's convivial notes to Calhoun did not mention that the Junto's bandwagon was planning to head up to Harrisburg.[15]

BEFORE THE JUNTO could turn its attention fully to Pennsylvania, it first had to consolidate Tennessee. How to do so caused the first quarrel in the Junto. When Pleasant Miller suggested running Jackson for governor, friends dismissed the idea for at least two reasons. First, it meant challenging William Carroll, whose popularity made Jackson's victory uncertain. Losing an election, any election, could bring a premature end to Old Hickory's political career. Second, Miller's proposal seemed more selfish than helpful. As the other members of the Junto suspected, Miller wanted to challenge Senate incumbent John Williams in 1823 and believed that if Jackson defeated Carroll for governor, it would weaken Williams supporters, the Erwin faction, in the legislature.[16]

Moreover, Miller's aspirations were at odds with a greater goal. Williams had joined the Erwins, and the Overton faction wanted to replace Williams in the Senate for that reason alone. The desired end was clear, but the means to it less so. Even as presidential elections were opened up to more Americans, Article I, Section 3 of the US Constitution gave state legislatures the authority to choose their senators, and that made Williams a formidable opponent the Junto doubted Pleasant Miller could defeat. Williams had prepared for the 1823 contest by persuading many legislators to support his reelection, promises all the more binding because they were made by men whose grasped hand was more sacred than a signed covenant. Pleasant Miller discovered this when he tried to pry away Williams men in a frustrating exercise that convinced Overton's people to find another candidate. They briefly backed former Tennessee congressman John Rhea, but honeyed words mixed with arm-twisting could push Rhea only to within three votes of Williams.[17]

The Junto had other reasons to find this situation troubling. Williams had once been Andrew Jackson's friend, but they had quarreled during the Creek War, and Williams had crossed Jackson over the Florida invasion. If Old Hickory's known enemy won reelection to the Senate, Jackson's popularity in Tennessee might be questioned nationally. It was at this pivotal point that William B. Lewis and John Eaton showed up to observe the Tennessee legislative session in September 1823 and decided to take a momentous chance, one so hazardous that discussions about it had become sharp disagreements in the Nashville Junto. Lewis and Eaton planned to end their support for an uninspiring contender to replace Williams. Rather, they wanted Jackson himself to challenge him. Junto dissenters from this plan had a strong counterargument, for the maneuver was perilous and the possible gain from it unclear. If Jackson lost, his presidential prospects would suffer enormous damage that would perhaps be irreparable. If he won, he would have to take firm positions in the Senate that were sure to alienate those best courted by vagueness. Voting as a loyal Republican, for instance, would alienate Federalists otherwise eager to form new allegiances amid their party's disintegration.

Winning a Senate seat also could forfeit Jackson's advantages as a Washington outsider. Just weeks earlier, John Eaton had unveiled a significant change of course in the Junto's campaign strategy by emphasizing Washington's corruption rather than touting Old Hickory's credentials as a man of the people. A series of essays written by Eaton and titled "Letters of Wyoming" appeared in Stephen Simpson's Philadelphia *Columbian Observer* during June and July as the most overt political productions of the Jackson campaign up to that time. John Coffee underwrote the entire project, not only for Simpson's paper but also, in the following year, to fund the republication of the articles in a pamphlet.

Eaton's use of *Wyoming*, taken from the valley of that name in northeastern Pennsylvania, was to emphasize Jackson's growing support in the state, but the letters also addressed concerns about America abandoning first principles. "Wyoming" warned that limited government, selfless service, and a resolve to preserve the liberty won by the Revolution were vanishing under the national government's current stewards, all puppets of patronage. The congressional caucus was nothing more than a tool of arrogant men reminiscent of European courtiers assuming an authority inappropriate for servants of the people in a sovereign republic. To "Wyoming," Jackson was the second George Washington, a hero who had returned to his plow after his wars were finished but who now should be summoned to save the people from petty politicians who had never fought for anything but their own preferment. The comparison of Old Hickory to George Washington, and the contrast of his republican simplicity to the glitter of Washington, DC, became a common theme for Jacksonites. They challenged any criticism of Jackson by invoking Washington the man and mocking the fatuousness of Washington the capital. Andrew Jackson, Eaton declared, had been a courageous, patriotic boy fighting in the Revolution, the only candidate for the presidency who could make that claim. He could be the last veteran of the Revolutionary War to serve as president and at a time when the country needed such a man the most.[18]

The "Wyoming" letters struck a chord with a large audience as pro-Jackson papers throughout the country either published excerpts from them or reprinted them verbatim. But the audience was also a problem. Eaton's 1817 biography had presented Jackson as above party and faction, but it had not explicitly named him as a presidential possibility. "Wyoming" did, repeatedly, and with forceful criticism of the existing order as well as the political methods that had brought it about. "With the exception of that veteran [Jackson] in his country's service," said "Wyoming," " . . . all have toiled through the winter at Washington, seeking by every species of art and finesse, to further their own views, and press themselves into favour. Why is not JACKSON *there*? Because he has a soul that towers above intrigue." Some in the Junto worried that making Jackson a senatorial candidate before the Tennessee legislature was not at all an example of towering above intrigue. A victory would undermine Eaton's blunt question: *Why is not Jackson there?*[19]

But Eaton and Lewis insisted that only timidity jeopardized Jackson's chances for victory over Williams. The chance of undermining Jackson's status as an outsider was offset by creating the image of Jackson as a statesman. It was an attitude that captured perfectly the spirit of a man who had risked death in a duel with the crackshot Charles Dickinson and had rolled the dice on the Chalmette Plain with Wellington's veterans. Andrew Jackson scratched out a letter to a friend in the legislature in September 1823 declaring he would neither seek the US Senate seat nor decline it, and he then pounded toward the state capital at Murfreesboro to drive home the latter part of the message's meaning. Sam Houston was there in the gallery as before, large and unsmiling, and when the voting started, the promised support for John Williams was nothing compared to the dazzle of Andrew Jackson's name. The mismatched brothers-in-law, Lewis and Eaton, had been right. The decision was for Jackson by a vote of 35–25, a comfortable margin of victory in the first of the Junto's many risky gambles on the path to the presidency. The tally was telling, but the event had the feel of a turning point for the man at the center of the effort. Jackson's trip to Murfreesboro made clear that he was serious about the quest his friends had been mounting.[20]

=====

WITH THE PANIC of 1819 providing a reason for frugality, William H. Crawford's budget cuts at Treasury reined in the War Department through army reduction, and Calhoun fumed over the ploy for being as clever as it was popular. It was popular because the cash-strapped government was reeling from the continuing financial burdens of the war, and it was clever because it undermined Calhoun's influence and ability to stay competitive for the 1824 campaign. Retaliatory moves to hurt Crawford would come soon enough, but none of them would be as devastating as what happened to him that autumn. At almost the same moment that Andrew Jackson took a step toward the presidency with the Tennessee legislature's nomination, William H. Crawford all but lost any chance of winning it.

For years he had been the preferred candidate of many Republicans in all sections of the country. His supporters controlled many of the nation's most prominent newspapers, which caused opponents to grouse that Crawford's editorial reach gave him an unfair advantage that was not properly republican. Crawford's supporters fought against that charge. They believed his withdrawal on behalf of James Monroe in the 1816 congressional caucus deserved consideration, which became a tacit promise to reward his gesture when Crawford's turn came after Monroe's second term. Supporters of Adams, Calhoun, and Clay disagreed with that reasoning, of course, and Andrew Jackson tended to apoplexy when contemplating it.

But that promise remained a powerful influence on men who admired Crawford for other reasons too. Those vying for the presidency in 1824 were seen as more different in personality than in philosophy, though the appearance of broad consensus among them was deceiving. Nevertheless, in a field of candidates who all embraced a national vision, Crawford stood out as the man who harkened back to the Jeffersonian promise of limited government, prudent foreign relations, and fiscal responsibility. Old Republicans were nostalgic for the late 1790s when despising John Adams and lauding Thomas Jefferson had been something of a pastime. They longed for the return of those olden days and the political certainties that had characterized them. Then, one knew who to support, who to oppose, what to believe, and how to keep those beliefs alive in the country's heart. Some of the old-school Republicans, as in Pennsylvania, gravitated to Andrew Jackson, but the large numbers of them in critical places like New York, Virginia, Illinois, and Ohio thought Crawford was the man with the courage and experience to stay the Jeffersonian course. For them, he had the heart of a lion and the temperament of a lamb, and they proudly wore the label "Radicals," after a French republican faction that had opposed Louis XVIII after Bonaparte's fall.

The usual sniping of political rivals should not distract from the reality that Crawford had many more friends than enemies, although those enemies, such as John Clark in Georgia, Ninian Edwards in Illinois, and Andrew Jackson in Tennessee, were often voluble and could be vicious. Jackson's enmity puzzled Crawford the most because he could not understand how a disagreement over

Indian policy could foster such enduring hostility. "With the man I have not had a direct quarrel," said Crawford, who was well aware that Jackson had developed a hatred for him that resembled an unhealthy obsession. Crawford chose not to acknowledge Jackson's "anger or his malignity" and wondered whether "this indifference to his anger is the head and front of my offending towards him."[21]

Crawford left the capital on September 2, 1823, claiming that he needed to escape its sweltering summer, though cynics suspected that politics was the real reason for the trip. His travel plans were vague, but some concluded he was on his way to Monticello to seek Jefferson's blessing. "Cannot two such citizens as Messrs. Jefferson and Crawford bear such good will to each other," asked the Richmond *Enquirer*, a Crawford paper, "as that one of them may pay a social visit to the other, without making it a ninth-day wonder?" Crawford did not head to Jefferson's home in Albemarle County but to James Madison's in western Virginia's cool foothills.[22]

Crawford was soon on his way to another friend's home, near Madison's, but by the time he reached Senator James Barbour's residence, he had fallen ill, and it was his misfortune to then fall into the hands of an incompetent local physician, who misdiagnosed as heart disease what was probably a minor complaint. He gave Crawford digitalis, which requires an unusually precise dosage. Too little is ineffective, but the slightest overage can be lethal. Crawford would have been luckier had it killed him right away. Instead, he went into violent convulsions, symptoms of not one but two massive strokes. The doctor watched in horror, expecting Crawford to die.[23]

After Crawford regained consciousness, a prisoner of a hopelessly broken body, the Barbour family thought he would die too. His legs were paralyzed, his hands were like grotesque claws, his eyes sightless, and his tongue was so thick nobody could understand the unsettling moans he occasionally exclaimed from either pain or exasperation. He existed in this state for eight weeks while his failure to return to Washington encouraged rumors that something was wrong. The more benign newspaper accounts speculated that "bilious fever" had laid him low. "He continues seriously indisposed," said one report at the end of October, adding the hardly encouraging detail that he "was able at times to sit up." Meanwhile, the doctor resorted to the approved and potentially deadly course of treatment for an invalid, tapping into Crawford's veins to bleed him no fewer than twenty times.[24]

James Barbour opened the door of Crawford's sickroom on the afternoon of October 14 and ushered in a guest, tall, spare, and stooped. His clothes were hopelessly unfashionable, as had become his habit; perhaps he was wearing a waistcoat with flapped pockets and a remnant of frayed embroidery once meant for decoration but now comical, had it not been for the man wearing it. At eighty years of age, Thomas Jefferson seldom ventured from his little mountain, but he had heard about his friend and made the taxing journey to see him. Jefferson sat silent and watched the rise and fall of Crawford's labored breathing. A bit of deafness mercifully kept Jefferson from hearing it, and after a time, he rose and turned to leave. Crawford was still his friend, and like all of Crawford's friends, Jefferson would persist in the fiction that nothing had really changed. But Thomas Jefferson had to know on his dreary return to Monticello that the man he admired, as well as the hope for a Jeffersonian revival, was all but dead.[25]

═══

BEFORE ANDREW JACKSON left for Washington in November 1823 to take his seat in Congress as Tennessee's newest senator, he conferred with friends about how he should behave during the trip and after arriving in the capital. Everything he and his friends did from this moment forward was designed to promote Jackson's presidential viability. In his fifty-sixth year, he possessed a natural dignity that he had lacked as a young man. And though the same temper that had defined much of his youth could reappear quickly in reaction to the right provocation, Jackson was determined to keep it in check. It had never been easy for him to do this, and it is a testament to his emerging political ambition that he was resolved to try in the fall of 1823.

Almost thirty years earlier Andrew Jackson had served in both the House of Representatives and the Senate, and neither had been happy experiences. He held the distinction of being the first and, at the time, the lone congressman from Tennessee after its admission to the Union in 1796, but he could barely wait for his term to end, and when he returned to Nashville, he had vowed to retire from public life. His Senate stint came very soon after this pledge. He was only thirty years old when he took his seat, the youngest of the Senate's thirty-two members, most fifteen to twenty years his senior. Federalists also dominated the Senate, making Republican Jackson part of a minority that comprised less than 30 percent of the chamber. More than youth, inexperience, and insignificance had made him miserable, though. He missed Rachel terribly, and elaborate Senate procedures chafed him. Perhaps he was a bit intimidated by his learned and eminent colleagues, including the presiding officer, Vice President Thomas Jefferson, who remembered Jackson as an angry young man sometimes unable to form coherent words because he would "choke with rage." Jackson had resigned in less than a year.[26]

Starting from Nashville in November 1823, Jackson traveled with fellow Tennessee senator Eaton, who had become Old Hickory's unofficial campaign manager. Already close because of their collaboration on Jackson's biography and Eaton's chatty reports from the capital, they became like father and son during the trip to Washington and the congressional session that followed. Jackson's former aide Richard Keith Call was Florida's new territorial delegate to Congress, and he rode with them. They all avoided any appearance of politicking, though their journey through east Tennessee where John Williams was highly popular featured gratifying expressions of approval from town committees holding public dinners in Jackson's honor. Jackson told Andrew Jackson Donelson in Nashville to dispel reports that east Tennessee was unhappy with his election.[27]

In western Virginia, another traveling companion joined the trio. Virginia state legislator David Campbell was on his way to Richmond for the Virginia Assembly's session and tried to persuade Jackson to come to the town and meet its influential men. Jackson refused. Such a visit would have the look of electioneering, and as they neared the state capital, Jackson, Eaton, and Call parted ways with Campbell to go around it. The Virginian watched the three men trail away on their roundabout route with a better grasp of things than he let on. Campbell was a merchant by occupation and knew the look of men planning to buy and preparing to sell. "I think," he told his family, "he has not yet lost hope of being the next president."[28]

Jackson and his companions stopped at Fredericksburg, where, for once, he did not object to a major reception. A troop of horse, a company of riflemen, and the famous Washington Guards escorted him into town to a booming artillery salute. Proceedings included the introduction of an eight-year-old boy who had been named after Jackson following the Battle of New Orleans. Jackson knelt and folded the tyke into his arms before holding him away to look into his eyes. The boy met the stare. Jackson admonished him to "be a good boy . . . and be always ready to fight the enemies of your country." He pulled from his purse a fifty-cent piece and pressed it into Andy's little hand. The coin at the time was worth about ten dollars in today's money, a small fortune for a boy not yet ten himself, but Andy would never part with it. He planned to wear it around his neck. At that moment and forever after he was a "thorough Jacksonite" who intended to go to Washington when Jackson became

An engraving of Jackson after a Thomas Sully portrait done about the time Jackson entered the Senate. Another of Sully's portraits would become the image on the twenty-dollar bill in the twentieth century. (Library of Congress.)

president to show him the pendant and return the hug. It was hard to say who was more affected. Jackson described the receptions on the journey as a kind of endless marvel, proof of his undiminished popularity, and a testament to the enduring power of his victory at New Orleans. These were signs pleasing to his friends and troubling to his enemies.[29]

In Washington, the three travelers took rooms at the Franklin House where Eaton had lodged since becoming a senator in

1818. It was a fine establishment owned and managed by William O'Neale. Jackson became friends with the loquacious O'Neale. His daughter Margaret's looks and vivacity reminded Jackson of his pretty Donelson nieces and his Rachel when young. Margaret was married to a navy purser named John Timberlake and stayed with her parents to help at the boardinghouse when he was at sea. Jackson liked to hear her play the piano, but John Eaton heard music in her voice. The young senator was a handsome widower. Timberlake was often at sea.[30]

———

BECAUSE ONE OF the principal reasons for placing Jackson in the Senate was to convince the political class that he had the dignity to be the president, he meant to charm new acquaintances and repair relations with even his most reviled enemies. In advance of his arrival, some commentators believed Washington was going to see the "real" Jackson, who was courtly, reserved, and unruffled by insults. But those familiar with the authentically real Andrew Jackson were not so sure. "Jackson has thus far acted with prudence," wrote Romulus Saunders, hinting that the act could fall apart at any minute. Saunders was a young North Carolina congressman whose quick temper and gruff manner made him an astute observer of a man posing as otherwise, but Jackson's friends were confident Jackson could manage the role of potential president. Sam Houston reported home that "the General is calm, dignified, and makes as polished a bow as any man I have seen at court," and Rachel heard from Eaton that her husband had made peace with most of his enemies in Washington. It was an impressive list with long fences to mend. Jackson had almost fought a duel with General Winfield Scott, had brawled with Tom and Jesse Benton in the summer of 1813, and had thought about shooting Henry Clay after the Seminole War debates, but one by one he restored "harmony & good understanding with everybody."[31]

Jackson confided to Winfield Scott that "whenever you shall feel disposed to meet me on friendly terms, that disposition will not be met by any other than a correspondent feeling on my part." Henry Clay seemed amused and puzzled. "Genl. Jackson has buried the hatchet," he said, "and we are again on good terms." Jackson understood that he needed not only to reconcile with Clay but to court him as well. Clay broke bread and raised a glass with Old Hickory at a small dinner Jackson arranged just for him, and the end of the convivial evening saw Jackson and friends conveying Clay to his lodgings in their finest carriage.[32]

Patching up things with Thomas Hart Benton was the most remarkable act of newfound harmony given that Jackson had actually tried to kill Benton ten years earlier and still carried the bullet from the fracas. Benton had left Tennessee for the Missouri Territory after the war and in Saint Louis became the editor of an influential newspaper pushing for statehood. As a reward for his labors, Benton was made one of Missouri's first US senators. He promoted internal improvements for the entire nation to help Missouri farmers get their crops to market. It made him an ally of Speaker Henry Clay, the foremost proponent of federal funding for projects that are now called infrastructure. A family tie bolstered the political one. Clay's wife, Lucretia Hart Clay, was Thomas Hart Benton's first cousin. Benton had hoped that Cousin Henry would become the next president, but that was before he saw the "real" Andrew Jackson charm the capital. *Missouri* derives from an Algonquin word meaning "river of big canoes," and in due course, the senator from Missouri saw no good in holding a grudge against a man apparently destined to paddle the biggest canoe of all. For brother Jesse, though, forgiving and forgetting were impossible, as was understandable. Having been held down, kicked in the head, and carved up with a knife was too much to forgive and too memorable to forget.

On January 8, 1824, Jackson was at the center of Washington's commemoration of the Battle of New Orleans. Congress voted him a gold medal to be struck and presented later in the session, and the day itself began with a ceremony in Jackson's rooms that his friends made certain newspapers across the country recounted. John Eaton ushered in Congressmen Charles F. Mercer of Virginia and Stephen Van Rensselaer of New York to give Jackson the two pistols that the Marquis de Lafayette had presented to George Washington, weapons Washington had carried in the Revolutionary War. Jackson as a young congressman had voted against an address of gratitude to President Washington and had always recalled the first president as too soft on the British and too aristocratic in his social customs. But that was all in the past and forgotten as the new, "real" Jackson responded to the gift of the pistols by declaring that "no man living entertains a higher veneration for the character, the virtues, and disinterested patriotism of the father of American liberty, than I do." The sentiment loosed a flood of Washington memorabilia from the family. Soon enough, George Washington Parke Custis, Washington's step-grandson, gave Jackson the general's spyglass, and Custis's sister Eleanor Parke Custis Lewis sent him a plate from the first presidential service. Newspapers made clear that Jackson planned to visit the fabled "Nelly" at her home outside the capital.[33]

The anniversary celebrations in 1824 ended with Louisa Catherine Adams staging a ball in Jackson's honor. Her husband hosted a dinner at least once a week, and she arranged a ball twice a month, even though these entertainments taxed her health, for like her husband, she did not like people very much. She was better at socializing than he was, at least, "a woman of great spirit" able to shoulder social burdens "with a high hand." Nevertheless, she was not a Jackson admirer, and the ball capping the New Orleans celebration was apparently her husband's idea, possibly because he thought the gesture would gain him support from westerners. Mrs. Adams did not skimp, and her ball would be remembered as the event of the season by the thousand people who came to sip punch and crane necks to gawk at the famous, especially General Jackson. Some even danced, the women in regency gowns and preposterously plumed caps, but the crush of people made it hard to breathe. John Quincy Adams stood uncomfortably to the side, doubtless nursing the hope that his backers could persuade Jackson to become his running mate. His wife did more than her part for the plan. She charmed Jackson by offering her arm and escorting him through the house to collar prominent Washington figures eager to be introduced to the evening's guest of honor. Jackson returned the favor with a gallant toast to her at the midnight supper, the perfect end to an affair that featured expensive wines, whiskey, and delicacies that only the urbane Adamses could have identified, let alone pronounced. Jackson was at his dignified best.[34]

But Jackson had no intention of quitting his presidential quest. He seemed a model of statesmanship and sacrifice, but privately he was still directing his campaign. Eaton arranged to have his 1817 biography of Jackson reprinted with additional material that made it an obvious campaign document. Junto member Pleasant Miller, who had nominated Jackson for president before the Tennessee legislature, wrote to contacts across the country, including North Carolina state legislator Charles Fisher. He praised Fisher for his stand in the North Carolina legislature against the congressional caucus. Miller admitted that he and Fisher differed about who should be the next president (Miller knew that Fisher supported John C. Calhoun), but they could agree that the hated caucus exemplified the political class's intolerable elitism. Miller hymned Old Hickory as "a man of Elegant manners, of first rate sense about all things" and a "man of integrity," but he avoided criticizing Calhoun. When the

Jackson juggernaut drove the secretary of war from the race, Jackson and the Junto did not want bad feelings to prevent his supporters from coming to their side.[35]

Meanwhile, John Overton and William B. Lewis continued placing items in newspapers. When Overton tired, Lewis would ghostwrite his essays in addition to cranking out letters trumpeting the virtues of General Jackson to scores of correspondents. A measure of necessity dictated Lewis's working behind the scenes. When Jackson had served as a treaty commissioner to the Chickasaw Indians in 1818, Lewis had tagged along to strike a secret deal with two Chickasaw headmen for the rights to a valuable salt lick on the land under discussion. It was a shady arrangement that was gradually coming to light in early 1823. The piecemeal revelations had done considerable damage to Lewis's reputation, and though Jackson did not turn on him, everyone knew that Lewis was better suited for quiet deeds of persuasion. He established another North Carolina contact after a visit from William Polk, the state's leading Federalist. Polk supported Crawford, having never forgiven John Quincy Adams for deserting the party to join Thomas Jefferson's Republicans in 1808. But after Lewis showed him Jackson's 1816 letter to James Monroe suggesting the president-elect appoint a Federalist to his cabinet, Polk began having second thoughts. Who would have imagined that Andrew Jackson would want to mend the animosities of the war by disregarding political parties? It suggested that Jackson would be open to Federalists serving in his administration, and Polk returned to North Carolina ready to persuade friends to support Old Hickory. That was the sort of result that made Lewis, no matter how tainted, indispensable.[36]

Through it all, Jackson kept up appearances, adapting to the nation's capital more seamlessly than the Junto expected. His letters to friends and family always declared his desire to stay above the fray and claimed ignorance about the presidential contest, but they also recited his and the other candidates' standing in each state with astonishing detail and precision. His popularity pleased but did not deceive him, which made him seem the most seasoned professional in a field purportedly full of them. He knew that more than a few denizens of Washington expected to see him "with a Tomahawk in one hand, & a scalping knife the other," but that did not matter. He was "getting on very smoothly." Only William H. Crawford remained unreconciled, and even if that was by Jackson's choice, the Georgian, who had been conveyed back to the capital the previous November, was not receiving guests. "When it becomes necessary to philosophise & be meek," Jackson told his nephew Donelson, "no man can command his temper better than I."[37]

CRAWFORD'S SLOW IMPROVEMENT at the Barbour manse had made him fit enough to return to Washington, but he remained frail even on his good days. The strain of pretending otherwise brought on relapses that disheartened the few visitors allowed to see him. Those friends brought out reports laced with lies that were avidly repeated by Crawford's supporters. They described his full and rosy cheeks, his buoyant spirits, and his sharp memory. But privately they whispered that he remained appallingly ill. Only his daughter Caroline could understand him, or at least pretend to, translating his slurred mumbles for guests. His hands were verging on necrotic, requiring Caroline to push his loosely held pen across official documents. Nevertheless, some hoped that Crawford's affliction was temporary and he would soon be his old self again. Perhaps some of them believed it.[38]

The loyalty of Crawford's friends during his ordeal was inspiring even as their thoughts about his health were wishful thinking. Their determination, however, to save Crawford's candidacy had them committing the kind of mistakes they smugly attributed to the amateurs of the Nashville Junto. New York senator Martin Van Buren had emerged as the most influential manager in Crawford's campaign, and after surveying the wreckage of the near fatal stroke, he concluded that the political damage to Crawford's candidacy could only be offset by having the congressional caucus make Crawford the official Republican nominee for president as soon as possible. He believed the move would provide a sufficient show of confidence to quell rumors about Crawford's health. Having little else to warm them in the bleak winter of 1824, Crawfordites quickly warmed to this idea. His nomination, they told one another, would guarantee his election. Only occasionally did hard reality intrude, as when some of his most stalwart supporters added the sobering caveat to their prediction—"if Mr. Crawford lives."[39]

When Congress assembled in December 1823, many doubted there would be a caucus for the upcoming election. Sam Houston thought Jackson's presence in Washington alone had so dampened enthusiasm for the caucus as to kill it. It had always had its critics, but they now broadened their attacks and increased their volume. Tennessee newspaper editorials railed against it as undemocratic, and the state legislature had followed Pleasant Miller's nomination of Jackson with resolutions condemning it as a relic of aristocratic privilege. Tennessee sought support for this view from other states with disappointing results, but it was evident to many that the tide had turned against the tradition they now derisively dubbed "King Caucus."[40]

The potential influence of the caucus deeply troubled the Nashville Junto, though, and Felix Grundy sponsored resolutions in the state legislature instructing Tennessee's representatives and senators not to attend it. Pointing out that western states with smaller populations were disadvantaged in the caucus was a persuasive argument and gained momentum among small states elsewhere. Jackson's supporters also reckoned that boosting his candidacy by resisting the antiquated caucus would make him viable enough to deny anyone a majority in the Electoral College. That would put the question before the House of Representatives, where each state delegation, regardless of size, had one vote, which would increase western clout. The Junto had to be careful, though, and not let the democratic impulse get out of hand. For example, Jackson men quashed the idea of holding a nominating convention in which each state would be proportionally represented according to its population. They wearily explained to those promoting the idea that proportional representation missed the very reason for killing the caucus: in such a convention, the West would be just as underrepresented compared to the more populous East.[41]

Calhoun, Clay, and Adams supporters mimicked the Junto's arguments after realizing that Jackson's men were mining a rich vein of discontent. Because so many Americans believed that the caucus thwarted the will of the people, many in Congress planned to steer clear of it. An added incentive for not attending was that it would taint Crawford supporters—the only people still clinging to the tradition—by showing them as blocking healthy competition from the heartland with a nomination engineered by Washington aristocrats. Soon Calhoun people in North Carolina were railing against the caucus, and Adams newspapers were heartily denouncing it in Massachusetts. The caucus became "monstrous in itself, and so repugnant to the spirit of our institutions, that it would be strange if it were tolerated." Caucus supporters were "like the Praetorian Guards of ancient Rome" who hoped "to meet at the Capitol, and there dispose of the empire to the best bidder." Daniel Webster was less dramatic but more original. Caucuses were wrong, he said, because "they make great men little & little men great."[42]

Van Buren and his cadre of Crawford supporters hoped that the criticism was campaign bluster that would disappear once the nomination was settled. They were a sad bunch, all the same, greatly discouraged by Crawford's health and fatigued by the growing up-roar against the caucus. Having little choice, they proceeded with plans to call the meeting by placing a notice in the *National Intelligencer* of February 7, 1824. Eleven congressmen from eleven states placed their names on this announcement, all of them Crawford supporters, but readers needed only glance elsewhere in the *Intelligencer* to see an announcement from 24 anticaucus congressmen declaring that 181 of their colleagues in both the House and the Senate would not be attending. This brazen rebuff by so many in Congress shocked the Crawford men, and they moved the date of the caucus. It encouraged suspicion that the caucus was being delayed because of Crawford's wretched health.[43]

On the evening of February 14, 1824, a thousand spectators in the House gallery watched as only 66 of the 261 eligible House and Senate members attended the last congressional nominating caucus in American political history. John Eaton's anonymous jabs in local papers had shamed wavering congressmen into staying away, and once the event began, everyone saw the wisdom in the decision. It was a gloomy affair marked by embarrassment over the meager turn-out and confusion about the way to handle it. Participants briefly considered adjourning, but the sad 66 finally resolved to carry on and nominate Crawford. The smattering of applause from the gallery was telling, and the funereal nature of the event was underlined by a clumsy ploy to win votes in Pennsylvania. The caucus chose the elderly Pennsylvania statesman Albert Gallatin to run as Crawford's vice-presidential candidate. Gallatin's Swiss birth called into question his eligibility, and he had not been the first choice. Martin Van Buren had attempted through Thomas Hart Benton to persuade Henry Clay to be Crawford's running mate. Crawford supporters had been working this angle for some time, some even sweetening the proposition with oblique but macabre references to a likely vice-presidential ascendancy, given Crawford's health. But

A Jacksonite political cartoon disparaging the congressional caucus nomination of William H. Crawford. Jackson, in full military regalia, stands above the snarling curs of the other candidates' lackeys in the press. (Library of Congress.)

talk like that made Henry Clay wince. He had not smiled when refusing. The behavior of Crawford's friends during his ordeal had been inspiring, but the behavior of his enemies and, now in their desperation, even some of his friends brought to mind jackals.[44]

Before the caucus met, opponents called it the "abortive Caucus," and Jacksonites kept up the criticism of it and its beneficiary, William Crawford, even after their tirades had dismantled its credibility and a country doctor had destroyed Crawford's viability. Jackson's hatred for Crawford had something to do with this. He had written John Coffee the day after the caucus's apparent failure about meeting with their mutual friend, editor William Savin Fulton, to encourage him to "use his pen in opposition to this usurpation of the rights of the people."[45]

The caucus nomination was a major mistake. Crawford papers used it to portray him as the only national candidate, but the din of derision drowned out even the most determined of these efforts. A Virginia editor recalled Milton's *Paradise Lost*. The caucus resembled for him the fallen angels gathering in Pandemonium, a meeting of "Satan and his peers." Others argued that the men who had participated in Crawford's nomination were now political pariahs who would pay at the next election. Those who stuck with Crawford, however, were something other than stubborn. Martin Van Buren believed Crawford was the only real Jeffersonian Republican in the race and the only man who could unify the party and thereby restore the country. To him, caucus opponents were disingenuous and hypocritical. They suddenly opposed the traditional method of picking the party's candidates only because this time around Crawford happened to be its favorite. And this much was, at least, true. What was not true was the groundless comfort Crawfordites took in believing Jackson's people were too disorganized to mount a meaningful campaign and that "the outcry [against the caucus] is mostly confined to the uninformed." As Crawford's friends soldiered on, they labored for a withered shadow of a once formidable man who would be a hopeless president if by some miracle he won the election and lived to be inaugurated. They came to resemble men engaged in a quest only because they could not find anything else to do. Jacksonites, however, were busier than ever, and purposeful.[46]

CHAPTER 7

1824

E VERY WEEK WHEN CONGRESS WAS IN SESSION, JAMES MON-
roe hosted a dinner, but they were large and impersonal affairs
that offered little chance for intimate conversation except for
cliques that might find themselves among the thirty or forty guests.
The president held these banquets "in a vast, cold hall," which
was bad enough. Worse, in the view of the attendees, was that no
women were invited.[1]

Dinners at the elegant Calhoun home Oakly, by contrast, were
"the pleasantest of the ministerial dinners, because he invited ladies." The house had been a wedding gift to John and Floride (pronounced "Florida") from her wealthy mother, and it was there, in
between Floride's elegant soirées, that her handsome husband laid
plans to succeed James Monroe as the next president of the United
States. No matter what one thought of a possible Calhoun presidency, at least the parties would be better.[2]

Enough people thought highly of John C. Calhoun to make them
believe it could happen for him in 1824. Some found him to be
"the most agreeable person in conversation in Washington," at least
of those in the cabinet, but others measured him from a broader,

almost epic perspective. William Wirt believed that Calhoun was "ardent, generous, high-minded, brave" and possessed "a genius full of fire, energy and light." He was "a devoted patriot—proud of his country, and prizing her glory above his life." Calhoun's appeal lay in the fact that he was an unabashed nationalist, a champion of economic development spurred by federally funded roads and canals and financed by a disciplined bank controlling currency and credit. Calhoun's America would have manufacturing protected by a tariff and encouraged by domestic consumption.[3]

None of this went unnoticed by Calhoun's rivals, including Clay and John Quincy Adams, and particularly Crawford, who by 1822 had come to view the dark, handsome man across the table in cabinet meetings as his most serious competition, particularly in all-important Pennsylvania, with its enthusiasm for tariffs and central banking.[4]

The earlier budget cuts angered Calhoun. He arranged for the founding of the Washington *Republican and Congressional Examiner* as a means of fighting back. His backing of the venture was an open secret. The *Republican* became the forum for a clumsy smear aimed at Crawford that ruined its perpetrator, the Illinois politician Ninian Edwards, and redounded poorly on its apparent progenitor.

The incident involved the "A.B." letters, so-called because they purported to be from a young clerk in the War Department who was protecting his identity by writing under those initials. The letters began appearing in the Washington *Republican* on April 19, 1823, to accuse Crawford of dishonestly reporting to Congress about government funds in western banks. The allegations resulted in an investigation by a select committee of the House of Representatives, which could find no malfeasance on Crawford's part but did discover the author of the letters to be Calhoun supporter Edwards, whom Monroe had recently appointed minister to Mexico. Congress summoned Edwards to return to Washington, and this gave him an opportunity to perjure himself by claiming under oath he was not "A.B." Rather than face the disgrace of being fired, Edwards resigned his appointment.[5]

Crawford proved vulnerable on another front. By the 1820s, he represented a diminishing cadre of Enlightenment disciples who embraced the belief that all men were perfectible. One result was that he had recommended during his brief tenure in President Madison's War Department changes in the policy that sought endless Indian land cessions. Crawford recommended reviving the plan proposed first by George Washington's secretary of war Henry Knox, another child of the Enlightenment who wanted to save his country from the stain of Indian extinction by persuading the natives to assume white culture.

Crawford went a step further by suggesting that intermarriage between Indians and white settlers could speed the process, something that had been happening on the American frontier since the beginning of European colonization. By the early nineteenth century, white views on race had changed, many viewing intermarriage and hence racial amalgamation with repugnance. A pro-Jackson printer published an earlier attack on Crawford's report in 1824, seriously damaging the Georgian's support in the South and the West.[6]

Southerners and westerners did not need specific incidents to argue for Indian removal rather than assimilation. Calhoun's supporters insinuated that it was only a small step from Crawford's idea of marrying Indians to marrying slaves. The allegation had force because Charleston, South Carolina, had recently and just barely foiled a rebellion among slaves that seemed to include trusted house servants with easy access to nurseries and ample opportunities to poison pantries. Southerners were in no mood to hear about the benefits of racial amalgamation or to be edified by Enlightenment rationalism.[7]

These attacks on William H. Crawford continued after Crawford nearly died from his stroke. As much as their persistence resulted from Calhoun's bitterness, it was also an example of a flaw in him that only worsened with age. He nursed grudges in childish and petty ways. His unabashed admirer William Wirt noticed this. "He is, at present, a little too sanguine," he said of Calhoun, "a little too rapid and tenacious." Calhoun also had an arrogant streak that led him to exercise bad judgment in trying to solve problems even when he saw them clearly. Calhoun knew that Pennsylvania along with New York was crucial to his candidacy, especially Pennsylvania if he lost New York. He did not sense that the place was slipping away from him, though, let alone that it was not tending toward Crawford. Even before the Georgian's stroke, Pennsylvania was moving toward Andrew Jackson. Calhoun would never understand exactly why.[8]

JOHN C. CALHOUN and his friends thought Pennsylvania was squarely behind him, a situation they expected the Republican state nominating convention to make official at its March 1824 meeting in Harrisburg. Calhoun was not alone in discounting Jackson as a candidate, but he was unique in counting him a friend, and nothing had happened since Old Hickory's arrival in Washington in December 1823 to change their relationship. The notion that Jackson's candidacy would end as soon as he realized he could not win comforted Calhoun, as did his calculation that Jackson being in the race hurt Crawford and Clay more than him or Adams. The assessment seemed smart, but it was quite wrong. Jackson's operatives worked tirelessly with Simpson and Duane as well as Henry Baldwin, James Buchanan, and M. C. Rogers to bypass party leaders and convince the rank and file of Pennsylvania Republicans that Old Hickory was a serious contender.

Calhoun had the backing of the "Family Party" led by Samuel Ingham, George M. Dallas, and John Sergeant. It was not actually a full-fledged political party but rather one of the many factions that comprised Pennsylvania Republicanism. But it was unquestionably the most influential faction. Its name derived from the practice of making appointments to government offices exclusively from "family," meaning a short list of dedicated men loyal to the faction and committed to its continued ascendancy. It was also called the Old School, which was a fitting label for men who had become complacent in their long domination of Pennsylvania politics. Among other things, they controlled Pennsylvania banking, which made them easy targets for accusations about enriching themselves at the people's expense, but acerbic charges did not trouble them much.

The Panic of 1819 gave more weight to the charges, though, and began to erode the Family Party's power and influence. Resentment over the politics of deference blossomed even as the Old Schoolers of the Family Party expected deference to endure forever. An incongruous mix of disaffected Republicans and untethered Federalists were sometimes called Amalgamators, but members of the new faction thought a better name was "New School." Whatever they were called, they were adversaries of the Old School who wanted more than economic reforms. They wanted broader participation in elections and more access to public office. When they took to calling themselves "Democrats," the Family Party thought it ironic because many of them were former Federalists.

Incongruity signaled a new type of political strength. Philadelphia's working-class voters read and believed Stephen Simpson's *Columbian Observer*, a Jackson paper, and western Pennsylvania farmers found Jackson appealing, and for not much more reason than he was a westerner and was assumed to have opinions similar to theirs. Scots-Irish in that part of the state heard Jackson promoters laud his Scots-Irish ancestry and were heartened by a man proud to be one of them. Calhoun was Scots-Irish too, but not particularly proud of it, and that showed. His supporters followed his lead and ignored the lower classes when they were not denigrating them as impoverished because they were shiftless and living in filth.[9]

But Jackson's support was not limited to the working and lower classes. In western Pennsylvania, Henry Baldwin of Pittsburgh personified the Amalgamators' cobbling together a Democratic faction of disparate elements. A native of Connecticut, Baldwin not only had been a Federalist but also served as one in Congress. His financial interests in a large iron foundry outside Pittsburgh also made him a protectionist eager for high tariffs, which ordinarily would have landed him in the Calhoun camp of the Family Party and, barring that, at least among the supporters of Henry Clay, whom Baldwin regularly praised. The East-West divide in Pennsylvania politics meant more to a man like Baldwin than did policy, though. The Family Party was a closed club of eastern Pennsylvania, so Baldwin and men like him found a different path to victory. Andrew Jackson looked like a winner, and with his dimming prospects in New York, Calhoun did not, and Clay even less so. For the time being, that was a good enough reason for men like Baldwin to throw in with Old Hickory, whatever he might think of tariffs and banks.[10]

The Jackson surge in Pennsylvania began with newspapers but soon featured public meetings so large that outdoor events "covered a four-acre lot." A Pittsburgh meeting put on by Baldwin and friends gave Jackson its resounding endorsement. Soon after that, the Dauphin County Democratic Committee in Harrisburg followed suit and appointed Henry W. Peterson to ask Old Hickory's permission to continue the push for his election. Peterson operated a tavern, which gave his letter an appropriately unpretentious aspect that offset its nod to old deferential habits. The barkeep's note to Jackson in Washington came as no surprise, for William B. Lewis had been in contact with some of the Family Party's enemies all along. On his advice, Jackson was ready to respond with his stock answer about never seeking office but always being willing to serve if called. Harrisburg's newspaper published Jackson's letter, and the Pennsylvania press picked it up, releasing a tide of approbation for Old Hickory. Ten thousand copies of the Dauphin Democrats' endorsement were soon in circulation. Almost nine hundred Philadelphians braved wet snow and icy temperatures to support Jackson in a mass meeting that pledged to promote his candidacy. Committees of correspondence sprang up to arrange pro-Jackson activities and establish contact with similar Jackson committees in other states. Stephen Simpson, with the help of the Nashville Junto, coordinated a ginned-up but seemingly spontaneous bustle.[11]

The Family Party finally stirred itself into action in the spring of 1823 by trying to convince the Republican convention in Harrisburg to nominate Calhoun. Delegates from Westmoreland County, however, dashed this plan by endorsing Jackson beforehand. Then the Family Party blocked a vote of any kind at the Harrisburg Convention that year. The same delegates who had been clamoring for an early Calhoun nomination now insisted that it was too early to nominate anyone from anywhere. While they thus bought themselves a year to regroup before the next convention in March 1824, the scent of desperation hung about their cause. Their year was also another year for Jacksonites, who did not need to regroup in the least.[12]

On the contrary, they redoubled their already successful efforts. Stephen Simpson organized Hickory Clubs throughout the state. In Philadelphia, he capitalized on the lingering misery caused by the economic panic and the contraction of credit with appeals to the city's skilled workers. If nothing else, he got them riled up. In preparation for the Harrisburg Convention of March 1824, the Family Party held a meeting of its own in Philadelphia to choose Calhoun delegates. Jackson men crashed it, and according to Family Party members, did so with "violence and audacity." It was likely an accurate description of how they took over the meeting and rammed through a slate of pro-Jackson delegates.[13]

Finally, grave doubts clouded the hopes of Calhoun men. When Family Party leaders convened two weeks before the Harrisburg Convention to plan strategy, they resembled shaken men in a shivering bunker. Even the news of Crawford's misguided nomination by the rump congressional caucus could not lift the pall. Instead, it only increased the alarm about Calhoun's prospects in contrast to Crawford's. George M. Dallas was a strong Calhoun man, but he believed it was time to cut his losses. From its presumably commanding perch, the Family Party had remained blissfully unaware of Jackson's grassroots movement, but Dallas thought it time to come to grips with the world as it was. Calhoun no longer had a chance in Harrisburg, and should he stagger on from that failure, he would lose the general election. Dallas quietly told his fellow party leaders that they must shift their support from Calhoun to Jackson, the only candidate who could beat Crawford. Not everyone was willing to swallow the pill just yet, but enough took the medicine to kill Calhoun's candidacy. It all but guaranteed Jackson's nomination in Pennsylvania.[14]

There would be no real drama at Harrisburg, and the only people surprised by what unfolded there in March 1824 were members of the political class, especially John C. Calhoun. Washington insiders had been clinging to the same sort of complacency that the Family Party had been shocked into abandoning. A week before the convention, Jackson heard from his Pennsylvania operatives that the state's old guard was coming around, so when Calhoun's diminishing support collapsed in the face of the Jackson juggernaut at Harrisburg, the result was an anticlimax. The nomination came to Andrew Jackson with a vote of 124 to 1, which was very nearly the acclamation that New Orleans newspapers had predicted for the country when the Tennessee legislature had nominated Jackson in the summer of 1822. The number made the few Family Party holdouts decide to support a bumptious backwoodsman as president, and they salvaged a particle of pride by having the convention nominate Calhoun for vice president.[15]

Calhoun's candidacy "is off!" marveled one of those seasoned professionals who up to the second he heard about Pennsylvania had thought Calhoun's candidacy was definitely "on!" Some Calhoun loyalists were alarmed by the prospect that the government would "become completely military if Jackson the general, and Calhoun Sec of War should be chosen President and Vice President." But many more were invigorated by the fact that "Andrew Jackson comes pure, untrammeled, and unpledged, from the bosom of the people."[16]

Staggered by his reversal of fortune, Calhoun retreated to his elegant home in the hills behind Georgetown to brood like Napoleon on Elba. "He does not look well," came one report, "and feels very deeply the disappointment of his ambition." He watched as his supporters in other states drifted away to Jackson. He only numbly accepted the vice-presidential nomination from the Harrisburg Convention. It would have galled him to know that Jackson's managers had not expected Calhoun to be on their ticket and were not happy about it. John Eaton worried that because both Calhoun and Jackson were from slave states, Calhoun could hurt Jackson in the North. Eaton also did not like the looks of Jackson's main rival in Pennsylvania winding up with a share of the spoils. Some might suspect that a secret deal between Jackson and Calhoun had predetermined the result, which would undermine Jackson's image as a political outsider above unseemly bargains. Calhoun understood at least that much, and before long he was countering rumors about an arrangement between his and Jackson's supporters.[17]

His brooding gradually abated. "He is full of the kindest feelings and the most correct principles," insisted William Wirt, "and another presidential term will, I think, mellow him for any service to his country." After all, most people did not expect Jackson to serve more than one term.[18]

═══

NOT SINCE GEORGE Washington had Americans considered some-one for the presidency who was mainly noted for his military career. Thus in 1824, questions inevitably arose. When opposition newspa-pers implied that Jackson's military exploits were overblown, Jack-son's newspapers simply published more accounts of Old Hickory's heroic deeds. That raised the issue of whether Jackson's military achievements alone entitled him to the presidency. Was the office a kind of reward for patriotism that eclipsed all other considerations? Or, as Henry Clay asked, did Jackson's ability to kill Britons merit any consideration at all in connection to the presidency?[19]

Thomas Ritchie in the Richmond *Enquirer* struggled to find the answer. His was a familiar "anxiety to avoid uttering a word which might wound the feelings of Gen. Jackson," but it was not healthy to let that uneasiness keep citizens "from a free investigation of his qualifications for the Presidential Chair." Ritchie nevertheless con-tinued to tiptoe as he mused that Jackson was competent for other pursuits more suited to "his genius . . . of that rapid, fiery and im-petuous order." The closest the *Enquirer* came to criticism was in wondering if Jackson's inexperience would make it easy for corrupt politicians to use him for their own ends. Such talk did not sit well with the Nashville Junto, nor did an Alabama editor's belief that he was too dictatorial to serve as president. Indiana senator Waller Taylor worried that "the People seem determined to have a military President, one whose every official act has shown a total disregard of the law and constitution when they interfered with his arbitrary and ambitious disposition."[20]

And that got to the heart of the matter. North Carolina congressman and William Crawford man Lewis Williams strived to emphasize the same point about Jackson's supposed unfitness for the job. He contacted Jackson's Tennessee critics for information about the vaunted military record reportedly speckled by autocratic behavior and an occasional murder. Williams reminded anyone who would listen that "even Washington was not made President on account of his military fame, but on account of his civil virtues." Jackson had "less military fame and no civil virtues at all." He told Jackson's enemy, the former Tennessee congressman Newton Cannon, that "if Jackson is chosen the government will be endangered or destroyed, . . . that Jackson will exalt the military above the civil power, . . . the peace of the country will be sacrificed, . . . all because Jackson won the battle of New Orleans."[21]

Cannon didn't need reminding. He was among Jackson's enemies in Tennessee who had been trying for months to convince the country that all was not as it seemed in Eaton's admiring biography and the glowing press reports of Jackson's dignified manner in Washington society and Senate deliberations. Old Hickory's defenders said Cannon's animosity stemmed from his losing large wagers at Clover Bottom, Jackson's horse track near Nashville. Cannon had a more sinister story as his reason. He had served on a jury that acquitted a man of murdering a friend of Jackson's. Old Hickory was said to have pointed at Newton Cannon after the verdict while muttering, "I'll mark you, young man." And Cannon was marked; he never forgot the incident. Jackson, he said in 1824, was "a Tyrant in every situation in which he has been placed."[22]

Lewis Williams and Newton Cannon would talk to anyone who would listen, but their audiences were small at first and shrank as time went on. Ohio editor Charles Hammond marveled, "How is it that no one speaks freely of this man?" The obvious answer was that many felt uncomfortable speaking ill of a national hero, but there was also the story of a man in a hotel barroom to consider. When his mild criticism of Jackson silenced conversation and stilled clinking glasses, the hotel owner's tone was quietly ominous when he said, "There is freedom of speech here but if any man says anything agin Andy Jackson we send daylight through him."[23]

That took place in western Pennsylvania, where Jackson men used methods they had first honed in Tennessee, including references to ventilating opponents. When Jackson's enemies claimed that his popularity at home was waning, the Junto staged huge rallies in Nashville and Knoxville and encouraged raucous public meetings in scores of villages and hamlets. Whether large or small, many of these events had a strangely threatening character about them, with declarations of support for Andrew Jackson including demands that Tennessee's elected officials and appointed staff pledge the same, or else. Meanwhile, newspapers from Maine to Mobile reported the large attendance and exceptional enthusiasm of these public meetings. Jacksonites soon took the show on the road. Occasionally, they held a mass meeting for no other reason than to generate positive stories for the press. Parades were another crowd pleaser, with their colorful banners, brass bands, and a standing invitation to boys of all ages to join the procession, shout slogans, and show off for local girls. It was fun to be part of something popular, rewarding to think it important. Jackson men never missed a militia muster and always carried to it a jug to pull on and stories to tell about Old Hickory eating acorns and killing Creeks.[24]

Men who had served under Jackson were enthusiastic supporters of considerable value. Because so few had fallen at New Orleans, their diaspora over the years created a large, extensive, ready-made network throughout the states. Stephen Simpson was one example, and others who had become prominent were now, like him, foot soldiers in the cause. Edward Livingston, Jackson's aide and attorney at New Orleans, worked doggedly for Jackson's candidacy in Louisiana. South Carolinian Arthur P. Hayne was another veteran of New Orleans and then of Florida. Arthur's brother Robert Y. Hayne was an admiring colleague of Jackson's in the Senate.[25]

The idea of establishing committees of correspondence also began in Tennessee but soon spread to Pennsylvania and other states. The Junto directed committees to print speeches favorable to Jackson and distribute them as pamphlets across states judged in play. They didn't waste money or time in those that were not. The speeches-cum-pamphlets lamented the waning of republican principles but assured that Jackson would revive them with the same resolve he had shown at New Orleans. They portrayed Jackson's deficiencies as strengths by hailing parochialism as purity. Jackson had never been to Europe, for example, and consequently, he had never learned the pretensions and pomposity of courtiers and courtesans, as had Adams, Crawford, and Clay. Rather than slurping at the government trough, Jackson had struggled to ensure the country's survival and protect its honor.

The frontier had toughened Jackson for any task; hardship and loss had hardened his resolve, but not his heart, which was as big as the country was great and as tender as sprouts in tilled earth. No pasty-faced politicians marinated in parliamentary protocol and talking flowery fluff could have beaten redcoats in Louisiana and were even less likely to reverse the erosion of America's virtue and will. Eaton, Overton, and Lewis never tired of the theme and were careful to keep it fresh. They became virtuosos, spinning hundreds of variations reprising its central motif in keys major and minor, sometimes mournful, always melodic. Editors from Maine to Mobile loved their copy for the way it filled columns and boosted circulation. Sometimes it came over the transom anonymously—the Junto never put too many markers on its work—but the ink-stained men in little offices of country sheets as well as the well-heeled publishers of big-city dailies got to where they could spot the work of this or that author.[26]

Jackson lacked support in the Washington press, but the preference of those newspapers for the traditional candidates played into another prominent theme of the Jackson campaign: that the nation's capital was out of touch. Sam Houston captured the mood when he wryly observed that Washington's editors "will not state facts, but make them to suit their own wishes." Outside of Washington, the presses turned to shape public opinion for Old Hickory. George Wilson, the editor of the Nashville *Gazette*, vehemently denied that his paper was a rag being subsidized by the Nashville Junto, of which he was a member. Such demurrals were less believable as he responded to every charge leveled at Jackson with a thunderclap of indignation. When Jesse Benton published a pamphlet stuffed with damning facts about Jackson's gambling, dueling, and shady land deals, Wilson's *Gazette* dismissed Benton as "suffering under derangement" and demanded that Thomas Ritchie apologize for publishing Benton's libels in the Richmond *Enquirer*. When criticism seemed inarguably steeped in truth, the *Gazette* asked "who of us are without our foibles" and clucked over petty attacks on the "people's candidate." Wilson insisted that people should become more acquainted with Old Hickory's illustrious military career, and he pointed the way with a syrupy review of the new edition of Eaton's biography.[27]

Pro-Jackson editors and the Nashville Junto became adept at turning flaws into favorables. Jackson was not reckless but brave, not impetuous but decisive, not dictatorial but confident in his leadership, not politically inexperienced but unsullied by politics as usual. Possibly the best example of the tactic was when Crawfordites tried to use Jackson's 1816 letters urging President-elect James Monroe to appoint a Federalist to his cabinet to discredit Old

Hickory as secretly supporting Hartford Convention traitors. The Junto responded with purpose and agility. Pennsylvania senator and Crawford supporter Walter Lowrie claimed to have copies of the letters with plans to publish them. A potentially serious misstep occurred when Jackson denied he had made the recommendation to Monroe. William B. Lewis knew this was not true—he had shown a copy of one of the letters to North Carolina Federalist William Polk a year before to gain his support—but he moved swiftly to defuse the issue by altering one of the letters to include the phrase "that monster party spirit." In Washington, Eaton published the copies with Lewis's addition, which turned the charge against Jackson's reliability as a Republican on its head by depicting him as above the footling concerns of patronage. He was a champion of merit blind to party affiliation.[28]

The Jackson men were a talented bunch, but even better, they were artful. Stephen Simpson's *Columbian Observer* in Philadelphia took the early lead as a regional hub for Jackson's cause. In Cincinnati, Elijah Hayward's *National Republican* and Moses Dawson's *Advertiser* found it easy to whip up support for Jackson in a part of Ohio still reeling from the Panic of 1819. It was the same in Alabama, where John Fitzgerald of the *Mobile Mercantile Advertiser* sometimes filled entire issues with positive stories about Jackson lifted from other papers. Fitzgerald added his own paeans, declaring that Jackson was owed the presidency for his service to the nation. He never tired of pointing out that only Jackson could "enter upon the duties of the Presidential office, untrammeled by a pledge of any kind, uninfluenced by any motive but the love of his country." Fitzgerald could get carried away, as when he compared Andrew Jackson to Jesus Christ because they had both coped with traitors. That sort of thing could bring even the most avid Jacksonites up short, but perhaps not. An enthusiastic supporter in Pennsylvania exulted after the state went for him in its October 29 election, "My God, and your God, . . . hath raised . . . up [Jackson] for to be a savior and a deliverance for his people."[29]

======

JACKSON'S SEEMING INDIFFERENCE about the campaign for the presidency was an affectation, but when he bared his soul to family, his words suggested he had been oversampling Fitzgerald's strange biblical analogies. "In this contest I take no part," he intoned to John Donelson. "I have long since prepared my mind to say with heartfelt submission, may the lord's will be done; If it is intended by providence that I should fill the presidential chair, I will submit to it with all humility, & endeavor to labour four years with an eye single to the public good"—but, of course, "it will be an event that I never wished, nor expected."[30]

Jackson's messianic musings belied his actual approach to the matter of his presidential bid. Jackson kept careful track of his standing in various states and was always ready with suggestions about how to improve it. The outward appearance of a conscientious senator going about his duties in an attentive way cloaked who he was when alone in his room with his pen, ink, and paper actively guiding efforts to win the presidency. His letters in the spring of 1824 to Junto members and Andrew Jackson Donelson, who had become the group's unofficial secretary, ranged broadly to discuss plans to publish Eaton's "Wyoming" letters as a pamphlet, Sam Houston's anonymous answer to a critical article in the Richmond *Enquirer*, and how a Tennessee congressman was writing pro-Jackson articles for general distribution.[31]

His candles guttered, and midnight oil sooted his lamp's chimney at the Franklin House as he scratched out letter after letter filled with counsel and calculations. Then the next morning, the "real" Andrew Jackson would walk with Eaton to the Senate, serious yet courteous, a diligent legislator weighing all bills before the chamber and always voting his conscience. The act worked like magic. "Jackson's conduct, here," reported Virginia congressman and Crawford supporter Charles Fenton Mercer, "has elevated him in the sentiment of all who had intimately watched him." After a Senate session and dinner with friends or (former) enemies, though, the "real" Andrew Jackson would retire to his rooms and shed his indifference along with his cloak. He scoured newspapers for praise and criticism and marked both for dispatch to his managers with directions to encourage the praise and punish the criticism.[32]

Outwardly, all was well, and inwardly all went smoothly, especially after Pennsylvania. But controversial questions before Congress spelled trouble in the spring of 1824. The specific issues for Jackson stemmed from the most prominent issues in American politics at the time: internal improvements and a protective tariff. In 1822, Jackson had praised President Monroe for vetoing the Cumberland Road Bill in language he would come to regret. "My opinion," he had said, "has allways been that the Federal government did not possess that constitutional power—That it was retained to the States respectively, and with great wisdom." At the time, the words had been music to the ears of Old Republicans who continued to insist that the Constitution was never meant to authorize such projects, the "necessary and proper" of Article I be damned. For their part, easterners had found Jackson's hymn to local control a lyrical refrain, because they caviled over paying for road and canal construction in a West that was steadily siphoning off their population and gaining greater political influence as a result. Two important constituencies had thus taken comfort in the words of a man famous for plain speaking.[33]

In early 1824, a piece of proposed legislation called the General Survey Bill came before Congress. It would give the federal government authority to fund internal improvements for military and commercial projects. Old Republicans were confident that Jackson, faithful to his earlier views, would oppose this bill. But Pennsylvania and many western states wanted federal spending on internal improvements to stimulate their postpanic moribund economies. Jackson accordingly joined the Senate majority to pass the General Survey. Old Hickory and his friends anticipated the reaction and had a defense at the ready against charges of inconsistency, if not bad faith. Jackson's position, they said, had not changed in the least. Rather, he had always believed the national government had the power to fund improvements if they were truly national in scope and had the support of the states involved.[34]

The protective tariff was a thornier problem. Three separate groups objected to it. Two were geographical in orientation and were motivated by economic complaints. Southerners had to buy all their manufactured goods from a protected northern market or foreign ones heavily taxed by high import duties. Northeastern shippers, as distinct from northeastern industry, feared that foreign markets would fight American protectionism by restricting American exports. Both groups took small comfort in explanations that American manufacturers needed a tariff to compete against better established foreign competitors. The third group, the Old Republicans, saw the protective tariff as a violation of the Constitution that, like internal improvements, improperly expanded federal authority. Tariffs were meant to raise revenue to fund government operations, not regulate commerce for the benefit of a favored few. If their purpose became a way to select winners in the economy, their consequence was inevitably to punish losers, an outcome that strict constructionists saw as not only odious but also extraconstitutional.[35]

When a proposal for a modest upward revision of the tariff came before Congress in 1824, Jackson had a narrow path to tread if he were to avoid angering significant portions of his core support and sustain his appeal for manufacturing constituencies in Pennsylvania,

New Jersey, Indiana, Ohio, and Illinois. In the end, though, he and Eaton reckoned that losing pro-tariff voters would be more injurious, and they both voted for protectionism. Theoretically, Jackson was in better shape regarding this vote, as compared to the internal improvements bill, because he had never expressed a firm opinion about the issue, and Eaton carefully crafted an explanation meant to mollify men nevertheless troubled by another seeming example of Old Hickory's apostasy. Eaton's production came out in the form of a letter to Littleton H. Coleman, an influential North Carolina physician. Though ostensibly a private communication, the note was for public consumption, but its publication met a mixed response and attracted a wider measure of attention than Jackson wanted. Eaton had tried to float the explanation that this 1824 tariff was not like others and thereby implied that Jackson's vote did not reveal a rigid principle on the issue. Rather, Jackson, per Eaton, declared that this tariff was a revenue raiser, not a commerce regulator, and that the monies collected by it would fund national defense and help retire the debt. It was the phrase that described the measure as "a careful and judicious Tariff," however, that struck even supporters as too cleverly drawn and critics as downright disingenuous. Henry Clay openly scoffed at the effort to have the matter both ways by contrasting Jackson's temporizing with his own unequivocal endorsement of an "injudicious tariff." Eaton took pride in his word-smithing, and he would remember Clay's attack. Jackson would remember it too.[36]

When Senators Eaton and Jackson left the capital for home in May, they took different routes in part to court different constituencies, Eaton to Philadelphia to cash in on the tariff vote and Jackson by way of Kentucky to control the damage it might have caused. Kentucky was Henry Clay country, and when large crowds turned out for Old Hickory in Louisville, some suspected it was more a result of campaign flummery than a sign of sincere affection.[37]

Jackson reached the Hermitage and a jubilant Rachel on June 4, but a letter from John Coffee soon arrived with troubling news about southern anger over Jackson's vote on the tariff. The path on the issue was even narrower than Jackson and Eaton had thought, and describing men angry about his vote as "ignorant" wasn't helpful. Insulting voters was stupid politics, and nobody in Jackson's inner circle was politically stupid.[38]

Jackson had much to study and much to puzzle over, including the unexpected gesture from a man he hardly knew and had reason to distrust. Martin Van Buren's desk in the Senate chamber happened to be near Jackson's, and during the itemized votes on the tariff, the little New Yorker had ambled over to strike up a conversation. Van Buren was to William H. Crawford what John Eaton was to Jackson, so Old Hickory listened to Van Buren's clipped words with more than a touch of skepticism. Van Buren spoke low to offer some counsel. Vote against the tariff on cotton bagging, he all but whispered, and Jackson dropped his wariness to follow the advice. It would please southern planters to know that Old Hickory had kept the price low on material used to bind their bales. Jackson watched Van Buren return to his desk, fidgeting and talking and scanning the chamber. He had the look of a man weighing his options to cut his losses.[39]

CHAPTER 8

ELECTION

A NDREW JACKSON'S TACTICS FORCED RIVALS TO FOLLOW HIS lead by seeking the nominations of state legislatures, too. Clay supporters scrambled to secure the endorsements of legislatures in Missouri, Kentucky, Ohio, and Louisiana. Crawford-ites had the Georgia legislature nominate him as insurance against the taint of the congressional caucus. Even Adams men importuned the Massachusetts legislature, whose regional allegiance put it, as expected, in his column.

For John Quincy Adams, such maneuvers were much against his nature. Before Congress adjourned in the spring of 1824, he attended receptions, dinners, and the theater and made himself un-characteristically accessible to ordinary citizens. Prospective visitors finding that they could drop in at his office at all hours of the day took him up on it with a vengeance. Between March and May 1824, Adams averaged almost 250 of these impromptu calls each month. It was a wonder that he found the time to stroll to the Capitol to observe congressional sessions. The House of Representatives might select the next president, after all, and all the candidates courted its members. It caused some, like Daniel Webster, to worry that "the

President's office may get to be thought too much the gift of Congress." Feeling under some political compulsion to waste time in the House gallery, Adams might have agreed.[1]

He knew what it looked like when he pretended to observe the House debate issues that he had little to do with and even less interest in, but he strained to maintain the fiction that he was merely a good citizen watching the turning wheels of government. During breaks, he chatted up members while pretending that he found the exchanges interesting. At the State Department, as Congress neared adjournment, most visitors were legislators paying customary courtesy calls on cabinet secretaries before departing for home, and Adams had always found those conversations tedious to the point of torture. But in this particular May, the visits gave Adams a chance to talk about strategy with supporters and feel out the friends of rivals. He took a keen interest in Andrew Jackson's backers. Adams still hoped that Jackson would become his running mate, especially when Adams realized that people found something magnetic about the tall, gaunt Tennessean. Adams could be as calculating as he was observant. A ticket topped by a New Englander and joined by a southerner from the West would be formidable, and given that the western southerner was wildly popular, the pair could be invincible. He pitched the idea to people he knew would take it back to Old Hickory, but Adams possibly suspected his pitching skills were not up to the task. Jackson did not refuse; he simply didn't answer. Helpless in the face of widespread affection for Old Hickory, Adams when alone with his diary at night wished he were better at this game.[2]

He was a man of legendary reserve who seemed supernaturally indifferent to popularity. Those traits made Adams both hard to get along with and poignantly inclined to effect reconciliations with men he had rubbed the wrong way. Adams had clashed with Henry Clay in Ghent, Belgium, when they were negotiating the peace to end the War of 1812, but the two had more or less made their own peace afterward, at least until the contest for 1824 began. They broke again when Adams suspected that Clay was behind an attack on him that was both unfair and clumsy. Its author was Jonathan Russell, who had also served on the peace commission in Ghent. Russell was a middling talent and someone with a tendency to act without thinking, speak without pausing, and, worst of all, write without doing either. He disliked Adams, which made him a member of a large club, but he was foolish enough to think he could tell a lie to injure Adams and help his friends Clay and Crawford, either of whom Russell preferred for the presidency. The episode featured everything John Quincy Adams hated about politics.[3]

In 1822, Russell was in Congress representing Massachusetts's Eleventh District when he claimed that Adams had not protected American interests at Ghent. Russell alluded to a letter he had written to then Secretary of State James Monroe in February 1815 outlining the details of Adams's flawed negotiating tactics. The prospect of bringing proud and overbearing John Quincy Adams up short was too tantalizing to pass up, and his enemies in the House of Representatives wanted the letter. It was nowhere to be found in the State Department's archives, but Russell provided a copy from his own files. It was a damning document that showed that Adams had been willing to grant Britain full access to the Mississippi River in exchange for New England fishing rights off the coast of Canada. By any estimation, the revelation meant the end of Adams's presidential quest, at least until the original letter suddenly turned up and was materially different from Russell's transcription. Adams never acted without thinking, never spoke without pausing, and always wrote skewering prose. He published a stinging rebuke that credibly pointed to Russell's dishonesty and painted him as both a fool and a knave. Jonathan Russell found out firsthand what the more sagacious knew about Adams by intuition. "There is no use in questioning his facts," Felix Grundy would say about him, "because he is always right. His memory never fails him. He is a very difficult man to argue with, because he always grows keener and sharper with every attack."[4]

Adams had no evidence of Clay's involvement, but Clay and Russell were friends. He assumed the Kentuckian was behind Russell's attack and used his refutation of Russell to recall that Clay had advocated only western interests at Ghent. Everyone believed what he wanted to about Adams and Clay by the end of the controversy, but it was indisputable that Russell had lied.[5]

Fellow New Englander William Plumer had been the only elector to vote against Monroe in 1820, casting his ballot instead for John Quincy Adams, a testament to his admiration for a man he thought gifted, learned, and virtuous. But Plumer knew Adams lacked "those popular talents which Crawford possesses." Adams, sighed Plumer, was "in general rather respected than beloved." Adams, late at night and alone with his diary, would have sighed too.[6]

"Respected but not beloved" could have been on the family's crest. John Quincy Adams had inherited more than his father's personality. He had the same compulsive desire for fame and approbation that had driven John Adams into frenzies of self-doubt and political immolation during his youth and middle age. For the elder Adams, who was slowly unraveling in his final years on his farm in Quincy, Massachusetts, the goads of ambition had mercifully abated to leave him relatively sanguine about the whip of history and the judgment of men. It was as if, though, the demon of ambition had left the soul of the old and palsied man to entwine around the heart of his son, spurring him to seek acclaim. Adams was a scholar by training and temperament who had the great misfortune to be the supremely talented son of a Founder. Because of that, the presidency was for him more than an office of enormous responsibility and obligation. It was the way to exorcise the demon and stop being "Johnny Q.," the comical child of a failed father. Johnny Q. would become the President Adams whose name would echo with those of Jefferson, Madison, even Washington. He would be the most lauded Adams, in the end.

When he went home late in the summer of 1824, he set his cap for New England's Republicans and Federalists by representing himself as the only northern candidate in the field. Though he drew criticism for trying to create a party of "renegade Federalists and half-breed Republicans," he looked at those large Jackson rallies and felt he had no choice. Adams returned to Washington that fall with the support of many northerners tired of the fabled Virginia Dynasty and eager to take their turn at having their own president. But he also had heard murmuring New England Federalists hedging their bets. Though Daniel Webster of the rafter-rattling voice never murmured, he was quieter than usual when he mused that Adams was indeed *their* man but that Andrew Jackson could very well be everyone else's. Webster knew that in politics, as in law, silence should be interpreted as tacit consent. The North keeping mum might not help Adams as much, but it would not hurt Jackson at all. When the time came, and the new steward of the federal trough took over, the meek would inherit their share of the slops.[7]

WILLIAM H. CRAWFORD's supporters tried to improve his chances during the summer and fall of 1824, but they could do nothing to improve his health. It remained precarious, despite cheerful reports to the contrary. Martin Van Buren, however, had a plan.

The New York legislature selected the state's electors on a proportional basis rather than winner-take-all, but pro-democracy advocates in the state had long wanted to have them chosen by a popular referendum. Van Buren's faction in the New York Republican Party opposed the change because it would have undermined its control of the process, a reflection of Van Buren's belief that iron discipline within a strong political organization made for stable as well as efficient government. Van Buren had built a machine on this principle that was called the Albany Regency for its confident dominance of the state's politics. Its members were colorfully labeled "Bucktails" for their way of identifying themselves by wearing that tanned part of a deer. Whether going by the colloquial label of forest ruminants or by the grand one of kingly prerogative, Van Buren's faction in New York was the best thing Crawford had going for him in an election marked by his invalidism and the iniquity of his enemies.[8]

Outside of New York, Crawford's supporters played their losing hand with traditional campaign techniques that Jacksonite innovations were rendering obsolete. North Carolina was an example of a Crawford stronghold withering on the vine as a result. While Crawford men wrote letters to one another and avidly read them, their man's strength ebbed among ordinary Tarheels. Jackson's surge roused the Crawford camp to organize its own public meetings, but nobody's heart was in them, and in the end, the Georgian's supporters were reduced to complaining about how unfair it was "this great and good man" was being treated so shabbily. The surviving Founders who considered themselves Jeffersonians supported him, but nobody could coax the two living embodiments of Jeffersonian government, Thomas Jefferson himself and his disciple James Madison, to endorse Crawford's candidacy. Like Monroe, both believed it inappropriate to take a public stand on the election. The innovations of amateurs and the ineffectiveness of traditions became a running theme for William H. Crawford.[9]

And as if the trouble was spreading uncontrollably, all was not well in New York either. Popular unrest over Bucktail rule became so great by mid-1824 that Governor Joseph Yates called a special session of the legislature to consider demands for reform. Regency maneuvering thwarted proto-Democrats in the legislature, but preserving the old way of choosing electors came at a price. Voters began counting the days to the next election with the aim of making Bucktails pay it.[10]

That was the background for Van Buren's heroic efforts to secure enough of New York's proportional electoral tally to place Crawford in the top three candidates who would go before the House of Representatives. The New York power broker would have seemed little more than a talented hack had it not been for authentic strains of statesmanship that guided his efforts while encouraging his followers and impressing his foes. Van Buren didn't just believe in Jeffersonian principles of limited government. He exalted them with a firm constitutionalism leavened by political pragmatism. In Van Buren's view, the national government had no more authority to fund internal improvements than it did to buy one man a house with another man's money. Such attitudes aligned him with Old Republicans of the South, and like them, he judged Crawford as the closest candidate to Thomas Jefferson still breathing, if only just barely.[11]

Van Buren did not know much about Andrew Jackson, and he thought the people close to Jackson were prone to say unpleasant things and to lie with alacrity. Assessing the Jackson phenomenon in New York, Van Buren feared Jacksonites were allied with DeWitt Clinton, New York's former governor and the Albany Regency's sworn enemy. Van Buren was also mildly alarmed by Jackson's growing popularity with ordinary voters, hence the fixation on keeping the presidential decision out of their hands. But after some calm calculations, Van Buren concluded that Old Hickory had little sway with the New York legislature. John Eaton had made the same judgment after a visit to New York that summer, leading to an absence of Jacksonite activity in Albany that reassured Van Buren. Clay and Adams, however, had solid support there, and that meant a division of the vote that could leave Crawford the odd man out. Van Buren's effort to prevent that from happening led to his proposal in the summer of 1824 that Henry Clay withdraw from the race and become Crawford's running mate.

This was the offer sweetened by implications that a Vice President Clay would soon profit from a President Crawford's death. Clay refused a proposal he found ghoulish, but political reality and inescapable mathematics also guided him. As the only "western" candidate other than Andrew Jackson, he knew that his chances against Jackson's growing popularity were slim, and the likelihood of his reaching a vote in the House of Representatives was even slimmer. If he withdrew, though, the entire West would go to Jackson, even Clay's Kentucky. Then the prospect of Jackson winning an electoral majority and gaining the presidency outright would be almost certain. The rise of the man baffled Clay as much as anyone. "I cannot believe," Clay wondered in a pensive moment, "that killing 2500 Englishmen at N. Orleans qualifies for the various, difficult and complicated duties of the Chief Magistracy." And yet, here they were.[12]

Rumors about a Clay-Crawford alliance had been circulating since the spring, and Jackson had branded the scheme as illustrating "the corruption of the times" with an apocalyptic vision that "nothing but the redeeming spirit of a virtuous people, who will arise in the majesty of their strength, and hurl these Demagogues of corruption from their confidence; can redeem our nation from woe, & our republican Government from destruction."[13]

Van Buren would have been puzzled at being described as subversive merely for trying to get his candidate before the House, but when the Jacksonite press exploded in a blaze of fury, it surprised everyone. The Nashville Republican accused Clay and Crawford of an unholy alliance that they had formed all the way back in 1816 to thwart the election of James Monroe. It had endured to smear Old Hickory over the Seminole War and now aimed to prevent the American people from choosing their champion. The Jacksonite furor over the suspected cabal of Clay and Crawford died away, but they didn't completely understand why Clay had refused Crawford and was remaining in the race.[14]

They would find out soon enough. Sam Houston was a true believer whose judgment that "Jackson is gaining" was as accurate as it was gleeful, but it did not merit his conclusion in early 1824 that Jackson "will be the next president." By that summer, most observers had concluded that the House of Representatives would pick Monroe's successor. The only question became which three men would be in final contention. As early as April 1824, Daniel Webster thought he knew the answer. He predicted that the three would be Andrew Jackson, John Quincy Adams, and William H. Crawford.[15]

═══

THE TERM PSEPHOLOGY wasn't coined until the mid-twentieth century, but the practice it names—the analysis of elections—is as old as the first canvass, when men stopped swinging cudgels and started counting pebbles as a more orderly way to conduct their collective affairs. It is an enormously complicated undertaking to figure out why an election turned out a certain way, when one considers it is often difficult to figure out how an election turned out, period. The seemingly straightforward business of casting votes and then counting them is beset by scores of variables, qualifiers, and conditions that complicate the entire affair with questions about fairness, probity, and participation.

The only certainty in 1824 was that John C. Calhoun would be the vice president. Everyone who knew anything about the field of presidential contenders and the states they were vying for had more or less deduced months before the fall of 1824 that the magic number of 131 in the Electoral College would elude them all. The purported amateurs handling Andrew Jackson even planned for that outcome with discussions about how to force a positive result in the House of Representatives. If Jackson received the most popular votes and was at least leading in the Electoral College at the end of the election, his managers insisted that the House had no choice but to choose him. One newspaper on October 20 minced no words: "The Constitution declares that a majority shall rule, and he who is the favorite of the people, and highest on the list, must be elected by Congress. . . . Nothing but intrigue and corruption can prevent it" and "will not fail to draw ruin and infamy upon those who will be known as the instruments." Nine days before the first votes were cast, the groundwork for a charge of corruption was in place if things did not turn out Jackson's way.[16]

It is helpful to recall how the election worked in 1824 to understand what happened that year. The rules were simple inasmuch as they were generally applied. The law required that the states choose their electors within a thirty-four-day window before the first Wednesday in December, which in 1824 fell on December 1. That meant the states could choose electors on any of the last four days of October and through all of November. The number of electors for each state was equal to its number of representatives in the House plus its two senators. The electors were to meet in their states on December 1 to cast their votes for president and vice president. The result of those twenty-four separate tallies would then be sealed and sent to Washington for formal counting and the declaration of results by the president of the Senate before a joint session of Congress on February 9. Beyond these rules, there was no standard held in common by the twenty-four states then in the Union, including who could vote and when. By 1824, most states had broadened the franchise to include most adult white males, but there was no such thing as a national corporate election, meaning that the states held their elections when they pleased between October 27 and December 1. A close race in the Electoral College meant little chance for determining a winner until most of the states had counted their votes, whether in the eighteen that held popular referenda or the six that still left the decision to their legislatures.[17]

As returns dribbled in from each state, trends could be discerned, such as who was the frontrunner and who was losing ground. Early successes could establish momentum for a candidate, shaping the votes of those states voting later, and though there is some evidence that the Jackson campaign tried to use the different election days to its advantage, it did not happen in 1824 to any great degree for several reasons. One was the fact that only a small percentage of eligible voters went to the polls. The contest in 1824 was the first seriously contested election since 1800, and because of that, it marked an increase in voter participation, but the average still was only a shade over 25 percent. A general nonchalance about a field of candidates all perceived as Republicans with no glaring policy disagreements separating them was the main reason for an indifference that belied the sound and fury of the campaigns, especially Jackson's. New Haven, Connecticut, reflected the national trend, as less than 280 of 1,000 eligible voters went to the polls. Admittedly, Connecticut was an Adams stronghold, but its low turnout can't be attributed to a lackluster candidate. Even Andrew Jackson's bastion of Tennessee followed the pattern. He had a smashing majority of 20,197 to 528, but only 27 percent of eligible voters cast a ballot.[18]

Another reason Jackson's lead in early returns did not build momentum was the effect of schedules, time, and distance. For example, Jackson was the clear frontrunner after Pennsylvania held its election on October 29 and gave him an early lead of 28 electoral votes, but he unexpectedly lost Ohio's 16 electoral votes to Henry Clay on the same day. Then on November 1, the New England states of Connecticut, Maine, New Hampshire, and Massachusetts held their elections, with all going to Adams for a total of

30 electoral votes. On that same day, Crawford won Virginia's 24 votes. Also on November 1, Jackson took Mississippi's 3 votes. Illinois voted on November 1 as well, but it was not a winner-take-all state. Two of its three districts went to Jackson, and the other to Adams. And though these early totals placed Jackson with a slim three-point lead over Adams, hard figures for returns usually took days to report, which meant they had little influence on other elections that happened to be bunched with them on the calendar.

Nevertheless, Ohio's Jackson operatives tried to generate momentum to influence voting in subsequent states. US congressman and staunch Jackson supporter Caleb Atwater had been among the most active partisans trying to steer fellow Buckeyes to Old Hickory. As the voting began in Ohio on October 29, Atwater smelled victory, prematurely, as it happened, for he had not reckoned on Henry Clay's still formidable strength in the state. Ohio required a candidate win only a plurality of the popular vote to take all of its sixteen electoral votes. Even after Old Hickory's men spread the lie that Clay had withdrawn from the race, he won a narrow plurality in Ohio, but it's entirely possible that Atwater's congratulatory letter to Jackson was not premature but part of a public plan to influence the vote in other states. Atwater dispatched a galloping express rider with a similar letter declaring Jackson's victory to DeWitt Clinton just before the New York legislature was to pick its electors. Atwater also sent messages to Indiana and Illinois announcing that Ohio had gone for Jackson, apparently in the knowledge that the state was too close to call or was probably going to Clay. In Indiana and Illinois, it may have worked, because Jackson took the former and won two of the three districts in the latter.[19]

The New York legislature began selecting electors on November 11. Martin Van Buren was cheered that the summer's special session had refused to open the selection of electors to a popular vote, and he remained hopeful that Crawford would hold the bulk of the legislature. DeWitt Clinton and a young political operative named Thurlow Weed, however, had been successfully generating enough support for Adams to rattle Van Buren's certainty about Crawford. Van Buren stalled for time and managed to deadlock the legislature for a full day while he frantically tried to save Crawford's candidacy one more time. He approached Clay supporters with a deal. In exchange for their giving the lion's share of electoral votes to Crawford, Van Buren would use his influence to give Clay more votes than he had expected, improving the Kentuckian's chances of finishing in the top three in the Electoral College. Clay's people were adamantly opposed to Crawford, however, and they did not trust Van Buren in any case. On November 12, a combination of Adams and Clay men all but squeezed Crawford out as the legislature awarded Adams twenty-five electors, Clay seven, and Crawford four. Clay's fortunes, though, became hostage to additional schemes before the electors could assemble to cast their votes on December 1. For reasons that were never clear, two Clay electors did not arrive in Albany to cast their votes on the appointed day, and one of his other five switched to Jackson. With the official meeting in some disarray, the Adams majority chose Adams supporters as substitutes for Clay's no-shows with the result that New York cast twenty-six electoral votes for Adams, five for Crawford, four for Clay, and one for Jackson.[20]

It was hardly a windfall for Old Hickory, but the overall trends during November pointed his way. On November 2, his ticket secured 52 percent of New Jersey's popular vote and thus won all eight of the state's electors. He likely would have been competitive even in Crawford's Georgia had that state's legislature not chosen the electors. North Carolina was another matter, though. Crawford had been expected to take the state before Jackson entered the race, but Calhoun's withdrawal and the efforts of people like William B. Lewis changed the situation. The result was a dramatic instance of

REPUBLICAN
ANTI-CAUCUS TICKET.
For President,
JOHN QUINCY ADAMS,
For
VICE-PRESIDENT,
Some tried and approved Patriot.

•

TICKET.

Col. Stephen Wright, *Norfolk.*
Dr. Henry W. Holleman, *Surry.*
Dr. John W. King, *Dinwiddie.*
Edward R. Chambers, *Lunenburg.*
Col. John Clarke, *Halifax.*
Benjamin Hatcher, *Manchester.*
Col. William B. Lynch, *Lynchburg.*
Col. James Callaway, *Franklin.*
John M. Martin, *Nelson.*
William B. Randolph, *Henrico.*
Philip Harrison, *Fredericksburg.*
Christopher Tompkins, *Mathews.*
Robert Lively, *Hampton.*
Hancock Eustace, *Stafford.*
John Shackleford, *Culpeper.*
Capt. John P. Duval, *Fauquier.*
John Rose, *Leesburg.*
Hon. Hugh Holmes, *Winchester.*
Col. Jacob Vanmeter, *Hardy.*
Thomas J. Stuart, *Staunton.*
Pere B. Wethered, *Greenbrier.*
Peter Mayo, *Abingdon.*
Enos Thomas, *Mason.*
John S. Barnes, *Monongalia.*

In the election of 1824, all the campaigns had electoral tickets printed in states where their candidates were viable. Listing the electors in advance made it easier for voters to choose the men who would vote for their preferred candidate. (Library of Congress.)

strange bedfellows, as Federalists such as William Polk linked arms with erstwhile Calhoun supporters such as Montfort Stokes.[21]

In North Carolina, it was the Jacksonites' use of Adams enthusiasts that was most striking. From earlier anti-Crawford efforts, Jackson and Adams men could lay claim to a slate of proposed electors on the artfully named "People's Ticket." It was a cynical label for a group picked by a small cadre of shrewd partisans, but it matched the theme of Jackson's campaign to paint Crawford as the candidate of elite Washington insiders. It suited Adams men because it bolstered their minority in North Carolina enough to help destroy Crawford's chances there. As time went on, though, they began to regret their alliance with Jacksonites who seemed ready to destroy everybody in their sights. Because of the Jackson campaign's superior organization, North Carolinians on November 11 gave the People's Ticket a whopping 56 percent of the popular vote, handing Jackson all fifteen of the state's electoral votes.[22]

Alabama's numbers turned out to be similar. Crawford and Adams had been strong until Crawford's stroke, and Adams became an odd sectional duck in contrast to the southerner Jackson, who won the state. Jackson easily took South Carolina, the one state that would persist in having its legislature select electors all the way to the Civil War. Clubby connections in Columbia did not even require schemes to hand Old Hickory the state.[23]

State after state, some small and a few large, rolled into the Jackson column to create a seemingly irresistible momentum. Some of it was earned by the cleverness of his talented amateurs. They had parsed the problem of Maryland and concluded that most of the state's electoral votes could be won by courting the most populous of its three districts. Jackson was most popular in the Baltimore area where the Panic of 1819 had devastated the urban working class, and his votes for a protective tariff and federally funded internal improvements helped him with state leaders eager for federal help. The problem was that Adams was also quite popular in Maryland, especially in southern counties and on the Eastern Shore. Jacksonites made a tactical decision to cede those areas to Adams and concentrate on the large population center of Baltimore. The result was startling. Adams edged Jackson in Maryland's overall popular vote, but the areas that Jackson won had larger electoral totals. Jackson took seven of the state's electoral votes, leaving Adams three and Crawford only one.[24]

Indiana had a sizable number of immigrants from New England, which gave Adams a good chance, even over Clay, who was popular with Hoosiers. Indiana, however, was a winner-take-all state that required a candidate to win only a plurality to take its five electoral votes, so when Jackson won 46.6 percent of the popular vote, it did not matter that Adams and Clay had a combined total of 53 percent. One or the other probably could have taken Indiana, but Jackson captured the state and its five votes.[25]

By the time the Louisiana legislature met on November 22, 1824, to choose the state's electors, Andrew Jackson had 96 electoral votes; John Quincy Adams, 82; William H. Crawford, 41; and Henry Clay, 37. Those totals ensured that the House of Representatives would decide the presidency, but they also made Louisiana crucial for Clay, because its 5 electoral votes would put him ahead of Crawford and place him in the top three for the House's consideration. Clay as Speaker wielded enormous influence in the House, and the dynamic as well as the vote in that body would have changed if he were among the candidates. Only Clay could beat Jackson and Adams in the House, and there was a better than good chance that he would win in such a situation.

It looked for all the world as if that would happen. Louisiana had always been a Clay stronghold. He had many close connections in the state house. A significant portion of the population was still Creole—people of French and Spanish descent—and they especially liked Clay for his business dealings in the region solidified by his brother and his cousin, both residents of New Orleans. Clay's brother and his oldest daughter, Susan, had married into the wealthy and influential Duralde family, and Louisiana's US senator Josiah S. Johnston became Clay's informal campaign manager in a state where personal affection and political affinity for Henry Clay were widespread.

Yet the entrance of the Hero of New Orleans put Louisiana in play, and when the state legislature convened to choose electors in late November, Jacksonites put into motion an aggressive plan. They vigorously courted a significant minority of the legislature that supported John Quincy Adams. In proposing a deal that sounded like Van Buren's to Clay in New York, they promised Adams a portion of Louisiana's split electoral vote if they would help block Clay. Just as it had in Ohio, a rumor conveniently surfaced out of nowhere that Clay had withdrawn from the race. Believing that lie, some of his supporters in the legislature switched to Jackson, and by the time the rumor was proved false, the legislature had voted. Finally, curious mishaps had the look of dirty tricks. Something prevented two Clay legislators from arriving in Baton Rouge before the vote was taken, and when it was taken, Clay was completely shut out. Jackson won three of the state's electors. Adams won the other two. Henry Clay would not go before the House.[26]

In some places, the talented amateurs supporting Andrew Jackson had merely been required to play upon his popularity. But in just as many key states, such as Louisiana, they had played the game better than the complacent professionals, who were no longer as smug as they had been months before. As the year came to a close, Adams and Clay supporters weighed the unpleasant prospect of scrambling for an invalid's votes to elect their accomplished statesmen in the place of a military hero widely admired for recent statesmanship that some suspected was an act. A South Carolina newspaper marveling over it all recalled Macbeth confronting Banquo's ghost: "Can such things be, And overcome us like a summer's cloud, Without our special wonder?"[27]

On the Cumberland, and expecting a better result, the Junto could have cried, "*Lay on, MacDuff!*"

CHAPTER 9

BARGAINS

FOR THE FIRST TIME IN HER LIFE, RACHEL JACKSON CAME TO the nation's capital. It was in late November 1824, and her stay would last for a little more than three months. Neither she nor her husband could stand being apart. "Whenever she is alone," Rachel's brother had confided to John Coffee, "she goes to crying." She also fretted that Jackson was not taking care of himself and would fall ill far away from her, while he worried that without him around she would work too hard and risk her health. He knew she wept, and thinking about that made him pensive as nothing else could. So Rachel Jackson came to Washington. They offered a simple explanation. When Jackson won the presidency, he would remain in the capital for his inauguration. As the First Lady in waiting, Rachel would be there too.[1]

She was happy to have him near, but she was still miserable over leaving Nashville and the vast array of tributaries formed by a dozen clans of siblings, cousins, nieces, and nephews, her mainstays all. It was good then that Jackson also brought a bit of home to Washington. Rachel's nephew and his ward, Andrew Jackson Donelson, accompanied the Jacksons to Washington, but the particular delight was the girl who came with him. Donelson was still boyish at twenty-five, but his good looks had a noticeable glow because he was a newlywed, his marriage to his lovely seventeen-year-old cousin Emily Tennessee Donelson only weeks old. As he had been his Uncle Jackson's aide in Florida, Donelson was to serve as his private secretary in Washington, and the couple had worn down her father's objections and tied the knot on September 16 so they could live together in the capital. Rachel looked forward to her niece's companionship, and she smiled at their happiness.

Rachel's unqualified love and his guardian's expectations had defined Andrew Jackson Donelson's childhood at the Hermitage. Donelson never minded the daunting burden of both the love and the expectations, as if to say that they were a small debt for grand memories, such as drifting off to sleep in a trundle bed as pets snoozed on the hearth and Uncle and Aunt Jackson played soft duets, she at the piano and he on a fiddle. The lad was taught never to forget that he was as much a Jackson by choice as he was a Donelson by birth. Old Hickory secured an appointment to West Point for him in 1816 and was soon reading young Donelson's complaints about the rough treatment cadets received from officers. Jackson was blunt. If someone laid a hand, or worse, a foot on Donelson, he was to "put him to instant death the moment you receive either." It was the code of someone careful about his name with an excitable sense of the importance of respect. "Never my son, outlive your honour," Jackson declared, "never do an act that will tarnish it." Either nobody tested Donelson's patience, or he kept from killing anyone who did. The young man fared well and graduated second in his class.[2]

At two years, Donelson's army career was brief, most of it spent as his uncle's aide until he resigned his commission in February 1822 to study law at Transylvania University in Lexington, Kentucky. Uncle Jackson viewed the law as a gateway to politics but counseled him to keep vague about political issues, advice born of his own past experiences. The Tennessee bar admitted Donelson in 1823, but his legal career would prove even briefer than his military one. His uncle's presidential campaign pressed him into service, first as the Nashville Junto's secretary and then as Jackson's when he became a senator. Donelson had Eaton's talent with a pen and brought with it the exuberance of youth that made him invaluable to his uncle. He was soon drafting many of Jackson's letters.[3]

In Washington, the close family group stayed at Jackson's familiar lodgings in the Franklin House, now called Gadsby's Tavern after its new owner, though William O'Neale remained its manager. John Eaton's friend and O'Neale's daughter Margaret Timberlake soon met Emily Donelson and thought the young bride a bit too precious. In return, Emily thought Mrs. Timberlake a striking beauty but a bit too coarse. Otherwise, she and Andrew enjoyed Washington's social life with its theater, receptions, balls, and soirées, where matrons cooed over the handsome bridegroom and gallants eagerly fetched the Tennessee belle punch and competed to make her smile. The Jacksons kept to themselves, content in their rooms "chatting & smoking our pipe." Rachel had never seen play-acting on a stage and did not intend to start now. At most, she consented to an occasional dinner party and would submit to the scrutiny of Washington ladies over afternoon tea. It was unsettling to think that most of them called on her because they were curious. It was worse to think that they might have heard things. During the campaign, there had been rumors that Crawfordites intended to exploit the questionable origins of Jackson's marriage, which had sent the Junto into a frenzy to counter anything that cropped up, whether true or not. As it happened, attacks had been limited and oblique, as in North Carolina where the Raleigh *Register* urged voters not to "place such a woman as Mrs. Jackson at the head of the female society in the U. States."[4]

Rachel Jackson probably did not know about these veiled and infrequent attacks, but in Washington, she had to realize that sidelong stares and the whispers of matrons glancing her way meant something, and most likely something unpleasant about her clothes, her grammar, her looks. Andrew Jackson knew that any interest in his and Rachel's past boded ill. His impulse was to murder anyone who soiled her name, but he also speculated that gossip was a tactic to provoke a show of temper and undo all the efforts to portray him as a calm statesman.[5]

The chatter was petty at best and thoughtlessly cruel at worst. One wag, for example, called Rachel "her majesty of two husbands." When she came to the Capitol one afternoon to see where her husband worked, she strained to dress fashionably to make him as proud of her as she was of him. Delaware representative Louis McLane saw only "an ordinary looking old woman dressed in the height & *flame* of fashion," which did not so much describe Rachel Jackson as reveal his ability to abandon any pretense of gallantry with piffling criticisms of a kind lady's appearance, age, and attire. But McLane was hardly done. No one, he said, would "be able to make her fashionable, and if she presides in the palace, her reign will be any thing but glorious." After all, he solemnly pronounced, once a woman "loses the high charm of immaculate chastity, . . . tears & repentance are her lot, and her fit occupation, constant devotion to make attonement [*sic*] for the injury to publick morals."[6]

Apparently, McLane had heard things, and thus he passed judgment from the Olympian perch of his Delaware congressional seat. He could not have known that not too many days would pass before he too became a Jacksonite on the way to becoming a Jacksonian, and in his lack of self-awareness alone, he was Rachel Jackson's inferior. She knew exactly who she was on the day she arrived at Gadsby's and on the day she went to the Capitol, and who she would be

A pious, shy woman, Rachel Jackson was stoic as she endured the stress of her husband's quest for the presidency, especially when their marriage came under attack during the 1828 campaign. (Library of Congress.)

as she counted down the days to the one that would take her home to the Cumberland.

IN THE WEEKS leading up to the fall elections of 1824, the country was treated to a spectacle at once inspiring and silly. It involved an authentic American hero from the Revolutionary War, a hero who happened to be a foreigner visiting the United States during the height of its political season. In that regard, the entire business gave the impression of bad planning. In 1823, Congress invited the Marquis de Lafayette to visit the country as the "Nation's Guest," and he had happily accepted. His name was Marie-Joseph Paul Yves Roch Gilbert du Motier, and he had long before renounced his noble title during France's embrace of revolutionary republicanism, but Americans knew him best simply as Lafayette, the lad who had been more than a friend to George Washington. Lafayette had become the son Washington never had.

Lafayette's visit was of profound importance to his hosts. Just a couple of weeks shy of his sixty-seventh birthday, he was an old man when he arrived in New York Harbor on August 15, 1824, carrying a cane and moving with a sobering deliberateness. But Lafayette was ageless in his invocation of America at sunrise, and he himself was a metaphor for the country as a light unto the world. When not yet twenty, he had joined the fight for American independence with a touching willingness of the heart, and in the years that followed, he became a folkloric figure, the centerpiece of admiring anecdotes and fond reminiscences. His lofty stature, in fact, caused the political class to pause once it had noticed the coincidence of Lafayette's visit with the presidential election.

To ordinary Americans, there was no reason to hold back. The nation anticipated Lafayette's visit as a way to revive its revolutionary virtue. Members of the founding generation were getting thin on the ground by the 1820s, and the leading figures of the next generation seemed pale shadows in comparison, their quest for office eclipsing everything that mattered, including the general welfare and individual liberty. When John Eaton as "Wyoming" capitalized on this discontent by comparing Jackson to Washington and emphasizing the boy Jackson's exploits in the Revolution, he linked his subject to both its premier hero and his youthful sidekick, the brave and irrepressible Lafayette. The association wasn't lost on George Erving, a respected diplomat and friend of William H. Crawford. Worried that Lafayette's visit would burnish the bona fides of the homegrown hero running for president, he tried to persuade Lafayette to postpone his trip. For the old Frenchman, though, the more compelling argument rested in advancing age and past hardships, both of which were hastening him to his end. He resolved to be the "Nation's Guest" before it was too late.[7]

Banquets and balls awaited him everywhere. Cities wheeled batteries into place for deafening artillery salutes, and small hamlets polished their little field pieces on courthouse squares to pop sharp reports upon his approach. Lafayette's entourage was modest enough not to merit the name—it consisted only of his son George Washington de La Fayette, a secretary, and a single servant—but his itinerary was ambitious, with travel charted through all twenty-four states. Mindful of the election, he resolved to show no favoritism to either places or people, and he only partly deviated from that intention, when occasion demanded it. His visit to New England, for example, included a stop to see John Adams in Quincy, Massachusetts. The meeting of the two relics of the Revolution was inspiring, and the chagrin of the candidates contending with the son of one of them was judged silly.[8]

Lafayette spent most of the rest of the year in the vicinity of Washington because of events rather than politics. The anniversary celebration of American victory at Yorktown occurred in October, and he visited Jefferson at Monticello. Just across the Potomac at Arlington House, he enjoyed long and lovely hours with George Washington's step-grandson, George Washington Parke Custis, the place congenial and Custis a raconteur with whom to share memories over his vast collection of Washington memorabilia. The scenes were heartwarming to many who read about them, but some reactions were cynical. A banquet for the Nation's Guest at Richmond, groused one of the town's merchants, surpassed "all the mock greetings which was ever bestowed on any of the adored sovereighns [sic] of Europe when returning from being banished, or otherwise on a tour of what are called their dominions." It was a minority view. Most of Richmond, like most of the country, had the feeling of experiencing something extraordinary, what one resident called "the La Fayette storm."[9]

Everyone vied for Lafayette's company, but the Jacksons saw him more often than most because the Nation's Guest was also the honored guest of Gadsby's Tavern during his time in the capital. When Lafayette arrived there and heard that General Jackson was in residence, the old man all but tossed away his cane to vault up the stairs to pay a call. Jackson, for his part, was already striding from his room and bounding down the stairs. The two almost went tumbling over each other. Rachel Jackson watched as "the emotion of revolutionary feeling was aroused in them both." Lafayette "delighted" her, "an extraordinary man" with the "happy talent of knowing those he has once seen."[10]

Congress hosted a lavish dinner on New Year's Day with the Nation's Guest given the place of honor. By then, the election results were in, and everyone knew that the names of Jackson, Adams, and Crawford would be before the House of Representatives for the presidency. For once Lafayette receded into the background as all eyes were trained on candidates and congressmen for signs of an alliance here or an alienation there. More than two hundred attendees at the elegant Mansion House Hotel spent their evening this way, exchanging booming greetings and murmuring mindless pleasantries. The volume of voices rose and fell, raucous laughter sometimes drowning out all else, but the traditional round of toasts to distinguished guests finally silenced the crowd for a time.[11]

Speaker of the House Henry Clay was surprisingly merry, his eyes twinkling and his voice so jolly that one would have thought he had won the election. His power in deciding it, though, was manifest—even though, or perhaps because, he was not among the final three—and everyone craned necks to watch him amble through the hall as much as they did to catch a glimpse of the Nation's Guest. Clay noticed that Jackson and Adams were seated at a table with an empty chair between them. He strode across the room and eyed it. "Well, gentlemen," he said in a theatrical baritone, "since you are both near the chair, but neither can occupy it, I will step in between you, & take it myself." Jackson, it was later said, chuckled, but Adams was startled and looked it. At the end of the evening, though, the little New Englander had a bigger surprise coming his way, also courtesy of Mr. Speaker Clay.[12]

———

AT THE END of the grand dinner for Lafayette, Henry Clay suggested to John Quincy Adams that they should talk. The remark must have surprised Adams, but he merely replied that he would be happy to meet at Clay's convenience. This otherwise casual exchange set the stage for a series of events so transformative that they rank with the most significant in American history.[13]

A few weeks earlier, when Clay had left Kentucky for Washington, the Louisiana returns that eliminated him from consideration by the House of Representatives were not yet widely known. Even so, he suspected he had lost and spoke to friends about his plans, which had the potential to be more consequential in defeat than in victory. The few people to whom he opened his mind knew his intentions before he left Kentucky. Clay could not support Andrew Jackson. William Crawford's uncertain health cast doubt on his effectiveness as president, making immaterial Clay's fondness and respect for him. That left John Quincy Adams, a man Clay mildly detested and had reason to believe returned the sentiment. They had disagreed so often while negotiating the peace with Britain in

Ghent that their relations moved rapidly from cautious reserve to icy civility. Clay, however, did not have the luxury of supporting a semi-invalid he liked and thus faced the quandary of opposing a man he didn't trust by allying with another he could barely abide. The one consolation was that Adams seemed willing to advance policies Clay thought would best serve the country's interests. If he could be sure that Adams would support internal improvements, the Bank of the United States, and a protective tariff, it would make him a palatable choice. Clay had made this plain to his Kentucky friends, but he kept his counsel after he arrived in Washington, and that created the unfortunate appearance that he was equally open to overtures from all candidates.[14]

As early as 1822, John Eaton had confided to the Nashville Junto his greatest fear. It was that Jackson would not win the election outright, and "the result will be a decision by the House of Representatives." Even before Louisiana had eliminated Clay, it was clear that the House was going to make the final decision, and Jackson's men had planned accordingly. As they saw it, their most cogent argument had to do with the numbers. Andrew Jackson came in first in the Electoral College with 99 votes, which was far short of the 131-vote majority necessary for victory. But it was the popular vote that had his supporters looking over columns of figures, adding them repeatedly, and checking the math. In the eighteen of twenty-four states that chose electors by popular vote, Jackson had won a total of 151,363 votes, almost 40,000 more than his nearest competitor, who was John Quincy Adams with 113,142, and 110,000 more than William H. Crawford's 41,032.[15]

According to the Constitution, only the electoral counts of Jackson's 99, Adams's 84, and Crawford's 41 were pertinent in referring the question to the House of Representatives. That didn't stop Jacksonites from seizing on both his plurality in the Electoral College and his plurality in the popular vote to demand his victory in the House. Aside from the fact that the House would not consider these factors, their logic was flawed, as was made evident by scrutinizing the case of Henry Clay. He had beaten Crawford in the popular vote by more than 6,000 votes (47,545–41,032), but Crawford had 4 more votes in the Electoral College, placing him with the other top two candidates before the House. Comparing the apple of popular votes to the orange of electoral ones was, in short, a pointless exercise, especially as it bore on the House's decision. Because of the complicated nature of the election, though, it would prove a highly effective one in shaping public opinion.

Jackson men, in fact, touted Jackson's plurality in the electoral and popular votes immediately. In a letter to John Overton on December 19, 1824, Old Hickory referred to himself as "having been supported by the majority of the people," which wasn't the case, but Jackson correctly assumed that this was not the time for subtlety. In retrospect, though, subtleties are essential to understanding the event. Historian Donald Ratcliffe has meticulously analyzed the elections that peopled the six state legislatures that chose electors in 1824 and has convincingly argued that John Quincy Adams would have won a plurality of the overall popular vote if those states' electors had been selected by popular referenda. Even in the eighteen states that did choose electors by popular vote, only 28 percent cast ballots for Jackson electors. That meant 72 percent did not vote for Jackson, or to be precise, they did not vote for electors pledged to Old Hickory. Neither the apple nor the orange produces a clear winner regarding popular preference. Jacksonite claims that he was the clear choice of the people in 1824 were never true.[16]

Nevertheless, Jacksonites intensively and persistently pressured House members with that very claim. The House would not take up the question of the next president until February 9, which gave not only the supporters of Jackson but also those of Adams and Crawford more than two months to cobble together the simple majority in the House vote necessary for victory. They also courted one another. Operatives for the three candidates met to make promises, seek pledges, bend the truth, and, if necessary, lie.

Crawford was reported as doing better or worse, health-wise, depending on the source. "You would be greatly hurt to see him," said Louis McLane, noting how Crawford had "lost his powers of speech," slurring many words and halting over others. He was "not that commanding man" he used to be. Others at least found Crawford cheerful. He was surrounded by his family and touched by "the exemplary fidelity of his friends." One of the most faithful was his chief assistant at the Treasury, Asbury Dickins. He occasionally carried Crawford's instructions to his chief operative Martin Van Buren, who was boarding in the same house as Louis McLane and New York congressman Stephen Van Rensselaer, but more for the fellowship than from conviction. Van Buren had not given up hope that he could secure enough states in the House to elect William Crawford. He had arrived in Washington determined to hold Crawford supporters together for that purpose, but his paramount aim was to keep New York's House delegation away from any bargains that could decide the question for Adams on the first ballot. Van Buren believed if Crawford could get past the hurdle of that first ballot, he could entice Adams and Jackson strays to come to his side.[17]

Growing incredulity and rampant rumors were Van Buren's biggest obstacles, though. That Crawford remained a contender despite his health led to speculation that he planned to release his supporters to Adams, or that Clay and Crawford were joining forces to block Jackson, or even that Crawford would endorse Jackson. The chance of any of these happening caused Andrew Jackson to snort over Crawford as "the great whore of babylon."[18]

Jackson could claim he was above grubbing for votes, but his friends were too busy to dissemble, and sometimes they were ham-handed negotiators, too obvious with a bribe and too ugly with threats. Ohio congressman John Sloane found himself sitting across a dinner table from Sam Houston, who mused between bites that Ohio would surely go for Jackson in the House vote. Sloane was an experienced politician in his mid-forties, a Jeffersonian who preferred Clay, and his response to Houston was measured. He had not spoken to others of his delegation, he said guardedly. Sloane believed Houston looked anxious as he spoke about "what a splendid administration it would make, with Old Hickory as President and Mr. Clay as Secretary of State." Later, as Houston bade Sloane farewell, he made doubly sure his offer had not been misunderstood. "Well, I hope you from Ohio will aid us in electing General Jackson," Sloane recalled him saying, with a winking repeat of the proposed deal, "and then your man (meaning Mr. Clay) can have anything he pleases."[19]

James Buchanan proved remarkably inept as a dealmaker. At the time, he was an insignificant Pennsylvania congressman visible mainly because he was also one of the state's former Federalists who had thrown in with Jackson at the start. During that December and January of furtive men trafficking in sly offers, he joined the game, sure that he could guarantee Jackson's election and earn the man's eternal gratitude. Buchanan first approached John Eaton to propose a strategy to counteract the damage caused by rumors that Jackson intended to keep Adams as secretary of state. Buchanan assured Eaton that if Jackson quietly pledged that Clay would be his secretary of state, Clay's friends would be Jackson's for the asking. Eaton listened impassively, and Buchanan correctly inferred that Eaton was choosing to pass. Buchanan persevered until Jackson granted him an interview, but the candidate was even more indifferent than Eaton. At most he insisted he had never said anything about keeping Adams at the State Department. Buchanan asked if he could repeat what Jackson had told him. Jackson said yes. Buchanan sallied forth and proceeded to tell anyone who would listen something Andrew Jackson had not said. In Buchanan's account, Jackson's careful demurral about not saying something became a declaration that he would not appoint Adams. A little over a year later, James Buchanan would awaken from the bad dream of this foolish ploy to find himself in a full-blown nightmare.[20]

Old Hickory's men heard the distressing news that the young Illinois congressman Daniel P. Cook intended to vote for Adams. Cook was Ninian Edwards's son-in-law and was grateful that Adams had refrained from condemning Edwards during the "A.B." investigation, but even before that, Cook had been among the few men in Washington who liked John Quincy Adams. At thirty years of age and in frail health, he suddenly found himself at the center of an unsettling effort to influence his vote. Illinois was a relatively new state of the Union, and its sparse population granted it only one representative, but because each state had one vote in the House election, Dan Cook by himself was as important as all of New York or Pennsylvania. Illinois had mostly gone for Jackson, and Old Hickory's men forcefully demanded that those general election results do more than guide Cook in the House vote. He should accept them as the verdict of the people—or else. Pennsylvania's Samuel Ingham, who had effortlessly shed his allegiance to Calhoun to support Jackson, took this tack. A rumored alliance of Adams and Clay would be unpopular, he muttered darkly to Cook, and it would hurt Cook's career to join it. Ingham watched the young man absorb this threat and saw someone not at all weighing his options to cut his losses. Ingham accordingly switched his mood and smiled benevolently. Cook, said Ingham, could be territorial governor of Arkansas if his vote helped Andrew Jackson become president.

For Daniel P. Cook, the offer of the whole world was insufficient to purchase his vote at the cost of his integrity. But Arkansas? Ingham knew when to drop it.[21]

THE RUMOR OF an Adams-Clay alliance was one of many, and it gained more credence than all others only because it turned out to be true. As it happened, the most important of all the meetings that January would be the one between John Quincy Adams and Henry Clay. On January 9, Clay sent Adams a note asking to call that evening, and Adams quickly responded. At Adams's home, the two met privately for several hours that night, and nobody else would ever know the precise details of their discussion. The detailed diary Adams kept with addictive regularity was remarkably vague about the meeting. He and Clay clearly reached an understanding behind the closed doors of Adams's study, but no evidence supports the charge that they struck a bargain. In fact, the most precise detail Adams recorded was that Clay did not ask for a single personal consideration.[22]

The statement rings true because it matches their respective characters. John Quincy Adams would never have consented to a brazen deal that traded anything of even footling value for Clay's support in the House vote. Adams was rectitude defined, whether it came to matters large or small. His stubborn insistence on keeping apparent enemies in government jobs during his presidency was proof of that. As for Clay, his motive for having the meeting was to obtain Adams's assurance to support a national agenda. Clay received such a pledge, but beyond that, he did not like Adams and would not have asked him for so much as a postmaster's post, even if the political costs of receiving it had been negligible. And in this case, the potential political costs were beyond calculation. Approached by men seeking Crawford's support, Martin Van Buren heard one say that Henry Clay was prepared to make Adams president whatever Crawfordites did. Without a trace of malice or a hint of desperation, Van Buren was matter-of-fact. The deed, he said, would "sign Mr. Clay's death warrant."[23]

Of course, the meeting and the discussion were horrible mistakes, and Clay's behavior both before and after January 9 compounded them. Logic pointed him toward Adams as soon as he knew that Louisiana had removed him from contention, and as noted, he had said as much to friends in Kentucky. Clay can be excused for keeping his counsel after returning to Washington, for he wanted to make sure before he made his preference known that he and Adams agreed on policy. During that time, though, he indulged an impish streak, relishing how all sides courted him and his friends. Perhaps more than mischief prompted him to make his former rivals dance to a tune that only he knew the steps to. "Since my exclusion from the H. of R.," he crowed, "I enjoy the rare felicity, whilst alive, which is experienced by the dead, if they then have a consciousness of what passes here—that of hearing every kind of eulogium and panegyric pronounced upon me."[24]

After January 9, Clay allowed two weeks to pass before he announced his decision to support Adams, which gave the appearance of cunning. In any case, his period of enjoyable courtship ended when news of his January 9 meeting with Adams made the rounds. Crawford's friends and Jackson's operatives stopped the flattery and began their attacks. These were love pats in comparison to what was coming.[25]

═══

WHEN HENRY CLAY announced his support for John Quincy Adams on January 24, 1825, the Ohio and Kentucky congressional delegations did the same. Adams's brightening prospects encouraged Crawfordites, who saw in them the chance of getting past a first ballot, which was one reason the news stunned Jackson men. Most of all, it made clear what had been going on during the latter half of January. Both Ohio and Kentucky had given their electoral votes to Clay, but Jackson had polled second in them, and that was expected to count for something when Clay no longer counted at all. Indeed, the Kentucky legislature had instructed the state's congressmen to vote for Jackson. Though framed as a directive, the legislature's dictate was nonbinding and consequently nothing more than a suggestion. Both in Washington and in Kentucky, grumbling men pondered the Kentucky delegation's political future.[26]

Clay's announcement caused Andrew Jackson to explode. He sputtered "that self-aggrandizement, and corruption, by many are attached to his motives—be that as it may, nothing can save him from the condemnation of all highminded men." Others were soon done with grumbling too. Lafayette's secretary heard that Jacksonites from Pennsylvania planned to march on Washington if the House elected Adams.[27]

Rather than marching anywhere, though, most Jacksonites scrambled to repair the damage. Gone in an instant were the characterizations of Crawford as a "whore," because he had just enough votes in just enough delegations to make him suddenly worthwhile as a friend. Crawford's supporters, though, had long memories and were unwilling to forgive. One Crawford man declared "they might as well think of turning the Capitol upside down as of persuading him to vote for Jackson." The Jacksonites were undeterred because they had little choice. Rachel Jackson even hoisted herself into a carriage and called on Mrs. Crawford, a sadly insincere social gesture that was as ineffective as the political ones. Crawford's supporters had met on January 18 to hear Van Buren reprise his strategy of holding firm, avoiding all deals, and resisting all entreaties. Clay's announcement could benefit the cause, for even if the Speaker did throw his support to Adams, Crawford could "avoid the odium and profit by it too." Getting past the first ballot was Van Buren's Holy Grail. Then he could make a case for Crawford as a compromise selection. Jackson's effort to pick up Crawford men fell flat.[28]

Pessimism and anger led Jackson's operatives to do something, anything to reverse the momentum. The procedure gave each state a single vote, regardless of the size of its delegation, with a simple majority deciding the victor. Jacksonites reckoned Adams already had twelve of the thirteen states needed to win the election on the House's first ballot. The day after Clay made his announcement, an anonymous letter appeared in the *Columbian Observer* accusing him and John Quincy Adams of rank opportunism in brokering a disgusting deal. The accuser claimed that in return for Clay's help in winning the House, Adams had promised to appoint Clay secretary of state. The letter also said that Clay's minions had offered his support to Jackson if he would match Adams's offer, but that Jackson's people were above bargaining for the presidency.[29]

The contents of this remarkable letter nearly unhinged Henry Clay. In Washington's most prestigious daily, the *National Intelligencer*, he labeled its author "a base and infamous calumniator, a dastard and a liar" and promised to "hold him responsible, as I here admit myself to be, to all the laws which govern and regulate the conduct of men of honor." It was a challenge to a duel. All Clay needed to know was whom he was going to kill. Close upon the publication of Clay's challenge—a "card" in the locutions of the day—Pennsylvania congressman George Kremer published a "card" of his own admitting that he had written the letter and was prepared to prove everything in it. Kremer unmasking himself shocked every person in the capital, including Henry Clay. Kremer was the nephew of Simon Snyder, the influential leader whose faction had controlled Pennsylvania's politics for a decade before his death in 1818. The family connection alone accounted for Kremer's place in the House, for he had little else to recommend him. Rather, he had the reputation of a contrarian who affected the manner of an eccentric, such as striding around the capital wearing a coat made of leopard pelts. Along with the peculiar garment, he wore a gruff anti-intellectualism and amused himself by lampooning learned men in the House. The joke was on him, though, for his high-pitched voice earned him the nickname "George Screamer," which was not only true but also rhymed. Clay had challenged an anonymous accuser to defend his honor only to discover that he had called out a man who didn't have any.[30]

It was also clear that Kremer was lying about writing the letter. In fact, it had the subtle cadences of John Eaton, the blunt force trauma of Sam Houston, or perhaps the unctuousness of William B. Lewis, but it had nothing of the screamer's buffoonery. As a pawn of the Jackson camp, Kremer had become part of a clumsy plot to force Clay and his followers to disprove the allegation of corruption by abandoning Adams. Clay had no intention of deserting Adams. He would never support Andrew Jackson, and after he discovered who his accuser was at least claiming to be, he ditched the idea of killing George Kremer too. Instead, Clay had Kremer investigated by the House to compel him to prove his charges.[31]

A House committee began its work immediately, but it had little to investigate. Kremer produced no evidence to substantiate his charges, and he even refused to produce himself when the committee invited him to appear before it. Like the original letter that had libeled Adams and Clay, a lengthy one explaining his demurral came from someone else's pen. The damage done to the reputations of Clay and Adams was not insignificant, but it would have been worse had not the episode devolved into a farce complete with a clumsy Falstaff. Jacksonites didn't mind. With practice, they would get better at the smear.

Louis McLane tried with all his might to avoid serving on the Kremer committee, for he despised Adams and disliked Clay, but he was dragooned into the job and learned much about Jacksonites as a result. Jackson's people, he said in some amazement, were "most violent & implacable." That was one way to describe men who told jokes without smiling and threatened mayhem while grinning. Clay smelled bad, they shouted. The stench of "downright bribery & corruption" was enough to put a starving man off his feed. What had happened in Adams's study on the night of January 9 would always be "as infamous as you can imagine." And "no matter what may be the result," said a Jacksonite, while grinning, "it will bring home to Clay such a political curse he can't outlive." He wasn't joking.[32]

═══

THE IMMENSE CROWDS filling the capital became throngs by February 9. Neither freezing temperatures nor heavy snow could keep the people away from the drama about to unfold in Congress. Louis McLane had unsuccessfully tried to have the House exclude spectators in the gallery, at least for the vote that was to decide the presidency. When Jackson supporters berated him for trying to conduct the vote in secret, McLane scoffed at the charge. He was Delaware's sole representative, he said, making Delaware's choice his and his alone. What could be secretive in that? He argued that he merely wanted the House of Representatives to make a dispassionate decision uninfluenced by the pressures that even a silent gallery would bring to bear. Fearing widespread outrage over a closed event, his colleagues disagreed. Citizens would watch their representatives choose their chief executive.[33]

Those congressmen in favor of open proceedings had a point, but even McLane's critics had to admit his logic concerning the House acting independently of all general election results made sense. What, after all, did the Framers of the Constitution intend? If the House were merely to ratify an Electoral College plurality, the House need not vote at all. An Electoral College plurality would be sufficient to select a winner, but that was explicitly not the case per the Constitution. Rather, the top three finishers in the Electoral College came before the House with none favored by any previous election result. As most would have argued, the Constitution meant for the House to start its considerations from scratch.

Jacksonites did not like the sound of this at all, but they took comfort in that, logical as it may be, it was only an opinion about a process in which every state had one vote. What really mattered was how persuasive each candidate's emissaries could be. States with few congressmen had attracted the most attention from all three candidates' operatives because it was simpler to line up a lesser number, and those with only one representative experienced increased pressure. Daniel P. Cook of Illinois, John Scott of Missouri, and Louis McLane of Delaware knew all about this.

It was peculiar, then, how the question ultimately devolved on New York, a state with one of the largest delegations, which was evenly divided between Adams and Crawford. Adams had firm commitments from ten states, and Henry Clay was confident about Cook from Illinois and Scott from Missouri. That meant Adams needed only one more state to win on the first ballot. The first ballot was crucial, as everyone, especially Martin Van Buren, understood, because those congressmen pledged to vote for Adams on the first ballot would be released for subsequent ones. If Adams suffered diminishing returns in the second or third ballot, Crawford could end up the winner in a House deadlocked over Adams and Jackson. In a play with a variety of possible plots leading to three different conclusions, Henry Clay was the director, but Martin Van Buren was doing the casting. Clay as Speaker controlled the House that would do the counting, but the New Yorker Van Buren seemed to control the one state that, in the end, would count.[34]

At noon on February 9, the Senate and the House gathered in the House chamber for the official tally from the Electoral College. It was a tiresome formality because everyone knew the totals, but it was played out with great deliberation for an excruciating two and a half hours. Senators moved about the floor, not wholly out of boredom. Some, such as Van Buren, continued to politick for their candidates in the House vote to come. From a field of six men, some of whom had not been official candidates, John C. Calhoun received a majority of the Electoral College vote for the vice presidency. As expected, the tedious counting of the presidential electoral ballots produced no majority. Senators then trailed out of the House chamber. It was 2:30 p.m. Before a hushed gallery of a thousand spectators who barely rustled, the House of Representatives, at last, commenced the business of choosing the next president.[35]

Each step was clear and straightforward, but they amounted to an elaborate process. State delegations followed a practice from the Continental Congress by arranging themselves in roughly geographical order, North to South along the East Coast, then South to North for the western interior. Each state had a box into which each member of a delegation placed his secret ballot. After all the votes had been cast, each state appointed one of its own to count them and prepare two duplicates of the state's ballot indicating the winning candidate. Both sets of twenty-four ballots were placed in two boxes and taken to the head of the House chamber, where a committee consisting of one delegate from each state would count them. This committee of twenty-four was evenly divided into two groups, each to count the true copies of the state ballots to ensure that the totals were the same. The two members chosen to head these two groups were Daniel Webster and John Randolph, the latter helpful because he was one of two representatives who had been in Congress the only other time this had happened. That was in 1801 when Thomas Jefferson and Aaron Burr had tied in the Electoral College.

New York was the key to everything because Adams had twelve states locked on the first ballot, and New York was the only remaining state whose choice was uncertain. To the very last minute available to him, Van Buren focused on one particular representative, his messmate Stephen Van Rensselaer, an old Federalist congress-man. Van Rensselaer did not care for Adams, and he did not think Crawford physically capable, which inclined him toward Jackson. With the state evenly divided between Crawford and Adams, Van Rensselaer's vote for Jackson would have made no difference, ex-cept to negate New York's vote entirely by leaving it tied. In one sense, that result would deliver to Van Buren his objective of get-ting past the first ballot. But it would also come at the cost of blunt-ing Crawford's momentum by depriving him of the chance to show that he could win a large state. Van Buren argued his case with Van Rensselaer, and at breakfast that morning, both he and his fellow Crawfordite Louis McLane felt sure that the onetime Federalist was in their camp. McLane had to leave early for the final meeting of the wretched Kremer committee at ten o'clock that morning, and Van Buren had to go to the Senate when Congress opened the day's session at eleven. That left Stephen Van Rensselaer alone for most of the morning, and what happened to him during that time and after he arrived at the Capitol has never been clear.

Van Rensselaer hailed from a family that, during New York's Dutch colonial days, had been part of the "patroon" class, the upper echelon of New York's most elite gentry. The honorific survived as a relic of a pastoral past that Washington Irving would romanticize in fiction but that remained very real to the people, such as Van Rens-selaer, clinging to a simpler time when everyone knew his place and purpose. It left Van Rensselaer the last of a breed freighted with the prudence common to all dying breeds. Despite his purported authority, he was retiring and diffident, polite to a fault, and in the first weeks of 1825, increasingly dismayed that his single vote as a member of New York's congressional delegation could choose the next president of the United States.

There are at least two colorful versions of what happened to this somewhat befuddled man on February 9. One tells of Henry Clay's dramatic intervention when Van Rensselaer arrived at the Capitol. Clay and Daniel Webster, it was said, sequestered Van Rensselaer in the Speaker's office and forcefully described the chaos that would result from an indecisive first ballot. Perhaps something like this occurred, and the word *chaos* would have jarred a large landowner reflexively afraid of social and political disruptions. Whether true or not, it is more believable than the story later told by Martin Van Buren, an invention rivaling any fiction Washington Irving ever hatched. Van Buren recalled how Van Rensselaer bowed his head and closed his eyes to pray for guidance during the poll of the New York delegation. Van Rensselaer opened his eyes and saw a printed ballot on the floor. The name on it was an answered prayer.[36]

The states completed their polling and transferred the results to the tellers, Webster and Randolph. They examined the ballots in a silence so complete that the galleries could hear them murmuring to each other, but not what they were saying. Both knew who had won the presidency as soon as they saw the New York ballot, but not until all results were counted did Webster pause, stand, and announce in his booming voice:

> *Mr. Speaker:* The Tellers of the votes at this table have proceeded to count the ballots contained in the box before them. The result they find to be, that there are
> For John Quincy Adams, of Massachusetts, 13 votes
> For Andrew Jackson, of Tennessee, 7 votes
> For William H. Crawford, of Georgia, 4 votes.[37]

At the other table, John Randolph rose and piped his concurrence with the tally in his shrill voice, varying Webster's words only by saying "states" rather than "votes." Their counting had taken a mere half hour, and the widely held expectation that the first ballot would be only the beginning of a long process had lulled everyone into a kind of torpor. When Henry Clay announced that Adams was the president-elect, the realization that it was all over had an "electric" effect. A smattering of applause rippled through the gallery. Low hisses answered. It was hardly a raucous response, but Clay was taking no chances. He slammed down his gavel and ordered the gallery cleared. Andrew Jackson Donelson, who had stationed himself in it from the start, was already shouldering his way through the crowd. He raced to Gadsby's with the news.[38]

The House adjourned. Stephen Van Rensselaer saw Louis McLane leaving the building and walked briskly to catch up with him, but McLane sprinted from the building, jumped in a crowded carriage, and returned to their boardinghouse. Back in his room, he heard Van Rensselaer's heavy tread on the steps and a tap on his door. The patroon entered. "Forgive me, McLane," he said softly, holding out his hand. McLane turned away. "Ask your own conscience, General and not me," Louis McLane said flatly.[39]

North Carolina senator Nathaniel Macon found William H. Crawford seated comfortably in his parlor, a cheerful fire warming the room against the blowing snow outside. Macon was "a solid, farmer-like man," a sage of the Senate and a keen observer of changing times. The campaign season had unfolded in ways that troubled him, marking the emergence of "new parties . . . not founded like the old, on the construction of the Constitution." Instead, they would be collections of self-interest, "the followers of men [rather] than principles." As it did every visitor, Crawford's appearance saddened him, particularly because of the news he carried. He wondered why Crawford seemed surprised to hear it.[40]

Other supporters drifted into the parlor that night, including Martin Van Buren and Louis McLane, still bitter about Van Rensselaer's "miserable wavering." Crawford's wife was curt with Van Buren, but he overlooked it and sat subdued, joining the others in a gathering that had the mood of a wake. The only cheerful person in the room was the one playing whist and occasionally cracking a joke. Crawford's dear Caroline, the daughter who had become his understanding ear as well as his voice to the world, always laughed appreciatively. It made William H. Crawford smile before he went back to squinting at his cards.[41]

———

ALSO THAT NIGHT, the Monroes held their weekly reception, and though everyone seemed drained by the experience, they were also grateful that despite the angry talk, broad recriminations, and grinding apprehension, the election, in the end, had "been decided with a calm dignity." The president's gathering was not festive, but it was uneventful, which was pleasant for people weary of events. "A kindred spirit pervaded the whole scene," the National Intelligencer reported. "The friends of the different candidates mingled together, and conversed with a good humor and frankness contrasted with the virulence and malignity which, in some parts of the country, had attended the discussion of this question."[42]

President-elect John Quincy Adams stood near the center of the room in the midst of a press of people offering congratulations. He received them with a drawn smile and stiff bows. He felt another press of people behind him and turned, just as Andrew Jackson stepped up to face him.

It had been a grueling day for them both. Adams had received the news of his victory with a mixture of elation and disbelief. Young Donelson had torn into Jackson's room at Gadsby's outraged and nearly in tears over what he had seen happen in the House. The general had calmed him down, despite his own disbelief. At Gadsby's, Rachel was the one elated.

The president's reception fell silent. Guests suddenly became conscious of the cramped space and instinctively backed away from the two men to create a small empty circle with them at its center.

The last bit of stray laughter and murmuring voices went quiet in the corners of the room. Adams looked up at the gaunt face. Andrew Jackson bowed low. He extended his hand. Adams took it.[43]

Official Washington pondered the scene. Possibly, just possibly, the suspicion that Andrew Jackson had been playing the statesman for political effect was groundless. With the bow and proffered hand, he had "shown equal nobleness and equanimity." A collective sigh of relief followed. In the Crawford parlor, though, with the mood of a wake, a fresh log lay on the fire as the host played whist and cracked wise. Crawford had not seen the encouraging tableau of traded bows and grasped hands at the Monroe reception, but he didn't need to. Caroline's thick-tongued father with his squinting eyes could see more than she, or anyone else, knew.[44]

CHAPTER 10

ALLEGATIONS

Weeks before the House vote, John Quincy Adams had made plans to maintain continuity and present a reassuring competency in the event of his victory. On January 18, he asked Samuel Southard to remain as secretary of the navy. He also requested that William H. Crawford stay at Treasury. Southard agreed, but Crawford declined. After the vote in the House made him president-elect, Adams had less than a month before his inauguration to select his secretaries, and as late as February 22, "rumors and speculation" were "still the order of the day as to the Cabinet." Such uncertainty was precisely the thing Adams wanted to avoid.[1]

On February 10, the day after the vote in the House, Adams offered Henry Clay the office of secretary of state. It was a choice he had revealed to a select few three days earlier. Adams expected them to protect the confidence, but someone talked, and when Clay asked for time to consider and commenced to do so, both he and Adams were surprised that all of Washington already knew about the proffer. Nearly universal condemnation followed. One of the more benign observers said that if news of Clay going to State was "true[,] Adams' Administration will be more tempestuous than any we have seen." More typical were the ones that minced no words. Louis McLane snarled that to compare Adams to Caesar was "to belittle the name of that mighty Roman tyrant." Harsh reactions came from across the country. A South Carolina Jacksonite attributed Adams's victory "to the treason of Mr. Clay," who was not only a traitor but a petty one at that. Clay "has sacrificed his antipathies to Mr. Adams on the altar of self-interest and is to receive as a remuneration, the office of Secretary of State." A Virginia jurist was blunt. "There was a corrupt bargain," he said.[2]

Less than two weeks after the House vote, the phrase "corrupt bargain" had already come to life. To Henry Clay's dismay, it would prove immortal. It is difficult to understand how he and Adams did not realize the consequences of their behavior during the pivotal days before Adams assumed office. Certainly, some factors that guided both men will remain forever hidden from modern scrutiny. But others, upon examination, appear rather obvious.

For one, it is important to remember that Adams likely felt great pressure to appoint his cabinet quickly to establish an aura of competency at the outset of his administration. That pressure in part explains his willingness to keep Southard at Navy, despite his close ties to John C. Calhoun, and his eagerness to have Crawford remain at Treasury, notwithstanding the virulence of the recent campaign. Because he was vacating State by assuming the presidency, Adams did not have the luxury of an acting secretary who could be kept on, nor did he have much leeway in choosing just anyone to head up the State Department. He knew Clay's talents as a hardheaded diplomat from his association with him during the treaty negotiations at Ghent in 1814. He did not like Clay, but he had developed a grudging respect for him, and he was confident that Clay would not be a weakling in foreign relations.

Clay knew that if he accepted the president's offer to head the State Department, he would "be much abused." But it was to be worse than that. It was the worst blunder of Clay's political career. He did not like Adams personally, but he was convinced that Adams would promote the right policies, especially the triple-pronged American System of a national bank, internal improvements, and a protective tariff. Clay had already aligned himself with the incoming administration by helping to elect it in the House, and there was no reason for him not to be a part of it, except for the impression it would create.[3]

But refusing to join the administration would have been awkward, too. In fact, growing criticism compelled Clay to make a bad political decision to uphold a point of moral courage. Accepting the State Department would run a high political risk, but refusing it would be a tacit admission to opponents of the administration that they were correct in their allegations about a disreputable deal. Refusal would also send the signal that mere criticism could dictate the administration's personnel and, by implication, its policies. Moreover, adversaries would have the tacit admission from Clay himself that they could direct his future with threats of character assassination.

When he heard the rumors about Clay, Andrew Jackson maintained the admirable equanimity he had displayed on the night of the House vote. But privately, he simmered. When Clay's fellow Kentuckian Richard M. Johnson confirmed that Adams had offered Clay the appointment, Jackson boiled over. He predicted to William B. Lewis that the Senate would not confirm Clay, but it was his rhetorical question that set the tone of political talk for the next four years: "Was there ever witnessed such a bare faced corruption in any country before?" He stormed, "So you see the Judas of the West had closed the contract and will receive the thirty pieces of silver—his end will be the same."[4]

Jackson wrote to Lewis about a week later implying that he was already preparing for the next campaign. He protested that he "would be happy at the result [of the election]" had it not been for the corrupt means of how Adams's victory was achieved, but now the people's liberty was at stake. His friends advised him to keep quiet about everything for the time being. They needed time to get things organized. John Eaton, for example, was raising money to establish a Jackson newspaper in Washington. Jackson, meanwhile, continued to write to the Junto and other friends, fulminating against "Judas" and the corruption that robbed him of the presidency, all the while protesting that he had never wanted to be president in the first place.[5]

Old Hickory's correspondence with Samuel Swartwout, the man primarily responsible for Jackson's victory in New Jersey, became increasingly important as the campaign for 1828 began in earnest. Jackson was incensed that Clay apparently was justifying his actions in helping to make Adams president by saying Jackson's being a "military chieftain" disqualified him from the presidency. Clay, railed Jackson, "never yet has risked himself for his country—sacrificed his repose, or made an effort to repel an invading foe." Therefore, Jackson insisted Henry Clay was unqualified to render a judgment on someone who had. Jackson realized, he told Swartwout, that the term "'military chieftain,' has for some time past been a cant phrase with Mr. Clay & certain of his retainers; but the vote with which by the people I have been honored, is anough to satisfy me, that the prejudice by them, sought to be produced availed but little." Swartwout published this letter in the New York National Advocate soon after receiving it.[6]

Since the original voting in the fall of 1824, Jackson's friends had argued that the House should honor the will of the people. They muted this line of argument after February 9 after Adams was elected, however, to avoid alienating House members who had voted for Crawford or Adams. Rather, Jacksonites targeted Henry Clay as a convenient villain. Jackson hated him anyway, so shifting the blame for his woes from Crawford to Clay was a natural move. Newspaper reports from Jackson-aligned papers across the country took up the refrain. The *Louisiana Gazette* was a good example. It opened a column with "DIED—politically, on the 9th inst. Mr. HENRY CLAY" and continued in mock mourning that "in the death of this gentlemen, we have to lament the loss of one whose career we have followed for twenty years with admiration and respect." Clay, "like Milton's favoured angel . . . has fallen." The *Gazette* placed a black border above and below the article that was headed by skulls and crossbones. The editor soon was using the consequences of Clay's behavior as a cautionary tale. The paper announced that it "would let him rest in peace, but the interest of our country requires that we elevate him as a beacon to warn the unwary." But proclaiming that its slanders were a public service was hollow as the *Gazette* began dwelling on the "corrupt bargain" and leveling attacks on the Adams administration, whatever its course.[7]

ANDREW JACKSON ATTENDED the inauguration of John Quincy Adams on March 4, 1825, and it was apparently the last time the two men spoke to each other for the rest of their lives. At one point, Jackson had been inclined to support Adams for the presidency, and even during the heated campaign season, Jackson had continued to think of the New Englander as a friendly acquaintance. Jackson's belief that Adams had made a deal with Henry Clay changed all that in an instant, and by the day Adams was to be sworn in, Jackson's hostility to him had become only slightly less vicious than that toward Clay.[8]

In a way unique to him, Jackson was able to rationalize his hatreds as rising from principled altruism rather than from petty or even grand grievances. The House vote had not given him the result he wanted, but he refused to consider that the ordinary course of politics was the culprit. A jumble of partisan enthusiasms, selfless principles, and selfish motives had shaped events, but that was not how Jackson saw it. He perceived a plot hatched by scheming blackguards working for Adams.

Adams supporters could have wished it had been so easy to wrangle thirteen states, each with unique electoral and demographic complexities, into a winning coalition. Jackson simply saw the complexities as corruption and believed an administration founded on it would continue its double-dealing unless checked by the forces of virtue. Indeed, opposing such a creation had to proceed from higher motives than disappointment and resentment. Defaming the perpetrators of such fraud was a righteous obligation, not a scurrilous enterprise. Andrew Jackson, as he himself saw it, had a duty to vilify the Adams presidency out of principle, regardless of its policies, and with complete disregard for its principal figure's reputation for spotless rectitude. Jackson's mission justified the actions of his supporters. Kentucky senator Richard M. Johnson swore that Old Hickory's men would oppose Adams and Clay even "if they act as pure as the angels that stand at the right hand of the throne of God." Even Thomas Hart Benton, who never believed the "corrupt bargain" accusation, endorsed obstructionism as justifiable to secure Jackson's victory in 1828.[9]

At his inauguration, Adams wore a plain black suit with trousers, not the knee-britches of his predecessors, a visible marker that he was the first president not of the Revolutionary generation. Yet any sign of discontinuity ended with his clothes. His address extolled the virtues of the Constitution and lauded the many advances in self-government and human freedom resulting from it. He lamented the spirit of party that could set citizens on angry paths, but he also expressed optimism. He was sure that Americans would recall that the general welfare and domestic tranquility were the government's primary purposes, noble aims that drew their power from the people's consent. Adams praised President Monroe for his comportment and achievements and announced that his primary goal as president would be to continue his predecessor's admirable bearing and policies. Adams closed on a note of understatement by remarking that his election had been somewhat unusual. But, he added, its uniqueness merely imposed a different rather than an onerous burden on the political system sure to be guided by Congress, the states, and "the candid and liberal support of the people, so far as it may be deserved by honest industry and zeal."[10]

Responding to these routine political incantations and occasionally eloquent appeals, the Jacksonites turned to the work of destroying the man who had uttered them. Adams's sincere desire to rise above partisan quarrels, "to break up the remnant of old party distinctions and bring the whole people together in sentiment" was buried from the outset under an opposition both adamant and unreasonable. Congress became the first forum for the opening moves by Jackson and his friends in the presidential campaign for 1828. John Eaton would approve of how John Randolph, as of December 1825 a Virginia senator, dragged "in [Clay and Adams] upon every question." Randolph liked to "torture them, to use an expression his own, as composed as a philosopher would to torture mice in an air pump." Moreover, the angry Virginian declared "that the Hickory of Tennessee is the only rod that can be successfully used to drive these money changers from the temple."[11]

As before, the Jacksonites used their newspapers across the nation to attack enemies relentlessly. In Philadelphia, Stephen Simpson's *Columbian Observer* imagined a conversation between Adams and Clay in which the president lectured Clay on his immorality, especially his gambling. It sent Clay into a pout. He hoped that Adams would "have no notion of shuffling me off now, after my intrigues and treachery to the people have placed you in the chair of state." It turned out that Adams had no such notion at all. Rather, the two planned to have Congress pass a law "to silence the cursed newspapers." After all, Adams observed, he had "some of the blood of my father in me," an unsubtle reminder that John Adams had signed the Sedition Act in 1798 to suppress dissent. Western newspapers reported that the election results had made Jackson supporters so angry that they planned to march on Washington and overthrow the corrupt Adams regime. Adams had activated militia, said one rumor, to prevent an insurrection. A Missouri Jacksonite declared that "the late occurrence in Washington, has excited alarm in the republican ranks throughout the United States." The House vote, he said, had occurred "for the pecuniary interest and aggrandizement of Mr. Clay."[12]

In places where Jackson lacked a press presence, his supporters either cultivated existing papers or founded new ones. Stephen Simpson received generous subsidies from John Eaton, which caused some embarrassment when the arrangement came to light, but such minor embarrassments were easily explained and mended. Jackson urged John Coffee to subscribe to the *Washington City Gazette* because it was the only paper in the capital not controlled by the Adams administration, a situation John Eaton was also working to change.[13]

Raising the banner of All Things Jackson became a tactic and rallying cry, as when the Nashville *Gazette* described at length a Jackson birthday celebration in Elkton, Maryland, with a pointed jab. At sunrise, said the paper, there were "seven volumes of heavy charged artillery, wadded with Clay." The toasts included "General Andrew Jackson—The People's President," and another to "The people of the United States—More disinterested and better judges of the qualifications of presidential candidates than their representatives."[14]

There was nothing too trifling for Jackson's operatives to leave unnoticed. John Eaton began criticizing the purportedly lavish lifestyle Adams planned to enjoy in the White House. The most delicious story, said Eaton, "makes even his friends look down." It related how the inventory of White House furnishings had included a billiard table purchased with taxpayer money.[15]

The billiard table "scandal" became a staple of the attacks on Adams for the next four years, even though its most damning detail—the use of public money for the purchase—was not true. Aside from a scrupulously honest man being defamed for supposedly raiding the treasury to buy gewgaws, the potentially heartwarming aspects of the affair never had a chance to shine under the shadow of the lie. The truth was that the playful side of John Quincy Adams, hidden in all other instances by his sour nature, unexpectedly emerged in the company of his sons, with whom he liked to play billiards. With fifty dollars of his own money, he purchased from a local merchant a used billiard table, indifferent to its lumpy felt and frayed edges but eager for the pleasure of sharing time with his boys. John Adams II was one of his father's secretaries and had mistakenly included the billiard table on a list provided to the House Committee on Public Buildings. It did not matter that Adams immediately sent word to the committee's chairman that he had paid for the table himself. A public correction did not appear for almost a year while the story became an embarrassment that would not die. Jackson newspapers also attacked Adams for even playing billiards, a pastime associated with gambling. Jacksonites masked their glee with pretended sorrow over the president's low morals while shrugging, as if to say, *What can you expect?* When Adams went home briefly in the spring of 1825 to visit his aged father and found himself too busy with personal matters to accept invitations to public dinners, Jacksonites shook their heads over the president's cold heart and ungrateful nature.[16]

Their treatment of Henry Clay was worse. Before the inauguration, Clay's most visible attacker George Kremer published an address to his constituents in Pennsylvania to explain his accusations of corruption and to repeat that he could substantiate them. Adams ignored him, but Kremer's renewing his claims after refusing to testify at the congressional investigation infuriated Clay anew. Friends confirmed his suspicion that Kremer was really a front for a ghostwriter, most likely John Eaton, but they urged him to forget the entire matter, accept the State Department, and move on. Kremer had not proved anything, and Clay had done nothing wrong in working for a candidate he preferred. "Although Mr. Clay might not like Mr. Adams very much," a New York newspaper sensibly observed, "he is perfectly justifiable in liking General Jackson less."[17]

If only everything had been so sensible, Clay would have let it go. But he knew that Kremer's address to his constituents did not have to be true to be effective. Jackson thought it convincing enough to have his Tennessee operatives circulate it. He and Kremer struck up a friendship and traded letters bemoaning the administration's continued intrigues as the Pennsylvanian became increasingly active in Jackson's cause. The attention paid to Kremer's address by newspapers gave it legitimacy, Jackson's endorsement made it seem authoritative, and the controversy over it kept the "corrupt bargain" allegation alive while eroding confidence in the administration. Clay knew that its odor would linger over his career even after its particulars were forgotten. He saw no other option but to rebut it with an address of his own.[18]

Clay had his address ready for national publication before the end of March as an open letter to his constituents.[19] In the lengthy piece, Clay defended himself against Kremer's charges and explained his reasons for opposing Jackson, a man who never had "exhibited, either in the councils of the Union, or in those of his state, or in those of any state or territory, the qualities of a statesman." He lacked "that prudence, temper, and discretion, which are necessary for civil administration." In closing, Clay was succinct: "Gen. Jackson fights better than he reasons." As for George Kremer, Clay avoided disparaging him and even applauded his rise from humble origins, which was disingenuous because Clay privately described him as an "old vulgar gross drinking half Dutchman half Irishman." But that had been Clay in a fit of anger. At this point, and publicly, he lamented how "others have availed themselves, and have made him [Kremer] their dupe and their instrument." He specifically mentioned the open secret that John Eaton had paid a late-night visit to Kremer's rooms.[20]

Jackson was not impressed. "The poor Devil H. Clay," he told John Coffee, "has come out with an adress to his constituents, in a begging cringing tone, to clear himself from the corrupt intrigue & management to procure for himself the office of sec of state—but he steers entirely clear of denying this charge—The various papers are commenting upon it." Perhaps the main impact of Clay's address was that it almost caused a duel between him and Eaton, until their exchanges turned foolish. When Eaton demanded that Clay retract the insinuation about Kremer's original letter, Clay pointed out that Kremer himself had admitted he did not write it. Clay had a counteroffer, though. If Eaton would give his word that his "nocturnal interview" with Kremer had nothing to do with the Pennsylvanian's literary productions, Clay would happily admit to being mistaken about Eaton as their author. Eaton refused to deny anything and seized on a lawyer's point, which was far afield from the one Henry Clay was trying to make. He crowed that because Clay had admitted he was not sure who was writing for Kremer, the implication was that he knew for a fact that nobody was. Going back on the offensive, Eaton chided Clay for tardiness in answering the demand for a retraction. In exasperation, Clay fell to lecturing. His official duties did not afford him the leisure Eaton enjoyed to write letters, but he certainly wasn't demanding explanations about Eaton's and Kremer's late-night conversations. If Eaton wished to keep mum about such things, the people could draw their own conclusions. It was John Eaton's turn to be exasperated. He had the entire exchange published in the press. Clay thought doing so was "silly."[21]

Clay had to suspect that his ordeal was only beginning, however, as Jacksonites turned private disagreements into public insults. It was part of a calculated plan to discredit through innuendo when facts fell short, and Clay was soon experiencing such treatment from Jackson men from all over. His friend and supporter Caleb Atwater, the representative from Ohio who had become Jackson's lead manager among Buckeyes, was not content to be Clay's former friend and supporter. Atwater became a belligerent enemy. He wrote a letter to Clay after the inauguration demanding to know whether support for Jackson would mean being "proscribed" by Adams. His pledge to keep Clay's reply confidential was far from congenial, accompanied as it was by a threat. "If you treat me as Mr. A[dams] did more than once, by not answ[ering] this," Atwater snarled, "I shall not trouble you agai[n] in the same way, during life." There is no record that Clay answered Atwater.[22]

Companions closer to home fell away. Kentucky governor Joseph Desha had been a friend of Clay's for years but broke with him over the election and joined efforts to organize "Jackson Dinners" as a counter to events for the new secretary of state when he returned home. That presented a most pleasing prospect to Old Hickory, and he seriously considered invading Clay's state to bask in the honor of tributes while sampling Kentucky cuisine. In the end, though, Jackson abandoned the idea, claiming it would look like electioneering, but, in truth, he worried about receiving a cold welcome from Kentucky. "It would be a feast to Clay & his friends," Jackson said, "was I to go there and the assemblage of people not greater, or the attention paid not more paid to him."[23]

Jackson need not have worried. The defections from Clay started as a trickle and became a flood as political allies and even a few close friends held dampened fingers in the wind and felt a breeze from Tennessee. Clay began receiving depressing reports about this, such as one about a "Capt. Moore" who had often been heard to "assert that Genl. Jackson had not a claim to the Presidency, and that his ignorance was such that 'he could not write three lines of English to save his life, but had the others to write those publications to which he had affixed his own name.'" The House's treatment of Jackson, however, changed Moore's attitude entirely: "Now [he] thinks the Genl. the most accomplished and diplomatic character."[24]

Up until the minute on March 7 that the Senate voted to confirm Henry Clay as secretary of state, Andrew Jackson believed it would not. He, Eaton, and twelve other senators voted against the confirmation, but twenty-seven votes gave Clay the post. Martin Van Buren voted with the majority to sustain friendly ties to the new administration, and many of his colleagues suspected that a similar motive, rather than enthusiastic agreement, was responsible for Clay's confirmation. By tradition, the Senate held these votes behind closed doors, but the controversy over Clay's appointment prompted it not just to disclose the tally but also to identify the yeas and nays. The extraordinary transparency had the effect of reinforcing the idea that something irregular had occurred in the election and its aftermath, something that had soiled everyone in the new administration, Clay most of all. He got the job he would grow to hate.[25]

———

THE SENATE ADJOURNED on March 9 until the end of the year, and Jackson and his family wasted no time leaving the capital for Nashville. Within a day they were in Baltimore, where citizens staged a grand ball and banquet. The city opened its largest halls and finest salons for collations, receptions, and speeches and even presented theater tickets to everyone, except Rachel, who was "indisposed." Pleading illness was probably an excuse to shrink from the public appearances she detested. Still, she received all the ladies who wanted to see her, their courtesy mixed with curiosity. She abided the curiosity because she could not rebuff the courtesy, but the family's departure from Baltimore on March 15, her husband's fifty-eighth birthday, must have been a great relief. Jackson swung into the saddle of a horse, but she with Andrew and Emily Donelson rode in a beautiful carriage. Baltimore found it hard to say goodbye, though, and a large group of citizens insisted on escorting them along the Frederick Road. Those people reluctantly parted and returned to the city only after treating their guests to one last dinner.[26]

It would take the Jacksons more than a month to reach Nashville, largely because of scenes like this one. Pennsylvania's anticipation of Jackson's visit resembled something close to "marks of madness" as Old Hickory and company entered the state that had set him on the path to certain victory just a year before. But now, the exertions of their hosts seemed an apology for victory having been far from certain after all. Jackson himself contributed to the bittersweet aura. His statements during the journey were possibly slips of temper, or perhaps they were only remembered that way, after subsequent events. People recalled Jackson "conversing freely respecting Mr. Adams, Mr. Clay, and the Presidential election." He was said to have declared that "he would not have the office of President of the U. States, if he had to obtain it by bargain, corruption, and intrigue as Mr. Adams had done."[27]

The Jacksons and Donelsons finally arrived in Nashville on April 13 to a hero's welcome. John Overton stood in the public square to address a large crowd that cheered, whistled, and stomped as he described Jackson's sacrifices during the war and his heroism at New Orleans. All grew silent when Overton reminded them how Jackson had starved so his soldiers might eat, had walked so his wounded could ride. Jackson's friend concluded by praising the Hero's dignity during the presidential campaign. He had never demonstrated a shred of "personal ambition" but had been willing, as always, to do his duty. Overton's reference to the election's result clearly conveyed his belief that dark forces had thwarted the will of the people.

The crowd's deafening response was not a cheer. It sounded like an angry lion, awakening.[28]

In the days that followed, Andrew Jackson's money would not spend, and his appetites would not go wanting, either for acclaim or victuals. Both were served up in heaping portions. Nashville invited him to a lavish dinner, an event that began with two companies of cavalry and a rifle company appearing at the Hermitage to escort him into town. The banquet's brimming tables matched the brimming mood after dinner. John Overton again delivered a few remarks to introduce the Hero, who rose to speak, his shock of white hair jutting upward, his brow knitted into what had become with age an expression of constant, mild worry. He was grateful, he told them, for the approbation they had settled on a fellow citizen who had only been brought forward for the presidency by well-meaning friends. Those good people had acted rather against his will and certainly had never expected him to sully their efforts with any overt ones of his own. In that, everyone who mattered had been gratified and vindicated, for the presidency was not an office ever to be sought, just as it was one that could never be declined. As Jackson spoke, it gradually dawned on his fellow diners what he was saying. George Wilson's Nashville *Gazette* had already endorsed Jackson for the 1828 election, but such gestures had become an appreciative staple, like laudatory toasts after an excellent meal. Now it was clear that Jackson fully intended to stand for the presidency again. The applause became a roar.[29]

LATE IN THE fall of 1825, Andrew Jackson sent an address to the Tennessee legislature resigning his US Senate seat. The Tennessee legislature had again nominated him for president, and he claimed the gesture required his resignation. In late 1823 and again in December 1824, Thomas Hart Benton had introduced in Congress a constitutional amendment to abolish the Electoral College and have the people elect the president directly. With Jacksonites arguing that the Electoral College and the House vote had thwarted the will of the people, and with Jackson an outspoken supporter of Benton's amendment, it would be inappropriate, he said, to vote in the Senate on a measure that could bear on his election to the presidency.[30]

His resignation was no surprise, but his actions in its aftermath were unexpected. Immediately after his announcement, he left the Hermitage for Murfreesboro to explain himself to the legislature, the people who had elected him. His appearance was portrayed as an act of civic concern, but its real purpose was political. Jackson planned to suggest that the legislature recommend another amendment to the Constitution that would bar any member of Congress from accepting a position in the executive branch within two years of leaving the national legislature. The Nashville *Gazette* explained the urgency behind the proposal. Unlike Jackson, said Junto member George Wilson, not all members of Congress could resist being "warped from the direct line of duty & honor." Some men could not resist their "all-grasping ambition." They would forever be in the thrall of their "avarice of the lust of power."[31]

Jackson had hardly dismounted from his horse in Murfreesboro before the speakers of the Tennessee House and Senate invited him to a joint session to be held on October 14. On that day, he arrived at the capitol shortly before noon and was escorted with ceremony into the House chamber. Senate Speaker Robert C. Foster expressed thanks for Jackson's service to the nation and said his visit to the legislature was a signal honor for the body, especially in light of Jackson's commendable behavior during the presidential election. Foster knew both the words and music to the Jacksonite tune about the will of the people, and he sang it with gusto while adding a coda of disgust over baseless charges that Tennessee's hero was nothing more than a "military chieftain."[32]

Jackson took his cue. He slowly rose to his feet and surveyed the leaders of his state, a pleasing prospect, he said, since so many friends and former comrades-in-arms were among them. They basked as he told them that their approval of his conduct during the election was most gratifying to him, and they solemnly nodded when he insisted it was simply his nature to be honorable. "It was impossible for me to have acted differently," he humbly avowed, "because it would have been at war, with all the declarations I had made; and all the principles upon which thro life I had professed to act." After all, "the situation" held "fearful responsibility, too many & too variant to be undertaken but thro the sanction and approbation of the country freely given, without which no man could hope to administer its affairs with satisfaction to the public, and credit to himself."[33]

These sentiments were published nationwide to great acclaim by Jackson's supporters, who used them to recruit new followers. Opponents, however, tried to put a different gloss on Jackson's actions by arguing that his resignation would mean "all chance for him hereafter will be at an end." Henry Clay received that kind of message from people trying to cheer him up. Jackson, said one particularly optimistic correspondent, would never "again be so near the first office in the Gift of the People, as he has been." Another friend assured Clay that "Genl. Jackson's Grooms have brought [him] on the turf too soon[;] he will be broke down in training." Crawfordites also came to a similar judgment, though less happily. After all, Jackson's waning meant "that the admin[istration] will be reelected easily." As for his part, Henry Clay might have taken small comfort had he not been more worried that "the General having tried to be elected president by going into the Senate, now means to make the experiment by going out of it."[34]

═══════

WHEN THE NINETEENTH Congress convened in early December 1825, Hugh Lawson White replaced Jackson as Tennessee's new junior senator. He was not just an accomplished jurist and state legislator. He was John Overton's brother-in-law and a power in Knoxville, a town that his father had helped found. He was east Tennessee's equivalent of John Overton, and his ascendancy to the Senate was a key step in the Jacksonite attempt to obstruct the Adams administration's every effort at governance. White was there to help Andrew Jackson become president.

The House still reeled from the excitement of how its predecessor had chosen Adams in February, and it started off rambunctiously when it undertook to elect a Speaker to replace Henry Clay. In the process, the House dealt Andrew Jackson a setback. The chagrin of southerners in general and Jacksonites in particular was palpable when John W. Taylor of New York was chosen on the second ballot. Taylor had been Speaker before. He had succeeded Clay in 1820, after the Kentuckian went into temporary retirement. At the time, Taylor had alarmed southerners during the Missouri Crisis by endorsing the territory's gradual abolition of slavery as a requirement for Missouri's statehood. Southern sectionalists were understandably suspicious when Taylor assumed the Speakership in December 1825. More importantly for Jacksonites, though, Taylor had always supported John Quincy Adams, who was already grasping for victories wherever he could find them. In fact, the president uncharacteristically urged Taylor to appoint friends of the administration to committees.[35]

The tensions within Congress over Taylor's election, however, were quickly set aside amid the dismay over President John Quincy Adams's first Annual Message (what today is called the State of the Union Address). Unlike his inaugural address, which mainly had contained platitudes, the first Annual Message called for a broad national program of improvement to be aggressively promoted by the federal government. Knowing that the message would set the tone for his presidency, Adams and his cabinet had labored over it for days, which at least made Adams realize his first important presidential state paper was a "perilous experiment." Treasury Secretary Richard Rush, son of the celebrated Philadelphia physician and an ardent nationalist, found it pitch perfect, but the secretary of war, Virginian James Barbour, and Attorney General William Wirt were sure that the message would alienate states' rights southerners. For that reason alone, Henry Clay, who found the message agreeable but quite impolitic, urged Adams to strive for more subtlety. The president only partly heeded this advice. The result was disastrous.[36]

Adams's address arrived in Congress on December 6, 1825, where the members of the Senate and House read it immediately (at the time, the Annual Message was not given as a speech by the president). It opened with an innocuous expression of "gratitude to the Omnipotent Disposer of All Good" for the many blessings enjoyed by the country. That suggested the document would follow the same boilerplate everyone had come to expect from Annual Messages, but the mood greeting this one was different. A considerable number of representatives and senators were still angry over the presidential election and were prepared to take issue with Adams's most anodyne words. It probably would not have mattered even if Adams had furnished a simple, straightforward report about routine items such as foreign affairs, trade, Indian treaties, and American commerce; even the most inoffensive expressions had an electric effect on Congress. Jacksonites in Congress who had already sensed blood in the political waters were ready to bare their teeth.

After the relatively harmless opening, Adams opened himself up to attack. His recommendation that Congress significantly expand the federal government's role in internal improvements was needlessly provocative. His professorial observation that "moral, political, intellectual improvement are duties assigned by the Author of

Our Existence to social no less than to individual man" was perceived as an unseemly attempt to make God Almighty a member of his administration. The secular perspective was no better. Adams's belief that the federal government had an obligation to interpret the constitutional concept of "general welfare" with maximum elasticity brought to mind Alexander Hamilton's intrusive Federalism. Adams's belief that the government had the right and the authority to improve the country's agriculture, commerce, manufacturing, and transportation with active involvement and commensurate spending repelled even those who had been inclined to put aside the nature of his election and give him a fair chance.

The congressional mood grew darker in contemplating the message's budget-busting wish list. Adams urged Congress to fund a broad range of scientific endeavors lest the United States fall behind Europe, in itself a reference that angered men who thought the United States superior to Europe. He wanted exploratory expeditions, a national university, and astronomical observatories, which he described as "light-houses of the skies," a phrase critics found both pretentious and preposterous. He wanted to enlarge the executive and judicial branches to keep pace with the country's growing population and prevent the president and the courts from being "confined to their primitive organization." He wanted Congress to pass laws promoting "the cultivation and encouragement of the mechanic and of the elegant arts, the advancement of literature, and the progress of the sciences, ornamental and profound." The failure to do so, he lectured, "would be treachery to the most sacred of trusts." Nations less free than the United States were exhibiting more resolve by advancing in these areas. Adams called on Congress to cast off the fetters of limited government and move to the front of an international parade of progress. Members of the United States government, he proclaimed, should not be "palsied by the will of our constituents."[37]

Adams's breathtaking Annual Message all but demolished what little goodwill he had among a dwindling cohort of reluctant supporters. His instruction to members of a representative government not to be "palsied" by the will of constituents did more than offend those mindful of their obligations to voters. It suggested the delusion of a man with, at best, a partial and possibly an illegitimate mandate. With his own pen, John Quincy Adams had given thoughtful men cause to condemn him. By abiding Federalists, James Monroe had made himself unpopular, but now, and despite his conversion to Jeffersonian Republicanism in 1808, John Quincy Adams wanted to embrace Federalists while betraying Jeffersonian principles of limited government. Moreover, he wanted everyone to embrace with enthusiasm initiatives that repelled many, and he was willing to censure those who objected as ignorant and even irreligious. Daniel Webster noted how Virginia was "in a great rage with the Message." The reaction was typical among Crawfordites, though, which meant it spread beyond the Old Dominion. The influential Old Republican from North Carolina Nathaniel Macon was aghast.[38]

As a young man, Macon had been an Anti-Federalist firmly opposed to North Carolina's ratification of the US Constitution. When his state joined the Union, Macon continued to oppose the central government's growing power. He had been in the Senate since 1815, where his persistent advocacy of limited government made him a Crawfordite. But Macon was also fair and highly principled, an unequivocal patriot rather than a mere rabble-rouser. It was understandable that Adams's message would trouble him, but the extent of his alarm was revealing. At no time, he recalled, "while the constitution was under consideration," had anyone claimed that the national government would have "the power to authorize banks, roads and canals." The expansion of the executive, the establishment of a naval academy, the absurd lighthouses of the sky, all would increase "executive patronage" and enhance the power of the presidency. The prospect was sobering: "A Government which has complete power over the purse & sword, with a patronage of millions of dollars cannot be easily kept in check by a constitution which by construction or implication can be made to mean whatever a majority may deem expedient or convenient." And just as Clay and Barbour had feared, Adams had awakened in Macon a southerner's vigilance about threats to slavery. "If Congress can make banks, roads, and canals under the Constitution," Macon had already warned, "they can free any slave." He feared that if Adams got his way, nothing would stop "the dreaded spirit of emancipation percolating up."[39]

Adams's message did not just distress southerners. It also made a deadly impression on many in the American heartland. People still in want from economic dislocations found the talk of astronomical observatories and national universities asinine. They needed jobs to put food on their tables, and farmers needed people who could afford their crops. Adams's proposals on tariffs and trade agreements could have offered sensible solutions to the nation's economic problems, but the clumsy way he presented his ideas allowed his enemies to portray them as frivolous while they denounced him for indifference to the plight of ordinary people.

The charge of corruption, the impression of coldness, the seeming embrace of Federalist principles, and the perceived call to ignore the will of the people suggested a government in disarray and helmed by elite incompetents. But one man, who happened to be a putative member of the administration, saw something worse, or at least he said he did. Ever since John C. Calhoun had been defeated in the Pennsylvania convention in the spring of 1824, many had speculated about his loyalties as he glided effortlessly into the vice presidency with no apparent ties to anyone. Cynics—Clay was one, and Crawford another—suspected that Calhoun was merely waiting to judge the durability of Jackson's popularity and that soon the South Carolinian would choose to "carry on business under the firm of the Hero." In a season of high opportunism, it was easy for observers to be cynical, even when—especially when—Calhoun took the high road of principle. His anger over Clay's appointment to the State Department and the implication that it designated Clay as Adams's successor rankled the new vice president. So Calhoun's reaction to the Annual Message could have been sincere in its alarm over violating the Jeffersonian ideal or a convenient way to justify his opposition to the administration he was part of. In any case, Calhoun soon was saying to trusted correspondents that Adams and Clay were worse than incompetent and dishonest. They were incipient tyrants.[40]

Less than a year into his presidency, Adams had a vice president drifting into opposition, a secretary of state under constant assault for being corrupt, Old Republicans angry at his Federalism, and Jackson partisans accusing him of tyranny and incompetence. Meanwhile, men of thoughtful opinions, such as Nathaniel Macon, were in transition from nebulous discontent over Adams's vision to open support for those opposed to it. Macon would never be a Jacksonite, but Adams's first Annual Message sent him on the road to becoming a Jacksonian. Jackson's supporters perhaps could not distinguish between the partisanship stimulating the one and the philosophy animating the other. At the outset of Adams's presidency, many had detected the ever so faint fragrance of blood. After his first Annual Message of December 6, 1825, an uncharted political sea was awash in it.

CHAPTER 11

MACHINE

T HE COMPOSITION OF THE NINETEENTH CONGRESS HAD TO trouble the Adams administration, despite the habit of everyone considering himself a Republican. William H. Crawford's retirement had simplified the division in the House of Representatives to give the president a slight majority there, while Jacksonites held only a paper-thin majority in the Senate. But predictions that this situation indicated more substantial majorities for the administration in the future ignored trends already evident in both houses. In the Senate, pro-Jackson numbers had more than doubled from 12 in the Eighteenth Congress to 25 in the Nineteenth, whereas Adams's supporters only increased by 7. Even in the House of Representatives, the president's majority was never more than 7 seats. Of greater relevance in the House was how 34 former Crawford men had gone over to Jackson and Adams had picked up only 21.

From a position of relative strength, Jacksonites planned to fight the administration over every one of its proposals, especially after discovering they could rely on Old Republicans such as Nathaniel Macon and John Randolph. In the spring of 1826, this alliance almost blocked a sensible foreign policy initiative meant to improve relations with new Latin American republics. The United States had received an invitation to participate in a hemispheric congress in Panama, and Adams found the idea so promising that he had made the mistake of mentioning it in his Annual Message. That alone put southerners on edge because Latin American liberation movements had embraced abolition, and the proposed congress would include the Republic of Haiti's black delegation. Suddenly the sensible idea of sending American representatives to Panama became a sectional controversy that Jacksonites gleefully exploited to thwart and embarrass the administration. Participation in the Panama Congress became one of Secretary of State Henry Clay's pet projects, and that made hobbling it even more enjoyable for his enemies. Clay could not imagine that domestic partisanship would undermine efforts to improve diplomatic relations and forge lucrative trade partnerships. He was quite wrong.[1]

Indeed, the fight over the Panama Congress proved how thin the administration's support was in the legislature. Jackson privately rallied his congressional troops by railing against the project as "dangerous and alarming" and warning that it "might lead to serious & embarrassing consequences." Senators John Eaton and Robert Y. Hayne accused the administration of trying to form "entangling alliances" and shamelessly stoked the fears of nervous southerners. That motive spurred the eccentric Virginian John Randolph's opposition, but he had other causes propelling him as well, including an abiding hatred of Henry Clay. He was an example of the diverse membership of a pro-Jackson movement forming among those who personally loathed the president and Clay as much as they disliked their politics. The proposed mission to the Panama Congress was the first measure of the Adams administration that Randolph openly opposed. He called it "a Kentucky cuckoo's egg, laid in a Spanish-American nest."[2]

Randolph was an Old Republican like Macon, and he could lay credible claim to having founded the rogue wing of Thomas Jefferson's party in the early 1800s, what Randolph called the "Tertium Quids," literally Latin for "third something." The faction came together in response to what it saw as Jefferson's drift from true Republican principles of limited government. Randolph at the time was earning the reputation of a firebrand on top of his existing one as an eccentric as odd mannerisms and a peculiar appearance warned of his nasty streak that could appear from nowhere. He likely suffered from Klinefelter syndrome, which prevented his passage through puberty, and the physical results became increasingly evident over the years. Randolph was at first an oddly old young boy and then an oddly young old man with a skeletal build. His beardless face had the exploded veins of an alcoholic and the wrinkled mesh of an opium addict. The psychological toll of his malady combined with the physical one of these vices made John Randolph a bundle of corrosive inner conflicts. He was a lawyer who never practiced law, a vile contrarian who could be sweetly agreeable, a man with the voice of a woman, and a warm friend who could become a dangerous enemy. "I think he is partially deranged," said one Adams man, "and seldom in the full possession of his reason."[3]

That opinion represented only one of two schools of thought on Randolph. The other recognized the brittle genius evident in Randolph's ability to speak for hours running on days while holding the Senate floor, a form of parliamentary legerdemain that anticipated the filibuster. Others merely saw oratorical "tricks" performed with the voice of "an opera girl." But after rattling on about nothing of any pertinence to the matter under consideration—"I never write out speeches," Randolph boasted—he would then pause, hesitate, and abruptly utter an incisive observation of resounding relevance while stabbing the air with a "spectral finger." Here is how the poet John Greenleaf Whittier described him:

Mirth, sparkling like a diamond shower,
From lips of lifelong sadness;
Clear pictures of majestic thought
Upon a ground of madness.[4]

Shrewd tacticians such as Eaton and Hayne, abetted by Randolph's ability to prolong debates, could manage small triumphs of obstruction. The argument over the American mission to the Panama Congress was a case in point. In the end, Jackson partisans and their unlikely allies were able to hollow out the administration's eventual victory by delaying the decision to send delegates until they were sure to miss the event. Adams and Clay won the vote, but Jackson's forces won the result. It was a theme of American governance for the remainder of Adams's presidency. Nathaniel Macon noted how every one of the administration's measures that it managed to push through was "approved, not by force of argument but votes."[5]

Clay became exasperated by the administration's difficulties early. Kremer's attacks had grated, but Randolph's were blunt, brilliant, and in the closing days of the debate on the Panama mission, defamatory. The shrill Virginian could open wounds when he put his mind to it, as John Eaton noticed with relish. On March 30, 1826, Randolph was in fine form and high dudgeon over a message from President Adams that seemed to lecture the Senate on protocol. "He was a professor, I understand," Randolph sneered. "I wish he had left off the pedagogue when he got into the Executive Chair." But it was not against "the evil genius of the American House of Stuart" that Randolph meant to take his deadliest aim. It was against the malodorous relationship between Adams and Clay, something Randolph likened to "the coalition of Blifil and Black George." Their coming together, he said in mock wonder, was like "the combination, unheard of till then, of the puritan with the black-leg."[6]

The reference shocked every man who heard it that afternoon in the Senate, and it rattled Henry Clay almost senseless when he heard about it. Henry Fielding's frolicsome novel *Tom Jones* featured ribald vignettes and lively characters, such as a hypocritical money-grubber named Blifil and a cowardly cheat called Black George. With his allusion to them, the senator from Virginia had called the president of the United States a fraud and his secretary of state a swindler. Adams shrugged it off as another example of a madman talking rubbish, but Clay measured the offense as warranting his gravest response. He challenged Randolph to a duel.

It took place just across the Potomac in Virginia on April 8, 1826, and afterward was universally regarded as discreditable. A sitting United States senator exchanging gunfire with the secretary of state suggested a self-indulgent disregard for the obligations that came with high office and the public trust. From that vantage, enemies could condemn Clay for engaging in the immoral practice of dueling while at the same time his friends believed the affair would "operate much against" him. Randolph added an unexpected trace of pathos to the episode when he privately told Thomas Hart Benton, Lucretia Clay's cousin, that he had no intention of making her a widow and her children orphans. The sentiment was that of a man trapped in a dangerous ritual. Meanwhile, Clay revealed how deeply his anger had eroded his sense of decorum and decency. He intended to kill John Randolph. Had he been a better marksman, he would have.[7]

As it happened, both men were inept with firearms. For all his verbal ferocity, Randolph had never fought a duel. Clay had been involved in only one previously, which had occurred more than two decades earlier. As they prepared to face off, Randolph was examining his pistol as if it were an exotic animal when he accidentally discharged it and caused a momentary delay while the seconds fussed over dueling etiquette. With his weapon reloaded and the two separated by the proper number of paces, they fired at each other. Randolph hit a stump behind Clay's legs, possibly on purpose, though it's doubtful he could have hit Clay if he had tried. Clay also missed Randolph. They both reloaded and repeated the drill. Clay fired first in the second round and sent a bullet through Randolph's billowing coat, indicating the seriousness of his intent but again missing his mark. Randolph gazed at the torn fabric and looked back up at Clay, who was waiting with his hands down, the spent pistol held limply in one, his face a blank. Randolph brought his pistol up but continued to raise its muzzle until it pointed skyward. He pulled the trigger, exclaiming in unison with the report, "I do not fire at you, Mr. Clay!" The two strode to meet each other halfway. As they shook hands, Randolph chirped, "You owe me a coat, Mr. Clay."[8]

The lighthearted conclusion to the deadly business seemed to promise better times ahead, but the moment of seeming reconciliation was so fleeting it did not last much beyond John Randolph's return to the Capitol. He resumed his attacks on Adams and Clay and would continue them for the next two years, though with a bit more care about his literary allusions. His oft-repeated theme that Andrew Jackson was "the only man in the nation who can be, & ought to be looked to, to rule the affairs of this Country" would have been tiresome had it not been given so many improvisational flourishes that appreciative Jacksonites knew only John Randolph could manage. They were certainly grateful he had managed to stay alive.[9]

━━

MEANWHILE, OUTSIDE OF Congress, Jackson men organized his supporters into something resembling a party machine geared to make already proven techniques more effective and to experiment with new ones. The advantages a partisan press could yield had been abundantly demonstrated throughout the country in the campaign for 1824. That lesson made the absence of a Jackson newspaper in

Washington a glaring deficiency. Even the knowledge that every newspaper had a strong political viewpoint could not diminish how things in print always seemed more valid. A paper claiming that patronage was corrupting government functions and that petty abuses were shattering restraints on power could do so with authority.[10]

The most promising opportunity to establish a Jackson paper in the capital was a faltering one called the Washington *Gazette*, whose editor John Silva Meehan was put up to purchasing and renaming it the *United States Telegraph*. It became a daily under its new moniker, the first issue appearing on February 6, 1826. Meehan ostensibly helmed the *Telegraph*, but he clearly lacked the means to pay the $30,000 that Adams papers reckoned as necessary to bring the *Telegraph* into existence. Meehan's principal contribution to the *United States Telegraph* was its motto, "Power is always stealing from the many to the few," and the Jackson camp did not wait long before easing him out. Meehan didn't object. He even played along with the fiction that his secret underwriters were placing someone on the paper's staff to assist rather than replace him.[11]

Only a few weeks passed before the "assistant" appeared and almost immediately took charge of the *Telegraph*'s operations. Duff Green was a westerner who had been the editor of the Saint Louis *Enquirer*, where he developed a distinctive style that mixed invective with alleged facts and always argued from seemingly unassailable authority. His ties to John C. Calhoun caused some Jackson men to doubt Green's motives, but Old Hickory liked him, and that was all that mattered. By the summer of 1826, Green had bought the *United States Telegraph* from Meehan through a mysterious scheme financed by shadowy backers, although they were clearly Jackson men. Under Green, the *Telegraph* quickly became a major influence on the Jackson press nationwide. It broadcast a coherent, disciplined, and persistent political message that battered the administration and barricaded Jackson's reputation. Americans heard it whether they were gathered at hearths in drowsy village inns or crowded into bars in busy hotels. Duff Green's way of mixing truth with lies to blur the one and cover the other was something genuinely new in American politics, a political witch's brew that addled the truth while titillating the senses. Andrew Jackson liked him.[12]

———

HENRY LEE IV had served in the southern theater during the War of 1812, which nominally made him a military subordinate of Jackson's. His martial exploits were not notable. But even had they been, they would have been minor compared to those of his illustrious father Henry Lee III, better known as the American Revolution's dashing cavalry commander "Light Horse Harry" Lee.[13]

Henry Lee IV was neither dashing nor particularly handsome, which was of little consequence except as it diminished his appeal to marriageable ladies from fine Virginia families. But he was also indolent, which made him wholly unsuited to the demands of a plantation with worn-out soil and a mansion going to seed. By the end of the War of 1812, the best years of the Lee family's impressive estate on Virginia's Northern Neck were behind it, and the mansion—stately Stratford Hall on the Potomac River—had become a burden with a checkered history. One of its most impressive architectural features was a massive stone staircase that descended from an exterior door. Philip Ludwell Lee had made the addition in the mid-eighteenth century, but its beauty was marred for the family when his little boy tumbled down the steps to his death in 1780.[14]

In 1817, Lee married a wealthy heiress named Anne Robinson McCarty, who, with her younger sister Elizabeth, was an orphan in possession of a spectacular inheritance. Henry used Anne's part to refurbish Stratford Hall and refill his coffers. He also became sixteen-year-old Betsy's guardian, which made him the manager of her assets. She came to live with them. The renewed grandeur of the mansion and the cozy nest it provided for this happy family promised a bright future, especially when Anne delivered a baby girl in early 1818. Henry proclaimed little Margaret Lee "beautiful," and Anne and Betsy filled their days doting on her. Margaret was only two years old, though, when the clumsy gait typical of all toddlers sent her hurtling down the same steps that had killed little Philip Lee forty years earlier. In 1820, the impressive stone staircase did more than kill Margaret; it snuffed out all happiness for her parents. Secluded in her room and unable to sleep, Anne began taking laudanum and was soon sneaking opium. Married to a distant and loveless addict, Henry buried himself in expensive amusements, but the worst of his diversions was Betsy. She was nineteen by then, a plump but pretty girl whose most fetching feature was flowing hair the color of chestnuts. Betsy proved an easy mark for Henry's seduction. With the mistress of the house a dope addict and her sister the mistress of her husband, the three of them made Stratford Hall a house of horrors.

When Henry Lee's other vices exhausted Anne's inheritance, he began using his authority as Betsy's guardian to embezzle from hers. By the time rumors had Betsy giving birth to a stillborn child, gossip was rampant about both illicit sex and misappropriated money. People could only frown over Henry Lee's license with his sister-in-law's person, but local authorities took a keen interest in his handling of her finances. The subsequent investigation turned over the rock of Stratford Hall and turned upside down the lives of the people who had been squirming under it. Anne McCarty Lee fled Virginia. Her husband, now dubbed "Black Horse Harry" Lee, slunk away to Fredericksburg, some forty miles distant but a lifetime removed from his ancestral heritage and its venerable family seat. He was the last Lee to own Stratford, which he gave up to cover his debts.[15]

In complete disgrace, he planned to write a history of the War of 1812 and even traveled to gather material for it before his few remaining friends managed to land him a regular job. In the fall of 1825, Chief Justice John Marshall and Vice President John C. Calhoun proved that the Lee name still carried some weight when they persuaded Postmaster General John McLean to hire Black Horse Harry to fill a lowly place in the US Post Office. In one respect, the appointment illustrated John Quincy Adams's insistence that previous and even current political loyalties should not bar any competent man from government service. McLean had been a staunch Calhoun supporter, for instance, and would become an open Jacksonite as time went on, but Adams refused to remove him. Similarly, Lee had supported Jackson in the 1824 race, and this was not held against him a year later. He would later claim it was, but Black Horse Harry talked freely about many things.

As an Andrew Jackson supporter working in a federal government run by John Quincy Adams, Lee found himself balancing his desperate need for a paycheck against the likelihood that its source would offend Old Hickory. The *Nashville Republican*, whose editor had sensitive antennae for detecting traces of disloyalty, attacked Lee as a turncoat who had accepted the job to help Jackson's enemies. Lee scrambled to suppress such notions. He wrote to Old Hickory to deny the charges and assert his unswerving loyalty, and in doing so, he found just the right phrases to turn Jackson's head. Jackson assured Lee that he did not blame him for taking a job he could not live without. From that slight glimmer of sympathy, Lee took considerable solace and began cultivating the good graces of Andrew Jackson.[16]

Despite Lee's disrepute, Jackson men would not let a talented scribbler languish long at the Post Office. They soon tapped him to write a column or two for the *United States Telegraph*, and Duff Green liked the work so much he suggested that Lee resume his historical writing projects and include among them a new biography of

Old Hickory. Lunging at the opportunity, Lee quit his government job and set out again on research journeys funded by generous Jacksonite subsidies. That was how he came to visit New York and had a chat with DeWitt Clinton that he dutifully reported to his new boss at the Hermitage. It was a sign of how Lee's research increasingly focused on current politics rather than historical events. He eventually traveled to Nashville to work with the men closest to Andrew Jackson in the quest for the presidency. There on the Cumberland, Henry Lee would fitfully try to put his life back together, beginning with Anne.

She had fled Virginia for a Tennessee spa famous for its mineral springs. In December 1811, the New Madrid earthquake had cracked open the earth not far from the Hermitage, and from the cleft flowed what entrepreneur William Saunders called "the Fountain of Health," waters that he claimed could cure everything from gangrene to gonorrhea, even drug addiction. At the Fountain of Health, Anne Lee had a modest room and took the waters in the hope of beating opium, but most significantly she met a kindly round lady who first called on her as a courtesy. The old lady did not visit Anne out of curiosity—she knew all too well how visits with that motive made the host feel—but because Anne seemed so wretchedly lonely.

It soon dawned on Anne that she would never know a more stalwart friend than Rachel Jackson, someone who also had felt the cutting whip of gossip. When Anne's husband arrived in Nashville, Rachel smoothed their reconciliation. Anne slowly relented and finally agreed to have Henry move into her modest room at the Fountain of Health. It was among the most incredible second chances in American history, and not only because Henry Lee could turn a phrase both political and poetical. Andrew Jackson heard music in Lee's political writing, but Rachel persuaded Anne to listen to

Henry's quiet cadences and finally let go of her dead child. Anne more than anyone might have thought their story beggared belief, especially as she slowly, reluctantly fell in love again.

———

In June 1826, before his travels took Henry Lee to Nashville, he visited Monticello. Ostensibly, he was trying to interview Thomas Jefferson for an eyewitness account of the Revolution in Virginia, particularly Light Horse Harry's role in it. However, Lee's letter to Andrew Jackson shows he was seeking more immediately valuable information, such as Jefferson's opinion of John Quincy Adams after the Annual Message. Jefferson was too ill to receive anyone when Lee arrived, limiting the visitor's historical investigation to Jefferson's papers. His political investigation proceeded through conversations with members of Jefferson's family. Lee reported to Jackson that they told him of the patriarch's contempt for the current administration and that Jefferson wanted Adams defeated in 1828. This was good news indeed, for even though it had not come from the horse's mouth, the source was close enough to it. That was the way Duff Green liked his details, and it was pleasing to see Henry Lee similarly turning hearsay into hard facts. That talent would make him a worthy addition to the team.[17]

Jefferson would never personally denounce Adams, for in early July it became clear that the Sage of Monticello was dying. Not only did the day of his passing, July 4, fall on the fiftieth anniversary of the adoption of the Declaration of Independence, but it also occurred just hours before John Adams's death in Quincy, Massachusetts. As the news of this spread, newspapers and citizens throughout America marveled over the stunning coincidence. Businesses were shuttered, church bells tolled, and minute guns in communities across the country commenced firing a report every sixty seconds well into the night of whatever day they received the news. Retrospectives on America's Jubilee deemed that the deaths of these two Titans made the day "doubly sacred" with a supernatural omen whose meaning could only be guessed. "They were lovely in their lives," intoned the Reverend Dr. Rowan of the Christopher Street Presbyterian Church in New York City, "and in their deaths they were not divided."[18]

Like all Americans, President John Quincy Adams mourned the loss of two peerless patriots, but the passing of these particular men was an intensely personal blow that saw him briefly set aside his usual cynicism. Adams admired his father as a man of Olympian stature whose passions and ideals had forged an inspiring intellect worthy of not just veneration but emulation. For John Adams, his son's winning the presidency had made him almost immorally proud. John Quincy could also look back fondly on Jefferson as his former mentor. In happier times in Europe, the teen had watched his father, all pepper and spice, and Mr. Jefferson, almost drowsy in speech, trade opinions on gardens, governments, and God. The scenes had etched awe and reverence in his memories of them. The hole their passing left in John Quincy Adams's world was too vast to measure, too gaping to fill.

Adams had known Jefferson was ill, but not until the capital was far along in its preparation for the fiftieth anniversary of the Fourth did he learn that his father in faraway Massachusetts was probably dying. Adams departed for home immediately but only had reached Baltimore before receiving the sad news. The journey to Massachusetts seemed no less urgent, though, which was strange, for it was no longer toward the wizened little man with the watery eyes but only to the numerous ceremonies that would recall him, and imperfectly at that. These were the sort of public obligations that John Quincy Adams found hard to bear in the best of times. Beginning on July 15, he attended "solemnities" in Dedham, Charleston, and Boston on consecutive days and was either so moved or so exhausted by these events that for the first time in his life he took communion.[19]

The deaths of Jefferson and Adams on the day of Jubilee took Jackson men aback because the most obvious beneficiary was John Quincy Adams. The passing of his father would remind citizens of the Founding and was likely to establish a sympathetic link to the son and revive dormant loyalties. Jackson supporters pondered a way to prevent this from happening and finally settled on claiming the mantle of the other dead Founder, the one Henry Lee had heard was opposed to John Quincy Adams. It was only a slight leap to interpret that purported opposition to the administration as overt support for Andrew Jackson, and because Jefferson was dead, it was all the easier to put words in his mouth. "Is this an omen that Divinity approbated the whole course of Mr. Jefferson," wondered Andrew Jackson, "and sent an angel down to take him from the earthly Tabernacle on this national Jubilee." Naturally following from this was the possibility that "the death of Mr. Adams" was "an omen that his political example as President and adopted by his son, shall destroy this holy fabric created by the virtuous Jefferson."[20]

Beguiled by the tactic of invoking Jefferson, Crawfordites across the country found a comfortable home in the Jackson camp just as most of them already had in the confines of Congress, but a bit more subtlety than Jackson's obvious comparison was needed. Old Hickory's operatives first had Andrew Jackson appointed chairman of the Nashville committee planning the commemoration of the deaths. Then from that position Jackson chose Nashville Junto member Felix Grundy as the eulogist for the town's ceremonies. Grundy crafted a piece worthy of Antony addressing the Roman throng. He spoke of the presidency of John Adams with faint praise, emphasizing how it had given Americans the chance to compare Adams and Jefferson and how the election of 1800 made clear their preference for Mr. Jefferson's mode of governance. When Jefferson was inaugurated, Grundy mused, he had laid out "those great and salutary principles upon which this government required to be administered," including "the support of the state governments in all their rights, as the most competent administrations for our domestic concerns, and the surest bulwarks against anti-republican tendencies." Warming to that theme, Felix Grundy made the bulk of his eulogy a campaign speech that lauded Thomas Jefferson as president and philosopher. In the balance of achievements, John Adams had merely helped with the Declaration of Independence but had sadly suffered a failed presidency.[21]

With the mantle of George Washington already on Jackson's shoulders, Thomas Jefferson's death provided the opportunity to tie another revered Founder to Old Hickory. Adams had only his father's legacy, which was that of an unsuccessful president who had suppressed dissent. Grundy's eulogy thus became a campaign speech for Andrew Jackson that celebrated Jefferson's virtues and implied that they were Jackson's as well. Crawfordites listening to the comparison were becoming easier to convince that it was valid and that Jackson was the inheritor of the Jeffersonian tradition of limited government and fiscal prudence.

———

DURING THE SUMMER and fall of 1826, Jackson newspapers promoted Jackson loyalists for Congress over men who had supported the Adams agenda. Reprising one of the tactics of 1824, Jacksonites formed committees in major cities and state capitals, but the one in Philadelphia unwittingly awakened a slumbering critic when it issued a circular listing reasons why everyone should vote for Old Hickory in 1828. Former Pennsylvania senator Jonathan Roberts thundered out of retirement to publish an open letter condemning Jackson as a military despot guilty of appalling crimes. Roberts was among those who had found Jackson objectionable during the

Seminole War investigation in 1819. At the time, Senator Roberts had told of Jackson swaggering around the capital with a menacing entourage and threatening to cut off the ears of John Wayles Eppes. His opinion of the general had not improved over the years. The prominent Philadelphia merchant Chandler Price, who led the Pennsylvania Jackson Committee, tried to dismiss Roberts as a partisan pest, and Jackson newspapers suggested that Clay had written the Roberts letter. But these were weak responses made no stronger by the boast that Roberts "had been literally torn to atoms by the Jackson writers in Philadelphia."[22]

Much to Jacksonite chagrin, Roberts proved tenacious enough to give the impression of a resolute man rather than a mere nuisance. He was one of the few people left in public life who hailed from the ranks of artisans rather than of attorneys, and his forthright manner was a hallmark of his character. "True courage," as he defined it, "consists in meeting danger with presence of mind, not with insensibility."[23]

When Roberts followed his initial attack of July 10, 1826, with another letter responding to Chandler Price's dismissiveness, he questioned Jackson's role in the victory at New Orleans, and that criticism instantly made him a real threat. The claim that Secretary of War James Monroe and President James Madison were equally if not more responsible for the victory and the implication that the posturing "Hero" was a glory-hunting blowhard infuriated Old Hickory and his supporters. Roberts swatted these angry hornets by reviving the charge that Jackson had threatened to carve up Eppes over the Senate report on the Seminole War. Adams administration papers gave these letters wide currency, which, to the Jackson men, made it sound as though Jonathan Roberts was begging for destruction. As tempting as assassination by smear was to the Jacksonites, calm ones among them had to admit that Roberts had never strayed from a narrow path in either his personal or public life.[24]

They did what they could. Jackson personally took on the Eppes story by writing directly to George Wilson, the editor of the Nashville *Gazette*, to refute it, in a way. He had never gone near the Senate during that visit to Washington, he said, but that was hardly a blanket denial that he had made the threat. He selectively recalled other aspects of the time he spent in 1819 in the capital. He insisted that he had met with no one in the government except President Monroe and Secretary of War Calhoun, but the truth was that he met with Secretary of State John Quincy Adams at least twice and had been a dinner guest at the Adams home.[25]

For his part, John Eaton tried to counter the "military chieftain" charges with elaborate arguments he could by now recite in his sleep, but having to revisit Jackson's conduct at the Battle of New Orleans was unsettling. Everyone in the Jackson camp was accustomed to defending the imposition of martial law and explaining the Dominic Hall controversy, but all of that had happened after the battle. A challenge to the military achievement on the Rodriguez Canal placed Jackson men on uncharted ground. Old Hickory helped gather evidence to sustain his status as Hero, and Eaton deployed it the best he could, but Jackson became quite touchy over this new and unexpected line of attack on a previously sacrosanct subject.[26]

And it was his obsessive vigilance about his record at New Orleans that embroiled Jackson in a foolish controversy with Secretary of the Navy Samuel Southard. He was a holdover from the Monroe administration whose loyalty to his former boss was tinged with affectionate regard. It was an unusual sentiment for Monroe to evoke because most of the former president's subordinates judged him well-meaning but dense. Southard was an unusual man, though, in his belief that a favor merited a measure of friendship in return. Monroe had never been anything but kind to him, and the same could be said for Southard's colleague John Quincy Adams. The two had served together in the cabinet only a few months, because Southard took office late in Monroe's presidency, but Adams recognized him as a quiet, competent administrator who kept his desk tidy, his department trim, and his habits modest. He was among the first men Adams asked to stay on, and Southard had given his hand on it, though with some reluctance. Southard was quiet, but not stupid, and he realized that the nature of Adams's election portended some disagreeable moments in his presidency's future. The one that occurred in the summer of 1826 was an example.

During a brief trip in July to escape Washington's heat, Southard was visiting Dr. John Spotswood Wellford near Fredericksburg, Virginia, and enjoying after-dinner wine with Wellford's neighbors. Local physician John H. Wallace was a confirmed Jackson supporter and bluntly declared that Old Hickory's victory at New Orleans alone qualified him for the presidency. Southard disagreed. Jackson's achievement at New Orleans was indeed commendable, he said, but the instructions, the men, and the materiel supplied by James Monroe had contributed to the victory. The exchange was hardly confrontational, and the two men retired the topic as a point of genial disagreement.[27]

Jackson heard about the conversation, and in the worst possible way. Dr. Wallace's recollection of his exchange with Southard made it seem less amiable, and either he irresponsibly mischaracterized Southard's remarks or simply garbled them. As a result, by the time the story reached the Hermitage, it had Southard describing Jackson as leaving New Orleans until Monroe ordered him back to defend the city. Jackson's temper detonated. The story mimicked the charge from that troublemaking Pennsylvanian Jonathan Roberts, which struck Old Hickory as beyond coincidence. Jackson detected a coordinated attack by sinister conspirators.[28]

He dashed off a letter to Sam Houston instructing him to visit Southard and demand the source for his vile calumny about New

Orleans. Jackson included another letter with the one to Houston, this one expressly for Southard, which Houston was to deliver by hand. It was Jackson's personal demand for Southard's source. Houston left for the capital with Jackson's epistolary bomb in his luggage, but he had hardly departed before Old Hickory had a new target. Another letter to Sam Houston followed him to Washington with instructions to find the good Dr. Wallace and obtain details about this disgraceful summer conversation.[29]

The reappearance of Jackson's temper dismayed John Eaton, Sam Houston, Hugh Lawson White, and other Jackson men in Washington. Houston took his time tending to the Southard matter, and letting it rest kept it from disturbing the off-year congressional elections. Jackson picked up two Senate seats for a total of 27 to Adams's 20 and gained a majority of 111 to 101 in the House. It was horrible news for the administration.

After it could not do any harm, Sam Houston finally talked with John Wallace, who apparently was surprised by the visit and alarmed over its potential meaning. As a consequence, Houston came away from it pensive. The affair was no affair at all, it seemed, in light of Wallace's more favorable account of his harmless sparring with Southard. Houston thought it best to return Jackson's letter with some gentle counsel from trusted friends, John Eaton foremost among them, to forget the entire matter. Houston assured his boss that he, Eaton, and others would handle it, but just in case Jackson felt compelled to communicate with Samuel Southard, "let it be in the mildest, calmest tone of expression." Houston tried to distract Old Hickory with a guarantee that Eaton's published letter responding to Jonathan Roberts was being well received.[30]

Jackson's impatience had already drawn him back to his desk, though, and the letter that resulted crossed Houston's reassuring one to him. He was anxious to hear Southard's response to his original message, which Houston had not delivered. A brooding

Jackson had convinced himself that Henry Clay was behind everything, and he was hell-bent on exposing the brigand "naked before the american people." Armed with proof of Clay's treachery, Jackson relished the idea of using it "to his political, & perhaps, to his actual destruction."[31]

As 1827 dawned, Jackson's imagination was summoning the phantoms of additional conspirators. Just twelve months earlier, he had noticed, in reference to the anniversary of the Battle of New Orleans, that "the 8th of Janry has this year passed without notice in the City of Washington," but at the time he had put a positive face on this omission. He had understood that it "might be dangerous now in Washington, to commemorate military chieftains." But the Roberts letters and the Southard conversation changed everything for him, and the absence of a January 8 event in 1827 could have set off another fulmination. His friends tried to prevent that by scheduling a commemorative banquet in the capital where Hugh Lawson White would make remarks appropriate to the occasion. Houston cheerily reported to Jackson that he could "not conceive the happy effect of our friend Judge Whites speech & toast." Houston also made his most direct reference yet to the damage a show of temper would inflict on Jackson's image as a calm statesman. Your friends, said Houston, are "fearful that you will let the administration; or their hireling miscreants, provoke you to some course; which; may eventually turnout to their advantage."[32]

This letter was on its way to the Hermitage when another from Jackson crossed it to cause consternation among his beleaguered confidants in Washington. Jackson had composed a new letter to Southard, which he included in his mail to Houston. Jackson ordered him to deliver it without delay. Nobody took much comfort in Jackson's assurance that this new letter to Southard was "calm & decorous."[33]

John Eaton read this most recent letter to Southard in which Jackson revisited the exchange with Wallace as reported to him, especially the galling part about Monroe having ordered him back to defend New Orleans. Jackson demanded that Southard tell Sam Houston the source for that falsehood. By now, Eaton and the others were deeply worried about a spreading controversy threatening to career out of control. Hugh Lawson White's "speech & toast" at the anniversary banquet had tried to end the loose talk about New Orleans by insisting that the battle was a Jackson victory achieved without any significant help from anyone else. While this could have mollified Andrew Jackson, it removed James Monroe from the event altogether, and he was soon rumored to be angry about the omission. Eaton did not care about the former president's feelings—he didn't trust Monroe and even suspected that he, rather than Clay, was behind Southard's story—but Eaton did fret over the widening circle of people for Jackson to target as conspirators. To lump the former secretary of war who was now the former president in with the current secretaries of the navy and state and describe them as an antagonistic cabal could make the accuser look unhinged. Eaton was therefore careful in the way he reported Monroe's anger to Jackson. He dismissed Monroe as "one of the coalition gentry," merely another member of the pretentious political class that included the corrupt Clay and the wine-sipping Southard. Eaton insisted that this so-called elite feared Jackson's victory in 1828 as inevitable and were becoming desperate. As Houston had done, Eaton warned Jackson to be on his guard, to "be cautious—be still—be quiet; & let your friends fight the arduous battle."[34]

Despite his efforts to blunt the mention of Monroe, Eaton soon had reason to regret having done so. Instead of convincing Jackson that the former president was feckless, it had the opposite effect: Jackson added Monroe to the list of people conspiring against him. Meanwhile, Houston stalled as long as he could before taking Jackson's second letter to Secretary Southard. The latter gravely accepted it, for like all of Washington, he knew of the controversy. He even knew that there had been an undelivered letter and after reading the one deemed acceptable, he had to wonder what the first one had said. In his response, Southard managed a level tone that explained he had never said that Jackson had left his post, that he had merely defended his friend James Monroe, and that he had never uttered a word criticizing Jackson.

Southard sealed this letter and gave it to Houston, but he refused to take it unopened because Jackson wanted it copied before its dispatch to the Hermitage. Among his multiplying suspicions was the belief that people were tampering with his mail, and he wanted to make sure that the Southard letter he received was the one Southard had written. Houston asked a flabbergasted Southard to open the envelope and place the letter in an unsealed one. Southard impatiently refused to do this. He gave the communication to Postmaster General John McLean to see to its delivery. He had no way of knowing at the time that he was handing over the letter to a secret Jackson supporter. At this point, though, Samuel Southard would have believed anything. Hoping to calm himself, Southard recounted the entire episode in a long aide-mémoire that consumed several nights of his time and many sheets of his stationery. It did not help that he would receive one more letter from Andrew Jackson, this one accusing Southard of lying about the conversation with Wallace.[35]

Southard tried to let it go, but Jackson would not. Newspapers managed to lower the tone when Jackson turned over the correspondence to Duff Green who published it in the *United States Telegraph* and thereby set off bickering among partisan editors. Green thought that the way Jackson had handled the incident reflected "much credit" on his patron. The pro-Adams Richmond *Whig* countered that Jackson's letters only proved his capacity for "violence and in-temperance," and if Jackson's grammar and spelling had gone uncor-rected by Green, they knew it would open some eyes.[36]

Samuel Southard at least knew the truth of that. As he sought the counsel of his friends, he showed Jackson's letters to one of them. Virginia congressman John Taliaferro found the substance and grammar to be "a vain, ungentlemanly production not worth even notice." Southard had to take notice, though. The prospect of Andrew Jackson as president had been distasteful to him in 1824. Now, he contemplated 1828. The letter with demands had made him angry. The one calling him a liar made him sick. The man who had written them could never be president.[37]

CHAPTER 12

INK

NEWSPAPERS STILL OPERATE THE WAY THEY DID IN THEIR HEY-day about a half century ago, but their profitability and status have dramatically waned. Even in the mid-twentieth century, radio was eroding the press's dominance in politics. Television ac-celerated the decline, and the Internet has all but completed it. In the early nineteenth century, however, newspapers were becoming the primary medium of political information, opinion, and debate. It was the result of innovative and relatively inexpensive printing processes, an increase in literacy, and a people hungry for news about politics now that more of them could vote. Even modest and unas-suming sheets in the most remote places achieved a prominence for readers who devoured the information they offered, regardless of its provenance or reliability.

The newspaper transcended the problems of private business concerns. It was an oddity in a free market—a profit-making entity perceived as a public service. The Constitution's First Amendment protected newspaper content, and the federal treasury subsidized the papers themselves through postal privileges, either in the form of subsidized rates or free delivery, on the assumption that informed people would make wise decisions at the ballot box. Thus newspaper publishers surmounted one of their greatest challenges, which was the business of placing their product into the public's hands. People expected newspapers to be a part of their daily lives. That became a reality by the early nineteenth century as the belief that government should sponsor the press's educational role led to a proliferation of post offices. It meant influence and profit for smalltown printers and big-city publishers alike.

The favor shown toward newspapers, in fact, started with the constitutional republic. In 1789, Congress and the executive departments relied on newspapers to publish statutes and other public business of the legislature. In the capital, fortunate newspapers won lucrative contracts to become the government's papers of record, and politicians won free publicity in return. Indeed, from the earliest days of the republic, local and national politicians understood newspapers not only as a means of disseminating information but also as an economical and efficient way to promote agendas and control political discourse. Political parties used newspapers to win office, and once members of that party held office, they used the public till to purchase additional press support, making newspapers another patronage recipient as well as an ancillary part of the government. The selection of a public printer to print laws and legislative journals became a time-consuming and contentious process that occupied Congress far more than it should have. And the more obvious abuses of this patronage raised fears that the press was not merely being used to promote good citizenship but was being corrupted to serve self-interested party aims with the public's money.

Immediately after the inauguration of John Quincy Adams in March 1825, his administration faced attacks focusing on the nexus of patronage, press, and post office. The accusation that the administration was using the mail for campaign activities exasperated Adams men because Jacksonites in Congress were obviously guilty of the charge themselves. They placed their franks (the free postage congressmen used to correspond with constituents) on wrapping paper they sent to constituents who, in turn, used it to mail pamphlets and newspapers postage-free. Another common charge was that the administration used its appointive power for political gain and to control public opinion.[1]

Thomas Hart Benton sponsored bills to remove such power from the executive, but when they failed to pass, charges continued to mount that Adams and his minions were using government appointments in exchange for support. The accusation struck men within the administration as most ironical. They knew that the overly scrupulous Adams would never use his power to help his cause. Instead, he allowed department heads and local federal officials to make their own appointments, a practice that saw Jacksonites "fattening on the loaves & fishes . . . allowing the very money which they receive at the hands of the admnson to hire men to abuse" it. Adams supporters were mystified that the president tried to mollify his enemies with appointments because the practice only "served to neutralize a few political opponents" and mostly "alienated the affections, and cooled the ardour of a host of friends."[2]

As secretary of state, Henry Clay wielded enormous patronage power through the award of printing contracts, and unlike Adams, he did not hesitate to reward loyalists and punish opponents. He retaliated against Amos Kendall's *Argus of Western America* by canceling all of its government printing contracts when it began attacking the administration. The howling of Jackson men became less credible when their members in Congress, in turn, rewarded Duff Green for his efforts. At the end of 1827, they ousted Joseph Gales and William Seaton of the *National Intelligencer* from their long-held position as Senate printers and selected the *United States Telegraph* just when Green sorely needed the lucrative plum to continue his campaign work. Clay could grimly recall that it had been him as Speaker in 1819 who had pushed for the law allowing each house of Congress to select its printer.[3]

The breadth and intensity of Jacksonite newspaper strategy forced opponents to scramble to explain their every deed and mount defenses against every assault. It prevented the Adams camp from forming a coherent program for reelection and made it easier for the Jackson party to get out its message—messages, really, because they varied depending on the region of the country. Jackson's managers wanted to convey information as widely as possible. Their masterful use of newspapers achieved this end with remarkable success. Their most enviable accomplishment was making manipulation passive rather than active. They acted as if they wanted to determine what people desired while actually nudging them to embrace what Jacksonites wanted. With that approach, the press could be portrayed as indispensable in educating voters even though in reality it was working to promote confidence in Jackson and subvert support for Adams and Clay.

=====

ONE OF THE most effective Jackson newspapermen started his journalistic career as a Clay partisan. Originally from Massachusetts, Amos Kendall came to Kentucky in 1814 at twenty-four years of age to work as a tutor, and it was Lucretia Clay who hired him to teach her children. Her husband was in Ghent negotiating the end of the War of 1812. Kendall spent about a year in the job, but he found the children difficult and stayed on only because "one of the principal inducements for accepting Mrs. Clay's offer . . . was the hope of profiting by Mr. Clay's friendship."[4]

By the time Henry Clay returned from abroad, Kendall had become the editor of the Frankfort *Argus of Western America*. He attached himself to the important Kentuckian with exceptional vigor, as Clay's almost immediate resumption of the Speakership in the

House of Representatives meant he had attractive favors to hand out. Kendall's support for Clay in the election of 1824 made the *Argus of Western America* an eloquent advocate, but everything the young man did carried the odor of opportunism. When the 1824 election wound up in the House of Representatives, Kendall reassured Clay that whatever his vote, "the *Argus* will not complain." When the majority of the Kentucky delegation voted for Adams against instructions from the Kentucky legislature, Kendall did not hesitate to let Clay know that people were urging him to drop his allegiance to him. But, Kendall claimed, he could not turn his back on a man whose family had shown him such kindness. Once when Kendal was quite ill, Lucretia Clay had nursed him back to health, and Henry Clay had aided him when Kendall's wife of five years died suddenly, leaving him with four small children. The plight of the mourning widower touched Henry's and Lucretia's hearts, and Clay loaned him $1,500 to get him past the rough patch. Two months later Kendall was asking for more.[5]

Not long after the election of Adams and the appointment of Clay, Kendall asked for even more. In April 1825 he bluntly requested a government post "with a liberal compensation attached to it." Such a sinecure would give him the means, he told Clay, to continue writing for newspapers and "take some pride in vindicating you from the aspersions with which your enemies would overwhelm you." Kendall went on editing the *Argus* and peppering Clay with letters while waiting impatiently for his patron to reward his loyalty, but when Clay finally offered him a post, Kendall sniffed that the salary was not nearly high enough. Clay likely suspected that the days of Kendall taking pride in vindicating him were numbered.[6]

It is difficult to say whether Jacksonites became Kendall's friends to encourage him to turn the *Argus* against the Adams administration or if they encouraged the turn because they were already his friends. Initially, Kendall refrained from attacking Henry Clay, but his final shred of loyalty was forgotten by the summer of 1826. There remained the awkward business of owing Clay money and the even more awkward business of selling out a man who kindly extended the loan's due date, but Kendall's new friends were working on that. In the meantime, Jackson supporter Governor Joseph Desha saw value in Kendall's relationship with Clay, for pretending to be Clay's friend was a way to mine him for information damaging to the administration. Kentucky senator Richard M. Johnson, a stalwart Jackson man, told Duff Green that if Kendall could pay off his loan, he would join the attacks on Henry Clay with brio. Green had no trouble finding someone who would help with Kendall's finances. Senator Martin Van Buren was in a generous mood, had some extra cash, and had been pondering his options now that William Crawford was finished.[7]

Freed from his financial obligation to the secretary of state, Kendall behaved like "a famished wolf." He opened a direct correspondence with Andrew Jackson while publishing in the *Argus* a series of public letters directed at Clay. They were cleverly constructed smears that posed questions that had no answers and posited rumors as verified facts. Kendall told Clay that one of the secretary's close friends had revealed the ruse about his having made a principled decision to support Adams. Kendall said this friend had told him three weeks before the House vote that Adams intended to appoint Clay to the State Department in exchange for his support. A few weeks of practicing this technique made Kendall pitch perfect at it. In a later public letter, he was able to assert without blinking an eye a plain falsehood that had Clay striking the bargain with Adams only after Jackson had honorably rebuffed Clay's overtures.[8]

Clay had documentary proof that showed he intended to support Adams as soon as he knew the Electoral College results in the fall of 1824. He had said as much in a letter to Francis Preston Blair before he met with Adams. Kendall almost certainly knew about this letter and apparently had seen its contents because Blair coedited the *Argus*. He had become a Jackson man, but he had not wholly cast off Clay, who was a friend of long standing. Yet Kendall safely gambled that Clay would not ask Blair to publish the letter. In it, Clay had indeed said he would support Adams, but he had described the decision as "a choice of evils." Making that phrase public would embarrass both the president and his secretary of state.[9]

Clay decided against publishing the letter, as Kendall suspected he would, but he did put out a lengthy pamphlet containing the sworn recollections of friendly witnesses. They independently related their knowledge of Clay's intention to support Adams regardless of personal considerations. This impressive production by Clay was nevertheless a waste of his time. Its length and the public's fatigue over an issue that most people had already made up their minds about meant that comprehensive explanations went unread. Clay's friends in Kentucky tried to help by having the legislature declare him innocent of all charges, but Jacksonites used the debate over the resolution to demand a full legislative investigation into Clay's behavior. The resulting testimony ultimately exonerated him, but Jacksonite newspapers, especially Kendall's *Argus*, reported on the event to emphasize the serious nature of the charge. Unlike Clay's methodical pamphlet, Kendall's coverage kept the "corrupt bargain" before the public in the worst way.[10]

In early 1828, Kendall began insisting that damning letters nobody had ever seen nevertheless existed and should be produced. They were purportedly messages from Clay to friends, including Blair, that had Adams promising the State Department in return for support. The ploy placed Clay in the impossible position of having to prove that Kendall's imagined letters were a figment rather than a fact. At the same time, Blair's keeping Clay's letter private led people to suspect the worst about it, and Clay's friends dolefully suspected that was Blair's intention. With Clay's permission, though,

Blair allowed a few trusted men to read Clay's letter and certify that
it contained no incriminating admissions. Kendall almost immediately suborned one of these men and garbled the letter's contents
to put Clay in the worst light. Kendall relentlessly pounded away.
He accused Clay of trying to bribe him with the State Department
job, a claim Clay easily disputed with Kendall's letters asking for
the post and then refusing it because the salary was too low. But the
first version with the accusation was the one that lingered in public
memory, while its documented refutation was buried under a deafening chorus of "corrupt bargain" and references to incriminating
correspondence that did not exist.[11]

"A vindictive temper" characterized Amos Kendall, said his
enemies, who were numerous. He had "no admiration of noble
qualities—no sympathy with suffering, no conscience; but a clear
head—a cold heart—a biting wit—a sarcastic humor—a thorough
knowledge of the baser parts of human nature, and a perfect familiarity with everything that is low in language, and vulgar in
society." Lucretia Clay would have never imagined it of the young
man who taught her children Euclidian geometry, but she had her
wounded husband as proof of Kendall's character.[12]

═══

FEW NEWSPAPER EDITORS could match Amos Kendall's vitriol and
penchant for the personal attack, but many Jackson editors were
more popular and probably more useful, in the end. Duff Green and
his *United States Telegraph* was one example, because of its ability to
spread centrally generated information about the latest story or attack far faster than the old technique of correspondence committees.
Green became highly skilled in lifting items from other papers and
integrating them into the *Telegraph* where they reached the paper's
extensive national audience. Overall, the *United States Telegraph*'s editor seemed born to politics, with the thrust and parry of it his second

nature. He was more than a disseminator of information. He gathered it in such a way as to make himself a central conduit and fount of political trends throughout the country. He became an indispensable figure in Jackson's operation in the capital, and many within the campaign recognized him as Old Hickory's political field general. Green's connections spanned to the East and West and reached from lowly clerks to influential legislators, but he was also able to maintain jovial relations with ordinary people, a folksy touch that made local Jackson men believe they were an important part of the team.

Adams and Clay supporters pulled no punches once they realized what Duff Green's ownership of the *United States Telegraph* meant. They described him as a scoundrel, a poltroon, a poseur, and a rabble-rouser. All their labels, however, struck Green as mildly amusing because they had the effect of transforming, by contrast, his scandalous attacks on Adams and Clay into measured and purportedly factual pieces pointing out the administration's failings. Green resorted to other innovations to defame without restraint, such as the weekly "Extra" that he began issuing in March 1828. It was quite popular, with print runs of twenty thousand by that summer. Extras were exclusively devoted to news about candidates and information about the pending election and thus served as guides and manuals for operatives in the field. The tactic proved effective enough to inspire imitation by the Adams press with the *National Journal* publishing a pamphlet extra called *We the People* and Charles Hammond's Cincinnati *Gazette* similarly bringing out a monthly called *Truth's Advocate*. Whether in the service of Old Hickory or "Johnny Q.," these Extras were free-wheeling exercises tailored for rural audiences that liked their politics to be ear-biting, eye-gouging fracases. That meant the publications trafficked in defamation and insults more zestfully than their parent newspapers, though observant readers of both would have found it hard to see much difference.

One result of the pamphlets was that the competence of candidates for high office was gauged according to personal characteristics and human frailty. Attacking Jackson, the Adams press dwelled on his educational deficiencies, printing examples of his amusing grammatical lapses in letters, some of them fabricated but many accurate. Peter Force's *National Journal* declared that Old Hickory's lack of formal education alone disqualified him for the presidency, and the New York *American* insisted that everyone knew people wrote letters for Jackson, and no one was deceived about his illiteracy. In response, Jackson's defenders filled countless newspaper columns with variations on the central theme that as long as Jackson understood the rights of the people and the duties of Congress, proper spelling was irrelevant. A satirical piece in the *United States Telegraph* described a cabinet meeting devoted entirely to President Adams conducting a spelling lesson. He admonished the secretaries to be especially careful with their spelling and grammar because they had never led troops in battle. Duff Green even invoked the "corrupt bargain" with a sally about Jackson's being ignorant, as in ignorant of "the simple words, bargain, intrigue, and management, as not to be able to spell them at all."[13]

Jackson's defenders even printed the letters of other prominent Americans to show that they too contained spelling errors, including letters written by Harvard-educated Adams. They painted Adams as an effete snob who had once made such an obscure literary reference in a toast to militiamen that he later had to explain it. The tale was true, pointing to a singular ability of Adams's supporters to have nothing go right. In another instance, their plans to print a collection of marginally literate Jackson letters went wrong when the printer carefully proofed them to correct all the misspelled words. It turned out like many other attempts to portray Jackson as an illiterate rube that comically went awry, and all of them tended to provoke people already suspicious of elite intellectuals. In sum, the attacks on Jackson were not helpful to Adams or harmful to Jackson, and in some quarters, they boosted him.[14]

======

DUFF GREEN DESPISED Henry Clay for personal as well as political reasons. Green thought the BUS was a foul nest of unscrupulous predators, and Clay's strong support of the institution would have been enough to provoke Green's ire, but the editor was also a cousin of Humphrey Marshall, an enemy of Clay's who had been the only person to fight Clay in a duel before John Randolph. Green's *Telegraph* sometimes nipped at Clay's ankles as if out of boredom, accusing him and other cabinet members of making frequent campaign trips on the public's dime. Other more severe charges crossed a libelous line. He suggested that the secretary of state came by his income dishonestly, such as by serving as the executor of a friend's estate only to embezzle from it to live in luxury.[15]

In June 1826, Duff Green revived the allegation of the "corrupt bargain" against Clay and Adams in the *United States Telegraph* by claiming he had proof that Clay had indirectly approached Jackson to offer the same deal he later made with Adams. Weeks passed with his readership's impatience to see Green's evidence mounting, so he set into motion a series of events that came close to smashing the "corrupt bargain" story and very nearly tarnished Andrew Jackson's credibility.[16]

It had all stemmed from someone in Jackson's inner circle, likely John Eaton, informing Green about James Buchanan's meeting with Jackson in either late December 1824 or early January 1825—the dates were muddled, which turned out to be significant. Possibly Eaton by the spring of 1826 really believed Buchanan had been an emissary from Henry Clay. Jackson was at least prepared to remember it that way. When Green learned this, he promised that summer to expose Clay, but months passed, and Congress went into recess.

That fall, Green wrote to Buchanan in Pennsylvania and ominously warned that he would not be able to keep his name out of the affair for much longer. James Buchanan read Green's letter with considerable alarm.[17]

Trouble always found Buchanan. Talent, intelligence, and hard work had seen him graduate from college with honors, but only after he had narrowly escaped expulsion. As a prosperous attorney in Lancaster, he seemed to thrive, but his ill-starred romance with Anne Coleman ended with a broken engagement, her untimely death, and her father's everlasting enmity. The experience, it was later said, made Buchanan into a confirmed and permanent bachelor, though whispers hinted at other reasons for his never marrying. For a time, his public career was mercifully uneventful. He entered politics as much to expand his law practice as to advance a political philosophy, and he was a Federalist mainly because his father had been one. Buchanan remained one for only as long as it wasn't a liability. By the time of the presidential contest of 1824, he had been in Congress four years performing mundane services such as serving on the House's agricultural committee while participating in his state's Jacksonite surge. He was still seen as an innocuous man when he went to visit Andrew Jackson weeks before the House vote. In his plan to help Jackson win the presidency, all he had wanted was Jackson's statement that he might appoint Henry Clay to his cabinet and bar Adams from his administration. That was how James Buchanan remembered it, vividly. Now he read and reread Duff Green's letter with mounting agitation. There was no mistaking it: trouble had found him again.

Buchanan promptly answered Green. He tried to buy time by claiming his absence from the capital during the congressional recess left him ignorant of any controversy. He implored Green to let him study the newspapers and not to reveal anything in the interval. Buchanan indeed recalled his meeting with Jackson, he said, but he also flatly declared that he had carried no authority to speak for Henry Clay or any of Clay's friends. In a pathetic attempt to end speculation about his part in the affair, Buchanan emphasized how Clay's behavior after the House vote was enough proof that he had struck a bargain with Adams.[18]

Green studied this letter with its direct declaration from James Buchanan denying that he had approached Jackson with a Clay proffer. The editor's alchemy required at least a particle of truth to make a lie seem golden, and Buchanan had not supplied it. Jacksonites were going to have to prove the "corrupt bargain" in some other way.

There was also a lack of evidence in Andrew Jackson's correspondence archive. He and Buchanan were friendly acquaintances but hardly friends, as would be expected between an established celebrity and an insignificant congressman nearly a quarter century his junior. Jackson had kept up a sporadic exchange of letters with Buchanan after returning to Tennessee in the spring of 1825, a correspondence that displayed an almost slavish allegiance on the part of the young Pennsylvanian. What those letters did not contain was a single mention of their January 1825 meeting, let alone details that were now being bruited as proof that Clay was a double-dealing huckster. In fact, their meeting had been an awkward event. Buchanan had asked Jackson to do something he would not and then later had vaguely mischaracterized what Jackson had said to him. Had Buchanan been brokering a deal for Clay, Old Hickory would have discussed it in these letters, particularly after he was convinced that Clay had been in a similar negotiation with Adams.[19]

In fact, not until the spring of 1827 did the matter dubiously reappear under the banner of new "facts." Making it even more questionable was an expanding cast of characters, specifically one named Carter Beverley. In March 1827, Beverley visited the Hermitage and heard Jackson state that he knew Clay had made a deal with Adams because an emissary from Clay had tried to strike one with him. It is possible Jackson did not know about the failure of Duff Green's efforts in this direction, but even if he was unaware that Buchanan had explicitly denied any connection to Clay, Jackson had to realize it was wrong to assert one because he himself knew that it was not true. To make matters worse, Jackson now deliberately embellished the January 1825 meeting for a loquacious man with a reputation for repeating private conversations overheard at dinner parties.

Trading in loose gossip was only one feature of Carter Beverley's untrustworthiness. Like Henry Lee, Beverley was one of those sons of Virginia who hailed from a good family but managed distinction only in disgrace. "It is in every farmer's power to live within his means," Beverley once sagely observed, as if to prove the rule by being its exception. The father of six children, and the wastrel husband of a long-suffering wife, he lost their patrimony to profligacy, left her destitute while he dodged creditors, and filled his days suing prosperous relatives. By the spring of 1826, he had embarked on an American walkabout in Mississippi, Tennessee, and Kentucky where rumors had him marrying a rich widow and riding rivers in well-appointed steamboats. His disrepute could not match that of "Black Horse Harry" Lee, but only because in courting shame, as in everything else, Beverley was a man of only middling ability.[20]

Nevertheless, in the spring of 1827, Carter Beverley was the man Andrew Jackson used to renew his attack on Henry Clay's rectitude. Not long after hearing Jackson's account of the January 1825 meeting, Beverley told it to a friend in a letter that quickly appeared in the nation's press and quite prominently in Duff Green's *United States Telegraph*. Beverley did not mention Buchanan by name, but he did not need to. Pro-administration newspapers openly called into question Carter Beverley's story. Peter Force sensibly observed that Clay did not need to notice this shadowy figure about whom next to nothing was known. "He may be a very responsible and veritable individual," said Force's *National Journal*. But the paper added,

"He may be directly the reverse." The editor of Virginia's Wheeling Gazette was blunter. He called Beverley's information a bald-faced lie. When Beverley responded with his favorite pastime of filing a lawsuit, this time for libel, the jury deliberated for all of five minutes before returning a verdict in favor of the Gazette.[21]

Clay neither took comfort in such developments nor saw the wisdom in Force's advice. Instead, he demanded that Beverley reveal his source. Failing in the courts and flailing before public opinion, Beverley asked Jackson to substantiate the story, and to the chagrin of Old Hickory's handlers, he did so. In a letter to the public published in newspapers throughout the country, Jackson named James Buchanan as Clay's emissary. Jackson waited until after he had named Buchanan to seek his corroboration, a request framed in typical Jackson fashion as a demand. Buchanan had reason to be befuddled as well as horrified. He felt compelled to publish his own denial absolving Clay of any involvement in the meeting with Jackson. That letter's appearance preceded the arrival of Jackson's demanding that Buchanan say the exact opposite.[22]

Someone was not telling the truth, and for once, a shadow of doubt began to descend on Andrew Jackson. Henry Clay wrote his own public letter to the press categorically denying Jackson's charges. Clay possibly sensed that the American people were finally going to see Jackson's true character. Old Hickory's "guardians ought to keep nearer to the Genl," he mused with a sense of wry satisfaction. The guardians would have agreed.[23]

The question for them became how grave the damage would be and how to go about recovering from it. Adams supporters were not happy that Buchanan had given Jackson a shred of cover by portraying the affair as a misunderstanding rather than a misrepresentation on Jackson's part, but anti-Jackson newspapers did everything but put Buchanan's public disavowal on their mastheads. When Carter Beverley's carelessness led to copies of his letters to Jackson falling into Clay's possession, and Clay published them, Jackson was said to be contemplating a duel. It did not help Jacksonite efforts to tamp down stories that they now had to worry that Jackson had become a prisoner of his temper.[24]

Hope rippled through the Adams camp as it pondered a major misstep that could cost Jackson the 1828 election. The incident "has blown up the combination," chortled one Virginia congressman, "and [has] put an end forever to the [charge] of bribery and corruption." Soon friends of the administration were opining that the evidence could be interpreted to indicate that Andrew Jackson had authorized Buchanan to make a deal with Clay. With such theories, they thought that at last they had the means to destroy Jackson's candidacy, once and for all.[25]

As they came to grips with the enormity of Jackson's mistake, his handlers worked day and night to limit its consequences, and to the dismay of Adams supporters, Jacksonites would amazingly find a way to turn the mistake to their advantage. First, they had Jackson express surprise at Buchanan's faulty memory while John Eaton repaired to his writing desk to draft a "clarification." Green's *United States Telegraph* brazenly claimed that Buchanan's letter actually vindicated Jackson's version of the event, but Green also knew this lie could only be pressed so far. He advised Jackson against pushing to have the House of Representatives investigate the charge.[26]

Whether Jackson was furious with Buchanan for not lying, or if he had really come to believe that Buchanan was not telling the truth is difficult to know. Jackson's friends were collecting affidavits—their standard technique for smearing opponents and defending Old Hickory—and John Overton was in contact with Tennessee congressman Jacob C. Isacks, who had been present during part of Jackson's meeting with Buchanan. Isacks said he remembered Buchanan's intentions the way Jackson did. Whether truthful or not, Isacks gave Jackson's alchemists what they needed to work their magic. They began lodging the claim that Buchanan's current denials only proved that he did not want to be implicated in any corruption. Repetition of this interpretation was crucial. Jackson anonymously contributed to a piece printed across the country that said Andrew Jackson always told the truth and consequently had no choice but to expose Clay's corruption.[27]

While Eaton labored on a convincing refutation of Buchanan and a defense of Jackson, Old Hickory clung to the original story that he had not misunderstood Buchanan at all. In fact, he wrote to John Coffee that he had proof that if released would "destroy Mr. Buchanan," but for that, he had "no wish, altho. he deserves it." He did not want a "dispute with Buchanan" to distract people from Clay's and Adams's corruption.[28]

On September 18, 1827, the *Nashville Republican* published Eaton's apologia. It attacked Henry Clay for many things. Not until eight paragraphs into the essay did Eaton address the Buchanan controversy. He supposed there might be a few seeming contradictions in the statements made by Jackson and Buchanan, but those differences were "principally verbal, and not material." Eaton assumed an even straighter face to put an even finer point on the matter. Jackson had never claimed that Buchanan came directly from Mr. Clay; instead, he could have been representing Clay's friends.

Having set up his props for his elaborate magic trick, Eaton moved the meeting with Buchanan to the time when Clay declared his intention to vote for Adams, which placed it near the end of January 1825. Buchanan remembered the meeting as taking place at the end of December 1824, and Jackson had always stated that it occurred in early January. Eaton, however, made the event contemporaneous to Clay's "corrupt" proffers to Adams, overtures that, he stated, Jackson had honorably dismissed. With a torrent of words to blur the real point of contention and a chronology neatly arranged to create the impression of cause and effect, Eaton avoided the reason for the controversy, which was that either Andrew Jackson or James Buchanan was lying. To the surprise of Adams supporters, this elision did not matter.[29]

Jackson's people did not banish Buchanan, though they kept him at arm's length, as if they believed Richard Maury's estimate of him as "little better tha[n] a Swindler." Buchanan still served a purpose after the election as Jackson's political operation became the Democratic Party. Twenty years after his embarrassing part in the "corrupt bargain" charges, Buchanan continued to insist that he had never been part of a deal proposed by Clay, but by then the history was ancient and the political climate much different. His seniority and controversies hobbling other aspirants gave Buchanan the Democratic Party nomination in 1856, and he was elected president just in time to preside over the disintegration of the United States that would lead to the Civil War. Trouble always found James Buchanan.[30]

———

As THEY INCREASED in number and in circulation in 1827 and 1828, Jackson newspapers varied their charges against the Adams administration to match a region's political complexion. For example, in areas hostile to Federalists, the press said the administration's program proved Adams was an unabashed Hamiltonian. Given his presidency's nationalist cast and centralizing tendency, the charge carried just enough truth to make it credible, though the claim that Adams had been a part of the "Hartford Convention party" was a cheap device to defame a patriot. Moreover, it especially maddened the president's supporters because they could counter it by pointing out how Jackson had recommended Federalists for Monroe's cabinet in 1816 and had courted them in 1824. They were routinely disappointed to find that the public was more interested in Adams's apostasy than Old Hickory's opportunism.[31]

The same sort of attacks named Henry Clay as a traitor to the heritage of Virginian republicanism, despite his always having been a plainspoken admirer of Jefferson and Madison. In Clay's case, the effort to tar him with a Federalist brush took a bizarre turn, thanks to Henry Lee and Thomas Jefferson's son-in-law. Lee had already demonstrated that Jefferson's passing made it easy to put words in the dead sage's mouth regarding Adams, but the Jackson camp soon prodded Thomas Mann Randolph to add that his father-in-law had disapproved of Henry Clay.[32]

Thomas Mann Randolph was likely the family member Henry Lee mentioned as conveying his father-in-law's endorsement for Jackson during Lee's visit to Monticello in the summer of 1826. Randolph published a statement in the Charlottesville *Virginia Advocate* that Jefferson had registered his "repugnance" for Henry Clay and his support for Andrew Jackson. As other newspapers reprinted this remarkable declaration from Randolph, a man with wide repute as an incorrigible alcoholic, Clay's friends told the secretary of state to ignore the ramblings of this "poor unprincipaled & besotted" wretch. For once, Clay took the advice.[33]

━━━

Isaac Hill exemplified the amalgam of newspaper editor and politician who, in his role supporting candidates and attacking their opponents, was an important part of the political culture of the 1820s. He frequently served in the New Hampshire legislature while working as a newspaperman, a trade he had learned as an apprentice to Joseph Cushing in Amherst. In 1809, Hill purchased the Concord *American Patriot*, soon renamed it the *New-Hampshire Patriot*, and used his political connections to land fruitful printing contracts from both state and federal governments. Hill was a persistent contrarian who supported Crawford in 1824 but switched to Jackson shortly after the election was finally decided. He turned the *Patriot* into such an enthusiastic advocate for Old Hickory's cause that it attracted a national following when Green began reprinting Hill's work in the *United States Telegraph*, and the *Telegraph's* network of newspapers followed suit. Hill's creative defenses of Jackson and his innovative attacks on John Quincy Adams soon made him a celebrity, and not just among politicians and operatives. Other Jackson editors, Green included, delighted in his description of Henry Clay as "a shyster, pettifogging in a bastard suit before a country squire."[34]

Though that example does not suggest it, Hill's *New-Hampshire Patriot* was more dignified than his campaign tracts, the most infamous of which was a biographical sketch of Andrew Jackson that included an incredible story about Adams based on an innocent truth that Hill wove into a salacious lie. During Adams's diplomatic service in Russia, his wife's maid had included gossip about Czar Alexander's voracious sexual appetite in a letter that the Russian government intercepted. The czar was highly amused by this portrayal of him as a great lover and asked Adams if he could meet the author. Adams obliged at his next audience. In the company of several retainers as well as members of his family and John Quincy Adams, the czar exchanged some meaningless pleasantries with the girl for all of ten minutes. Hill transformed this harmless anecdote into a titillating story about Adams procuring, in the worst sense of the word, an innocent American virgin for the czar. The Adams press would not reprint such a tale but expressed outrage at it for being "more base and despicable than any language can describe," which meant people everywhere could not wait to read it.[35]

In a way, Hill was brave to serve as Jackson's champion in New Hampshire, for it was hard to swing a cat in the state without hitting an Adams man. Henry Clay stripped Hill of his federal government printing contract, and in 1827 the *Patriot* also lost its contract with the state. Hill was undeterred, and he even managed to win a seat in the state senate that same year. On January 8, 1828, he delivered the main oration at Concord's commemoration of the Battle of New Orleans, lauding Jackson throughout. Abel Parker, an elderly veteran of Bunker Hill, however, wasn't buying any of it. Parker wrote an open letter to Hill that the Adams papers published. He criticized Hill for attempting "to raise to the Presidency of the United States, a man on whom no real republican can reflect without . . . horror" and asked, "What evidence have you, that General Jackson is a republican, or that he ever had a shred of republican blood running in his veins?" Parker's opinion was typical of New Hampshire, but Hill knew it was atypical for the rest of the country, and that was where his exciting stories about Adams as a procurer of American virgins for Russian czars were being reprinted with good effect. Like Amos Kendall, Isaac Hill expected a government appointment from the Jackson administration when the time came for gratitude in service to the cause. Like Kendall, he would not be disappointed.[36]

THE SHEER NUMBER of American newspapers—861 by 1828—marked a significant increase from even the 1824 contest. The Nashville Central Committee that was established as the Junto's heir in March 1827, and its auxiliary branches, encouraged editors and financed new papers. As with every other aspect of the campaign, Jackson supporters proved much more adept than Adams men at raising the necessary capital for these endeavors, even after Adams men realized too late the new importance of money in politics. North Carolina alone had nine new Jackson papers by the middle of 1827. Ohio's five Jackson papers in 1824 were joined by eighteen more by 1827.[37]

The use of newspapers in the campaign of 1828 was the most revolutionary aspect of a revolutionary year in American politics. Partisan newspapers enlisted in campaigns openly and avidly, and their editors could be strident or subtle, the former sounding alarms over the fate of the republic should it fall into the wrong hands, the latter falsely lamenting the need to point out the unsavory nature of an opponent. Operatives working for centrally controlled campaigns called on newspaper editors the way modern sales representatives drop in on clients, systematically lining up support and making sure everyone stayed in line. Meanwhile, because they were cheaper to produce and inexpensive or free to mail, the reach and influence of newspapers gave those wielding legislative power or executive contracts unique ability to direct the sentiments of the entire country as newspapers became just another form of traditional political tracts. The power of such organizing principles was incalculable. The Unitarian minister William Ellery Channing marveled with some trepidation about how "men of one mind, through the whole country, easily understand one another, and easily act together." It allowed them to assume "the uniformity of a disciplined army." Pro-Adams newspapers knew this but knew little about how to accomplish it. "Organization is the secret of victory," conceded the New York *American*. "By want of it we have been overthrown."[38]

With such advantages, the press supporting Andrew Jackson gained momentum as his campaign embraced the maxim that organization would deliver victory. One of the most talented politicians of his time had known this all along, and he might have achieved triumph if his preferred candidate in 1824 had stayed healthy. As it was, Martin Van Buren had seen William Crawford fall and then fail and could only console himself that nobody could have done better for the Georgian. Dampened for a while in the wake of defeat, the old organizing principle simmered in Van Buren's soul, dormant but not dead. Knowing Van Buren's mind in the final year of the campaign, the politically astute would also have known the reason that former Crawford newspapers began to boost Old Hickory. It was because Martin Van Buren had become an enthusiastic Jacksonite.

CHAPTER 13

MAGICIAN

A PLEASANT MAN, MARTIN VAN BUREN HAD COUNTLESS friendly acquaintances from all across the political spectrum. He never let yesterday's disagreement stand in the way of tomorrow's alliance, plainly admitting that "it had never been my practice to continue the war as long as my adversary desired it, but always to be prepared for peace."[1]

This much was true. Shortly after New York sent him to the United States Senate in 1821, Van Buren visited Schenectady to dine with Joseph Yates, whom the Albany Regency intended to run for governor. Yates was a prominent state politician and jurist from the Mohawk Valley, but he lacked the widespread appeal of DeWitt Clinton and also had a suspicious nature, even with friends, such as his other dinner guests, as well as foes, such as Senator Van Buren. They had disagreed for years, but the chance to put a potential ally in the governorship required the new senator to prepare for peace with an old adversary.[2]

The gathering was lively, as these events always were with Van Buren part of the mix. Sparkling conversation and harmless flirtations complemented the courses. Elizabeth Yates was not as pretty as

Yates's first wife or as rich as his second, but she brought her politically influential family, the De Lanceys of Westchester County, into Yates's service, which made up for all other shortcomings. Elizabeth impressed Van Buren as a serious soul tempered by an endearing innocence, a simple nature residing in a sheltered aristocrat. During dinner, one of their number mischievously brought up a past disagreement between Van Buren and his host. "Ah," Yates said, "that was at a time when I did not understand Mr. Van Buren as well as I do now!" Elizabeth turned to her husband and quietly asked, "Are you sure you understand him now?"

Everyone, including Martin Van Buren, erupted in laughter, but he quickly noticed that Elizabeth Yates was crestfallen at having said something stupid, or worse, uncivil. He acted chivalrously that evening when he eased away Elizabeth's embarrassment by pretending she had scored the wittiest remark of the night.[3]

With such behavior, he resembled Henry Clay, who shared with Martin Van Buren the belief that gallantry involved spying the homely girl at a party and giving her a wink. Clay was also pleasant by habit and, when they had opportunity to come into contact, reciprocated the New Yorker's fondness for a fellow bon vivant, even if they disagreed about many people and many things. Professional courtesy required more than mere civility between such men, but they carried out even their liveliest disputes without losing the respectful warmth of kindred spirits.

Those similarities of a personal character were as far as the resemblance went, however, for Van Buren and Clay did not merely disagree about politics; they approached the workings of politics from entirely different vantages. Van Buren predicted at the end of 1824 that Clay's plan to elect Adams in the House would seal his political doom. He had foreseen that consequence, in part, because of the Kentucky legislature's instructing the state's congressional delegation to support Jackson. That Clay did not even attempt to influence events in Kentucky struck Van Buren as careless. Going to the Senate in 1821 removed Van Buren physically from the daily affairs of New York's state government, but his Albany Regency did not strike its colors or its operatives doff their Bucktails because he was in Washington. Van Buren remained in touch with lieutenants in Albany to fight DeWitt Clinton, and he traveled back to his state when necessary, as during the governor's race, to support his faction. Controlling New York—or at least trying to—was not a matter of pride but a necessity, unless one wanted to risk the receipt of awkward instructions from home.

Van Buren's implacable enemies regarded him as a political hack for this very reason, and they gave him the moniker of "Little Magician" as an insult and called his political operation the "Regency" to tarnish it with proto-Democrats. To them, the Albany Regency was a machine based wholly on cupidity and self-interest, and its leader was nothing more than a crafty boss. He was an "artful, cunning intriguing, selfish, speculative lawyer . . . a political electioneerer and intriguer" always moving "in so cautious, sly, and secret a manner, that he can change at any time, as easily as a juggler or a magician can play off his arts of legerdemain." Martin Van Buren, they snorted, was the "Little Non Committal Magician."[4]

But whether people admired the Little Magician for his political skill or detested the "Red Fox of Kinderhook" for his shenanigans, all would have profited from hearing Elizabeth Yates ask the more than pertinent question: Did any of them really understand Martin Van Buren?

═══

IN THE CAMPAIGN of 1824, Martin Van Buren had made a series of miscalculations, but bad luck had forced many of them on him. The wretched health of his candidate had blocked all the traditional avenues to victory in an ordinary canvas, but Van Buren had also

After honing his organizational skills in New York politics and as William H. Crawford's unofficial campaign manager, Martin Van Buren was called the Little Magician. His contributions to Jackson's campaign helped deliver Old Hickory a landslide victory in 1828. (Library of Congress.)

faced a rising spirit of democracy that discredited the congressional caucus. Saddled with a stroke victim and having to resort to the worst of methods to save the man's candidacy, Van Buren should have taken comfort in retrospect. Up to a point, William H. Crawford had been the man to beat mainly because Crawford was Van

Buren's man. Even after Crawford's illness and the missteps it compelled, Van Buren managed to put him before the House in ways that seemed rather magical and held hope for a happy ending, at least until the first ballot. After that was over, the Little Magician felt more like Sisyphus than a sorcerer.

He seemed to fail so completely because he had come so far. Martin Van Buren was born in 1782 in the village of Kinderhook. Situated southeast of Albany, it ranked among the oldest Dutch colonial settlements. Originally known as Kinderhoek or "children's corner," it remained clannish with English a second language for most families. Before humble origins were considered a political advantage, Van Buren's enemies described his youth as worse than lowly for having been spent in a tavern. But his father, Abraham, actually was an innkeeper, and his inn's watering hole was an unremarkable appendage rather than the primary purpose of his business. Abraham Van Buren also held political posts in Kinderhook, all of them minor, but many of them instructive for young Martin, who grew up observing the art of persuasion and the value of congeniality. While absorbing these lessons, he also developed habits of tidiness and order that were rooted in his cultural background but became defining elements of Martin's character. In adulthood, he exhibited a near fixation on the organized life as the guide for all personal and public activity. Like a man for whom a crooked picture is a disquieting distraction that compels straightening, Van Buren saw political problems as things to be set right by transforming erratic variables into predictable constants. The successful politician, in his view, was a man fixing crooked pictures with a spirit level.

Martin's mother, Maria, saw talent in her middle child as a sign of impending greatness. She acquired for him as elaborate an education as the children's corner could provide, but as he later conceded with regret, the local academy was not the most impressive educational institution. He had a nimble mind, though, and a local law practice took him on for clerking duties while allowing him to read a bit of law. Martin was fourteen years old.

Six years later, he moved to New York City to study under William Van Ness, who had once lived in a town near Kinderhook. William's older brother John was a New York congressman whose most avid supporter was young Martin, since boyhood "a zealous partisan" of Jeffersonian Republicanism. By the time Martin arrived in New York City, William Van Ness was a successful attorney with important connections that included Vice President Aaron Burr. (Van Ness later served as Burr's second in his duel with Alexander Hamilton.) These first associations with influential people began a pattern in young Martin's life. Decades could pass, but he always recalled a favor and always repaid a kindness, as in 1827 when he helped secure John Van Ness a central place in Andrew Jackson's campaign for president. By then, all of them were important.[5]

Van Buren was admitted to the New York bar in 1803 and went home to practice law with his older half-brother James Van Alen. He had the manners, attire, and polish of a gentleman, but never the attitude of a snob. Political partisanship never triggered his temper, and local Federalists remained friends, many for a lifetime. Almost everyone liked him in return, in fact. Everyone admired his hard work on local political projects and noticed his willingness to shoulder even drudgery with good cheer.

He stood about five-foot-six, if he held his slight physique especially upright, but his face had agreeably arranged features that women tended to find winsome. He combined magnetism with antique charm, and no matter how famous or accomplished he became, he was always invariably kind. It was the reason that Hannah Hoes loved him during their childhood, adored him as her husband, and devoted her life to him up to the hour she died. That was in February 1819, when she was only thirty-five, still youthful even while tuberculosis was remorselessly hollowing her out. Four little boys, the oldest eleven, clustered around Martin, all shattered like their father. He never remarried.

In the early 1800s, Van Buren was a rising star in New York politics, serving in the state senate and then as the state's attorney general. He attracted the attention of rivals and discovered that politics was an adversarial game that many men took too personally. New York governor DeWitt Clinton's pet project, the Erie Canal, was more than a magnificent engineering achievement. It was an expensive undertaking that attracted men of questionable honesty and careless accounting practices. Criticism about that could goad Clinton into tantrums, and when Martin Van Buren offered criticism of his own, Clinton's enmity threatened to pull down the curtain on the Little Magician before he had pulled off his first real trick.

In response, Van Buren did not reach for a wand but for his spirit level. His talent for organizing a political movement and mobilizing voters stemmed in part from his personality but also from experience: he had seen how factional squabbling in little Kinderhook could stall and sometimes ruin the most beneficial projects. Factions without discipline were too fluid. They encouraged voter volatility and made men fickle. As Van Buren saw it, the Republicans of the children's corner had to start acting like adults to form disciplined organizations, and those of New York had to start living up to the state's motto as the place of empire. Loyalty to the party and obedience to its leaders were crucial. A disciplined, organized party's vigor was the press, its lifeblood the patronage, its musculature the people armed with ballots, and its mind the principles of the Founding as long as its leaders adhered to them.[6]

By 1820, Van Buren had organized a formidable faction in opposition to Clinton with the aim of wresting away his grip on the state government. With his colorful Bucktails—Van Buren knew the power of symbols—he directed a focused campaign to gain control of the New York legislature. He was so successful that opponents coined the name "Albany Regency" to decry the monarchical tyranny of upstarts they had previously lampooned as clowns wearing ruminants' rears. The dominance of the upstarts in the legislature allowed them to place their leader in the US Senate and watch voters send him to the state constitutional convention in 1821. New voters joined Van Buren's party, and in 1822 they elected for governor Bucktail Joseph Yates of the convivial dinner party.[7]

———

From the start, old Washington hands marveled over Senator Van Buren's charm and congeniality, especially when considered alongside his relative youth and inexperience on the national stage. William H. Crawford's embrace of Jeffersonian principles of limited government—which was why Van Buren supported him in 1824— should have alienated all Federalists. But Van Buren was able to rope more than a few of them into Crawford's camp, apparently through his pleasantness, as he lodged with a number of the eventual converts at a Georgetown boardinghouse.[8]

Crawford's stroke, more than Jackson's unexpected popularity, upset Van Buren's best-laid plans, but the younger man persevered in a losing cause because he found the alternatives disagreeable. He had met Andrew Jackson only once before he found himself in the row in front of Old Hickory's desk in the Senate chamber, and the physical proximity had not given Van Buren a favorable impression. John Quincy Adams had embraced James Monroe's idea of tempering Republican ideals and courting Federalists, and Van Buren thought both men had their politics and philosophy upside down. He believed that Federalists should have to abandon their principles for access to a winning team. In any case, Jackson and Adams had ties to DeWitt Clinton—Jackson had even praised him as a possible president—which meant that either a President Adams or a President Jackson could result in an unstoppable Clinton.

The sly dog Clinton had run for governor as, of all things, the "People's Party" candidate, which was just a way to demagogue against Van Buren's Regency. Worse, from Van Buren's perspective, was that naive Old Hickory or wily Adams might put Clinton into the cabinet. Van Buren shuddered at the thought.

When Adams won on the first ballot in the House of Representatives, Van Buren's desolation was complete. At home, DeWitt Clinton won the governorship, and in Washington, men advancing a philosophy Van Buren loathed had carried the day. He put on a cheerful public face, but privately he was inconsolable, as he plainly showed in Crawford's parlor the night of the House vote. He had a way of carrying "himself with an air of cold grandeur" when his world fell apart, as when Hannah had died, but this defense mechanism was counter to his nature and thus temporary. He put aside his distaste for Adams and decided to give the man a decent chance, but that resolve did not survive the jolt of Adams's Annual Message. Van Buren could not support the president's centralizing measures and see hated Hamiltonian Federalism revived.[9]

This stance naturally led him to closer ties with Adams's other opponents, including the Jacksonites, but Van Buren moved cautiously. He was too familiar with the interplay of politics to invest much indignation in the "corrupt bargain" charge. All of the candidates had been maneuvering, cajoling, dangling carrots, and swinging sticks. Adams had simply come out the winner in the second oldest profession, and how that had happened was of less interest to Van Buren than what to do about its consequences for the country. He had his doubts about Jackson men. They were too free-wheeling with facts and too extemporaneous with tactics to suit him. Jackson himself seemed a walking problem as well. "Leading politicians inclined to the opinion," he later recalled, "that Gen. Jackson's strength could not stand the test of a four years exposure to the public scrutiny." And Jackson's politics—his recommendations to

Monroe in 1816 about appointing a Federalist to the cabinet, his boosting DeWitt Clinton in the New York governor's race, and more recently his votes for the Tariff of 1824 and internal improvements—raised suspicions. Van Buren did not know what to make of the old man.[10]

Prudence did not stay his hand altogether. To oppose the administration's Federalist program, Van Buren needed a coalition comprising more than vengeful Jacksonites. He looked to Crawford supporters from 1824 and the Calhoun wing of the party, two groups that had found common cause in opposing the Panama mission. As for Jacksonites, Van Buren kept his distance and played the coquette while he quietly proselytized for Jackson's cause. Nearing the end of 1826, he more openly opposed Adams administration initiatives, causing most people to infer his inclination was for Jackson and some to suspect he was already in the Jackson camp. He frequently met with possible Jackson supporters and applied his philosophy of making peace with former enemies, even DeWitt Clinton, whom Van Buren feared might support Adams if only to spite him and the Bucktails. The path was narrow, with perils on either side. Bucktails were livid over the rapprochement with Clinton, and Crawfordites balked over pressing their cheeks to Calhoun men's jowls, but Van Buren worked efficiently to join together disparate men by convincing them of the desperate nature of their problem. He spent Christmas of 1826 with John C. Calhoun with this goal in mind.[11]

The South Carolinian was a bigger mystery to Martin Van Buren than Andrew Jackson, and he became the exception to Van Buren's rule about finding something to like in everyone, if possible. After their Yuletide visit in 1826, Van Buren would only pretend to trust Calhoun. He kept up the pretense because he needed Calhoun's supporters, but he very much wanted to lose Calhoun. He laid plans to diminish Calhoun's influence in the Jackson movement and put into motion actions to oust him from Jackson's inner circle. The result could be too easily interpreted as a bald power play between two ambitious rivals competing against each other for political ascendancy, with the Little Magician the more cunning and Calhoun more the victim.

Calhoun became devilishly difficult to understand the minute he went into Monroe's cabinet. His work at the War Department was impeccable, but ambition corroded his finer instincts and nurtured a conspiratorial nature. His willingness to compromise his principles was never more evident than in his eventual acceptance of Jackson's 1818 invasion of Florida. In cabinet discussions, Calhoun argued with principled enthusiasm for Jackson's punishment, but the repercussion for doing the right thing soon had him rethinking his stance to rationalize the wrong of lying about it. The episode was a turning point for Calhoun, and if not on an epic scale, at least as a Faustian bargain. It only remained for him to choose his devil.

For a time, determining which devil he had settled on was all but impossible. After he was knocked out of the 1824 race, Calhoun was so guarded that many believed he was supporting Jackson, but just as many believed he was for Adams. He remained cautious even after the inauguration, when he became Adams's vice president. Normal expectations would have presumed his loyalty to the administration. The next year, however, in June 1826, Calhoun wrote directly (and privately) to Andrew Jackson to reveal his concern over the Adams administration's threatening the people's "liberty" while corruptly fortifying its incumbency with government patronage. Possibly Calhoun believed this, but he surely knew that the patronage accusation had become a common theme in the Jacksonite assault on Adams and Clay. Calhoun solemnly expressed the hope that Jackson would "be the instrument, under Providence, of confounding political machinations and of turning the attempts against the liberty of the country, into the means of perpetuating our freedom."[12]

It was an extraordinary communication. Even though the American political process did not institutionally guarantee the election of a president and a vice president in philosophical accord—Thomas Jefferson had been John Adams's vice president, for instance—the absence of adversarial parties in the 1820s suggested it would occur as a matter of course. With the Federalists fading away, everyone who vied for high office was presumably in the same camp. In the absence of fealty, whether owing to contradictory ideas or clashing personalities, the proper course of conduct was to resign. Calhoun did not resign. In the summer of 1826, he not only portrayed himself as politically sympathetic to the enemies of his administration but also offered himself as a mutineer. Jackson, who regarded disloyalty a mortal sin, was not at all fazed by Calhoun's to his chief. Jackson instead assured Calhoun that they were in complete agreement about the threat to the nation's freedom John Quincy Adams and his gang of accomplices posed. Moreover, Jackson said he expected "to march hand in hand" with Calhoun in the cause of the people. Old Hickory was sure that the administration's "hireling presses" would predictably send "the missiles of slander" at Calhoun, but he predicted that they "will fall harmless at your feet."[13]

The administration's supporters in Congress already suspected Calhoun's inconstancy. When he used his appointment power in the Senate to make anti-administration men the chairmen of key committees, pro-Adams senators used the brief window of their majority to strip Calhoun of this prerogative. And everyone knew that Duff Green had been a Calhoun man in 1824, so his arrival in Washington to take over the Jackson paper the *United States Telegraph* confirmed their suspicions about shifting alliances.[14]

Calhoun's opposition infuriated Henry Clay, especially when it emboldened John McLean to pack post offices with Jacksonites. Clay was exasperated that the fastidious Adams would neither fire McLean nor overrule his appointments. As for Calhoun, there was little Adams could do, even had he wanted to. The best administration supporters could manage was to fulfill Jackson's predictions about a hireling press hurling missiles of slander. At the end of 1826, the pro-administration Alexandria *Phoenix Gazette* accused Calhoun of jiggering contracts to receive kickbacks when he was secretary of war. Calhoun's demand that the House of Representatives investigate the allegation seemed to play into the administration's hands when Speaker of the House John W. Taylor, an Adams man, appointed a committee hostile to Calhoun. The committee belabored its deliberations to keep the charges in the newspapers for weeks. A vaguely worded report finally exonerated Calhoun, but the impression lingered, as it was meant to, that the vice president had done something wrong so cleverly that it could not be proved.[15]

Through it all, Duff Green defended Calhoun in the *United States Telegraph*, and the effort was quickly interpreted as a ploy to keep Calhoun viable as Jackson's vice president. Men such as John Eaton had never been happy about the pairing of Jackson with Calhoun and had only abided it to refrain from crossing the Pennsylvanians who liked Calhoun. More troubling to Calhoun, though, was a new presence in the Jacksonite organization. As 1827 dawned, the pieces of Calhoun's complicated mosaic finally indicated a discernible pattern of self-interest, and Martin Van Buren knew why he neither liked nor trusted the man. Van Buren felt the same about the man's talented crony Duff Green, whose defense of Calhoun could possibly hurt Jackson's candidacy. It did not take Van Buren long to discover that Green would never be running the *Telegraph*, let alone own it, had Jacksonites not loaned him large sums of money. Coin changing hands always made things simpler by making retribution surer. The vice presidency for 1828 and the editorship of the *Telegraph* meant a great deal to Calhoun and Green, which was a weakness. The Little Magician gazed northward toward New York. There, yesterday's enemy had become today's ally, and possibly could be more. DeWitt

Clinton for vice president would undo the crafty Calhoun, while locking up the Empire State for Old Hickory. Martin Van Buren mulled the possibility.[16]

═══

IN MID-JANUARY OF 1827, Sam Houston believed that Van Buren intended to throw in with Jackson's campaign, and by that spring, everyone else believed it too. "Van Buren's Panacea" was the mocking term the Adams press tried to hang on a development of grave concern to the administration, for the Little Magician was soon bringing over powerful politicians who had been adamantly opposed to Jackson in 1824. Even so, Jackson did not immediately welcome Crawford's former manager into his camp. Van Buren was noted for being "in his element when he is engaged in political intrigue," and this did more to worry Jackson than encourage him. Jackson's neighbor Alfred Balch was a close friend of Van Buren's, though, and he talked up the New Yorker's talent and vouched for his sincerity. William B. Lewis and Van Buren began writing to each other regularly.[17]

Balch did not have to exaggerate, for Van Buren was not just talented but genuinely magical in his ability to become ubiquitous, prominent, and indispensable while keeping his distance from Andrew Jackson. There is no record of Martin Van Buren ever visiting Nashville or meeting with Jackson during the 1828 campaign. Van Buren watched and weighed during 1826 before openly climbing aboard the Jackson bandwagon in the first part of 1827, but afterward, he managed to work for Jackson while remaining in the background. He corresponded directly with Jackson on matters of only the utmost importance, in part because he had cannily discerned that too much information tended to provoke Old Hickory's temper. Anger was a variable very much in need of becoming a tranquil constant.

The controversies over Buchanan and Southard were examples of how to lose an election, and Van Buren from afar joined the effort of Jackson's close associates to shorten his leash. John Eaton tirelessly counseled Jackson not to state a position on any issue and warned that people seeking his opinion meant only to hurt his candidacy. But it was a tedious chore, and Eaton must have been grateful for Van Buren's help. Jackson would raise his hackles over opposition attacks, Eaton would emphatically counsel Jackson to leave everything to his friends, and Van Buren would chime in with the same advice. When Duff Green urged Jackson to come to Washington and personally inquire about his correspondence from the War of 1812 that had gone missing, Van Buren grimly assessed the possible results. He quickly wrote to Jackson that the trip would be a terrible idea. "The reasons agt. such a step are manifold," Van Buren said.[18]

Jackson understood he could count for protection on a new network of committees that radiated from Nashville to important cities such as Cincinnati, Philadelphia, Louisville, and New York. The original Nashville Junto had performed well, but it was fundamentally provincial in character. And it was probably no coincidence that the new organizational model sprang up at the same time Van Buren joined the Jackson campaign. On March 17, 1827, Jackson's most ardent supporters met in Nashville where they were superintended by Jackson's neighbor Edward Ward and inspired by Jackson's friend William L. Brown's "animated and eloquent address." They established the Nashville Central Committee to direct the campaign and to correspond with other committees throughout the country. The most important of these would be a twenty-four-man committee in Washington, DC, which soon ranked with Nashville's in importance. Van Buren was the driving force behind the formation of the Washington Central Committee and responsible for John Van Ness becoming its chairman. Senators Thomas Hart Benton and John Eaton also sat on it.[19]

Adams supporters derisively called the Nashville Central Committee the "Whitewashing Committee," which was an accurate description of its activities, but rumor also had it that "one of the principal duties of the Committee at Nashville is to keep the Genl. cool—by keeping from [him] all papers & Letters calculated to incite him," and that was only partly correct. All of Jackson's committees kept eyes open and ears cocked for dirt on John Quincy Adams and Henry Clay. John Eaton traveled throughout the Northeast and Mid-Atlantic to bolster supporters and mine the landscape for damaging information. Henry Lee took breaks from writing Jackson's biography to do the same, as did Ohio congressman Caleb Atwater. These were not impromptu, haphazard searches. Instead, there was a purpose and plan behind them. Everyone regularly reported to the Nashville Central Committee and often directly to Old Hickory. Confirmations of corruption by the hypocrite Adams and the blackguard Clay always made him cheerful. Even Van Buren was willing to risk the chance that some intelligence would set the old boy off. Jackson's temper was the only surety, the one constant, that Van Buren always hoped would vary.

═══

WHEN MARTIN VAN Buren came to Washington in 1821, he planned to restore an alliance between New York and Virginia that had been pivotal to the election of Thomas Jefferson in 1800. Van Buren believed that such an arrangement would make Crawford all but invincible, but there was always more to the idea than that. Van Buren envisioned a permanent national political party whose alliances could diminish sectional disputes and whose discipline could guarantee victory in elections. In 1822, he directed Bucktails in the House of Representatives to push Virginian Philip Barbour's election to the Speakership. The gesture seemed politically incongruous because the incumbent Speaker, John W. Taylor, could presumably claim the loyalty of a fellow New Yorker. But Taylor was also a supporter of DeWitt Clinton, which for Van Buren made him a faux Republican. Clinton men, he muttered, were closet Federalists. Barbour was elected.[20]

In May 1824, with the Crawford candidacy in shambles, Van Buren made a pilgrimage to Monticello to ask for help from the man he admired more than any other in the world. Thomas Jefferson would not break his rule about remaining aloof from a presidential election, but he freely conversed with his guest. Jefferson would later place the same fears he enumerated to Van Buren in a consoling letter to Crawford after the House vote, but he had known after standing by the Georgian's sickbed that all was lost. The growing power of the judiciary promised the tyranny of the robe, federally funded internal improvements put the government up for sale to special interests, and the protective tariff favored some by picking the pockets of others. It was all resurgent Federalism and marked the peculiar triumph of Alexander Hamilton from the grave. Van Buren could not have agreed more. The defeat of William H. Crawford, the only man Van Buren trusted to turn back this threatening tide, was made doubly bleak because of it.[21]

In 1827, Van Buren returned to the idea of the Virginia–New York axis as the best way to unite a party in opposition to the Adams administration, but it would not be easy. Crawford men in Virginia had long memories and kept a short list of enemies, some so short they held only one name. They recoiled at the thought of Andrew Jackson. The idea of making him president was beyond comprehension. Added to the visceral reaction was a principled one. Jackson's behavior in Florida in 1818 appalled strict constructionists who thought his unauthorized attack on Spanish posts was an unconstitutional act that deserved punishment rather than plaudits. They had said so in their newspapers and Congress during the 1819 investigation. Those were blunt instruments, but Thomas Ritchie was like a skilled surgeon with his Richmond *Enquirer*. He was one of the few editors during the 1824 campaign who regularly attacked Andrew Jackson.

Thomas Ritchie did not doubt that Jackson was a patriot, but neither did he doubt that Jackson's tendency to tantrums and his stubborn streak made him unsuited for the presidency. Moreover, Ritchie believed that if Jackson gained the office, he was likely to fall under the influence of unscrupulous men willing to stroke his vanity and take advantage of his inexperience. Worse, if left to his resources, Jackson's decisiveness and autonomy, so admirable on a battlefield, were likely to be dangerous in the executive office. Confronting a measured opinion such as Ritchie's, a Jacksonite political operative had little recourse, but the Little Magician knew that Thomas Ritchie and the Richmond *Enquirer* were crucial elements to forging his intersectional alliance.[22]

On January 13, 1827, Van Buren drafted one of the most important letters he would ever write. With a tone of urgency, he warned Tom Ritchie that the country's failure to tame sectionalism would destroy them all. Reinvigorating the Republican Party was the only way to prevent the "prejudices between free & slave holding states" from shattering the Union. Sectionalism was poison, and the growing animosity between the North and South made evident by the Missouri Crisis should alarm Americans more than anything, including the possibility that Andrew Jackson as president would occasionally lose his temper. "Party attachment in former times furnished a complete antidote for sectional prejudice," Van Buren said, but he pointed out how James Monroe's foolish attempts to placate Federalists had made those attachments vestigial to the point that the demon of sectionalism ran rampant. Andrew Jackson could revive that spirit and renew those attachments. His "election as the result of a combined and concerted effort of a political party, holding in the main, to certain tenets & opposed to certain prevailing principles," could save the nation.[23]

Van Buren did not say the crucial point to Ritchie, but he did not have to. His unspoken and deeper meaning would be apparent to a southerner. This restored Republican Party that joined "the planters of the South and the plain Republicans of the North" would ignore slavery to avoid sectional arguments. Achieving the delicate balance between human bondage in one place and human freedom in another was to be no small political trick, but it was also morally monstrous. No historian since has been able to determine Martin Van Buren's bedrock views on the matter. Did he want to suppress the slavery issue from a sincere belief that it endangered the Union? Or did he callously weigh it as just another variable—as it had certainly proved to be in the Missouri controversy—one that had to be made into a constant by ignoring its evils? Was that the only way to remove its disruptive effect on public discourse and political health?[24]

———

LIKE OTHER OPERATIVES in Jackson's cause, Martin Van Buren also traveled with a purpose. After Congress adjourned in March 1827, he toured the South to convince Crawfordites that Andrew Jackson was not just a safe choice but the only reasonable one. South Carolinian congressmen William Drayton and James Hamilton Jr. traveled with him to ease introductions and provide moral support. Drayton wielded the kind of social influence common among wealthy Low Country planters whose sons usually became successful Charleston lawyers. Hamilton commanded the respect of Charlestonians for his leading role as mayor in suppressing Denmark Vesey's slave revolt in 1822. Van Buren's friend New York congressman and Crawfordite Churchill C. Cambreleng rounded out the group; his worth lay in the fact that he was a native North Carolinian. They started south in March 1827 with Van Buren planning to speak to every important southerner he could find. The primary reason for the trip, though, was to visit William H. Crawford. Hamilton sent Jackson an optimistic appraisal of their plan with the standard counsel that only two things were required of him to ensure his election: "keep in good health and keep quiet." Jackson newspapers were already touting the combination of Jackson, Crawford, and Calhoun that would sweep the South for Old Hickory.[25]

In Charleston, Van Buren met with Calhoun stalwarts and attended a dinner for fellow senator and Jacksonite Robert Y. Hayne, but his small group did not tarry before heading to Savannah, Georgia, where an interview with Crawford was meant to give Van Buren the chance to secure his blessing. The Little Magician found the older man little changed physically because his enfeeblement had persisted and the hope for his full recovery had waned. But Van Buren knew that Crawford's mind, though not as sparkling, retained a bit of its former luster. His appointment to Georgia's superior court had been a gesture of charity by the state government, and though the travel was taxing, Crawford's eyes were lively, and his return to the bench seemed to agree with him mentally. Van Buren acted as if the visit was for him a treat, but Crawford knew what the little New Yorker's arrival in Savannah portended. Van Buren was careful to soothe away the memories of Jackson's vitriol by shrugging it off as the way of politics in a competitive world. During their talk, Crawford seemed to mellow regarding Jackson. He had one immovable reservation, though. He could not abide John C. Calhoun, he said, and his eyes became more than lively. He would not stomach him as Andrew Jackson's running mate. Van Buren nodded, whether in agreement or understanding was hard to say. Time would tell.[26]

Thanks to Martin Van Buren, Crawford proved unexpectedly useful to Jackson's campaign. The Georgian's friends were fiercely loyal to him, and even his tepid endorsement of Jackson was helpful. Adams newspapers understandably viewed this change with unfeigned incredulity as they recalled the insults Jackson had once showered on Crawford. The formerly great man was now not merely willing to shrug off the past as just the way of politics in a competitive world. Crawford still dreamed of a place on the national stage, perhaps a return to the Senate or even an independent Calhounesque run for the vice presidency to undo the crafty Calhoun himself. Crawford got word indirectly to Jackson not to trust Calhoun. During the 1824 campaign, he sputtered, Calhounites had trafficked in the "military chieftain" charge as much as anyone.[27]

Van Buren headed for North Carolina at a more languid pace after his meeting with Crawford. In Raleigh, he spent several days with prominent Crawford stalwarts who listened with great interest to the news that Crawford had come into Jackson's camp. They hated Adams more than they disliked Jackson, and it was good to know that their former leader agreed.[28]

Van Buren was beaming by the time he stopped in Richmond on his way back to Washington. The visit to the Virginia capital was in part celebratory—Thomas Ritchie had agreed to endorse Jackson and to bring the *Enquirer* with him—but it was also to address an important organizational matter that could tie the state even more resolutely to Van Buren's cause. He needed trustworthy people and known quantities, and he thought Duff Green to be neither because he suspected the editor would always put Calhoun first. Van Buren asked Ritchie to come to Washington and found a new Jackson paper in the nation's capital. Ritchie did not have to ponder this decision. He refused as if by reflex.[29]

Ritchie's decision disappointed Van Buren because it delayed his plans to diminish Calhoun's influence. But it also meant that Ritchie would not be in place to help guide the evolution of the Jacksonite campaign into a Jacksonian form of governance. It was ironic that for the 1828 campaign Thomas Ritchie used the *Enquirer* to persuade Virginia's Crawfordites to shift their allegiance to Old Hickory because he was committed to upholding states' rights.

Afterward, during Jackson's presidency, the principles that defined Jeffersonian and Madisonian republicanism were to be set aside. The rise of westerners such as the Kentuckian Francis P. Blair and the transplanted westerner Amos Kendall muddled the fundamental beliefs of men like Ritchie and Crawford, beliefs in limited government and decentralized authority. The westerners would mouth the doctrines of the Jeffersonian tradition, but their hearts were in contradictory policies that opposed states' rights in some instances and insisted on national preeminence in others. And they would want national expansion, even if it required a large military establishment to realize it, and even if it risked invigorating sectional quarrels to the point of political crisis and possible violence.[30]

But Ritchie would not leave Richmond, which was home. The feeling came naturally to Virginians, which defined them as committed localists in a national setting. It was the reason Martin Van Buren believed Virginia could be a counterweight against the otherwise irresistible and conflicting forces of centralizing nationalism, southern sectionalism, and fervid democracy. At the time, though, when the election of 1828 preoccupied him, Ritchie's refusal disappointed Martin Van Buren. Years later, when sectional conflicts made the country increasingly ungovernable, failing to bring Ritchie to Washington could be seen as more than a missed political opportunity. It was another small, and at the time imperceptible, turn of the gears toward disunion and civil war.

═══

VAN BUREN'S SOUTHERN tour made northerners apprehensive about promises he might have made that would be inimical to their interests, and he planned to allay those fears during journeys through the North and Northwest. Meanwhile, he brought into Jackson's campaign the Albany *Argus,* which under the adroit editorial guidance of Edwin Crosswell was the Regency's premier voice and one of the most influential newspapers in New York. For Crawford's 1824 run, Van Buren had coordinated the press across a country with a rudimentary communication network, bad roads, and irregular mails. Now he applied the same methods to bring current Jackson papers into line while financing new ones with the campaign's war chest, to which Van Buren added impressive sums through direct appeals to possible donors. He expected all Jacksonites in Congress to contribute cash as well as use franking privileges to send pamphlets and newspapers to influential constituents. The Little Magician raised and spent more money in Jackson's cause than had any previous presidential election operation.[31]

The result was an extraordinary level of coordination and innovation. Thomas Ritchie brought into the mix not only the *Enquirer* but also his political connections with Virginia's leaders. Called the Richmond Junto and often incorrectly likened to the Albany Regency, the Richmond clique was smaller, less organized, more exclusive in membership, and in decline by 1828, which meant it had less influence on Virginia politics than its enemies claimed. But it was a tradition upheld by Virginians worth knowing, and Van Buren coordinated its activities with those of the Albany Regency, the Washington Central Committee, and the Nashville Central Committee.[32]

Van Buren's influence extended into both houses of the Twentieth Congress that convened at the end of 1827, where the simplest questions became "a fair test of the strength of parties." Jacksonites had increased their majority in the House, and for Speaker, they replaced administration man John W. Taylor with yet another Virginian, this time Andrew Stevenson, who packed twenty-one of the House's twenty-eight committees with Old Hickory's supporters. The Senate canceled printing contracts with the administration's *National Intelligencer* and gave them to Duff Green's *United States Telegraph*. The ousted Joseph Gales and William Seaton muttered about Van Buren that "there is nothing more elastic than the creed

of a thorough going party-man" and labeled him "a finished elec-
tioneer." Van Buren would have cheerfully acknowledged the
point while challenging its importance. Without party organization,
and the victory it ensured, one could never implement principles.[33]

The party, in fact, was the problem, because officially there wasn't
one, a lingering effect of the Era of Good Feelings. Van Buren thought
for a time that the way to distinguish the Jacksonite movement and
make it the sole claimant on Republican loyalty would be to stage a
national convention to nominate Jackson as the party's candidate.
Van Buren still rejected charges that the congressional caucus was a
vestige of elitism. But he also realized a convention would be "more
in unison with the spirit of the times" while effectively serving the
purpose of the caucus, which was to unify behind a candidate and
focus against an opponent, in this case, the administration. A convention would unite "Genl. Jackson's personal popularity with the
portion of the old party feeling yet remaining." The administration
would refuse to participate, allowing true Republicans to take control of the party. It was the perfect means of uniting "the planters of
the South and the plain Republicans of the north."[34]

But Van Buren ultimately abandoned the plan. He gauged Jackson's appeal as sufficient without a convention, and there were difficulties, too. The complicated details of organizing Jacksonites in
the states to choose delegates proved daunting, and it also revealed
the apparent problem that the coalition Van Buren was putting
together was a diverse, conflicted group. Gathering such people together promised to cause arguments best left silent. For example,
Calhoun men would eagerly embrace the convention to secure his
vice-presidential bid on Jackson's ticket. Van Buren himself found
that idea alone troubling enough to ax the scheme.[35]

Questions about Jackson's running mate remained unanswered
into 1828. Van Buren tried to put them aside as a distraction. He
continued his pretense as Calhoun's friend. And though his dislike

for the man only grew, Van Buren knew a break would alienate the Calhoun wing of the coalition. Van Buren's idea of supplanting Calhoun with DeWitt Clinton could secure New York, but which man would bring in the most votes remained a question.[36]

A friend told Van Buren that the vice-presidential question was "a very subordinate concern," but the Little Magician disagreed. In fact, he sat up nights worrying about it. Important elements of the coalition had hinted they would not support Jackson if Calhoun were on the ticket. Worse was that Calhoun's insistence about being on the ticket revealed his intention to follow Jackson as president. Neither Van Buren nor Jackson's inner circle wanted that to happen. Yet Van Buren finally decided that DeWitt Clinton's willingness to swallow his considerable pride and take second place on a Jackson ticket was a complication rather than a solution. Calhoun was a bother; DeWitt Clinton, even though at temporary peace with Van Buren, was a threat. Jackson was in bad health and could die in office. Van Buren was confident that Clinton would quickly revive their differences and turn on Van Buren and the Albany Regency from a much higher perch than the New York governor's chair. Clinton was "disposed to quarrel with his best friends & [was] on good terms only with his decanter."[37]

The line of least resistance was to accept Calhoun. When Clinton people tried to strike a deal with Jackson's handlers behind Van Buren's back, it sealed Van Buren's decision to support Calhoun. Then a report from Albany rocked the Jackson campaign. Clinton's friends in New York proposed him for the presidency at just about the time that Van Buren was warning Jackson against becoming embroiled in the vice-presidential question. Van Buren was worried about Clinton not solely for personal reasons. Clinton could potentially destroy everything by peeling off parts of Van Buren's fragile coalition, especially wavering Crawfordites, and thereby reelect Adams. Van Buren was still weighing this prospect when another shocking report came from New York. On February 11, 1828, DeWitt Clinton died suddenly from an apparent heart attack. The Little Magician had to marvel over the hand of Providence and the wisdom of Jefferson. The Great Disposer of all things had disposed of a ruinous development. The other had sagely observed, "How much pain the evils cost us that never happened."[38]

MOST OF MARTIN Van Buren's plans for Andrew Jackson worked like gears in beautiful clockwork. He had corralled most of the leading Crawford men from the last election, and they now appeared enthusiastic about Old Hickory. He was devising ways to neutralize any impact John C. Calhoun might have on a Jackson presidency. He had greatly expanded the Jacksonite newspaper network, refined its message, and coordinated activities through Jackson committees ranging from Nashville to Washington to New York City to Henry Clay's Kentucky and beyond. He had attended to a thousand minor details and made dozens of major decisions. And DeWitt Clinton was dead.

Van Buren would later claim that he and Andrew Jackson were virtual strangers throughout this entire episode. "There had been no personal intercourse between us, nor any correspondence or communication in any form, save a formal letter from him introducing one of his friends," he would assert. Oh, perhaps there had been "one or two letters to him and the Nashville Committee in reply to calls for my opinion as to the proper course to be pursued in respect to certain points in the canvass," but otherwise, Martin Van Buren, by his own estimation, had been only an interested observer in the titanic efforts and significant innovations that brought the rise of Andrew Jackson to its apex in the campaign for 1828. "The first information he received of my determination to support him," remembered Van Buren, "which was early formed, could therefore, as has been elsewhere stated, have been only derived from the newspapers or from the letters of others."[39]

This fantastic concoction of half-truths, evasions, and outright claptrap would have perplexed the men who watched Martin Van Buren make a party and create modern politics. Elizabeth Yates could well have posed her question to its subject to inquire whether he understood himself. Perhaps his answer would have had something to do with magic. He had, after all, pulled off the best trick imaginable. Nobody else in the world could have vanished while remaining at center stage.

CHAPTER 14

MUD

I N THE SPRING OF 1827, THE LOUISIANA LEGISLATURE INVITED Andrew Jackson to come to New Orleans in January 1828, for the thirteenth anniversary of the battle that had made him famous. He almost never accepted these types of invitations. He was disinclined to travel, and his managers advised him against public appearances where his temper could get the better of him. By this point, attacks by the Adams press irritated him, and his health had also become a concern; one day it was middling, the next wretched, but it was never good. He dosed his maladies with mercury-based patent medicines that locked his bowels as often as they freed them while bluing his teeth and damaging his gums. Hemorrhoids became a chronic complaint, sometimes making it impossible for him to sit a horse. Left to himself, he nursed grudges and dreamed of violence against his enemies. Jackson told John Coffee "how hard it is to keep the cowhide from some of these villains." Old Hickory's increasing irritability so concerned his handlers that their repeated cautions about keeping quiet had become a rote drill, tiresome but necessary, for they knew a show of temper would only encourage the administration's operatives to more provocations.[1]

Criticism of Jackson's performance at the Battle of New Orleans and new voting arrangements in Louisiana, however, convinced his managers to make an exception. Following the 1824 election, like other states, Louisiana altered its method of choosing electors from legislative fiat to a popular vote. Though they were putative defenders of democracy, the change was not welcomed by Jacksonites, because Creoles in New Orleans still brooded over Jackson's dictatorial behavior after the Battle of New Orleans. Jackson's men decided that an anniversary visit could mend fences in the city, produce a favorable climate in the state, and generate national publicity to remind everyone why Jackson was indispensable. Accordingly, the invitation had not just come out of the blue. William B. Lewis had encouraged Louisiana to extend it.[2]

The Nashville Central Committee worked with operatives in Louisiana to organize the trip. It included complimentary conveyance for Jackson and his party as well as free freight for the Hermitage's cotton crop going to market in New Orleans. Opulently appointed for the passage, the steamboat *Pocahontas* was to arrive in Nashville in late December 1827 to commence what resembled—ironically enough for the nation's champion of democracy—a royal progress. As fall on the Cumberland passed into winter, Rachel Jackson reluctantly agreed to make the journey, as did John Overton, who rarely ventured from his home, Traveler's Rest. Overton had at last married in 1820, his bride a widow with children whom Overton was raising as his own, and he looked forward to treating them to an adventure that he himself anticipated with relish. He wanted to see Jackson's triumphal return to New Orleans as much as anyone, even as much as William B. Lewis, the ramrod for the junket. Sam Houston, who had recently replaced the term-limited William Carroll as Tennessee's governor, packed his bags too, and Carroll did as well, which would have been surprising, given their earlier feud, if Jackson did not seem so likely to win the presidency.[3]

The most unlikely companion on the river journey to New Orleans, though, was James Alexander Hamilton, the third son of Alexander Hamilton. How young Hamilton and his brother, Alexander Hamilton Jr., became part of Martin Van Buren's political organization was almost beyond comprehension. Van Buren's association with the Van Ness brothers alone should have made him anathema to the Hamilton brothers because William Van Ness had served as Aaron Burr's second in the duel that killed their father in 1804. Aside from that awkward personal connection, everything about Van Buren's political philosophy conflicted with their father's design for an active central government that would reduce states to mere administrative entities.[4]

The Hamiltons nevertheless drifted into the orbit of the Albany Regency. Their hostility to DeWitt Clinton was one spur. Van Buren's extraordinary charm made the change more comfortable than it might have been, and the result was an alliance that the Little Magician found most useful. James A. Hamilton had many Federalist friends in New York and New England with warm feelings for the son of their dead leader. Hamilton was facile with a pen and a fount of felicitous phrases. Van Buren had Hamilton's newspaper editorials published as pamphlets to distribute in Federalist enclaves as a means of courting Hamilton's politically untethered friends, many of whom were eager to recoup something of their old political influence.

By the fall of 1827, Van Buren sensed that his ties to Jackson through William B. Lewis and Alfred Balch and even his direct correspondence with Old Hickory were insufficient to promote the level of trust that would redound to Van Buren's benefit after Jackson became president. The best way to cement a bond with Jackson was through a charming intermediary, and to that end, Van Buren dispatched James Alexander Hamilton to Tennessee. The meeting was intended by Van Buren to be seen as a coincidence, and Hamilton turned up as a wandering stranger at the Hermitage with a convoluted story to explain his presence. Hamilton thought Andrew Jackson a courtly gentleman on their first meeting in December 1827, but Old Hickory's high regard for DeWitt Clinton disturbed Van Buren's lieutenant, as did Old Hickory's estimation of Van Buren as cunning. Hamilton did not shrink from gently criticizing Clinton and warmed to the task of dispelling Jackson's reservations about Van Buren. A wandering stranger he might have been, but James Alexander Hamilton's pedigree seems to have dazzled the men and women in Jackson's entourage and to have intrigued Old Hickory himself. Everyone looked forward to Hamilton's company on the trip.

After Hamilton met Old Hickory in Nashville and traveled with him on the *Pocahontas*, Van Buren encouraged him to write important men with reassuring descriptions of Jackson's piety, character, and temperament. Hamilton would prove artful in emphasizing Jackson's religious life, which started a popular trend in the Jacksonite press. When he published a letter describing how Jackson not only attended the local Presbyterian church but also had devotionals at home, editors across the country told of Jackson praying twice daily with his family in addition to saying grace at meals. The Albany *Argus* printed a letter purportedly written by a chaplain during the Creek War attesting to Jackson's piety.[5]

Hamilton met a courtly gentleman, but the trip to New Orleans allowed him to see the side of his host that kept his managers on edge. The *Pocahontas* was late to arrive at the landing on the Cumberland, and Lewis went into a strange panic. Lewis had mapped out an ambitious schedule to have Jackson arrive in New Orleans on the morning of January 8, 1828, the anniversary of the battle. The tardy steamboat did not bode for a good start to a potentially bad idea. All sighed in relief when the *Pocahontas*, at last, appeared two days after Christmas. Jackson was ill, but he had grown accustomed to feeling bad. He and his large party clambered aboard, with the crew hefting luggage as passengers found their staterooms. The steamboat's whistle pierced the silence, and its chimneys chuffed smoke into the frigid air. They were on their way.[6]

Jackson had insisted that the boat make only one stop to avoid any appearance of electioneering, but Natchez greeted the *Pocahontas* on January 4 with gratifying cheers and adoring addresses. Jackson's former aide Arthur P. Hayne had gone ahead to oversee arrangements in New Orleans, but he had come back up to Natchez to join the steamboat on the final leg of Jackson's trip to the Crescent City. Lewis was glad to see him. Hayne was among the few who could make pointed suggestions to Jackson without risking his ire—Charlestonian charm, it seemed—and he used the uneventful days on the Mississippi to counsel Jackson about his public remarks at the celebration in New Orleans. Stay on the military exploits, Hayne stressed, and play up leaving his farm to serve his country, a deed worthy of George Washington, America's other Cincinnatus. Jackson liked the sound of it.[7]

The boat ride was peaceful, and the decks were pleasant for strolls when the traces of green swamp grass and cypress signaled warmer climes. Lewis beamed while Houston drank, Carroll flirted, and Hamilton observed. A day or two north of New Orleans, a faster steamboat came alongside the *Pocahontas*. Its pilot then threw on all steam and pulled briskly ahead. After gaining some distance, the boat made a lazy turn across the *Pocahontas*'s bow and headed back upriver. It then turned to steam past the *Pocahontas* again. The maneuver was playful enough to cause some amusement, and when it was several times repeated, interest grew in the boat's impressive show of speed. Jackson was on deck and was neither amused nor impressed. He sent for his rifle, and while waiting for it, he shouted to the other steamboat that he would shoot the pilot if he continued to show such disrespect. Hamilton was nearby, incredulous.

Much of what he had seen on his journey was alien to him, as when Emily Donelson visited the Hermitage on horseback with a baby in her arms, blithely explaining that it was easier to cross streams that way. On this trip, though, the courtly gentleman of the Hermitage now struck him as quite dangerous. Hamilton rushed belowdecks to the Jackson stateroom where he found Rachel resting. He blurted out what was happening. With a slight smile, she calmly told Hamilton "to say to the General I wish to speak to him." He charged up to the deck and breathlessly gave Jackson the message. He saw the old man's face soften. Andrew Jackson hurried below. Nobody saw him again, at least not until the other, exasperating steamboat had resumed its passage down the river. Possibly James Alexander Hamilton reported this incident to Martin Van Buren, but probably not. He certainly never included it in his reassuring letters to other prominent men.[8]

The New Orleans trip was a triumph. The *Pocahontas* arrived, as William B. Lewis had planned, on the morning of January 8, and scores of boats escorted it to the Chalmette Plain where a hundred-gun salute was followed by speeches and other ceremonies. All returned to the city for an elaborate dinner and more speeches, which set the pace for a four-day extravaganza of continuous celebrations, parties, balls, banquets, and church services. Immediately after the *Pocahontas* headed back upriver with its weary but happy passengers, Louisiana Jacksonites held their convention in New Orleans to choose a slate of electors and to attack John Quincy Adams as an aristocrat. It was the beginning of a deluge of support in other states that extended to administration strongholds. Kentucky Jacksonites chose January 8 for their convention to approve a slate of electors, and South Carolina's James Hamilton Jr. proposed that Congress commission a painting of the Battle of New Orleans for the Capitol rotunda. The best Adams supporters could do was tactlessly ridicule the celebration at New Orleans by claiming that only stupid plebeians had participated or that the January 8 dinner had been so undersubscribed that organizers had to lower the price from six dollars to three. Peter Force's *National Journal* returned to the tired theme of Jackson's illiteracy by insinuating that someone with talent was drafting Old Hickory's speeches. "If the Hero continues to improve this rapidly," the newspaper sniffed, "he will soon be the most accomplished writer in the language."[9]

Sarcasm was an eastern affectation that did not play well in the rest of the country. Jacksonites could not have produced better copy for their cause.

———

IN THE SPRING of 1828, Martin Van Buren orchestrated a significant congressional maneuver he believed necessary to seal Andrew Jackson's election. The high stakes were the only reason he was willing to take the risk of tackling the protective tariff. Depicting Jackson as opposed to protectionism had played well in the South, but Van Buren feared it would hurt Old Hickory in Pennsylvania and states in the Northwest, such as in Ohio, and even parts of the West, especially Kentucky with its thriving hemp agriculture. These places that produced wool as well as hemp and other raw materials to export and supply American manufacturers competed with imports. Any measure designed to court those groups, however, promised to anger equally formidable and necessary constituencies whose objections were grounded in either sectionalism or commerce. Southerners chafed at purchasing manufactured goods in a protected market that made items artificially expensive, and they caviled over policies that injured their regional economy to aid the North's. At the same time, manufacturers objected to the artificially higher prices for domestic raw materials, which was a protective tariff's purpose.

In short, whether in the North, the South, or the West, who was being protected by a protective tariff made it popular in one place and despised in another.[10]

Van Buren believed that Jackson's victory or defeat could hinge on this issue, and consequently, he resolved to take it away from John Quincy Adams. Others shared Van Buren's concern. Henry Baldwin, for example, knew that Adams's active support for a protective tariff was one of the few things that made him popular in Pennsylvania. Baldwin had tried to distract pro-tariff Pennsylvanians from focusing on Jackson's supposed opposition by emphasizing his military achievements, but Baldwin had to doubt the tactic's effectiveness. As for Jackson, he still had no firm opinion on the matter, and John Eaton had advised him to remain quiet about it. At most, he could perhaps make vague references to his vote in the Senate for the mildly protectionist 1824 tariff, which he had described at the time as "judicious," much to Henry Clay's disgust. In the weeks before states opened their polls for the 1828 election, though, Van Buren did not think ambiguity and references to tepid support in the past would be enough. Perhaps he was right, but even he did not realize the demons the tariff issue could unleash.[11]

As early as the summer of 1827, it was being rumored that Jacksonites in Congress intended to introduce a protective tariff in the certainty that the Deep South would join northern manufacturing districts to kill it. This analysis of the maneuver dismissed it as a cynical gesture that would allow Jackson men to avoid southern ire while claiming that at least they had tried to help wool and hemp growers in New England and the West. The tariff's self-interested sponsors were said to have taken much satisfaction in the clever maneuver that would see New England importers blocking the bill as well. The region that almost universally supported John Quincy Adams could then be blamed in the West and Northwest for opposing a measure that was never meant to reach Adams's desk in the first place.[12]

That same smug attitude greeted the measure the following spring precisely because it was Van Buren who revived it. A Van Buren deputy in the House, Silas Wright Jr., introduced a bill that seemed deliberately fashioned to make it dead on arrival. According to the plan, at least as southerners understood it, the bill was supposed to conciliate Jackson's northwestern supporters while generating implacable opposition in New England because it would levy stiff duties on raw materials imported to that region. New England's opposition would allow most of the blame to fall on Adams men. Calhoun participated in the scheme, persuading fellow southerners to help with initial maneuvers that blocked amendments that might placate New England's objections. When the amendments all failed, and the House passed the bill anyway, doubters were confirmed in their suspicions that they were dealing with a symbolic gesture to score political points with certain constituencies. Southerners who had voted for the bill in the House seem to have assumed that similar attempts to amend the bill to make it agreeable to New England would also fail in the Senate, where the bill would die as a result. Whether it would do so with a whimper or a bang was of little concern.

What happened next has never been completely clear. In one version, enough New Englanders surprised everyone—presumably even Martin Van Buren but certainly John C. Calhoun—by voting for the bill and securing its passage in both the Senate and the House. In another, Van Buren very much intended to put the bill on the president's desk, which meant the behavior of New England did not surprise him in the least. As matters unfolded in the Senate, the troubling revelation dawned on doubters that Van Buren's ploy was not an empty gesture at all.

The only section of the country that stood to lose in Van Buren's game was the South, but he knew that the vast majority of southerners would never vote for John Quincy Adams in the presidential election. The South would sulk—nobody could say how much—but the gains elsewhere would be worth the grief. Once he was willing to accept that, Van Buren needed only to find a way to make the bill attractive to New England textile manufacturers. Accordingly, the Little Magician worked behind the scenes to persuade senators from the West and Northwest to accept amendments increasing duties on manufactured wool. That meant the textile mills in New England stood to see a net gain offsetting the duties on the importation of raw wool. The result was a legislative *abra* that saw the bill pass in the Senate and a complementary *cadabra* for the same result in the House. To everyone's surprise, except apparently for Van Buren and his lieutenants, representatives from the states whose senators had supported the palliative amendments did the same in the lower chamber. After a blur of roll calls and hammered gavels, the Tariff of 1828 passed Congress on May 19 and headed up Pennsylvania Avenue to the White House, where John Quincy Adams promptly signed it into law. Irate southerners could not believe what had happened to them at the hands of their most trusted political allies in the North and the West. They were already calling it the Tariff of Abominations.[13]

South Carolinians were angrier than even the Little Magician had expected. They denounced him as a double-dealing dog and stopped their ears to his meek explanation that the New York legislature had instructed its congressional delegation to vote for the bill. The explanation was worse than disingenuous because Van Buren obviously thought they were all too stupid to know he had dictated the "instructions" Albany sent to Washington. South Carolina Jacksonites such as James Hamilton Jr. and the Hayne brothers tried to reassure themselves and convince others that it was all a nefarious administration plot hatched by Adams and his corrupt co-conspirator Clay. Old Hickory would fix everything, they promised fellow South Carolinians, once he was in office, but it is doubtful they believed the part about Adams and Clay. It was almost as hard for southerners to believe that the men who had done this to them would be willing to undo it later.[14]

By the summer, Carolina hotheads were speaking of secession with an enthusiasm that began to alarm Calhoun as much as it did Van Buren. In Richmond, Thomas Ritchie considered the possibility that South Carolina's recklessness posed a real danger to Andrew Jackson's chances in 1828, and he nervously asked Calhoun for his views on the subject, something Calhoun himself was having a hard time coming to terms with. During that summer, he had started to gather his thoughts for a seminal essay on the subject of tariffs, states' rights, and constitutional restraints that would appear anonymously in December, after the election, as *The South Carolina Exposition and Protest*. His reply to Thomas Ritchie, however, was measured—or guarded, depending on the perspective. Calhoun said he thought South Carolina would remain moderately opposed to the tariff. As for himself, he declared his support for both the Union and Andrew Jackson's election. Ritchie published Calhoun's tempered observation and unqualified pledge in the Richmond *Enquirer* and hoped for the best.[15]

Assurances that President Andrew Jackson would make things right soothed most southerners, but South Carolina's rash talk reminded Martin Van Buren why he did not care for the state or its people. Even in their anger they were inconstant, as Calhoun proved with a response that Van Buren judged as more opportunistic than cautious. So the tall, dark man with the fixed stare planned to support the Union and Andrew Jackson? Van Buren had no choice but to believe him for the moment, but he did not trust that Calhoun's answer would weather even a slight squall, let alone a major storm.

In due course, Martin Van Buren would know before anyone else in the nation's capital who wrote *The South Carolina Exposition and Protest*, with its prescriptions for nullifying federal law, challenging federal authority, and threatening the sanctity of the Union. And because Van Buren knew, Andrew Jackson would know too.[16]

———

IN THEIR EFFORTS to demonstrate Old Hickory's boundless popularity, Jacksonites resorted to silly gimmicks that have become staples of modern politics but were novelties in the late 1820s. State conventions that formally nominated Old Hickory featured the pointless demonstrations of fervid enthusiasm and rousing campaign songs like "The Hunters of Kentucky." Carefully managed straw polls produced majorities for Jackson, duly publicized in the aftermath, and pamphlets attacked Adams and offered plaudits for Jackson from Maine to the Mississippi. In politics, as in comedy, timing is everything, which Jackson men instinctively knew. North Carolina Jacksonites always waited to hold counterdemonstrations after Adams meetings to show that their numbers were greater. Organizers in cities held rallies for laborers to hear speeches about Jackson's sympathy for their plight. And in small rural clearings where sputtering pine torches threw ghostly shadows against dark woods, gaggles of men gathered to pull on jugs, munch free barbecue, and squint at men standing on tree stumps—hence the term "stump speeches"—to give Adams and Clay hell while making hard promises of the vague milk and honey in General Jackson's promised land.[17]

Communities large and small erected "Hickory Poles," and operatives hawked trinkets such as snuff boxes, ribbons, and Jackson tokens of metal and wood, hickory preferred for the latter, of course. Everything, including fine plate as well as cheap crockery, bore an image of Jackson. Some looked like him, more or less. For the serious supporter wanting more substantial paraphernalia, the campaign had sturdy canes carved out of hickory to sell at rallies. Portrait painter Ralph E. W. Earl produced an endless supply of likenesses, some of which, like the mug on beer mugs, looked like Andrew Jackson, more or less. In the spring and summer of 1828, Nashville bookshops began selling the work of famous engraver James B. Longacre, who had etched a special version of an Earl portrait. By that fall, thanks to advertisements in the Jackson press, it had become a prized item throughout the country, three dollars for the print alone and only six dollars for the discerning Jacksonite who wanted a frame, too. The ongoing demand convinced Earl to order five hundred copies to sell himself.[18]

Adams men tried to match this enthusiasm, but their skills fell short, and it was hard for an Adams supporter to get into the spirit of the thing. President Adams publicly acted as if the election was not happening, but his best efforts to sustain his dignity and personal detachment were easily painted by his enemies as coldness and indifference. Henry Clay urged supporters to become more organized on the local level, and a few heeded his advice to hold conventions and issue pamphlets, but the degree of desperation in the Adams camp was revealed by an attempt to persuade former Presidents Madison and Monroe to serve as Adams electors in Virginia. They declined.[19]

Postmaster General John McLean continued to work against the administration, but Adams continued to resist removing him. In another sign of desperation, Clay suggested that Adams get rid of McLean by appointing him to the Supreme Court. Various technicalities complicated the ploy, however, the most glaring of which were the lack of an opening on the court and the fact that Martin Van Buren chaired the Senate Judiciary Committee. Bouncing between hope and despair, the administration left McLean at the Post Office. It was, at least, more dignified to suffer political treachery than turn the Supreme Court into a pen for partisans.[20]

Dignity turned out to be in short supply. A spring reception at the White House attracted a mixed crowd, which included a reporter for Duff Green's *United States Telegraph*. Russell Jarvis was a former Massachusetts lawyer who some believed had joined the newspaper trade solely to pester John Quincy Adams. At the reception, the president cordially received Jarvis, his wife Eliza, and her sister Hannah Cordis, but amity unraveled from there when Jarvis led the ladies into the East Room. Adams's son, John Adams II, was conversing with a Reverend Mr. Stetson, who motioned toward Eliza and asked young Adams who she was. "The wife of one Russell Jarvis," Adams said loudly enough for Jarvis and his companions to overhear, "and if he knew how contemptibly he is viewed in this house they would not be here." Jarvis later claimed he took the remark as insulting to his wife.[21]

Young Adams was his father's private secretary, and a few days after the reception he had just delivered a communication from the president to the House of Representatives when Jarvis pounced on him, slapped his face, and twisted his nose. Stunned by the assault, Adams was trying to defend himself when Maryland congressman Clement Dorsey stepped in to separate the two. The Jackson-dominated House briefly pretended to some outrage over someone beating up a presidential messenger on the premises, and it even went through the motions of a congressional inquiry. But Jacksonites made plain that President Adams had requested the inquiry, which was a shabby way to smear the son as a coward hiding behind his daddy's office. The investigation concluded that Jarvis was wrong, but it absolved him on the basis that he was not aware that physical violence in the House chamber on a member of the executive branch was, technically and if one wanted to be fussy about it, against the rules. This disgraceful response by the national legislature to a violation of basic law and common decency was followed by Jackson newspapers turning the event into a kind of parody. It became the story of an effete son of a corrupt aristocrat getting his well-deserved comeuppance at the hands of a real man defending his wife's honor. It wasn't really funny, but churlish allegories seldom are.[22]

Adams supporters took temporary comfort in a belief that their attacks on Jackson were not in the least allegorical but were rooted in events as real as they were ugly. Many Americans still believed Aaron Burr was a traitor, and it was tempting for Adams and Clay supporters to tar Jackson with the brush of Burr's allegedly nefarious schemes. Because it had all happened some twenty-five years earlier, Jackson at first dismissed this tactic as the hopeless thrashing of deluded men. His managers, however, were not so sanguine. Stories linking Jackson to Burr threatened his candidacy because they could damage his image as a peerless patriot.

Henry Clay knew this, which was why he tried to track down letters that purportedly proved Jackson's complicity in Burr's scheme. Clay never was able to unearth any documentary evidence, but he had no reason to believe it didn't exist. Plenty of people alluded to such evidence or breathlessly repeated anecdotes with nodding certainty. Someone always knew of someone who knew someone who had seen the damning items or had personal knowledge of Jackson's involvement. When Jackson's old nemesis Andrew Erwin made a similar claim, though, the smoke of accusations suggested a fire was blazing somewhere, and by the spring of 1828, newspapers supporting Adams began talking about treason and Andrew Jackson with a conviction that was unsettling to the Jackson campaign.[23]

With Jackson on the verge of a titanic explosion in response to the accusations, the Nashville Central Committee stepped up. It gathered affidavits attesting to Jackson's lack of knowledge regarding Burr's plans and even summoned John Coffee from Alabama to help in the effort and provide a sedative influence on his old friend. The committee reassured operatives across the country that the accusations were baseless. Jacksonites also mounted an attack on Henry Clay by reminding everyone how Clay had represented Burr before a grand jury in Kentucky. This much was true, but Duff Green's *Telegraph* published a letter from "a gentleman of Kentucky" claiming that Clay had also been a coconspirator in Burr's schemes, which was a lie. Privately, Coffee convinced Jackson to keep calm, but Old Hickory could promise forbearance only "untill the month of November passes." Jackson warned that "beyond that period I give no pledges." Nervous operatives in Nashville told John Eaton about the old man's latest dark mood, and Eaton wearily wrote one of his stock letters to Jackson about tranquility and the wisdom of letting friends handle everything.[24]

———

JACKSON WAS CORRECT in his original assessment about Burr being old news of only slight interest to a few people and irrelevant for everyone else. The same was true about almost all the old allegations that the Adams papers unearthed. There was the story about Jackson's breach of dueling etiquette when he killed Charles Dickinson in 1806. It was true that Jackson had taken two shots by not counting his misfire on the first. But overzealous editors painted Dickinson as "an amiable, intelligent, and highly respectable young man" who fired in the air (in fact, he severely wounded Jackson) only to have Jackson snarl a demand for "concessions or die!" before shooting "THE MAN DEAD ON THE SPOT!"[25]

They tried to revive the story about Jackson threatening to cut off the ears of Senator John Wayles Eppes, but Susan Decatur, the commodore's widow, wrote Jackson a letter attesting that she knew that he had never done any such thing. Adams men could sputter that Mrs. Decatur could not know the truth about her husband's encounter with Jackson, but they were wasting their ire. The pretty widow's recollection had likely been nudged by the charming widower Martin Van Buren, a frequent caller and solicitous friend.

People applauded Jackson's gallant refusal to publish her letter lest it hurt her efforts to secure a pension from the spiteful, malevolent Adams administration, but then the Jacksonites decided to take no chances and published it anyway.[26]

Adams editors combed through accounts of the Creek War to condemn the execution of John Wood with romantic descriptions of a brave youth sacrificed by a venomous and vindictive commander. The story of poor Wood was a sad one, but melodramatically inflating it served only to diminish its impact and give Jackson's defenders the opportunity to explain the meaning of mutiny again. John Eaton had removed references to Wood in later editions of his biography of Jackson after the original, but in 1828 he had publisher Mathew Carey reinsert Wood in a new edition published specifically for the campaign.[27]

Of all the new attacks about old events, however, four set off alarms in the Jackson camp. One was the "Coffin Handbill" that denounced the execution of the six militiamen at the end of the War of 1812. It was the most striking image of the entire campaign and marked the one time that Adams supporters were able to match the Jacksonites' talent for effective propaganda. The second was a credible charge of slave trading that revealed Jackson as morally compromised. The third was an equally credible charge that he had treated Indians inhumanely in battle and duplicitously in negotiations. And the fourth attack was of such a personal and ugly nature that it enraged Jackson's friends almost as much as it did the man himself, while going far to discredit the people who mounted it.

Efforts to revive the case of the six executed militiamen at first focused on John Harris, one of the six and a Baptist minister who was said to have written a heart-wrenching letter to Jackson pleading for clemency. Harris had in fact been a clergyman, but that was the only part of the new version of the story that was true. He had not written any letter, the militiamen had mutinied, and these events

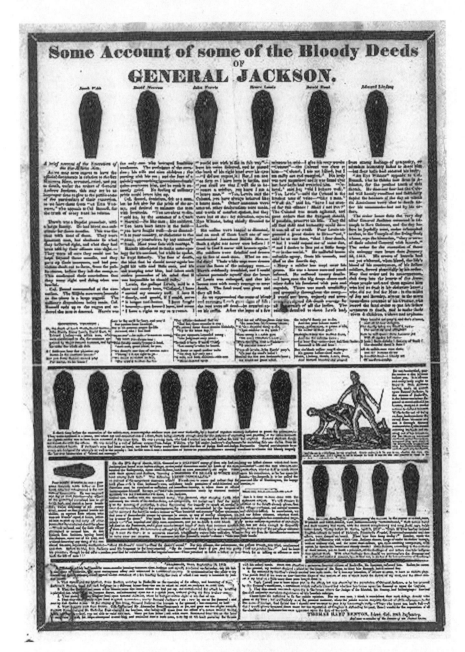

"Some Account of some of the Bloody Deeds of General Jackson" was the creation of editor John Binns. His stark depiction became known as the "Coffin Handbill" and was arguably the most controversial campaign document of the 1828 campaign. (Library of Congress.)

had occurred in Mobile while Andrew Jackson was in New Orleans. John Binns, the editor of the Philadelphia *Democratic Press*, did not let these particulars deter him from relentlessly promoting the story. Binns produced the Coffin Handbill that became an iconic campaign document that ever afterward served as the gold standard for negative politics.[28]

Born in Ireland, Binns had spent a fair amount of time in English prisons for his involvement with radical Irish independence movements before he migrated to America in 1801. In 1807, he founded the Philadelphia *Democratic Press* as a stalwart Republican organ that supported Crawford in 1824 and was responsible for spreading the story that Jackson had recommended Federalists for Monroe's cabinet. His politics as well as the news that Clay was awarding him printing contracts made Binns a pariah in Jacksonite Philadelphia. The contracts were a mixed financial blessing. They bound Binns to the administration while barely making up for the losses sustained by his unpopular newspaper. His subsequent effort to discredit Jackson became the personal project of a man angry about enemies ruining his livelihood. His Coffin Handbill was a delicious mixture of blunt imagery and direct language that was copied and reproduced by numerous printers for a half year before the election. Binns published it as a broadside, that day's version of a campaign poster. It was perfect for mounting on tavern walls, sticking in shop windows, and pasting on lamp posts. Underneath a stark illustration of large black coffins, a narrative chronicled the fate of the six militiamen, all named and all lamented. Later versions increased the body count to include John Wood, Alexander Arbuthnot, Robert Ambrister, and Charles Dickinson, but the common element to each was the image of the coffins. The text was translated for distribution among immigrant populations—the Dutch handbill was aimed at Martin Van Buren's part of New York along the Hudson—but the coffin was universal, and "the honest and unsuspecting Dutch people" as well as other ethnic groups did not need much more than the image itself to understand the content.[29]

Jacksonites alternated between outrage and contempt for the handbills, but their effectiveness was a point of real concern that merited numerous pamphlets to refute the charges. The Albany *Argus* accused Binns of having forged the Harris letter and derisively labeled him the "maker and vender of coffin handbills for the house of Braintree [Adams's birthplace]," but the critics could not dampen Binns's enthusiasm. He continued to produce the handbills, sent them out in bulk for fifty cents per hundred, and varied the theme with another handbill, "Monumental Inscriptions," that provided obituaries of the men Andrew Jackson had killed. Jackson men could wryly observe that "the Adams men are remarkably fond of coffins" and mock "the most ridiculous coinage of their brains," and they could describe Binns as an "impudent dog" employed "at extra wages by the administration," but Binns did not care. Ignoring the notion about imitation being the sincerest form of flattery, Baltimore editor Dabney S. Carr printed his own coffin handbill with the text, "Sacred to the memory of Sir E. Pakenham and 2500 Officers and Soldiers of His Majesty the King of Great Britain who, on the Eighth of January, 1815, were cruelly shot to death by Andrew Jackson, a sanguinary military chieftain." In the same vein, Isaac Hill was pugnacious: "Pshaw! Why don't you tell the whole truth? On the 8th of January, 1815, he murdered in the coldest blood 1,500 British soldiers for merely trying to get into New Orleans for Booty and Beauty." The Jackson press liked the sound of that and reprinted variations of it all over the country.[30]

Duff Green managed what he believed was the neatest trick by putting together a "supplement" to the Coffin Handbill with such care that his *United States Telegraph* seemed to have nothing to do with it. Instead, it was attributed to Virginia congressman John Taliaferro, whose name appeared at the end of the narrative. To this day,

"Pedlar and His Pack." A Jacksonite cartoon derided John Binns for demanding money from the Treasury while carrying his infamous coffins along with Henry Clay and John Quincy Adams. (Library of Congress.)

it is sometimes cited as a production of the Adams camp, despite its unbelievable charges about Jackson being a cannibal who had the six militiamen disinterred and sent to New Orleans for his dinner. Green's excess was meant to make Binns preposterous, but for once, Green misread the source of the handbill's power. The palaver was beside the point. The point was the coffin.[31]

The accusation that Andrew Jackson had been a slave trader was as sensational and as damaging as any charge John Binns ever leveled at Old Hickory. Americans knew that enslaved African Americans labored on the farms at the Hermitage, but they also knew that two of the other three candidates in the 1824 campaign had owned slaves, too. Slave trading, however, was considered a dirty business, because the traders bought and sold human beings under awful conditions.

Jackson brought the accusation on himself in 1828 by accusing his enemy Andrew Erwin of slave smuggling and perjury and thereby provoking Erwin to declare that Jackson had made his fortune in the buying and selling of people. The charge was sobering. Almost all slave owners bought and sold slaves as part of a plantation's business, and more humane owners limited the practice to avoid breaking up families or placing people in harmful situations. But a slave trader thought nothing of breaking up families and cared less about the fate of his commodity. He cheerfully delivered up man, woman, and child to either a benign buyer or vicious brute as long as the price was right and the money ready. Andrew Erwin was correct that at several times in his life Jackson had traded in people for profit, particularly in Natchez and New Orleans. Jackson had evidently forgotten about papers recording these transactions that were in the Bank of Nashville, but Erwin learned of their existence and secured a true copy of at least one.[32]

Against this evidence, Jackson's defenders scrambled to contrive explanations. They insisted that he had been merely a silent partner in such transactions and even implied that he had known only about vague commodities being purchased and sold, not slaves. It was a lie. Jackson's friends also attempted to create an irrelevant controversy about Erwin having stolen his evidence, and Jackson newspapers smeared Erwin as Henry Clay's puppet and hatchet man, citing the family connection of Erwin's son marrying Clay's daughter, and reviving the charge that Erwin illegally smuggled slaves from outside the United States.[33]

By the time elections began in the fall, though, Americans everywhere knew this sordid story, which was expanding to include accounts of Jackson mistreating slaves. For instance, a group of supporters in Harrisburg, Pennsylvania, nervously weighed the charge that Jackson had marked his human merchandise by cutting off ears. The Jackson press could do little more than laud his benevolent attitude toward his slaves. Duff Green cooed that "as a master he is humane and indulgent" whose slaves were "well clothed, and well fed." He was not "disposed to treat them with severity" and would "not permit others to do it."[34]

These were at best particles of truth in an awful story. Jackson did insist that overseers treat slaves humanely, and he always had their injuries tended and illnesses nursed, but he was also occasionally harsh, especially with runaways. Recent archaeological work at the Hermitage has mottled claims that the plantation had large brick dwellings for slaves. Investigators now speculate that those were improvements that more than coincidentally occurred in tandem with Jackson's political ambitions. A bit of brick and mortar might have been more show than real, a gesture that sought to buy some time while the South mortgaged its morals against a solution in the future, one always promised to come soon, just not that day.[35]

THE THIRD CHARGE revolved around the Treaty of Fort Jackson signed in August 1814, which was notorious for its enormous land cession that victimized Creek allies who had submitted to it because of Jackson's coercive threats. In the years following, Jackson frequently served as a government agent in negotiations for land cessions from southern Indian nations, securing highly favorable arrangements for the United States and sometimes resulting in lucrative land acquisitions by Jackson and his friends.

It was true that Andrew Jackson had made ruthless war on Creeks and Seminoles, but Americans were willing to accept the necessity of war without mercy against a merciless foe. A defenseless enemy, however, was another matter, and stories about killing warriors who were wounded or willing to surrender and sanctioning the slaughter of innocents were troubling. It also gradually came to light that Jackson wanted all Indians east of the Mississippi River moved west of it, and people in parts of the country that had not seen an Indian in years believed the idea inhumane. Jackson's managers and his press countered with ambiguous accounts of Jackson's fondness (though tempered by common sense) for Indians. But, they claimed, the survival of the different tribes as distinct peoples dictated their removal. In early 1828, Jackson told a Georgia member of the House Committee on Indian Affairs that the only way the national government could protect Indians from state encroachment was to remove them. It sounded most sensible to Georgians who were eyeing Cherokee land rumored to have gold in it.[36]

But of all the Jacksonite stories seeking to counter criticisms of Old Hickory's behavior toward Indians, the most effective was the touching one of Lyncoya, the baby Jackson had brought into his and Rachel's home during the Creek War. In this heartwarming account, the child lived with the Jacksons as a son, was educated by a tutor along with their adopted son, Andrew Jr., and was enrolled in local schools. According to Jackson's defenders, Jackson even considered obtaining an appointment to West Point for Lyncoya, but before he did so he asked the boy what he wanted to do with himself. Lyncoya wanted to learn a trade, it was said, so he was apprenticed to a Mr. Hoover in Nashville to become a saddler. In Nashville, though, Lyncoya became ill, and the diagnosis was dire—consumption, and well advanced. The Jacksons brought Lyncoya home. Rachel nursed him until he died on June 1, 1828. Lyncoya was fifteen, possibly sixteen years old.[37]

He was an obscure figure until the news of his death began appearing that summer in Jackson papers throughout the country. Old Hickory seems to have supplied the details to Henry Lee who drafted an obituary that was first printed in the *Nashville Republican* and then reprinted in the *United States Gazette* and the New York *Evening Post,* for starters. It was as much a biography as a death notice, because it included information about how Lyncoya came to the Hermitage and curious details transparently designed to paint cultural behavior as instinctual. The child had fashioned a longbow "after the manner of the Indians" when only five and "was in the habit of dressing his head with all the feathers he could pick up." Lyncoya had never lived with Indians, but he still acted like one, according to the story that announced his death. The meaning was subtle enough to abide quietly in the shadow of the obituary's larger and more immediate purpose, which was to show Andrew Jackson's fatherly affection and kindness for an orphan, regardless of race. But the other meaning was still there. Something innately different about Indians made their assimilation difficult at best and perhaps impossible in a real world taken on its own terms. It was to say that Lyncoya, like all Indians, would have been happier with his own kind. Most of all, they would all be happier living somewhere else.[38]

═══

THE PERSONAL ATTACKS against Andrew Jackson revealed the desperation of his opponents. Pro-administration newspapers scrutinized his irregular marriage and the charge by Rachel Jackson's first husband that she had committed adultery. But a new aspect of this discreditable approach was aimed at Jackson's mother, Elizabeth. Charles Hammond took the lead on this front in both his Cincinnati *Gazette* and its sister publication, one of those "extras" put together for the campaign, the candidly named *Truth's Advocate and Monthly Anti-Jackson Expositor*. His publications were lurid enough to attract readers who liked that sort of thing, but Hammond's operation, like that of John Binns, was an example of how little the administration funded supportive newspapers. Clay knew Hammond—to his embarrassment later on—and managed to drum up some money to supply him with a new set of printer's type, which was how he was able to launch *Truth's Advocate* in 1828.[39]

Adams's friends probably should have saved their money, for much of the information that Hammond placed in his extra was only half true and some of it was outright fiction. Hammond covered land fraud schemes, the six militiamen, the execution of John Wood, the killing of Charles Dickinson, Caesarism, treason with Burr, and a litany of purported scandals topped by lengthy examinations of Jackson's personal life, especially his marriage.

Hammond was something of an anomaly, considering his tactics. He was well educated, thoughtful and had been deemed a talented lawyer before turning to the newspaper trade, a career that saw him tilting at a broad array of windmills. He opposed the War of 1812 and the policies of Henry Clay, but he gradually came to see Clay as the best hope for the economic development of the West, which led him to support Clay in 1824. During that campaign, Hammond developed a morbid fascination with Andrew Jackson that was mostly informed by a kind of blind terror over the possibility that he could become president. In his view, Jackson was "the victim of strong passions and prejudices, . . . a fit instrument for others to work upon, subject to be governed by flatterers, and still inclined to hate every man of talents who has firmness to look through him, and speak of him as he deserves."[40]

During the 1828 campaign, Hammond became fixated on bringing down Jackson by any means possible. He resorted to tactics so unseemly that it was hard to believe that a reflective intellectual such as Charles Hammond could be capable of them, but he was one of those people for whom politics sometimes required great evil to attain a greater good. He never liked John Quincy Adams, but he liked Andrew Jackson less, and his attachment to the administration became a classic case of embracing the enemy of an enemy. He tirelessly defended Adams and Clay against the Jackson press, despite his exhaustion when surveying the endless charges of corruption leveled against the administration. Each new allegation became like "the heads of the fabled dragon" he sighed. "Indeed for One lie contradicted two new ones are immediately got up."

Binns conceded that "these Jacksonians are excellent politicians."
He didn't mean it as a compliment.[41]

In the summer of 1828 Hammond claimed to have information
from a respectable elderly man living in Ohio that Andrew Jackson
was not the son of Andrew and Elizabeth Jackson but was actually the son of a prostitute named Fanny Jennings and a mulatto
slave. The story was beyond fantastical. It was intended to sway
those voters who would be repelled by a candidate with a racially
mixed ancestry. The story understandably enraged Andrew Jackson
by making him a bastard and his mother a whore. As he saw it,
his real mother was a figure deserving reverence, a selfless patriot
who lay in an unmarked grave outside Charleston, South Carolina,
because she had taken sick on a British prison ship and the red-
coated miscreants had thrown her corpse in with a bunch of riffraff.
In response to Charles Hammond's slander, Jackson and his friends
mounted a frenzied campaign to clear her name with their usual
methods of collecting affidavits lauding her character. William B.
Lewis was stunned by the baseness of the charge. He told John Coffee that "the floodgates of falsehood slander and abuse have been
hoisted and the most nauseating filth is poured in torrents on the
head of not only Genl Jackson but all his prominent supporters."
He mirrored Jackson's dark mood when he muttered, "The friends
of Messrs. Adams and Clay have long since lost all sense of decency
as well as reverence for character."[42]

Andrew Jackson would always believe that the "friends" of Clay
were doing his bidding and that he was the real author of the attempt "to blacken the character of an ancient and Virtuous female."
As early as 1826, years before his mother was targeted for abuse,
Jackson made clear to Clay that attacks on his wife would not be
tolerated. John Eaton carried this menacing message to Clay at the
State Department. Confronted with the charge that he was feeding

slanders about Rachel to Charles Hammond, Clay was not flustered but obviously surprised. Yes, he told Eaton, he knew Hammond, but he had never discussed Mrs. Jackson with him. Something about Clay's candor and his surprise convinced John Eaton that the man was telling the truth. Eaton told Jackson this, but Jackson did not believe him.[43]

Hammond's stories about Jackson's marriage were the reason the Nashville Central Committee was formed. Its pamphlet defending the marriage and Rachel Jackson's honor caused detractors to dub it the Whitewashing Committee. John Overton coordinated a response to Hammond that emphasized common themes made coherent and solid by repetition. He gathered statements of respectable women to include in an essay framed by his own recollections, for it was a peculiar fact of their lives that Overton had known Rachel even before the three of them had lived at the widow Donelson's on the Cumberland. A quirk of the underpopulated frontier had seen Overton briefly boarding at the Kentucky home of Lewis Robards's mother. There he had seen the husband's jealousy and had sensed that it sometimes found expression in abuse. Overton sketched these events within the long-accepted chronology of Rachel's separation, Robards's tantrums, and the reluctant but obvious love that bloomed between her and young Andrew Jackson. Everyone in Nashville, Overton vowed, believed that Rachel had been groundlessly divorced, but divorced nonetheless, and that she had been free to marry Andrew Jackson.[44]

It was a masterful effort, and it was also Overton's final flourish for a campaign that he had started more than a decade earlier and nursed through its infancy and the disappointment of 1824. His work was less conspicuous in Jackson's second presidential campaign that began immediately after the House vote in 1825, but the cause for his obscurity rests in other reasons than inactivity, as would later come to light. The interconnected committees, the coordinated press, and the tactical touches of Martin Van Buren seemed to push Overton into the background if not completely out of the picture in his friend's final quest for the presidency. But when it came to Rachel Jackson, John Overton's pen and his person were all and forever in service to her occasion.

The gentle woman her husband's enemies branded an "American Jezebel" preserved a quiet dignity throughout the years-long ordeal, and the toothless old knight defending her achieved a measure of nobility as her champion. Others ostensibly on her side searched for the bottom along with Hammond. Duff Green was not alone among pro-Jackson editors who were digging for dirt on Louisa Catherine Adams, and some of what they found, such as it was, made it into print. Her British birth and rumors that she and Adams had consummated their marriage before taking their vows were meant to offend and scandalize. Lacking anything else, editors resorted to the false charge that Mrs. Adams was illegitimate.[45]

Andrew Jackson always asserted, "*I never war against females*" and denounced any man who did. But his seemingly resolute instructions that "female charecter never should be introduced or touched by my friends" was not quite so forceful when qualified by his adding "unless a continuation of attack should continue to be made against Mrs. J." Attacks on other women, he said, should only happen "by way of Just retaliation upon the known guilty." With such caveats, Jackson's sentiment was not as noble as it should have been. He was convinced that Henry Clay and Charles Hammond were trying "to arouse me to some desperate act by which I would fall prostrate before the people." He burned for his vindication before the people, and if it could only be purchased at incalculable costs, so be it. He had never counted them when it counted, whether in Alabama with starving soldiers facing hostile Indians or ragtag dirty shirts standing behind the Rodriguez Canal. The men now trying to do him in with every weapon at hand, including his wife's reputation, were to "be disappointed."[46]

Rachel Jackson looked like a luffed sail as they all entered the fateful fall of Jackson's final push for the presidency. Nobody could shield her from the stories. She had known as much from the moment all those years before when her steadfast champion had come with the news about the divorce that had not happened. "The Enemyes of the Genls," she told a friend in a lament hued by her Bible, "hav Dipt their arrows in wormwood & gall & sped them at me."[47]

═══════

QUESTIONING THE CHARACTER of political opponents was not new in the 1820s, nor was it novel to search their pasts for embarrassing lapses in judgment and behavior. Yet, the cold calculation of Jacksonite accusations, especially those they embellished or invented, shocked Adams supporters. Early on they struggled to defend against what they considered baseless charges, and the passing of time did not improve their situation. Instead, valid charges about Jackson's misconduct and legitimate concerns about his temperament did little to injure him, while skillful and relentless invective against Adams managed to create the impression that a principled statesman was a corrupt schemer. As the election of 1828 neared, frustrated administration supporters fought Jacksonites' vicious tactics with acrimonious rhetoric of their own in a desperate effort to find something, anything that would call into question Andrew Jackson's fitness for the presidency. That effort gradually drove otherwise thoughtful men to act thoughtlessly. They resorted to extravagant claims about Jackson that much of the public dismissed as groundless, and they leveled personal charges against his marriage that many people thought were crass and unfair. In the age-old political game of digging for dirt and slinging mud, Jackson supporters managed to elevate the dubious tactic and the unfounded accusation to a kind of debased art. When Adams men tried to follow suit, they seemed to sink low and aim lower. As the country prepared to elect its next president, the question of character was much in consideration. The facts guiding public deliberation, however, were not at all clear, having been muddied along the way.

CHAPTER 15

TRIUMPH

A S AMERICANS PREPARED TO GO TO THE POLLS IN THE FALL of 1828, the sense that a large and irresistible political force was on the verge of its moment was palpable. The country had done more than divide during the campaign. People confronted the consequences of losing this election with more gravity than they had felt in almost three decades. Jacksonites had promised to end corruption in Washington and dismantle its haughty aristocracy. Adams supporters had sounded alarms over a government headed by a military chieftain with a history of impulsive behavior. These differences bred fundamental disagreements about the culture and direction of the country. With Americans enthralled and involved, voter turnout from a broader franchise would reflect a renewed, intense interest in politics. More states had taken the choice of electors away from legislatures to place it in the hands of the people, and that too encouraged greater participation. In 1824, the trend of waning interest in presidential elections reached a low ebb with little more than a quarter of eligible voters going to the polls. In 1828, almost 58 percent of eligible voters planned to cast a vote in the general election.[1]

The rise of Andrew Jackson was central to these events and had gone far in causing them. The Battle of New Orleans gave Jackson iconic status, which shielded him from attacks that would have injured a less revered figure, and his popularity made criticism of him seem base and petty, the dross of politics in the worst sense of the word. His reputation alone made him a viable candidate before the Nashville Junto existed, but a convergence of other factors had made his rise possible.

The new political alignments taking shape after the war with Britain were among the most significant. Federalists never recovered from their opposition to the War of 1812, but what happened to them as a result—a steady disintegration—was most important in how it affected Republican unity. Lacking a common opponent, Republicans found new ones in their own ranks as they drifted into factions linked to leaders who called themselves Republicans but without the glue of commonly held principles. It was how John Quincy Adams and Henry Clay parted ways with William H. Crawford and John C. Calhoun. Adams and Clay had an agenda featuring a national bank, federally funded roads, and a protective tariff, but Crawford harkened back to Jeffersonian purity of limited government. Calhoun's nebulous nationalism tending toward states' rights and sectionalism rounded out the political incoherence, which created the impression that 1824 was not about issues but personalities. The American people did not care much for that, as most eligible voters showed by staying home.

Even without the Nashville Junto and its appendages in the press and in politics, Andrew Jackson could have participated in the election of 1824 as a bona fide American hero. With Eaton scribbling and the Junto organizing, though, his military exploits were burnished in a widely read biography and recounted in pamphlets and friendly newspapers. His lack of political experience made him an outsider at a time when the squabbling Republican factions seemed guided by their self-interest rather than his selfless patriotism. He wore the mantle of George Washington while Washington, DC, wore the stain of politicking and patronage.

Jackson's geographical remove from the capital helped in other ways too. Being a westerner gave him the advantage of the region's growing influence in national politics. New England feared the West would drain eastern populations and alter the country's commercial landscape, but it was the widening franchise as part of western settlement that produced a new type of voter different from citizens in the East and alien to the elite classes of established politics. The entrenched system at first dismissed these people as ignorant pioneers barely able to govern themselves, let alone the country, but their numbers proved too large to ignore. The congressional caucus was an early casualty of the new reality, and other traditional political practices soon followed its fate. Rather abruptly, the nation's original political system, in operation for three decades, paused, stumbled, and finally collapsed. That was how a political fledgling could be considered at all, but for Andrew Jackson, who also could count on a culture of adulation and the cachet of a hero, it made him unexpectedly viable in the election of 1824. Four years later, he seemed invincible.

The Jacksonite campaign that came to life immediately after the House vote of February 1825 adjusted its message and honed its techniques. While criticizing the Adams administration for a cold political professionalism, which in reality did not exist, Jacksonites portrayed themselves as more interested in reflecting the will of the people. It was an effective ploy that disguised the fact that they had become far more professional in the coldest sense. They realized that old political traditions endured as new ones were aborning. Professions of deference to ordinary voters had become obligatory, but the Adams campaign only half-realized that, as was shown in the clumsy way it tried to emulate the popular tactics of Jacksonites.

Old Hickory's operatives went on and on about "the people," but they also focused on influential figures at the local level, the Sam Inghams and Samuel Swartwouts and Henry Baldwins of this state and that. These were the men who had always been essential in winning rank-and-file support and deciding local vote tallies.

Thus were Jacksonites able to promote themselves as simple vessels of the popular will even while aggressively shaping it. They created a candidate who appealed to American voters from all geographical sections and economic classes by tapping into the growing dissatisfaction with the status quo. They used the press, public meetings, and propaganda to convince Americans that Andrew Jackson understood their problems and could solve them. By 1828, multitudes had come to believe that as president he would reinvigorate the spirit that had won American independence and had enshrined American liberty.

That was the central idea, and the new methods used to make it irresistible were revolutionary. It is impossible to overestimate how much the use of vigorous local and national committees benefited Jackson's candidacy. Jacksonites quietly organized their efforts around committees that were local but controlled by ascending tiers of authority, from neighborhoods to precincts to counties to states to nation. Paradoxically, centralized control became the management method of Jacksonites, whose most attractive quality for average voters was an embrace of localism and decentralized government.

It was not the only paradox. In a sense, the man the people were poised to make president in 1828 never really existed. The actual Andrew Jackson had been groomed to fit an image as managers either changed his behavior or kept him quiet, while they revised accounts of his past to make him the ideal candidate for a new era. Local mass meetings and barbecues featured stump speakers familiar to their neighbors outside of a political setting and therefore doubly influential when speaking in one. Partisan newspapers delivered the disciplined message that lauded Jackson as a flawless hero and castigated Adams and Clay as corrupt bargainers. Convinced that they were in the right, editors were not insincere when they acted as boosters while proclaiming their journalistic purity. Duff Green, Isaac Hill, Amos Kendall, and scores of others became skilled operatives as well as editors, men who knew how to take the pulse of the public as well as quicken it.

Even more striking about the pamphlets, newspapers, mass meetings, and network of committees was the way they could make hard facts into hazy fancies tailored to appeal to different constituencies in different regions. The result was a coalition of diverse interests combining behind Andrew Jackson's candidacy that upon close inspection made little political sense. Tariff advocates could possibly coexist with states' rights diehards. Supporters of internal improvements and a central bank could perhaps cooperate with zealous democrats preaching a new type of politics on the frontier. But these combinations, interesting in the abstract, were discordant in reality, and the forging of them to win an election hinted at potential chaos in trying to govern them after it. The friendships and alliances among the Jacksonites were likewise puzzling because they were strained by personality clashes or formed as opportunities of the moment. How much and for how long the magic bond of Jackson's popularity and appeal could hold together an organization built by temperamental leaders and their ambitious lieutenants remained to be seen.

Jacksonites on the verge of victory in the fall of 1828 did not worry about it, though. Some would become Jacksonians, others would not, but as the shadows lengthened, the leaves turned and started to fall, and the polls began to open, all of them were as one, and like Andrew Jackson, eager for their moment.

ONLY HABITUAL APPREHENSIVENESS could have made Martin Van Buren doubt the inevitability of Andrew Jackson's victory as states opened their polls in November 1828. "We shall beat them greatly," he had predicted in August, but one never knew, as that cold February day in 1825 had taught him. Until the last moment, he was tying up loose ends into constants and fretting over the appearance of unexpected variables. There was little he could do, for example, about a popular movement against Freemasonry sparked by the 1826 disappearance of William Morgan in upstate New York. Morgan, it was said, had intended to reveal Masonic secrets, and the reaction to his alleged kidnapping grew in force until the Anti-Masons were on the verge of becoming a political party. Andrew Jackson was a Mason; John Quincy Adams was not. The Adams camp had pointed this out in rural parts of New York to taint Old Hickory for belonging to a cult of elitists willing to commit murder to keep their secrets. But in November 1828, Anti-Masonry's anger was still incipient and its day had not yet arrived. Looking back, Van Buren would again be reminded of Jefferson's maxim about the pain caused by evils that never happened.[2]

In the spirit of taking no chances, however, Van Buren decided to leave the Senate. His friends convinced him that if he ran for governor of New York, his name on the ticket would pull voters to Jackson, and he reluctantly agreed. Jackson's victory in New York was narrow enough—twenty electors to Adams's sixteen—to commend the wisdom of the move. The election that made Jackson president put Van Buren in Albany as the state's governor, at least for a time.[3]

By the middle of November, as results rolled in from across the country, it became increasingly apparent that Jackson had not only won but had done so in a landslide. Henry Clay wrote to a friend before the Kentucky tally was final that if the state went for Jackson, it "will mortify and distress me." It did. Pennsylvania voted for Jackson by a two-to-one margin. Jackson took Ohio, and John Sloane, the adamant Adams supporter who had initiated a House investigation of the six militiamen incident, lost his congressional seat. Henry Clay sent condolences, but reminded Sloane that there were more important things to worry about. Jackson's election meant that "no greater calamity has fallen to our lot since we were a free people." Even so, Clay bristled over last-gasp plans to persuade electors to switch their votes to another man. Jackson's election was a blow so profound that Clay could hardly endure it. But to thwart it and the will of the people with arcane chicanery would not save the country. It would only demolish trust in the government and its systems. It would be *corrupt*.[4]

The will of the people, after all, was clear. As expected, Adams took New England and won part of New York's electoral votes, 6 of Maryland's 11, all of Delaware's 3, and all of New Jersey's 8, but Jackson won everything else easily. With the popular vote counted, and the Delaware and South Carolina legislatures on record for their electors, Jackson crushed Adams by a two-to-one margin in the Electoral College, with 178 to 83. The popular vote tally, though a bit narrower, still represented an overwhelming Jackson victory with his 647,286 to Adams's 508,064.

With Jackson's election assured, the Hermitage became a beehive. He received letters from Washington urging him to come to the capital right away. Except for the period before George Washington's first term, every president-elect had been in the capital when Congress opened the sealed boxes and officially tallied the states' electors. That meant that every victor after 1789 was notified immediately and could begin setting up an administration rather than making a taxing trip to the March 4 inauguration.[5]

The sensible plan appealed to Jackson and his advisers—their new label abruptly changed from "managers" had a nice resonance— but Rachel Jackson wrung her hands at the prospect. What would she wear? If they left for Washington soon, nothing suitable would be ready. But her concern about a wardrobe cloaked something else. The whispers over all those years had become more than she could bear. She could not catch her breath. She used a woman's prerogative about clothes and fashion to raise the possibility of staying behind, at least for the time being. She proposed to join the General later. Neither her friends nor the president-elect's advisers would hear of it.[6]

EPILOGUE

Rachel Jackson died between ten and eleven o'clock on the night of Monday, December 22, 1828. She was sixty-two years old.

Almost immediately sentimentalists, her husband among them, set her death at the doors of newspaper editors who had dredged up her past, but Rachel Jackson's past had always been scarred by gossip, and she did not need newspapers to remind her of it. Others blamed Andrew Jackson for Rachel's death, musing that he could have spared her the pain caused by the gossip and, by inference, saved her life. He had only to settle for a placid retirement where they both could have spun out their years in her haven of the Hermitage, forgetting the world and by the world forgotten. Both views were emotional nonsense. What had happened to Rachel Jackson in the campaign of 1828 was most unseemly, and some of it had been vicious, but it wasn't lethal. And Andrew Jackson's faults did not include killing his wife by exposing her to slander. In September 1828, Edward Livingston castigated the knaves who hurled mud at a defenseless woman and sensibly addressed the consequences of letting such people control public discourse. "Men of respectability will withdraw from the degrading contest," he warned, and " . . . the vile and worthless alone will fill your offices."[1]

Rachel Jackson's health had been declining for more than a year. Symptoms indicated heart disease. A visitor to the Hermitage in 1827 described her as having grown more than stout. Worse, she had become chronically short of breath and wheezed between words as she spoke. The slightest exertion fatigued her. Her family had to notice this, but perhaps her calm kindness made it less obvious. Henry Lee felt the warmth of her smile as she visited his Anne to pet, cosset, and soothe a poor creature fighting dope, depression, and degradation all at the same time and often feeling wretched and alone. Rachel fretted over Anne being "somewhat deraingd" by the stubborn addiction, but she refused to let her feel alone in sadness and shame.[2]

Such deeds, for those fortunate enough to see them, revealed a soul "like those fountains which, rising in deep and secluded valleys, flow on in the frost of winter and through summer's heat." She was, Jackson explained with plaintive simplicity, "the partner of my life." To her, he was all the world and more, and her only concern was how her past could tarnish his fame and how her dowdy appearance might make him ashamed. On the last journey of her life in January 1828, the trip down the Mississippi on the *Pocahontas*, she had overheard the ladies of their party asking James Alexander Hamilton to disembark early at New Orleans and purchase fashionable bonnets for them. Rachel shyly took him aside and asked him to buy her one too. He rather ungallantly remembered her as "ugly," but her face, as he discovered, could tame a temper no other mortal dared cross. The fabled Helen could only have wished for as much.[3]

Just weeks after her husband won the presidency, Rachel was planning the afternoon meal with the Hermitage's cook when she felt a stabbing pain deep in her chest. She screamed and collapsed. Andrew Jackson was writing a letter when he heard her being carried to their bedchamber. He rushed to her side and summoned a doctor, who found her in "excruciating pain" that radiated from her chest into her left shoulder and arm. She could not catch her breath. Over the three days remaining to Rachel Jackson, her husband only left her for a few minutes when he had to. He dropped all plans of traveling to Washington if it meant leaving her.[4]

The final crisis came unexpectedly after she had insisted he get some sleep in another room. Her cry brought him back to see the unthinkable. As Rachel Jackson lay lifeless, Jackson insisted that her physician bleed her, but no blood came. Her heart was not beating. She was placed on an improvised bier. Everyone but Jackson finally retired. He sat alone with her as the hours crept toward dawn.

Nashville had set aside December 23 for a full day of festivities ostensibly commemorating the anniversary of Jackson's 1814 night attack on Villeré Plantation during the New Orleans campaign. But it was actually to be a celebration of his election that would end in the evening with a grand banquet and ball. The news about Rachel brought all preparations for these events to a stop and instantly transformed the town into a place of mourning. The following day, a committee and the mayor called for all businesses to close on December 27, the day of the funeral, and for churches to toll their bells between one and two in the afternoon, the hour for the services at the Hermitage.[5]

On the afternoon of the twenty-seventh, the weather matched the event. A soft drizzle fell from a gray sky. Andrew Jackson watched vacantly and seemed not to hear the doleful voice of the preacher reading scripture. Thousands had traveled for miles to attend, but the throng was silent and kept a respectful distance from Rachel's rose garden as she was buried. Emily Donelson had seen to it that her aunt was dressed in a white satin gown purchased for the inaugural ball. Rachel had never wanted to attend it. Her dearest wish was to never again leave the Cumberland, but she did not want to live without him.

In the end, she would not have to do either. An authority even more imposing than her husband thought it was time that Rachel Jackson should have everything she wanted.

———

ACCORDING TO MARTIN Van Buren, shortly after Andrew Jackson reached Washington in February 1829 he sent a letter to Albany offering the New Yorker the post of secretary of state. Van Buren claimed the offer came as a surprise. Whether or not that was true— with Van Buren, one could never be sure—it did surprise him that the prospect of serving in Jackson's cabinet was no longer so desirable. In some cases, Jackson's selections caused criticism because of the questionable caliber of the people, such as John Eaton for the War Department. In that case, the problem was not just that it looked like Jackson was favoring a crony. Eaton had married the daughter of his innkeeper, the buoyant Margaret Timberlake, whom Emily Donelson had found pretty but coarse. Margaret had been widowed when her husband took sick at sea and died far from home. Eaton's attentions during John Timberlake's long absences had led to talk. Timberlake's death seemed convenient, and the hasty marriage in its wake seemed indecorous. There were sure to be social difficulties.

The grumbling about the new administration from other men pointed to another problem: how to govern with a coalition made for campaigning. Some who had sweated in the trenches and others who had opened their treasuries to put Jackson in the presidency brooded over their sudden expendability. A number of southerners, especially in Virginia and South Carolina, felt displaced by the ascendancy of Van Buren and were in a venomous mood. James Hamilton Jr., who had impishly needled Adams men while pledging to his fellow South Carolinians that Jackson would dismantle the Tariff of Abominations, fairly spat at Van Buren that taking the State Department would amount to Van Buren cutting his own throat.[6]

Van Buren thought that much of this discontent was an overreaction stemming from the incredible newness of what had happened in 1828 and the uncharted ground that consequently lay ahead. He resolved to accept Jackson's offer. After resigning as governor of New York, the Little Magician journeyed to Washington, which he found strangely quiet when his carriage pulled up to his hotel after dark. His conveyance had hardly rocked to a stop, though, "before it was surrounded by a crowd of applicants for office," all talking at once and shoving papers toward him as he signed the hotel register. They followed him up the stairs to his room, jabbering and elbowing. Having invaded Van Buren's room, they jostled one another to catch his eye. He was recovering from a mild illness, and the trip had tired him more than usual because of it, but he was patient, for he knew the mosquitoes swarming around him better than they knew themselves. These office seekers were a breed of insect more prevalent than ever in the fetid lowlands of the Potomac. The new administration had come into office on the promise of throwing scoundrels out, which meant other scoundrels would have their chance. Van Buren was grateful for the chance to escape them by insisting that he pay his "respects to the President within the hour."[7]

When Van Buren arrived, the White House was dark and seemed empty. "A solitary lamp in the vestibule" glowed. Jackson was in his office with "a single candle" inadequately lighting the room while throwing his wan face in high relief. He was seemingly alone, but Van Buren caught sight of another man in the shadows. Van Buren recognized him. It was William B. Lewis. The news was spreading that Lewis was to become an auditor in the Treasury. Van Buren could have heard the grumbles becoming growls.[8]

Incredibly, considering all that had passed between them in the interim, it was Van Buren's first meeting with Andrew Jackson since 1825 when they had parted immediately after the House vote that made Adams president. He found Jackson much changed—older, he thought, and haggard. The old man's appearance should not have surprised anyone. He had just recently led a morose entourage to Washington, DC, every member of which was in mourning. Andrew and Emily Donelson were part of the group. He was to become his uncle's secretary. She was to serve as Jackson's official hostess, the announcement reminding everyone of the awful absence in their party. Emily's cousin Mary Eastin came to brighten moods, to the extent possible. Meanwhile, Jackson insisted on no balls, no parades, no banquets, no ceremonies on the way to the capital.

When they approached Washington on February 11, 1829, they were met outside the town by a waiting carriage. Jackson wearily crawled into it and entered the capital unnoticed. He took rooms at the National Hotel, which winking men dubbed the "Wigwam," and spent the days before his inauguration conferring with congressional Jacksonites. Convinced that the outgoing president in some way, even if only by indirection, had contributed to the death of Rachel, he refused to call on John Quincy Adams, who, in turn, would refuse to attend Jackson's inauguration. Meanwhile, Old Hickory remained secluded in the Wigwam, where he formed his controversial cabinet, mulled other appointments, and worked on his inaugural address. Henry Lee was there to help. He had become an indispensable factotum and valuable wordsmith, but his presence caused as much whispering as that of the new Mrs. Eaton.

Van Buren might have noted that the quiet of the dim room was a stark contrast to the raucous house a few weeks following Jackson's inauguration. When the big day finally came, people who had been pouring into Washington for weeks erupted into a kind of marvelous frenzy. They cheered Jackson as he walked with a military and civilian escort from his hotel up Pennsylvania Avenue to the Capitol, and they erupted in a deafening roar when he emerged on the East Portico to take the oath of office. He bowed to the "majesty of the people," some of whom later quite majestically ravaged the White House in a celebration that Washingtonians judged much more frenzied than marvelous.[9]

All was quiet now, though, except for the low hum of office-seeking mosquitoes here and there in the town. That night, Van Buren, Lewis, and Jackson sat in his office with its single candle a pinpoint of light in an ocean of darkness. Jackson noticed his visitor's glassy gaze from the recent illness and his fatigue from the trip. He abruptly ended their interview with the insistence that Van Buren get some sleep. They would resume the next day, he said.[10]

Possibly his own weariness made the old man look old and ill, and perhaps it was the flickering candle that made his eyes look haunted under a furrowed brow. Van Buren had thought the house seemed empty as well as dark. He did not know the half of it.

═══

JOHN OVERTON ATTENDED Andrew Jackson's inauguration, but he withdrew from public life afterward and only visited his friend once in the White House. His communication with Jackson, however, remained brisk, which we can infer because of the number of items Jackson kept and the few particles of it that Overton did not destroy.

After all, he resolved to burn the Jackson section of his archive. His reasons, according to family lore, were grounded in a desire for privacy and the likelihood, from what he had seen in the political campaigns, that even the most innocent content of that archive could be twisted by artful interpretations to hurt his friend. The letters were more than artifacts and even more than a chronicle. They were a physical appendage of a life spent in friendship and service, and destroying them must have been something like an amputation.

It is a myth of fiction that when an old man nears death his life spools out in a grand chronological recollection. Old men are forgetful and both the small and great things of their past can fall through cracks of memory while other incidents, events, and people randomly snag and remain vivid. Usually these things relate to times of excessive anger and prodigious passion, but they can be offhand remarks long forgotten by their speakers but recalled by the one who heard them, perhaps because the words were pleasant or irritating. Watching the sheaves of paper curl at their edges and then briefly blaze up to become ash might have sent Overton's mind reeling back over the political campaigns, the military exploits, the lieutenants and enemies, the law, the judging, the land speculations. But possibly not. Landing his friend in the presidency was old news to this old man.

The urge to recall the beginning, though, is irresistible. Youth is the best prize of all, which is why old men shake their heads when they see youngsters blithely wasting it. The fire of the blazing letters, even in the darkest of studies, could feel like sunshine, like it had been on the Cumberland, where his friend of the tousled red hair and gangly limbs leaned in silhouette against the door jamb of the widow Donelson's blockhouse. They watched as the "sprightly young woman" went to the well, swinging a bucket at her side. She left in her wake an intoxicating perfume. It carried the slight fragrance of earth.[11]

ACKNOWLEDGMENTS

We are profoundly grateful to friends and colleagues who have encouraged us through the long process of researching and writing this book. They, along with us, have had to live with the General through good times and bad, have had to endure his explosive temper, his moments of warmth, and his overweening ambition. We thank them all for putting up with him as well as us.

Specifically, we would like to thank our dear friend Leslie Fruecht Bentley for sharing part of her summers with us and, more importantly, listening to the endless stories about General Jackson, his Rachel, and the quest for the presidency. We would also like to thank the "Eight Musketeers (now Ten)" for continuing to include us in the dinners and parties that had to be less jolly because we often brought Old Hickory along.

Scholars, many of them also friends, have made our task easier by providing their encouragement and expertise. Professor Kathryn E. Holland Braund was always available to read bits of the manuscript, but more importantly, her vast knowledge of the Creek Indians, especially the "Shee Coocys," added a richness to our understanding of these people that we could not have found anywhere else. Dr. Daniel M. Feller and Dr. Thomas M. Coens of the Andrew Jackson Papers at the University of Tennessee, Knoxville, generously provided us with a previously unknown set of documents bearing specifically on the short, tragic life of the Creek child Lyncoya. We are in their debt. We recall a grand November afternoon with Dan, boating around Saint Petersburg, looking for treasures on Shell Island, and sampling the local cuisine while gazing at the Gulf of Mexico.

Other scholars also provided expert counsel for this project. Jacksonian scholar Tom Kanon of the Tennessee State Library and Archives pointed us to numerous documents that were invaluable to this study. Marsha Mullin of Andrew Jackson's Hermitage gave generously of her time early in the project to answer questions and provide leads for possible sources about the people closest to Old Hickory. We would also like to thank the kind, helpful staffs of the Manuscript Reading Room of the Library of Congress; the Historic New Orleans Collection; the Southern Historical Collection of the University of North Carolina; the Rare Book and Manuscript Library of Duke University; the Georgia Department of Archives and History; the Alabama Department of Archives and History; Albert and Shirley Small Special Collections Library, University of Virginia; the Swem Library of the College of William and Mary; the Massachusetts Historical Society in Boston; and the Filson Historical Society.

This book could not have happened without the vision, meticulous attention to detail, cheerful encouragement, and keen editorial eye of our editor at Basic Books, Daniel Gerstle. We would also like to thank Dan's helpful assistant, Alex Colston. Sandra Beris oversaw production with efficiency and grace, and Christina Palaia's deft copyediting made her suggestions always cogent just as her grammatical vigilance has improved our prose. As usual, our agent Geri Thoma and her assistant Andrea Morrison provided just the right combination of support and advice along the way.

About halfway through this project, Jeanne's mother passed away. Sarah Daniel Twiggs was always our most enthusiastic cheerleader as we toiled and biggest booster once a book was published. We feel her loss sorely. And though we are truly orphans now, we have the encouragement and love of three wonderful brothers. To them, we have dedicated this book.

DAVID AND JEANNE HEIDLER
Colorado Springs, Colorado

ABBREVIATIONS

ADAH   Alabama Department of Archives and History, Montgom-
ery, Alabama.

AHR   *American Historical Review.*

AJP   *The Papers of Andrew Jackson.* Edited by Daniel M. Feller,
Harold D. Moser, et al. 10 vols. Knoxville: University of
Tennessee Press, 1980–2016.

AR   *Alabama Review.*

ASPFR   *American State Papers, Foreign Relations.* 6 vols. Washington,
DC: Gales and Seaton, 1834.

ASPMA   *American State Papers, Military Affairs.* 7 vols. Washington,
DC: Gales and Seaton, 1832–1861.

Duke   David M. Rubenstein Rare Book & Manuscript
Library, Duke University, Durham, North Carolina.

FCHQ   *Filson Club History Quarterly.*

FHQ   *Florida Historical Quarterly.*

FHS   Filson Historical Society, Louisville, Kentucky.

GDAH   Georgia Department of Archives and History, Atlanta,
Georgia.

GHQ   *Georgia Historical Quarterly.*

HNOC   Historic New Orleans Collection, New Orleans, Louisiana.

IMH   *Indiana Magazine of History.*

JAH   *Journal of American History.*

JER   *Journal of the Early Republic.*

JSH   *Journal of Southern History.*

LOC   Manuscript Division, Library of Congress, Washington, DC.

LOV   Library of Virginia, Richmond, Virginia.

MDHS   Maryland Historical Society, Baltimore, Maryland.
MHR   *Missouri Historical Review.*
MHS   Massachusetts Historical Society, Boston, Massachusetts.
MVHR   *Mississippi Valley Historical Review.*
NCHR   *North Carolina Historical Review.*
NEQ   *New England Quarterly.*
NWR   *Niles Weekly Register.*
NYPL   New York Public Library, New York, New York.
PMHB   *Pennsylvania Magazine of History and Biography.*
PML   Pierpont Morgan Library, New York, New York.
PSQ   *Political Science Quarterly.*
RKHS   *Register of the Kentucky Historical Society.*
SCHM   *South Carolina Historical Magazine.*
SCHS   South Carolina Historical Society, Charleston, South
         Carolina.
SHC   Southern Historical Collection, University of North
         Carolina, Chapel Hill, North Carolina.
THQ   *Tennessee Historical Quarterly.*
TSLA   Tennessee State Library and Archive, Nashville, Tennessee.
UGA   Hargrett Rare Book and Manuscript Library, University of
         Georgia Libraries, Athens, Georgia.
UVA   Albert and Shirley Small Special Collections Library,
         University of Virginia, Charlottesville, Virginia.
VHS   Virginia Historical Society, Richmond, Virginia.
VMHB   *Virginia Magazine of History and Biography.*
W&M   Swem Library, College of William and Mary, Williamsburg,
         Virginia.

NOTES

Introduction

1. Robert J. Dinkin, *Campaigning in America: A History of Election Practices* (Westport, CT: Greenwood Press, 1989), 3; Jeffrey L. Pasley, "'A Journeyman, Either in Law or Politics': John Beckley and the Social Origins of Political Campaigning," *JER* 16 (Winter 1996): 531–569.

2. G. P. A. Healy, *Reminiscences of a Portrait Painter* (Chicago: A. C. McClurg, 1894), 149.

Prologue

1. Frances Clifton, "The Life and Activities of John Overton" (master's thesis, Vanderbilt University, 1948), 68–69.

2. Clifton, "Life of John Overton," chap. 4; Henry A. Wise, *Seven Decades of the Union* (Philadelphia: J. B. Lippincott, 1976), 100–101.

Chapter 1: Hickory

1. See Jackson to Daniel Smith, November 11, 1807, in *AJP*, 2:176, for his estimation of Wilkinson and his altered opinion of Jefferson. Burr is quoted in James Parton, *Life of Andrew Jackson* (New York: Mason Brothers, 1860), 1:361.

2. Blount to Jackson, November 11, 1812, in *AJP*, 2:339.

3. Jackson to George Washington Campbell, November 29, 1812, Jackson to Tennessee Volunteers, December 31, 1812, in *AJP*, 2:344, 348.

4. See "Letters of John Coffee to His Wife, 1813–1815," *Tennessee Historical Magazine* 2, no. 4 (December 1916).

5. For biographical information on Coffee and his relationship with Jackson, see Aaron M. Boom, "John Coffee, Citizen Soldier," *THQ* 22 (September 1963).

6. Jackson to Monroe, January 1, 1813, in *AJP*, 2:351.

7. Wilkinson to Jackson, January 22, 25, 1813, Armstrong to Jackson, February 6, 1813, in *AJP*, 2:358–361.

8. Jackson to Grundy, March 15, 1813, Wilkinson to Jackson, March 1, 1813, in *AJP*, 2:374–375, 385.

9. Jackson to Armstrong, March 15, 1813, Jackson to Felix Grundy, March 15, 1813, Jackson to William B. Lewis, March 15, 1813, in *AJP*, 2:383–386, 388.

10. Jackson to Blount, July 31, 1813, in *AJP*, 2:416.

11. Gregory A. Waselkov, *Conquering Spirit: Fort Mims and the Redstick War of 1813–1814* (Tuscaloosa: University of Alabama Press, 2006).

12. Jackson to Tennessee Volunteers, September 24, 1813, in *AJP*, 2:428.

13. Ibid., 429.

14. Jackson to Lewis, October 24, 1813, Andrew Jackson Papers, LOC; John Reid to William B. Lewis, October 24, 1813, in Parton, *Life of Andrew Jackson*, 1:432.

15. Jackson to Rachel Jackson, December 29, 1813, in *AJP*, 2:516.

16. Jackson to John McKee, January 30, 1793, in *AJP*, 1:40; Robert V. Remini, *Andrew Jackson and the Course of American Empire, 1767–1821* (New York: Harper & Row, 1977), 70–71.

17. Stanley F. Horn, *The Hermitage, Home of Old Hickory* (Richmond, VA: Garrett & Massie, 1938; reprint edition, New York: Greenbert, 1950), 123. Jackson probably sent home at least two other orphan Creeks who died as children. See Kathryn E. Holland Braund, "Reflections on 'Shee Coccys' and the Motherless Child: Creek Women in a Time of War," *AR* 64 (October 2011): 278–280.

18. Jackson to Blount, November 14, 1813, in *AJP*, 2:453.

19. Jackson to Blount, December 26, 1813, in *AJP*, 2:504; Blount to Jackson, December 22, 1814, in Parton, *Life of Andrew Jackson*, 1:479.

20. Jackson to Rachel Jackson, December 29, 1813, Jackson to Carroll, February 17, 1814, in *AJP*, 2:515, 3:31.

21. Jackson to Willie Blount, March 31, 1814, in Andrew Jackson, *Correspondence of Andrew Jackson*, ed. John Spencer Bassett (Washington, DC: Carnegie Institute, 1926–1935), 1:489–492.

22. Washington (Kentucky) *Union*, April 19, 1814; Pinckney to Early, April 2, 1814, in *Washington City Gazette*, April 16, 1814.

23. Frank L. Owsley, *Struggle for the Gulf Borderlands: The Creek War and the Battle of New Orleans* (Gainesville: University Press of Florida, 1981), 90–91.

Chapter 2: Hero

1. Jackson to Manrique, July 12, 1814, September 9, 1814, Report of John Gordon, July 20, 1814, Jackson to Robert Butler, August 27, 1814, in Jackson, *Correspondence*, 2:15, 17, 32, 44–45; Jackson to John Reid, September 18, 1814, Andrew Jackson Letters, Duke; *NWR*, October 15, 1814, October 22, 1814; Nicolls to Lafitte, August 31, 1814, Jean Lafitte Papers, Duke; Arsène Lacarrière Latour, *Historical Memoir of the War in West Florida and Louisiana in 1814–15*, ed. Gene A. Smith (Gainesville: University Press of Florida, 1999), 35–39.

2. For analysis of Mobile's importance, see: David S. Heidler and Jeanne T. Heidler, "'Where All Behaved Well': Fort Bowyer and the War on the Gulf," in *Tohopeka: Rethinking the Creek War & the War of 1812*, ed. Kathryn E. Holland Braund (Tuscaloosa: University of Alabama Press, 2012), 182–199; David S. Heidler and Jeanne T. Heidler, *Old Hickory's War: Andrew Jackson and the Quest for Empire* (Baton Rouge: Louisiana State University Press, 2003), 44–46; Jackson to John Armstrong (Monroe), September 5, 1814, Monroe to Jackson, October 21, 1814, in *AJP*, 3:127–128, 170–171; Unknown person to Andrew Jackson, November 20, 1814, Telamon Cuyler Collection, UGA; Frank L. Owsley Jr., "Jackson's Capture of Pensacola," *AR* 19 (July 1966): 182–185; John Sugden, "The Southern Indians in the War of 1812: The Closing Phase," *FHQ* 60 (January 1982): 296–297; John Innerarity to James Innerarity, November 10, 1814, in John Innerarity, "Letters of John Innerarity: The Seizure of Pensacola by Andrew Jackson, November 7, 1814," *FHQ* 9 (1931): 128–130.

3. Thomas C. Kennedy, "Sibling Stewards of a Commercial Empire: The Innerarity Brothers in the Floridas," *FHQ* 67 (January 1989): 279–280.

4. Jackson to Rachel Jackson, November 15, 1814, same to same, November 17, 1814, Jackson to James Monroe, November 20, 1814, in *AJP*, 3:186–188, 190–193.

5. Marquis James, *The Life of Andrew Jackson, Complete in One Volume* (Indianapolis: Bobbs-Merrill, 1938), 247.

6. Jackson to Mayor Nicholas Girod, January 27, 1815, Andrew Jackson Items, HNOC; Jackson to Lafitte, n.d., Jean Lafitte Papers, Duke; Rachel Jackson to Robert Hays, March 5, 1815, Jackson Papers, LOC.

7. *Raleigh Register and North-Carolina Gazette*, May 31, 1816; *Illinois Gazette*, July 1, 1820.

8. *Daily National Intelligencer*, October 3, 1815; John William Ward, *Andrew Jackson: Symbol for an Age* (New York: Oxford University Press, 1955); William C. Cook, "The Early Iconography of the Battle of New Orleans, 1815–1819," *THQ* 48 (Winter 1989): 218.

9. *Daily National Intelligencer*, May 20, May 25, 1815.

10. *Daily National Intelligencer*, August 18, 1815; Providence (Rhode Island) *Patriot, Columbian Phenix*, August 26, 1815.

11. Chillicothe (Ohio) *Supporter*, August 1, 1815.

12. *Maryland Gazette and Political Intelligencer*, February 23, 1815; James, *Jackson*, 266.

13. Vanderlyn to Ralphiel [sic] Earl, April 2, 1819, Vanderlyn Letter, PML; John James Audubon, *Journal of John James Audubon, Made During His Trip to New Orleans in 1820–1821*, ed. Howard Corning (Cambridge, MA: Business Historical Society, 1929), 149.

14. Frances Clifton, "John Overton as Andrew Jackson's Friend," *THQ* 11 (March 1952): 27.

15. Carroll to Jackson, October 4, 1815, in *AJP*, 3:386–387; Andrew Hynes to Jackson, October 24, 1815, Anthony Butler to Jackson, November 7, 1815, Jackson Papers, LOC.

16. William B. Lewis to Lewis Cass, February 28, 1842, William Berkeley Lewis Letters, 1838–1845, MHS; Gabriel L. Lowe Jr., "John Henry Eaton, Jackson's Campaign Manager," *THQ* 11 (June 1952): 100.

17. Memorandum of Daniel Webster, December 1824, in Daniel Webster, *Private Correspondence of Daniel Webster*, ed. Fletcher Webster (Boston: Little, Brown, 1857), 1:371. By inferentially promoting Monroe, "Andrew Jackson," Marquis James would write, "had disposed of the cloud-castle of his aspiring friends." See James, *Jackson*, 272. Also see *Albany Daily Advertiser*, November 28, 1815.

18. *Daily National Intelligencer*, October 4, 1814.

19. New York *National Advocate*, May 20, 1815.

20. Jackson to Livingston, July 5, 1815, in *AJP*, 3:371. Hayne's sentiments are from his letter to Reid on September 13, 1815, which is quoted in John McDonough's excellent essay on the provenance of the Andrew Jackson Papers. See "Introduction" in Library of Congress, Manuscript Division, *Index to the Andrew Jackson Papers* (Washington, DC: Government Printing Office, 1967). It is available online at https://www.loc.gov/collections /andrew-jackson-papers/articles-and-essays/andrew-jackson-papers-provenance.

21. Memorandum, August 22, 1815, Andrew Jackson Letters, Duke.

22. William W. Woodward to Reid, November 22, 1815, Jackson Papers, LOC; Jackson to Carey, August 28, 1815, Hayne to Jackson, January 24, 1816, in *AJP*, 3:371, 4:5.

23. James, *Jackson*, 274.

24. Jackson to Reid, January 15, 1816, Jackson to Nathan Reid Jr., February 8, 1816, in *AJP*, 4:3–4, 8–9; Jackson to Alexander Dallas, February 4, 1816, quoted in McDonough, "Introduction."

25. Maury to Jackson, February 8 and 17, 1816, Jackson Papers, LOC; Jackson to Nathan Reid Jr., February 8, 1816, quoted in Samuel G. Heiskell, *Jackson and Early Tennessee History* (Nashville: Ambrose Print Company, 1918), 2:78–79.

26. Eaton to Jackson, March 20, 1817, in *AJP*, 4:104; Jackson to Abram Maury, April 22, 1817, in Jackson, *Correspondence*, 6:462.

27. Jackson to Reid, January 15, 1816, in *AJP*, 4:4.

Chapter 3: Image

1. John Reid and John Eaton, *The Life of Andrew Jackson, Major-General in the Service of the United States, Comprising a History of the War in the South, from the Commencement of the Creek Campaign, to the Termination of Hostilities Before New Orleans* (Philadelphia: M. Carey and Son, 1817), v. References to the several editions of this book indicate which is being cited by the date of publication, i.e., Eaton, *Biography* (1817). Some changes between the first and subsequent editions are significant in that they reveal the concerns of the Jackson presidential campaigns.

2. Eaton, *Biography* (1817), 17.

3. Robert V. Remini, "Andrew Jackson Takes an Oath of Allegiance to Spain," *THQ* 54 (Spring 1995): 9–10.

4. Robert V. Remini, "Andrew Jackson's Adventures on the Natchez Trace," *Southern Quarterly* 29 (1991): 37–38.

5. Affidavit of Thomas Hart Benton, Franklin, Tennessee, September 10, 1813, Thomas Hart Benton Papers, LOC.

6. Boom, "John Coffee," 234.

7. Eaton, *Biography* (1817), 18.

8. *New England Palladium*, May 3, 1814.

9. Eaton, *Biography* (1817), 154; Jackson to Willie Blount, March 31, 1814, in Jackson, *Correspondence*, 1:489–492; Jackson to Thomas Pinckney, March 28, 1814, Jackson to Rachel Jackson, April 1, 1814, John Coffee to Jackson, April 1, 1814, in *AJP*, 3:52–56; Thomas Kanon, "'A Slow, Laborious Slaughter': The Battle of Horseshoe Bend," *THQ* 58 (Spring 1999): 10–11; Owsley, *Struggle for the Gulf Borderlands*, 79–81.

10. Eaton, *Biography* (1817), 155.

11. Eaton, *Biography* (1817), 186; Jackson to Overton, August 10, 1814, Jackson Papers, LOC.

12. Act of March 3, 1815, in *Statutes at Large*, 13th Cong., 3rd Sess., 3:228–229.

13. Jackson to Coffee, December 4, 1815, and February 2, 1816, editorial note, in *AJP*, 3:394–395, 4:6.

14. Jackson to Coffee, February 17, 1814, George Doherty to Jackson, March 2, 1814, Jackson to Thomas Pinckney, March 6, 1814, Jackson to Willie Blount, March 10, 1814, in *AJP*, 3:32–33, 37–38, 41, 42–43.

15. Jackson's General Order to John Wood, March 14, 1814, in *AJP*, 3:48; *American Watchman*, May 4, 1814.

16. *American Watchman*, May 4, 1814, quoting the *Nashville Whig's* March 15, 1814, report from Fort Strother.

17. Eaton, *Biography* (1817), 142–143; *New England Palladium*, May 3, 1814; *Scioto Gazette*, April 7, 1814.

18. *Daily National Intelligencer*, March 24, 1815.

19. Louis de Toussard to John Clement Stocker, January 9, 1815, Louis de Toussard Letter, HNOC; Heidler and Heidler, "Fort Bowyer," 194–195; Owsley, "British and Indian Activities in Spanish West Florida During the War of 1812," *FHQ* 46 (October 1967): 121.

20. Bartholomew Shaumburg to James Wilkinson, January 25, 1815, Shaumburg Letter, HNOC.

21. Captain Laloire to Jacques Philippe Villeré, January 29, 1815, Jacques Philippe Villeré Papers, HNOC.

22. Connecticut *Courant*, reprinted in the Hallowell (Maine) *Gazette*, September 20, 1815.

23. Matthew Warshauer, *Andrew Jackson and the Politics of Martial Law: Nationalism, Civil Liberties, and Partisanship* (Knoxville: University of Tennessee Press, 2006); Eberhard P. Deutsch, "The United States versus Major General Andrew Jackson," *American Bar Association Journal* 46 (September 1960): 966–972; Jonathan Lurei, "Andrew Jackson, Martial Law, Civilian Control of the Military, and American Politics: An Intriguing Amalgam," *Military Law Review* 126 (Fall 1989): 133–145; Jackson to John Coffee, April 28, 1815, Edward Livingston to Jackson, September 15, 1815, in Jackson, *Correspondence*, 6:454, 457; Jackson to Francis Preston Blair, June 28, 1842, Jackson Letters, Duke.

24. Memorandum of letter to Secretary of War, c. April 27, 1815, Jackson to Secretary of War, April 28, 1815, Alexander Dallas to Jackson, July 1, 1815, in *AJP*, 3:349–351, 375–376; Alexander Dallas to Jackson, March 14, 1815, in Jackson, *Correspondence*, 2:190.

25. Eaton, *Biography* (1817), 255.

Chapter 4: Caesar

1. Crawford to Commissioners, March 14, 1816, Office of Secretary of War Relating to Indian Affairs, Letters Received, National Archives.

2. Crawford to Jackson, March 8, 1816, in Jackson, *Correspondence*, 2:235–236; Jackson to Crawford, June 10, 1816, Jackson to Crawford, June 16, 1816, Meigs to Jackson, August 7, 1816, in *AJP*, 4:43–45, 55–56; Thomas P. Abernethy, "Andrew Jackson and the Rise of Southwestern Democracy," *AHR* 33 (October 1927): 71; Crawford to Jackson, May 21, 1816, War Department, Letters Sent, National Archives.

3. Jackson to Lewis, June 25, 1814, in Jackson, *Correspondence*, 6:433.

4. Vicente Pintado to Josef de Soto, April 29, 1815, Vicente Sebastian Pintado Papers, LOC; Benjamin Hawkins to Jackson, July 17, 1815, Speech of Tustunnuggee Thlucco, September 18, 1815, in Benjamin Hawkins, *Letters, Journals and Writings of Benjamin Hawkins*, ed. C. L. Grant (Savannah, GA: Beehive Press, 1980), 2:742, 754–755; John D. Milligan, "Slave Rebelliousness and the Florida Maroons," *Prologue* 6 (Spring 1974): 6–7.

5. Vicente Pintado to John Innerarity, September 27, 1815, Pintado to Antonio Bocarro, February 9, 1817, Pintado Papers; Mark F. Boyd, "Events at Prospect Bluff on the Apalachicola River, 1808–1818: An Introduction to Twelve Letters of Edmund Doyle, Trader," *FHQ* 16 (October 1937): 76; Crawford to Jackson, March 15, 1816, Jackson to Zuniga, April 23, 1816, Jackson to Crawford, April 24, 1816, Jackson to Crawford, June 9, 1816, in *AJP*, 4:15–16, 22–23, 25–26, 43–45; Jackson to Crawford, May 12, 1816, Jackson to Crawford, June 2, 1816, Jackson to Crawford, June 15, 1816, War Department, Letters Received, National Archives; Zuniga to Jackson, May 26, 1816, *ASPFR*,

4:556; Clinch to Gaines, May 9, 1816, War Department, Letters Received, National Archives; Daniel Patterson to Jairus Loomis, June 19, 1816, Loomis to Patterson, August 13, 1816, Patterson to Benjamin Crowninshield, August 15, 1816, Letters Received by the Secretary of the Navy from Captains, 1805–1861, National Archives.

6. Jackson to Graham, January 14, 1817, Graham to Jackson, February 1, 1817, in *AJP,* 4:84–85, 86–87.

7. Jackson to Graham, February 26, 1817, James Monroe Papers (microfilm), NYPL; Division Order, April 22, 1817, in *AJP,* 4:113; Monroe to Jackson, August 4, 1817, in Jackson, *Correspondence,* 2:319.

8. Winfield Scott to Jackson, October 4, 1817, in *AJP,* 4:142.

9. Calhoun to Jackson, December 29, 1817, in Jackson, *Correspondence,* 2:343; General Orders, December 29, 1817, in John C. Calhoun, *The Papers of John C. Calhoun,* ed. Clyde Norman Wilson et al. (Columbia: University of South Carolina Press, 1959–1988), 2:42.

10. William Gibson et al. to David B. Mitchell, February 8, 1817, Telamon Cuyler Collection, UGA; Archibald Clarke to Edmund P. Gaines, February 26, 1817, ASPMA, 1:682; William Gibson to David B. Mitchell, July 31, 1816, Creek Letters, Talks, and Treaties, 1705–1839, GDAH, 3:876.

11. Calhoun to Gaines, December 16, 1817, ASPMA, 1:689; Calhoun to Jackson, December 26, 1817, in *AJP,* 4:163.

12. Jackson to Monroe, January 6, 1818, in *AJP,* 4:166–167; David S. Heidler and Jeanne T. Heidler, "Mr. Rhea's Missing Letter and the First Seminole War," in *America's Hundred Years' War: U.S. Expansion to the Gulf Coast and the Fate of the Seminole, 1763–1858,* ed. William S. Belko (Gainesville: University Press of Florida, 2011), 103–127; Daniel Feller, "The Seminole Controversy Revisited: A New Look at Andrew Jackson's 1818 Florida Campaign," *FHQ* 88 (Winter 2010): 309–325; Monroe to Calhoun, January 30, 1818, in Calhoun, *Papers,* 2:104.

13. Ernest F. Dibble, "Captain Hugh Young and His 1818 Topographical Memoir to Andrew Jackson," *FHQ* 55 (1977): 321–324; Jackson to Gaines, June 2, 1818, Jackson Papers, LOC.

14. Jackson to Rachel Jackson, April 8, 1818, in Jackson, *Correspondence,* 2:357.

15. John Quincy Adams, *The Diary of John Quincy Adams, 1794–1845,* ed. Allan Nevins (New York: Longmans, Green, 1928), 196; editorial note, in Calhoun, *Papers,* 2:354; Harry Ammon, *James Monroe: The Quest for National Identity* (New York: McGraw-Hill, 1971; reprint edition, Charlottesville: University Press of Virginia, 1990), 421.

16. Monroe to Jefferson, July 22, 1818, in James Monroe, *The Writings of James Monroe,* ed. Stanislaus Murray Hamilton (New York: G. P. Putnam's Sons, 1898–1903), 6:63.

17. Calhoun to Charles Tait, July 20, 1818, September 5, 1818, Tait Family Papers, ADAH; Jackson to Gaines, August 7, 1818, Calhoun to Gaines, September 1, 1818, ASPMA, 1:744–745.

18. Joseph Pizarro to George Erving, August 29, 1818, in *Narrative of a Voyage to the Spanish Main, in the Ship* Two Friends, introduction by John W. Griffin (reprint edition, Gainesville: University Presses of Florida, 1978), 282–284; Adams to Onís, August 24, 1818, Adams to George Erving, November 28, 1818, in John Quincy Adams, *Writings of John Quincy Adams,* ed. Worthington Chauncey Ford (New York: Macmillan, 1913–1917), 6:444–446, 474–475; Adams to Erving, December 2, 1818, ASPFR, 4:547; Richard Rush to George Washington Campbell, February 2, 1819, George Washington Campbell Papers, TSLA; Samuel Flagg Bemis, *John Quincy Adams and the Foundations of*

American Foreign Policy (New York: Knopf, 1949), 313, 317, 323–324; Lester D. Langley, *Struggle for the American Mediterranean: United States–European Rivalry in the Gulf-Caribbean, 1776–1904* (Athens: University of Georgia Press, 1976), 21.

19. Jackson to Calhoun, October 23, 1818, in Calhoun, *Papers*, 3:229; Deborah A. Rosen in *Border Law: The First Seminole War and American Nationhood* (Cambridge, MA: Harvard University Press, 2015) argues that Jackson knew the legal implications of what he had done as early as the taking of Saint Marks (p. 32). For Jackson's evidence gathering and affidavits, see: Hugh Young to William Bibb, September 1, 1818, Governor William W. Bibb Papers, ADAH; Affidavit of Joachim Barrelas, September 18, 1818, Affidavit of George Skeate, September 18, 1818, Affidavit of William Cooper, September 18, 1818, Affidavit of Charles Le Jeune, September 18, 1818, ASPMA, 1:716–717.

20. *National Advocate*, July 14, 1818; William W. Bibb to Charles Tait, September 19, 1818, Tait Family Papers.

21. Eaton to Jackson, December 14, 1818, in Jackson, *Correspondence*, 2:403; Johnson to Joseph Desha, October 29, 1818, Joseph and John R. Desha Papers, LOC.

22. John Quincy Adams, *Memoirs of John Quincy Adams, Comprising Portions of His Diary from 1785–1848*, ed. Charles Francis Adams (Philadelphia: J. B. Lippincott, 1874–1877), 4:224.

23. Clay's January 20, 1819, speech, in Henry Clay, *Papers of Henry Clay*, ed. James F. Hopkins, Mary W. M. Hargreaves, et al. (Lexington: University of Kentucky Press, 1959–1992), 2:636–660; David S. Heidler and Jeanne T. Heidler, *Henry Clay: The Essential American* (New York: Random House, 2010), 141–142; *Annals of Congress of the United States* (Washington, DC: Gales and Seaton, 1834–1856), 33:742, 1072; Deborah A. Rosen, "Wartime Prisoners and the Rule of Law: Andrew Jackson's Military Tribunals during the First Seminole War," *JER* 28 (Winter 2008): 571; Jonathan Roberts, "Notes and Documents: Memoirs of a Senator from Pennsylvania: Jonathan Roberts, 1771–1854," ed. Philip S. Klein, *PMHB* 62 (July 1938): 399.

Chapter 5: Two Washingtons

1. *Annals of Congress*, 33:655–674; L. W. Meyer, *Life and Times of Colonel Richard M. Johnson of Kentucky* (New York: Columbia University Press, 1932), 181–182; David S. Heidler, "The Politics of National Aggression: Congress and the First Seminole War," *JER* 13 (Winter 1993): 501–530; James Campbell to David Campbell, January 27, 1819, Campbell Family Papers, Duke; James Wilson to E. Jackson Jr., January 23, 1819, James Wilson Collection, UGA; Jonathan Barrett to John Holmes, February 16, 1819, John Holmes Papers, NYPL.

2. Jackson to William B. Lewis, January 25, 1819, January 30, 1819, Jackson Papers, LOC; Adams, *Diary*, 209–210; Jackson to Andrew J. Donelson, January 31, 1819, James Gadsden to Jackson, April 15, 1819, in Jackson, *Correspondence*, 2:408–409, 415.

3. Jackson to Pleasant Miller, June 9, 1823, William Blount Papers, LOC; Roberts, "Memoirs," 403.

4. *Annals of Congress*, 33:256–266; Webster to Jeremiah Mason, February 23, 1819, Jeremiah Mason Papers, MHS.

5. Hubert Bruce Fuller, *The Purchase of Florida, Its History and Diplomacy* (Cleveland, OH: Burrows Brothers, 1906), 264–265.

6. Jackson to William B. Lewis, March 26, 1819, William B. Lewis, PLM.

7. Rosen, *Border Law*, 94; Monroe to Richard Rush, March 7, 1819, in Monroe, *Writings*, 6:91; George Erving to Crawford, June 8, 1819, William Harris Crawford Papers, Duke.

8. [John Overton], *A Vindication of the Measures of the President and His Commanding Generals, in the Commencement and Termination of the Seminole War* (Washington, DC: Gales and Seaton, 1819); Clifton, "Overton as Jackson's Friend," 26–27.

9. Jackson to Eaton, November 29, 1819, Editorial Note, in *AJP*, 4:340, 359; King to Jeremiah Mason, February 7, 1819, in Rufus King, *Life and Correspondence of Rufus King*, ed. Charles R. King (New York: G. P. Putnam's Son, 1894–1900), 6:205; Memorial of Maj. Gen. Andrew Jackson, presented February 23, 1820, ASPMA, 1:754–759; Shaw Livermore Jr., *The Twilight of Federalism: The Disintegration of the Federalist Party, 1815–1830* (Princeton, NJ: Princeton University Press, 1962), 62–64.

10. Eaton to Jackson, March 11, 1820, in *AJP*, 4:360–361.

11. Albert Gallatin to George Washington Campbell, August 18, 1819, Campbell Papers, TSLA; William P. Cresson, *James Monroe* (Chapel Hill: University of North Carolina Press, 1946), 322–323; editorial note, in *AJP*, 4:338; Jonathan Russell to Henry Clay, n.d., Russell Family Papers, MHS; Jackson to Calhoun, August 24, 1819, Letters Received, Secretary of War, Indian Affairs, National Archives; Christopher Vandeventer to Jackson, November 22, 1819, Calhoun to Jackson, March 15, 1819, in *AJP*, 4:338, 365; Jackson to Calhoun, December 11, 1819, in Calhoun, *Papers*, 4:477; Calhoun to Jackson, December 24, 1819, in John C. Calhoun, *Correspondence of John C. Calhoun*, ed. J. Franklin Jameson (Washington, DC: Government Printing Office, 1900), 165–166; Bemis, *Foundations of American Foreign Policy*, 352; Wirt to John Coalter, October 25, 1819, "Letter of William Wirt, 1819," *AHR* 25 (July 1920): 693.

12. See July 12, 1817.

13. Gallatin to George Washington Campbell, August 18, 1819, Campbell Papers, TSLA.

14. Abernethy, "Southwestern Democracy," 67; Charles G. Sellers Jr., "Banking and Politics in Jackson's Tennessee, 1817–1827," *MVHR* 41 (June 1954): 66; Michael F. Holt, *The Rise and Fall of the Whig Party: Jacksonian Politics and the Onset of the Civil War* (New York: Oxford University Press, 1999), 5; Murray N. Rothbard, *The Panic of 1819: Reactions and Policies* (New York: Columbia University Press, 1962), 47.

15. Jackson to John C. Calhoun, August 20, 1823, in Calhoun, *Papers*, 8:236. See also Lewis L. Laska, "'The Dam'st Situation Ever Man Was Placed In': Andrew Jackson, David Allison, and the Frontier Economy of 1795–96," *THQ* 54 (Winter 1995): 338, 343–344.

16. Sellers, "Banking and Politics in Jackson's Tennessee," 64–66; R. A. Halley, *John McCormick Lea: A Biographical Sketch* (Nashville, TN: Cumberland Press, 1904), 3.

17. Andrew Hynes to Blount, December 30, 1814, quoted in *Providence Patriot, Columbian Phenix*, February 4, 1815; Anita S. Goodstein, "The Big Business of Nashville, 1780–1860," *Business and Economic History* 11 (1982): 27–29; Abernethy, "Southwestern Democracy," 68; Coffee to Jackson, December 27, 1815, Jackson to Coffee, February 13, 1816, in *AJP*, 4:8, 11.

18. J. Roderick Heller, *Democracy's Lawyer: Felix Grundy of the Old Southwest* (Baton Rouge: Louisiana State University Press, 2010), 1.

19. Daniel Feller, *The Jacksonian Promise: America, 1815–1840* (Baltimore: Johns Hopkins University Press, 1995), 43; Lewis to Jackson, July 15, 1820, Jackson to Lewis, July 16, 1820, in *AJP*, 4:376–379; Abernethy, "Southwestern Democracy," 67.

20. Jackson to John Coffee, July 26, 1821, in *AJP*, 5:83; John L. Lawrence to Jonathan Russell, August 18, 1819, Russell Family Papers.

21. Robert E. Corlew, *Tennessee: A Short History* (Knoxville: University of Tennessee Press, 1981), 159, 162, 170; Heller, *Felix Grundy*, 160; Paul H. Bergeron, *Antebellum Politics in Tennessee* (Lexington: University Press of Kentucky, 1982), 2.

22. Jackson to Livingston, May 17, 1815, in *AJP*, 3:357.

23. Rabun to Jackson, June 1, 1818, September 1, 1818, Governors' Letterbooks, GDAH; Adams, *Diary*, 206.

24. Roger J. Spiller, "John C. Calhoun as Secretary of War, 1817–1825" (PhD diss., Louisiana State University, 1977), 244, 255–256, 260; C. Edward Skeen, "Calhoun, Crawford, and the Politics of Retrenchment," *SCHM* 73 (July 1972): 142, 145–147; Crawford to Tait, November 7, 1819, Tait Family Papers; John H. Eaton to W. S. Hamilton, March 5, 1821, John Henry Eaton Letters, LOC.

25. Adams, *Diary*, 195; Monroe to William H. Crawford, May 23, 1821, Crawford Papers, Duke; Calhoun to Jackson, January 25, 1821, in Calhoun, *Papers*, 5:572–573; Jackson to Monroe, February 11, 1821, in *AJP*, 5:10.

26. Jackson to Coffee, March 1, 1821, in *AJP*, 5:14.

27. Arthur William Thompson, *Jacksonian Democracy on the Florida Frontier* (Gainesville: University of Florida Press, 1961), 1; Herbert J. Doherty Jr., "The Governorship of Andrew Jackson," *FHQ* 33 (July 1954): 6–8; Jackson to Callava, July 12, 1821, in *AJP*, 5:68–69; Jackson to Calhoun, July 17, 1821, in Calhoun, *Papers*, 6:262.

28. For Jackson's relationship with his nephew, see: Mark R. Cheathem, *Old Hickory's Nephew: The Political and Private Struggles of Andrew Jackson Donelson* (Baton Rouge: Louisiana State University Press, 2007).

29. Doherty, "Governorship of Jackson," 9; Jackson to Calhoun, in Calhoun, *Papers*, 6:291–293.

30. Doherty, "Governorship of Jackson," 14–16, 23; Jackson to George Bowie and Henry Marie Brackenridge, September 22, 1821, in *AJP*, 5:102–103.

31. Jackson to Monroe, October 5, 1821, Jackson to Philip P. Barbour, January 22, 1822, in *AJP*, 5:110–111, 137–138.

32. Jackson to Francis Preston, February 19, 1822, Jackson to George Gibson, January 29, 1822, "Friend" to Jackson, October 29, 1821, Jackson to Monroe, March 19, 1822, in *AJP*, 5:112–113, 139, 151, 161.

33. G. Eustis to John B. Davis, November 23, 1821, John Brazer Davis Letters, 1819–1837, MHS.

34. Jackson to Lewis, March 19, 1822, Samuel Ragland Overton to Jackson, August 1, 1821, in *AJP*, 5:89, 151, 159.

35. *Richmond Enquirer*, July 30, 1822.

36. J. T. McGill, "George Wilson," *Tennessee Historical Magazine* 4 (September 1918): 158; Heller, *Felix Grundy*, 160.

37. Lowe, "John H. Eaton," 102; Heller, *Felix Grundy*, 159–160; Corlew, *Tennessee*, 170–171; Richard P. McCormick, *The Presidential Game: The Origins of American Presidential Politics* (New York: Oxford University Press, 1982), 149; Norman K. Risjord, *The Old Republicans: Southern Conservatism in the Age of Jefferson* (New York: Columbia University Press, 1965), 185; editorial note, John Sommerville to Jackson, February 4, 1822, in *AJP*, 5:141–143.

38. Louis R. Harlan, "Public Career of William Berkeley Lewis," *THQ* 7 (March 1948): 15–16.

39. Lewis to Lewis Cass, February 28, 1842, William Berkeley Lewis Letters, MHS; Albert Ray Newsome, *The Presidential Election of 1824 in North Carolina* (Chapel Hill: University of North Carolina Press, 1939), 90–91.

40. George McDuffie to Charles Fisher, January 13, 1823, Fisher Family Papers, SHC.

41. Kim T. Phillips, "The Pennsylvania Origins of the Jackson Movement," *PSQ* 91 (1976): 497–498; Jeffrey L. Pasley, *"The Tyranny of Printers": Newspaper Politics in the Early Republic* (Charlottesville: University Press of Virginia, 2001), 389; Sean Wilentz, *The Rise of American Democracy: Jefferson to Lincoln* (New York: W. W. Norton, 2005), 245.

42. Jackson to Richard Keith Call, June 29, 1822, in *AJP*, 5:199.

43. Mark R. Cheathem, *Andrew Jackson and the Rise of the Democrats, a Reference Guide* (Santa Barbara, CA: ABC-Clio, 2015), 79; Charles Grier Sellers Jr., "Jackson Men with Feet of Clay," *AHR* 62 (April 1957): 543; William G. Morgan, "The Decline of the Congressional Nominating Caucus," *THQ* 24 (1965): 245–255; William G. Morgan, "The Origin and Development of the Congressional Nominating Caucus," *Proceedings of the American Philosophical Society* 113 (April 1969): 184–196.

44. Houston to Jackson, August 3, 1822, in *AJP*, 5:211–212.

45. Jackson to Andrew Jackson Donelson, August 6, 1822, in *AJP*, 5:213; *New Orleans Gazette*, August 31, 1822.

Chapter 6: Solon

1. Jeff Broadwater, *George Mason: Forgotten Founder* (Chapel Hill: University of North Carolina Press, 2006), 233.

2. Gaillard Hunt, ed., *The Writings of James Madison, Comprising His Public Papers and His Private Correspondence, Including Numerous Letters and Documents Now for the First Time Printed* (New York: G. P. Putnam's Sons, 1900–1910), 8:394n2; Frances Anne Baker (Fanny Kemble), *Journal of a Residence in America, in One Volume* (Paris: A. and W. Galignani, 1835), 246.

3. Kemble, *Journal*, 246.

4. Ticknor to William H. Prescott, January 26, 1825, in George Ticknor, *Life, Letters, and Journals of George Ticknor, with Illustrations* (Boston: Houghton Mifflin, 1909), 1:349–350.

5. Wirt to unknown, January 2, 1819, William Wirt Papers, Duke; Russell to Lydia Russell, January 1, 1823, Russell Family Papers.

6. Ticknor to Prescott, January 26, 1825, in Ticknor, *Life, Letters, and Journals*, 1:350; George R. Russell to Amos Binney Jr., December 26, 1821, Binney Family Papers, MHS; John L. Lawrence to Jonathan Russell, March 29, 1822, Russell Family Papers.

7. Lawrence to Russell, March 29, 1822, Russell Family Papers; Philip S. Klein, *Pennsylvania Politics, 1817–1832: A Game Without Rules* (Philadelphia: Historical Society of Pennsylvania, 1940), 119; Harry L. Watson, *Liberty and Power: The Politics of Jacksonian America* (New York: Hill and Wang, 1990), 50–52; Glyndon Van Deusen, *The Jacksonian Era, 1828–1848* (New York: Harper & Row, 1959), 10–11; Richard P. McCormick, *The Second American Party System: Party Formation in the Jacksonian Era* (Chapel Hill: University of North Carolina Press, 1966), 113; Lee Benson, *The Concept of Jacksonian Democracy: New York as a Test Case* (Princeton, NJ: Princeton University Press, 1960), 8; Merrill D. Peterson, ed., *Democracy, Liberty and Property: The State Constitutional Conventions of the 1820s* (Indianapolis: Bobbs-Merrill, 1966), 126.

8. Watson, *Liberty and Power*, 50–52; McCormick, *Second American Party System*, 113; Benson, *Concept of Jacksonian Democracy*, 8; Peterson, *State Constitutional Conventions of the 1820s*, 126; Donald Ratcliffe, "The Right to Vote and the Rise of Democracy, 1787–1828," *JER* 33 (Summer 2013): 233, 245, 250; Tom W. Smith, "The First Straw: A Study of the Origins of Election Polls," *Public Opinion Quarterly* 54 (Spring 1990): 23; Donald Ratcliffe, *The One-Party Presidential Contest: Adams, Jackson, and 1824's Five-Horse Race* (Lawrence: University Press of Kansas, 2015), 21; Holt, *Rise and Fall of the Whig Party*, 8.

9. Newsome, *Election of 1824 in North Carolina*, 24–31; Donald J. Ratcliffe, "The Role of Voters and Issues in Party Formation: Ohio, 1824," *JAH* 59 (March 1973): 857–860; Ratcliffe, *One-Party Presidential Contest*, 14–15.

10. Webster to Jeremiah Mason, January 10, 1822, Mason Papers; Alexander Smyth to unknown, January 18, 1822, Alexander Smyth Papers, Duke.

11. Andrew Hynes to Clay, June 30, 1822, John W. Overton to Clay, January 16, 1822, in Clay, *Papers*, 3:156, 361.

12. Eaton to Jackson, January 11, 1823, in *AJP*, 5:241; Houston to Overton, December 10, 1822, in John Overton, *Dear Judge: Selected Letters of John Overton of Travellers' Rest*, ed. Fletch Coke (Nashville: Travellers' Rest Historic Museum House, 1978), 65.

13. Eaton to Jackson, January 11, 1823, Houston to Jackson, January 19, 1823, in *AJP*, 5:236–238, 241.

14. Lowe, "John H. Eaton," 102; Jackson to Monroe, February 19, 1823, in *AJP*, 5:251; Carroll to Clay, February 19, 1823, in Clay, *Papers*, 3:385.

15. Editorial note, Jackson to H. W. Peterson, February 23, 1823, Jackson to John Coffee, March 10, 1823, April 28, 1823, Jackson to William Savin Fulton, April 4, 1823, in *AJP*, 5:252–253, 258, 268–269, 272–273; Jackson to Calhoun, August 20, 1823, in Calhoun, *Papers*, 8:236.

16. Corlew, *Tennessee*, 171; Heller, *Felix Grundy*, 159; Charles W. Crawford, *Governors of Tennessee, 1790–1835* (Memphis: Memphis State University Press, 1979), 139.

17. William B. Lewis to Lewis Cass, February 28, 1842, Lewis Letters; Miller to James K. Polk, August 18, 1823, in James K. Polk, *Correspondence of James K. Polk, 1795–1849*, ed. Herbert Weaver, Wayne Cutler, et al. (Knoxville: University of Tennessee Press, 1969–1996), 1:19–20; Thomas M. Coens, "The Formation of the Jackson Party, 1822–1825" (PhD diss., Harvard University, 2004); Bergeron, *Politics in Tennessee*, 3; McCormick, *Second American Party System*, 227; Lowe, "John H. Eaton," 102–103.

18. Gordon T. Chappell, "The Life and Activities of General John Coffee," *THQ* 1 (June 1942): 144.

19. [John Henry Eaton], *The Letters of Wyoming, to the People of the United States on the Presidential Election and in Favour of Andrew Jackson* (Philadelphia: S. Simpson & J. Conrad, 1824), 4–5; Robert P. Hay, "The Case for Andrew Jackson in 1824: Eaton's *Wyoming Letters*," *THQ* 29 (1970): 139–151; John Lauritz Larson, *Internal Improvement: National Public Works and the Promise of Popular Government in the Early United States* (Chapel Hill: University of North Carolina Press, 2001), 154; Robert P. Hay, "The Presidential Question: Letters to Southern Editors, 1823–24," *THQ* 31 (1972): 183.

20. John Spencer Bassett, "Major Lewis on the Nomination of Andrew Jackson," *American Antiquarian Society Proceedings* 33 (1923): 28–29; Abram Maury to Jackson, September 20, 1823, Jackson to Maury, September 21, 1823, in *AJP*, 5:297–299.

21. Crawford to Tait, n.d., quoted in J. E. D. Shipp, *Giant Days or the Life and Times of William H. Crawford* (Americas, GA: Southern Printers, 1909), 152.

22. Richmond *Enquirer*, September 12, 1823.

23. *Boston Weekly Messenger*, September 25, 1823; Chase C. Mooney, *William H. Crawford, 1772–1834* (Lexington: University Press of Kentucky, 1974), 241.

24. Alexandria *Gazette*, October 31, 1823.

25. William Wirt, *Memoirs of William Wirt, Attorney-General of the United States*, ed. John P. Kennedy (Philadelphia: Blanchard and Lea, 1851), 2:176–177n; James Henry Rigali, "Restoring the Republic of Virtue: The Presidential Election of 1824" (PhD diss., University of Washington, 2004), 57–58, 66; Wilentz, *American Democracy*, 241–242; Dumas Malone, *The Sage of Monticello*, vol. 6 of *Jefferson and His Time* (Boston: Little, Brown, 1981), 432.

26. Eleanore Bushnell, *Crimes, Follies, and Misfortunes: The Federal Impeachment Trials* (Urbana: University of Illinois Press, 1992), chap. 2; Daniel Webster Memorandum, December 1824, in Webster, *Private Correspondence of Daniel Webster*, 1:371.

27. Lowe, "John H. Eaton," 103; Jackson to Donelson, November 16, 1823, in *AJP*, 5:319.

28. Campbell to James Campbell, December 5, 1823, Campbell Family Papers.

29. *NWR*, December 13, 1823, January 3, 1824; Jackson to Rachel Jackson, November 28, 1823, Jackson to John Overton, December 5, 1823, in *AJP*, 5:320, 321.

30. Lowe, "John H. Eaton," 103.

31. Henry Clay to Benjamin W. Leigh, October 20, 1823, Clay, *Papers*, 3:501; R. M. Saunders to Bartlett Yancey, December 20, 1823, Bartlett Yancey Papers, SHC; Houston to Abram Maury, December 13, 1823, Sam Houston Papers, LOC; Eaton to Rachel Jackson, December 18, 1823, in *AJP*, 5:327.

32. Jackson to Scott, December 11, 1823, in *AJP*, 5:326; Clay to Peter B. Porter, December 11, 1823, in Clay, *Papers*, 3:535.

33. *NWR*, January 24, 1824; Jackson to Edward George Washington Butler, January 20, 1824, editorial note, in *AJP*, 5:341–342; Natchez *Mississippi State Gazette*, February 21, 1824.

34. Ticknor to Prescott, January 16, 1825, in Ticknor, *Life, Letters, and Journals*, 1:349; Paul C. Nagel, *John Quincy Adams: A Public Life, a Private Life* (New York: Knopf, 1997), 287–288; *Niles Weekly Register*, January 24, 1824, March 20, 1824; Natchez *Mississippi State Gazette*, February 21, 1824; Jackson to Edward George Washington Butler, January 20, 1824, in *AJP*, 5:341; Lynn Hudson Parsons, *The Birth of Modern Politics: Andrew Jackson, John Quincy Adams, and the Election of 1828* (New York: Oxford University Press, 2009), 84; Ratcliffe, *One-Party Presidential Contest*, 142.

35. Miller to Fisher, January 3, 1824, Fisher Family Papers.

36. Clifton, "Overton as Jackson's Friend," 29; Polk to Cass, February 28, 1842, William Berkeley Lewis Letters; Harlan, "Career of Lewis," 9–10, 17; Newsome, *Election of 1824 in North Carolina*, 91–92.

37. Jackson to George Washington Martin, January 2, 1824, Jackson to Donelson, March 19, 1824, in *AJP*, 5:334, 378.

38. Thomas W. Cobb to Bartlett Yancey, December 8, 1824, Yancey Papers.

39. Henry Clay to William Creighton, January 1, 1824, in Clay, *Papers*, 11:166; Daniel Webster to Jeremiah Mason, December 22, 1823, Mason Papers; R. M. Saunders to Bartlett Saunders, January 2, 1824, Yancey Papers; Beecher to Thomas Ewing, January 2, 1823, Thomas Ewing Family Papers, LOC; Mooney, *Crawford*, 241; George Tucker to William Tunstall, December 20, 1823, William Tunstall Jr. Papers, Duke; John L. Lawrence to Jonathan Russell, January 7, 1824, Russell Family Papers.

40. Henry Clay to J. B. Stuart, December 19, 1823, Henry Clay Papers, Duke; Daniel Webster to Jeremiah Mason, December 22, 1823, Mason Papers; Jonathan Russell to John L. Lawrence, January 17, 1824, Russell Family Papers; Houston to Abram Maury, December 13, 1823, Houston Papers; George McDuffie to unknown, January 7, 1824, Albert Ray Newsome, ed., "Correspondence of John C. Calhoun, George McDuffie, and Charles Fisher, Relating to the Campaign of 1824," *NCHR* 7 (October 1930): 485; Coens, "Jackson Party," 77–78, 96; Ratcliffe, *One-Party Presidential Contest*, 151.

41. Coens, "Jackson Party," 111, 145–150; *Charleston Mercury and Morning Advertiser*, April 12, 1824.

42. *Washington Republican and Congressional Examiner*, December 2, 1823; Thomas E. Jeffrey, *State Parties and National Politics: North Carolina, 1815–1861* (Athens: University of Georgia Press, 1989), 26; *Massachusetts Spy and Worcester Advertiser*, October 29, 1823, December 17, 1823; Webster to Ezekiel Webster, December 4, 1823, in Daniel Webster, *The Papers of Daniel Webster*, ed. Charles M. Wiltse, Harold D. Moser, et al. (Hanover, NH: Published for Dartmouth College by the University Press of New England, 1974–1988), 1:337.

43. John Elliott to David Blackshear, September 4, 1822, in Shipp, *Crawford*, 172; R. M. Saunders to Bartlett Yancey, January 2, 1824, Yancey Papers; James F. Hopkins, "Election of 1824," in *History of American Presidential Elections, 1789–1968*, ed. Arthur M. Schlesinger Jr. (New York: McGraw-Hill, 1971), 1:370.

44. Robert V. Remini, *Martin Van Buren and the Making of the Democratic Party* (New York: Columbia University Press, 1959), 47–49; Alvin Laroy Duckett, *John Forsyth: Political Tactician* (Athens: University of Georgia Press, 1962), 32; Hay, "Presidential Question," 253; Lowe, "John H. Eaton," 107.

45. George Blake to John B. Davis, February 10, 1824, Davis Letters; Jackson to Coffee, February 15, 1824, in *AJP*, 5:358.

46. Remini, *Van Buren and the Making of the Democratic Party*, 51–52; David Campbell to James Campbell, January 27, 1824, Campbell Family Papers; Thomas Hart Benton, *Thirty Years' View; or, A History of the Working of the American Government for Thirty Years, from 1820–1850* (New York: D. Appleton, 1854–1856; reprint edition, New York: Greenwood Press, 1968), 1:49; *The Virginian*, February 27, 1824; Carter Beverley to Robert Garnett, April 7, 1824, Robert Marion Papers, Duke; John Brevard to Willie Person Mangum, March 10, 1824, Willie Person Mangum Papers, LOC; William Robards to Hutchins G. Burton, March 7, 1824, Hutchins Gordon Burton Papers, SHC.

Chapter 7: 1824

1. Ticknor to Prescott, January 16, 1825, in Ticknor, *Life, Letters, and Journals*, 1:349.

2. Ibid. Oakly would become Dumbarton Oaks under subsequent owners.

3. William Wirt to William Pope, November 12, 1824, in Kennedy, *Memoirs of Wirt*, 2:161.

4. Culver H. Smith, *The Press, Politics, and Patronage: The American Government's Use of Newspapers, 1789–1875* (Athens: University of Georgia Press, 1977), 57.

5. Remini, *Van Buren and the Making of the Democratic Party*, 58–59; Adams, *Memoirs*, 6:390; Newsome, *Election of 1824 in North Carolina*, 112–113; Adam A. Leonard, "Personal Politics in Indiana, 1816–1840," *IMH* 19 (March 1923): 16–17; Monroe to William Wirt, September 27, 1824, in Monroe, *Writings*, 7:37–38.

6. Theresa Strouth Gaul, ed., *To Marry an Indian: The Marriage of Harriett Gold & Elias Boudinot in Letters, 1823–1839* (Chapel Hill: University of North Carolina Press, 2005), 8; Rigali, "Election of 1824," 145, 155, 170–171.

7. Thomas Cooper, *Strictures Addressed to James Madison on the Celebrated Report of William Crawford Recommending the Intermarriage of Americans with the Indian Tribes* (Philadelphia: Jesper Harding, 1824); Rigali, "Election of 1824," 120, 125, 132, 143, 166–167; Nashville *Gazette*, July 21, 1819. Denmark Vesey allegedly led the slave conspiracy, but its scope was at the time and has always been a matter of conjecture.

8. Wirt to Pope, November 12, 1824, in Kennedy, *Memoirs of Wirt*, 2:161; John Niven, *John C. Calhoun and the Price of Union* (Baton Rouge: Louisiana State University Press, 1988), 100–101.

9. Phillips, "Jackson Movement," 491–496; McCormick, *Second American Party System*, 139; Klein, *Pennsylvania Politics*, 121; George McDuffie to Charles Fisher, January 7, 1823, Fisher Family Papers.

10. Erasmus Wilson, *Standard History of Pittsburg* [sic] [,] *Pennsylvania* (Chicago: H. R. Cornell & Co., 1898), 759; Robert D. Ilisevich, "Henry Baldwin and Andrew Jackson: A Political Relationship in Trust?" *PMHB* 120 (January–April 1996): 41–43; Klein, *Pennsylvania Politics*, 124, 173; Herman Hailpern, "Pro-Jackson Sentiment in Pennsylvania, 1820–1828," *PMHB* 50 (1926): 197.

11. Wilson, *History of Pittsburg*, 479; Jackson to Peterson, February 23, 1823, in *AJP*, 5:253; *NWR*, November 15, 1823; Klein, *Pennsylvania Politics*, 123–124; Ratcliffe, *One-Party Presidential Contest*, 122.

12. Phillips, "Jackson Movement," 495–499; Ratcliffe, *One-Party Presidential Contest*, 122–123.

13. Ratcliffe, *One-Party Presidential Contest*, 123, 126–127.

14. Margaret Bayard Smith to Mrs. Samuel Boyd, April 11, 1824, in Margaret Bayard Smith, *The First Forty Years of Washington Society*, ed. Gaillard Hunt (New York: Charles Scribner's Sons, 1906), 164; Klein, *Pennsylvania Politics*, 122–123, 157, 161; Ratcliffe, *One-Party Presidential Contest*, 124; McCormick, *Second American Party System*, 139; John M. Belohlavek, *George Mifflin Dallas* (University Park: Pennsylvania State University Press, 1977), 23.

15. Jackson to John Coffee, February 22, 1824, in *AJP*, 5:362; Phillips, "Jackson Movement," 506–507.

16. Henry Seawell to Thomas Ruffin, March 1, 1824, Thomas Ruffin Papers, SHC; Lewis Williams to Newton Cannon, March 13, 1824, Newton Cannon Papers, LOC; *New-York Patriot and Morning Advertiser*, March 23, 1824.

17. Smith to Boyd, April 11, 1824, in Smith, *First Forty Years*, 164; Mark H. Haller, "The Rise of the Jackson Party in Maryland, 1820–1829," *JSH* 28 (1962): 311; Eaton to Chandler Price, March 14, 1824, Calhoun to John Pendleton Kennedy, March 20, 1824, in Calhoun, *Papers*, 8:579–580, 596–597.

18. Wirt to Pope, November 11, 1824, in Kennedy, *Memoirs of Wirt*, 2:161.

19. Henry Seawell to Thomas Ruffin, Thomas Ruffin Papers.

20. Reprinted in the Wilmington *Delaware Gazette*, March 19, 1824; Charles H. Ambler, *Sectionalism in Virginia from 1776 to 1851* (Chicago: University of Chicago Press, 1910), 130; *Cahawba Press and Alabama State Intelligencer*, June 7, 1823; Taylor to Archibald Austin, March 11, 1824, Austin-Twyman Papers, W&M.

21. Lewis Williams to Newton Cannon, March 13, 1824, Cannon Papers.

22. John E. Harkins, "Newton Cannon, Jackson Nemesis," *THQ* 43 (Winter 1984): 357.

23. Hammond to Clay, April 1824, in Clay, *Papers*, 3:730; Hailpern, "Pro-Jackson Sentiment," 196.

24. Editorial note, in *AJP*, 5:295; Coens, "Jackson Party," 191–192; Ratcliffe, *One-Party Presidential Contest*, 264; Calvin Jones to Duncan Cameron, May 6, 1824, Cameron Family Papers, SHC.

25. William B. Hatcher, *Edward Livingston: Jeffersonian Republican and Jacksonian Democrat* (Baton Rouge: Louisiana State University Press, 1940), 290.

26. Coens, "Jackson Party," 182–183; M. J. Heale, *The Presidential Quest: Candidates and Images in American Political Culture, 1787–1852* (New York: Longman, 1982), 58; John Overton to nephew, February 23, 1824, in John M. Lea, "Biographical Sketch of Judge John Overton," *Proceedings of the 10th Annual Meeting of the Bar Association of Tennessee* (Nashville: Marshall & Bruce, 1891), 183–184.

27. Houston to Abram Maury, December 13, 1823, Houston Papers; Jesse Benton, *An Address to the People of the United States on the Presidential Election* (Nashville: J. Norvell, 1824); Nashville *Gazette*, September 24, 1824; Jackson to John Coffee, September 23, 1824, in *AJP*, 5:442; Nashville *Gazette*, August 7, 1824, September 24, 1824, October 20, 1824.

28. Ratcliffe, *One-Party Presidential Contest*, 165–167; Lowe, "John H. Eaton," 111–114; Coens, "Jackson Party," 41; *NWR*, April 24, 1824, May 1, 1824, May 8, 1824; Klein, *Pennsylvania Politics*, 166–168; Cheatham, *Jackson and the Rise of the Democrats*, 80; Jackson to Donelson, January 18, 1824, Jackson to Monroe, April 10, 1824, Jackson to Kremer, May 6, 1824, in *AJP*, 5:339, 390, 402; *The Missionary* (Mount Zion, Georgia), May 31, 1824.

29. *Mobile Mercantile Advertiser*, January 9, 1824; Smith, *Press, Politics, and Patronage*, 58; Robert P. Hay, "John Fitzgerald: Presidential Image-Maker for Andrew Jackson in 1823," *THQ* 42 (Summer 1983): 140–146; Ratcliffe, "Role of Voters and Issues," 863.

30. Jackson to John Donelson, February 9, 1824, in *AJP*, 5:355.

31. Jackson to Donelson, April 4, 1824, Jackson to Lewis, May 7, 1824, in *AJP*, 5:388–389, 405.

32. Mercer to William Gaston, May 6, 1824, William Gaston Papers, SHC.

33. Jackson to James Lanier, May 15, 1824, Jackson to Monroe, July 25, 1822, in *AJP*, 5:208, 409.

34. James Kehl, *Ill Feeling in the Era of Good Feeling: Western Pennsylvania Political Battles, 1818–1825* (Pittsburgh, PA: University of Pittsburgh Press, 1956), 212; Abernethy, "Southwestern Democracy," 75.

35. Risjord, *Old Republicans*, 209; Ratcliffe, *One-Party Presidential Contest*, 30.

36. Jackson to Coleman, April 26, 1824, in *AJP*, 5:398–400; Martin Van Buren, "The Autobiography of Martin Van Buren," in *Annual Report of the American Historical Association for the Year 1928*, ed. John C. Fitzpatrick (Washington, DC: Government Printing Office, 1920), 240.

37. Eaton to Jackson, June 22, 1824, in *AJP*, 5: 419–420; *The Microscope*, June 5, 1824.

38. Coffee to Jackson, June 8, 1824; Jackson to George Wilson, August 13, 1824, editorial note, in *AJP*, 5:412, 433–434; Joseph Gibbs to Louis McLane, July 25, 1824, Louis McLane Papers, LOC; Horn, *The Hermitage*, 66.

39. Remini, *Van Buren and the Making of the Democratic Party*, 53, 55; Robin Kolodny, "The Several Elections of 1824," *Congress and the Presidency* 23 (Fall 1996): 152.

Chapter 8: Election

1. Nagel, *John Quincy Adams*, 288; Daniel Webster to William Gaston, September 8, 1824, Gaston Papers.

2. Rigali, "Election of 1824," 187–188; Nagel, *John Quincy Adams*, 288; Adams, *Memoirs*, 6:254, 293.

3. Russell to Lydia Russell, January 31, 1822, Russell Family Papers.

4. James Freeman Clarke, *Anti-Slavery Days: Sketch of the Struggle Which Ended in the Abolition of Slavery in the United States* (New York: John W. Lovell Company, 1883), 43.

5. Carter and Prentiss to Russell, June 24, 1822, Ralph Lockwood to Russell, June 27, 1822, John L. Lawrence to Russell, June 28, 1822, Barney Smith to Russell, August 2, 1822, Russell Family Papers; Clay to Russell, April 19, 1823, in Clay, *Papers*, 3:409; NWR, July 27, 1822.

6. William Plumer Jr. to Salma Hale, April 5, 1820, in Everett S. Brown, ed., *The Missouri Compromises and Presidential Politics, 1820–1825: From Letters of William Plumer, Jr.* (St. Louis: Missouri Historical Society, 1926), 47.

7. *New York Post*, October 28, 1824, quoted in Rigali, "Election of 1824," 195; Nagel, *John Quincy Adams*, 289; Paul C. Nagel, "The Election of 1824: A Reconsideration Based on Newspaper Opinion," *JSH* 26 (August 1960): 318. William Plumer Jr. to William Plumer, December 7, 1824, in Brown, *Missouri Compromises*, 119.

8. Everett S. Brown, "The Presidential Election of 1824–1825," *PSQ* 40 (1925): 394; Jonathan H. Earle, *Jacksonian Antislavery & the Politics of Free Soil, 1824–1854* (Chapel Hill: University of North Carolina Press, 2004), 57; Gerard Leonard, *The Invention of Party Politics: Federalism, Popular Sovereignty and Constitutional Development in Jacksonian Illinois* (Chapel Hill: University of North Carolina Press, 2002), 37.

9. David Gordon to Albert G. Ruffin, September 11, 1824, Francis Ruffin Papers, SHC; Unknown to H. G. Burton, July 9, 1824, Burton Papers; Samuel Whitcomb Diary, May 31, 1824, June 1, 1824, MHS; Thomas Jefferson to Judge William Johnson, June 12, 1823, Jefferson Letter, SCHS; Albert Gallatin to Jean Badollet, July 29, 1824, in Henry Adams, *The Life of Albert Gallatin* (Philadelphia: J. B. Lippincott, 1879, reprint edition, New York: Peter Smith, 1943), 598–599; Remini, *Van Buren and the Making of the Democratic Party*, 59–62.

10. Remini, *Van Buren and the Making of the Democratic Party*, 64; Rigali, "Election of 1824," 249.

11. Earle, *Jacksonian Antislavery*, 57; Rigali, "Election of 1824," 242, 252.

12. Remini, *Van Buren and the Making of the Democratic Party*, 65; Kolodny, "Elections of 1824," 153; Ratcliffe, *One-Party Presidential Contest*, 219; Aaron Burr to Levi McKeen, November 12, 1824, in Mary-Jo Kine, ed., *Political Correspondence and Public Papers of Aaron Burr* (Princeton, NJ: Princeton University Press, 1983), 2:1189; Raymond Walters Jr., *Albert Gallatin: Jeffersonian Financier and Diplomat* (New York: Macmillan, 1957), 324; Clay to Francis T. Brooke, March 6, 1824, Clay to Josiah S. Johnston, August 31, 1824, Clay to Peter Porter, September 2, 1824, Clay to Francis Preston Blair, January 25, 1825, in Clay, *Papers*, 3:674, 821, 835, 4:47; also see Willie P. Mangum to William Polk, February 8, 1824, Brown-Ewell Family Papers, FHS.

13. Jackson to Andrew Jackson Donelson, April 17, 1824, in *AJP*, 5:396.

14. *Nashville Republican*, October 2, 1824, October 30, 1824; McCormick, *Presidential Game*, 121–122.

15. Houston to Robert Williams, February 4, 1824, Houston Papers; John Eaton to George Washington Campbell, January 29, 1822, George Washington Campbell

Papers, LOC; Samuel D. Ingham to William Gaston, April 24, 1824, C. T. Mercer to William Gaston, May 6, 1824, Gaston Papers; Benjamin Watkins Leigh to Henry Lee, November 29, 1824, Benjamin Watkins Leigh Papers, VHS; Webster to Jeremiah Mason, April 19, 1824, in Webster, *Papers*, 1:357.

16. *Nashville Republican*, October 20, 1824.

17. *Daily National Intelligencer*, February 10, 1825; Ratcliffe, "Right to Vote," 233, 245, 250; Smith, "First Straw," 23; Ratcliffe, *One-Party Presidential Contest*, 21; Holt, *Rise and Fall of the Whig Party*, 8; Lillian B. Miller, *"If Elected—": Unsuccessful Candidates for the Presidency, 1796–1968* (Washington, DC: Smithsonian Institution Press, 1972), 76.

18. *Connecticut Herald*, November 2, 1824.

19. McCormick, *Second American Party System*, 261–262; Atwater to Jackson, June 24, 1824, in *AJP*, 5:421; Peter Porter to Henry Clay, January 14, 1825, in Clay, *Papers*, 4:16.

20. Remini, *Van Buren and the Making of the Democratic Party*, 75–82; McCormick, *Second American Party System*, 116; Joel H. Silbey, *Martin Van Buren and the Emergence of American Popular Politics* (New York: Rowman & Littlefield, 2002), 45.

21. Ratcliffe, *One-Party Presidential Contest*, 185–186; Kolodny, "Elections of 1824," 153–154; McCormick, *Second American Party System*, 128–129.

22. Charles Fisher to Carson, January 6, 1824, B. B. Smith to Charles Fisher, February 7, 1824, Fisher Family Papers, SHC; McCormick, *Second American Party System*, 203; Newsome, *Election of 1824 in North Carolina*, 40, 137–138, 147–152; Samuel King to Duncan Cameron, February 28, 1824, Cameron Family Papers, SHC; Ratcliffe, *One-Party Presidential Contest*, 192–194; William S. Hoffman, *Andrew Jackson and North Carolina Politics* (Chapel Hill: University of North Carolina Press, 1958), 2–3.

23. Thomas P. Abernethy, *The Formative Period in Alabama, 1815–1828*, 2nd ed. (Tuscaloosa: University of Alabama Press, 1965), 132.

24. Ratcliffe, *One-Party Presidential Contest*, 188; Kolodny, "Elections of 1824," 153.

25. Ratcliffe, *One-Party Presidential Contest*, 179; Thomas William Howard, "Indiana Newspapers and the Presidential Election of 1824," *IMH* 63 (September 1967): 189–192, 206; Leonard, "Politics in Indiana," 17, 22, 29.

26. Heidler and Heidler, *Henry Clay*, 155; Ratcliffe, *One-Party Presidential Contest*, 215; McCormick, *Second American Party System*, 313–314; Clay to Francis T. Brooke, December 22, 1824, in Clay, *Papers*, 3:900; David Corbin Ker to Jackson, November 23, 1824, in *AJP*, 5:450.

27. The quotation is from William Shakespeare's *Macbeth*, Act 3, Scene 4, in *Charleston Mercury*, November 20, 1824.

Chapter 9: Bargains

1. Pauline Wilcox Burke, *Emily Donelson of Tennessee*, ed. Jonathan M. Atkins (Knoxville: University of Tennessee Press, 2001), 84.

2. Jackson to Donelson, December 28, 1818, in *AJP*, 4:263; Charles Faulkner Bryan Jr., "The Prodigal Nephew: Andrew Jackson Donelson and the Eaton Affair," *East Tennessee Historical Society's Publications* 50 (1978): 93–96; Harriet Chappell Owsley, "Andrew Jackson and His Ward, Andrew Jackson Donelson," *THQ* 41 (Summer 1982): 126–127.

3. Mark R. Cheathem, "'High Minded Honourable Man': Honor, Kinship, and Conflict in the Life of Andrew Jackson Donelson," *JER* 27 (Summer 2007): 272; Jackson to Donelson, May 20, 1822, in *AJP*, 5:188.

4. Rachel Jackson to Elizabeth Kingsley, December 23, 1824, Jackson to William Berkeley Lewis, December 27, 1824, in *AJP*, 5:457, 459; Newsome, *Election of 1824 in North Carolina*, 135.

5. Jackson to Charles P. Tutt, January 9, 1824, in Jackson, *Correspondence*, 3:373–374.

6. Ratcliffe, *One-Party Presidential Contest*, 231; McLane to Catherine McLane, December 9, 29, 1824, McLane Papers.

7. Robert P. Hay, "The American Revolution Twice Recalled: Lafayette's Visit and the Election of 1824," *IMH* 69 (March 1973): 44–46, 51, 56–58, 60; George Erving to William H. Crawford, June 26, 1824, William Harris Crawford Papers, LOC.

8. Anne C. Loveland, "Lafayette's Farewell Tour," in *Hero of Two Worlds: The Art and Pageantry of His Farewell Tour of America, 1824–1825*, ed. Stanley J. Idzerda, Anne C. Loveland, and Marc H. Miller (Hanover, NH: University Press of New England, 1989), 63–66.

9. William Wallace to unknown, February 12, 1825, William Manson Wallace Papers, Duke; J. W. Baker to Nicholas Trist, December 2, 1824, Nicholas P. Trist Papers, SHC.

10. Rachel Jackson to Elizabeth Kingsley, December 23, 1824, in *AJP*, 5:456.

11. Charleston *Southern Patriot and Commercial Advertiser*, January 11, 1825; editorial note, in Clay, *Papers*, 4:2; McLane to Catherine McLane, January 2, 1825, McLane Papers.

12. Louis McLane to Catherine McLane, January 13, 1825, McLane Papers.

13. Editorial note, in Clay, *Papers*, 4:2.

14. Clay to George McClure, December 28, 1824, Clay to Francis Preston Blair, January 8, 1825, in Clay, *Papers*, 3:906, 4:9–10; McCormick, *Presidential Game*, 127.

15. Eaton to George Washington Campbell, January 29, 1822, Campbell Papers, TSLA.

16. Jackson to Overton, December 19, 1824, in *AJP*, 5:455; Ratcliffe, *One-Party Presidential Contest*, 3; Donald Ratcliffe, "Popular Preferences in the Presidential Election of 1824," *JER* 34 (Spring 2014): 55.

17. Romulus Saunders to Bartlett Yancey, December 10, 1824, in A. R. Newsome, ed., "Letters of Romulus M. Saunders to Bartlett Yancey, 1821–1828," *NCHR* 8 (1931): 447; Louis McLane to Catherine McLane, January 31, 1825, McLane Papers; Adams, *Memoirs*, 6:493; Van Buren, *Autobiography*, 150; Remini, *Van Buren and the Making of the Democratic Party*, 85–86; Duckett, *Forsyth*, 33.

18. Jackson to John Overton, January 10, 1825, Jackson to Coffee, January 5, 1825, January 6, 1825, in *AJP*, 5:5–8, 14.

19. Parton, *Life of Andrew Jackson*, 3:57.

20. Klein, *Pennsylvania Politics*, 179–181; Lowe, "John H. Eaton," 118.

21. Klein, *Pennsylvania Politics*, 181–182; Louis McLane to Catherine McLane, January 31, 1825, McLane Papers; Adams, *Memoirs*, 6:495; Ratcliffe, *One-Party Presidential Contest*, 244–245.

22. Clay to Adams, January 9, 1825, Adams to Clay, January 9, 1825, in Clay, *Papers*, 4:11; Adams, *Memoirs*, 6:464–465.

23. Van Buren, *Autobiography*, 150.

24. Clay to Benjamin W. Leigh, December 22, 1824, in Clay, *Papers*, 3:901.

25. *Charleston Mercury and Morning Advertiser*, January 20, 1825, January 21, 1825; Albert D. Kirwan, *John J. Crittenden: The Struggle for the Union* (Lexington: University of Kentucky Press, 1962), 68–69; Adams, *Memoirs*, 6:479; James Buchanan to Thomas Elder, January 2, 1825, in James Buchanan, *The Works of James Buchanan*, ed. John Bassett

Moore (Philadelphia: J. B. Lippincott, 1908–1911), 1:120; Nathaniel Macon to Charles Tait, January 9, 1825, Nathaniel Macon Papers, Duke; Brown, "Presidential Election of 1824–1825," 400.

26. Francis Preston Blair to Henry Clay, February 11, 1825, in Clay, *Papers*, 4:66; John McKee to Samuel Brown, January 26, 1825, J. A. Ware to Samuel Brown, January 29, 1825, Samuel Brown Papers, FHS; Henry Clay to J. B. Stuart, January 15, 1825, Henry Clay Papers, Duke.

27. Jackson to William B. Lewis, January 29, 1825, in *AJP*, 6:22; Ratcliffe, *One-Party Presidential Contest*, 258; Adams, *Memoirs*, 6:482.

28. Brown, "Presidential Election of 1824–1825," 401; Saunders to Yancey, January 18, 1825, in Newsome, "Letters of Romulus M. Saunders," 451; Ratcliffe, *One-Party Presidential Contest*, 246; Remini, *Van Buren and the Making of the Democratic Party*, 87.

29. Philadelphia *Columbian Observer*, January 25, 1825.

30. *Massachusetts Spy and Worcester Advertiser*, February 16, 1825; Clay to Gales and Seaton, January 30, 1825, George Kremer's Card, February 3, 1825, in Clay, *Papers*, 4:48, 52.

31. Daniel Webster to Ezekiel Webster, February 4, 1825, in Webster, *Papers*, 2:20; George Logan to Littleton Waller Tazewell, February 7, 1825, Tazewell Family Papers, LOV; Thomas W. Cobb to Henry Jackson, February 6, 1825, Jackson and Prince Family Papers, SHC; John J. Crittenden to Clay, February 15, 1825, in Clay, *Papers*, 4:68.

32. Louis McLane to Catherine McLane, February 6, 1825, McLane Papers; John Campbell to David Campbell, January 28, 1825, Campbell Family Papers; Thomas J. Green to William Polk, January 29, 1825, Brown-Ewell Family Papers.

33. Louis McLane to Catherine McLane, February 5, 1825, McLane Papers; *The Microscope*, February 19, 1825.

34. Henry R. Warfield to Daniel Webster, February 3, 1825, Webster to Warfield, February 5, 1825, in Webster, *Papers*, 2:18, 21–22; Mary W. M. Hargreaves, *The Presidency of John Quincy Adams* (Lawrence: University Press of Kansas, 1985), 39–40; Newsome, *Election of 1824 in North Carolina*, 167–169, 172; Alan S. Weiner, "John Scott, Thomas Hart Benton, David Barton and the Presidential Election of 1824: A Case Study in Pressure Politics," *MHR* 60 (1966): 481–482; William E. Foley, "The Political Philosophy of David Barton," *MHR* 58 (1964): 287.

35. Merrill D. Peterson, *The Great Triumvirate: Webster, Clay, and Calhoun* (New York: Oxford University Press, 1987), 124; Asbury Dickins to John Binns, Asbury Dickins Family Papers, LOC. Since the passage of the Twelfth Amendment in 1804, providing for separate electoral votes for president and vice president, the concept of an official running mate for presidential candidates had not fully developed.

36. Remini, *Van Buren and the Making of the Democratic Party*, 86–87; William B. Fink, "Stephen Van Rensselaer and the House Election of 1825," *New York History* 32 (1951): 326–327; Van Buren, *Autobiography*, 151–152; McLane to Catherine McLane, February 9, 1825, McLane Papers.

37. *Daily National Intelligencer*, February 10, 1825.

38. Ibid.; Burke, *Emily Donelson*, 103.

39. Smith, *First Forty Years*, 192.

40. Samuel G. Goodrich, *Recollections of a Lifetime or Men and Things I Have Seen: In a Series of Letters to a Friend, Historical, Biographical, Anecdotal, and Descriptive*, 2 vols. (New York: Miller, Orton and Mulligan, 1866), 399; Macon to Bartlett Yancey, December 26, 1824, in Edwin Mood Wilson, *The Congressional Career of Nathaniel*

Macon, Followed by Letters of Mr. Macon and Willie P. Mangum with notes by Kemp P. Battle (Chapel Hill: University of North Carolina Press, 1900), 73.

41. McLane to Catherine McLane, February 9, 1825, McLane Papers.

42. Washington, DC, *Columbian Star*, February 12, 1825; *Daily National Intelligencer*, February 11, 1825.

43. Adams, *Memoirs*, 6:502; *Daily National Intelligencer*, February 11, 1825.

44. Smith, *First Forty Years*, 180.

Chapter 10: Allegations

1. Romulus Saunders to Bartlett Yancey, February 22, 1825, Yancey Papers.

2. Adams, *Memoirs*, 6:505; Clay to Adams, February 11, 1825, in Clay, *Papers*, 4:63; John Campbell to David Campbell, February 20, 1825, Campbell Family Papers; McLane to Catherine McLane, February 21, 1825, McLane Papers; Mathurin G. Gibbs to Isaac Ball, February 16, 1825, John Ball Papers, SCHS; William Brockenbrough to Albert G. Ruffin, February 19, 1825, Francis G. Ruffin Papers.

3. Clay to James Erwin, February 24, 1825, in Clay, *Papers*, 4:82.

4. Jackson to Lewis, February 14, 1825, in *AJP*, 6:29–30.

5. Jackson to Lewis, February 20, 1825, in *AJP*, 6:37.

6. Jackson to Swartwout, February 22, 1825, in *AJP*, 6:40–43.

7. *Louisiana Gazette*, February 28, 1825, March 1, 1825; Joseph G. Tregle Jr., *Louisiana in the Age of Jackson: A Clash of Cultures and Personalities* (Baton Rouge: Louisiana State University Press, 1999), 170–171.

8. Lynn Hudson Parsons, "In Which the Political Becomes Personal, and Vice Versa: The Last Ten Years of John Quincy Adams and Andrew Jackson," *JER* 23 (Autumn 2003): 426.

9. Johnson quoted in Ratcliffe, *One-Party Presidential Contest*, 256; see Benton, *Thirty Years' View*, 1:47.

10. John Quincy Adams Inaugural Address, March 4, 1825, *Journal of the Executive Proceedings of the Senate of the United States, 1815–1828* (Washington, DC: By Order of the Senate, 1828), 3:431–436.

11. Adams, *Memoirs*, 6:474; William B. Lewis to Lewis Cass, February 28, 1842, Lewis Letters; Eaton to Felix Grundy, April 2, 1826, Felix Grundy Papers, SHC.

12. Nashville *Gazette*, April 16, 1825; *The Microscope*, May 21, 1825; Thomas Hardeman to John Overton, June 24, 1825, in Nicholas P. Hardeman, "Fighting Words from the Frontier: Thomas Hardeman on the Election of 1824–1825," *MHR* 73 (April 1979): 356, 359.

13. Simpson to Jackson, November 3, 1825, Jackson to Simpson, November 23, 1825, editorial notes, Jackson to Coffee, July 23, 1825, August 2, 1825, in *AJP*, 6:92–93, 97, 119–120, 123–124.

14. Lewis Williams to Bartlett Yancey, April 4, 1825, Bartlett Yancey Papers; Nashville *Gazette*, April 16, 1825.

15. Eaton to Grundy, April 2, 1826, Grundy Papers, SHC.

16. Edwin A. Miles, "President Adams' Billiard Table," *NEQ* 45 (March 1972): 31–35; Tobias Watkins to James B. Davis, June 23, 1825, Davis Letters.

17. *New-York Daily Advertiser*, March 5, 6, 1825; Clay to Robert Walsh Jr., February 18, 1825, John Binns to Clay, February 27, 1825, Francis Preston Blair to Clay, March 7,

1825, in Clay, *Papers*, 4:75, 84–85, 91; Jeremiah Mason to Daniel Webster, February 20, 1825, in Webster, *Papers*, 2:28.

18. Jackson to John Coffee, March 2, 1825, John Coffee Family Papers, LOC; Kremer to Jackson, March 8, 1825, in *AJP*, 6:48–49.

19. Clay's Address, March 26, 1825, in Clay, *Papers*, 4:143–165.

20. Clay's Address, March 26, 1825, Clay to James Erwin, February 24, 1825, in Clay, *Papers*, 4:82, 143–165.

21. Jackson to Coffee, April 24, 1825, in *AJP*, 6:65; Eaton to Clay, March 28, 1825, Clay to Eaton, March 30, 1825, Eaton to Clay, March 31, 1825, Clay to Eaton, April 1, 1825, Eaton to Clay, April 2, 1825, Clay to Francis T. Brooke, April 6, 1825, in Clay, *Papers*, 4:191–192, 196–197, 198–202, 207–208, 221.

22. Atwater to Clay, March 16, 1825, Clay to John Sloane, April 22, 1825, Clay to Charles Hammond, May 2, 1825, in Clay, *Papers*, 4:114–115, 282, 318.

23. Desha to Jackson, June 8, 1825, Jackson to Coffee, July 23, 1825, August 2, 1825, in *AJP*, 6:83–84, 92–93, 97.

24. Christopher C. Graham to Clay, August 31, 1825, in Clay, *Papers*, 4:608–609.

25. *Senate Executive Journal*, 18th Cong., 2nd Sess., 441; *Daily National Journal*, March 9, 1825; Remini, *Van Buren and the Making of the Democratic Party*, 91; *Daily National Intelligencer*, March 9, 1825.

26. *Daily National Intelligencer*, March 16, 1825; *NWR*, March 19, 1825.

27. *Pennsylvania Intelligencer*, March 1, 1825; *Truth's Advocate*, July 1828; Parton, *Life of Andrew Jackson*, 3:108.

28. Nashville *Gazette*, April 22, 1825.

29. Editorial note, Jackson's response to Overton and Nashville citizens, April 16, 1825, in *AJP*, 6:62–63.

30. *NWR*, December 27, 1823; *Washington Republican and Congressional Examiner*, December 23, 1824; Jackson to Robert Coleman Foster and William Brady, October 12, 1825, in *AJP*, 6:108–110.

31. Jackson to Robert Coleman Foster and William Brady, October 12, 1825, in *AJP*, 6:108–110; Nashville *Gazette*, October 29, 1825.

32. Editorial note, Robert Coleman Foster to Jackson, October 14, 1825, in *AJP*, 6:105–106, 111–113.

33. Jackson to the Tennessee General Assembly, October 14, 1825, in *AJP*, 6:113–114.

34. Lewis Williams to Bartlett Yancey, April 4, 1825, Willie P. Mangum to Bartlett Yancey, January 15, 1826, Yancey Papers; Hugh Mercer to Clay, April 7, 1825, William Creighton Jr. to Clay, November 14, 1825, in Clay, *Papers*, 4:228, 825; Peterson, *Great Triumvirate*, 146.

35. *Register of Debates in Congress* (Washington, DC: Gales & Seaton, 1825–1837), 2:795; Bemis, *Foundations of American Foreign Policy*, 555; Robert Pierce Forbes, *The Missouri Compromise and Its Aftermath: Slavery and the Meaning of America* (Chapel Hill: University of North Carolina Press, 2007), 191.

36. *Register of Debates*, 7:59–64.

37. James D. Richardson, ed., *A Compilation of the Messages and Papers of the Presidents* (New York: Bureau of National Literature, 1902–1904), 2:299–317.

38. Webster to Jeremiah Mason, December 11, 1825, Mason Papers.

39. Macon to Yancey, December 26, 1824, December 8, 1824, January 29, 1826, Yancey Papers; William E. Dodd, *The Life of Nathaniel Macon* (Raleigh, NC: Edwards & Broughton, 1903).

40. Clay to James Brown, May 9, 1825, in Clay, *Papers*, 4:336; Daniel Walker Howe, *What Hath God Wrought: The Transformation of America, 1815–1848* (New York: Oxford University Press, 2007), 249–250; Calhoun to Mahlon Dickerson, April 7, 1827, quoted in Michael Birkner, *Samuel Southard: Jeffersonian Whig* (Rutherford, NJ: Associated University Presses, 1984), 73.

Chapter 11: Machine

1. Randolph B. Campbell, "The Spanish American Aspect of Henry Clay's American System," *Americas* 24 (July 1967): 10.

2. Jackson to James K. Polk, May 3, 1826, Jackson to John Branch, March 3, 1826, in *AJP*, 6:141, 166; William Gaston to John H. Bryan, April 1, 1826, Gaston Papers; Eaton to William Hamilton, February 26, 1826, Eaton Letters, LOC; *Register of Debates*, 2:402.

3. Massachusetts senator Elijah Mills is quoted in Henry Adams, *John Randolph* (Boston: Houghton Mifflin, 1884), 263.

4. Roberts, "Memoirs," 406; *Register of Debates*, 2:402; John Greenleaf Whittier, *The Poetical Works of John Greenleaf Whittier* (Boston: Ticknor and Fields, 1868), 1:287.

5. Campbell, "Spanish American Aspect," 12; Macon to Bartlett Yancey, March 31, 1826, Yancey Papers.

6. *Register of Debates*, 2:400, 401.

7. Helen McLeod to Donald McLeod, September 1826, McLeod Family Papers, VHS.

8. Seconds' Account, April 10, 1826, Benton to Tucker, July 16, 1826, Henry Clay Family Papers, LOC.

9. John Eaton to Andrew Jackson, May 5, 1826, in *AJP*, 6:169.

10. *United States Telegraph*, March 28, 1826.

11. Adams, *Memoirs*, 7:113; John McDonough, "John Silva Meehan: A Gentleman of Amiable Manners," *Quarterly Journal of the Library of Congress* 33 (January 1976), 4–5; also see William D. Johnston, *History of the Library of Congress* (Washington: Government Printing Office, 1904), 1:213.

12. Editorial note, in *AJP*, 6:92; Chappell, "John Coffee," 144.

13. John Marshall. *The Life of George Washington* (London: Richard Phillips, 1807), 5:655.

14. Paul C. Nagel, *The Lees of Virginia: Seven Generations of an American Family* (New York: Oxford University Press, 1990), 207.

15. Ibid., 206–208.

16. Jackson to Lee, October 7, 1825, in *AJP*, 6:104–105; Smith, *Press, Politics, and Patronage*, 66.

17. Lee to Jackson, July 1, 1826, Jackson Papers, LOC.

18. New York *Evening Post*, July 8, 1826; Albany *Argus*, July 18, 1826; for an analysis of the commemorations in 1826, see Andrew Burstein, *America's Jubilee: A Generation Remembers the Revolution After 50 Years of Independence* (New York: Knopf, 2001).

19. Nagel, *John Quincy Adams*, 312–314; James Traub, *John Quincy Adams, Militant Spirit* (New York: Basic Books, 2016), 335–336.

20. Nathaniel Macon to Bartlett Yancey, December 24, 1826, Yancey Papers; Jackson to Call, July 26, 1826, in *AJP*, 6:191.

21. Felix Grundy's Eulogy, August 3, 1826, *A Selection of Eulogies, Pronounced in the Several States, in Honor of Those Illustrious Patriots and Statesmen, John Adams and Thomas Jefferson* (Hartford, CT: D. F. Robinson and Norton & Russell, 1826), 282–297.

22. Alexandria *Gazette*, July 21, 1826; *Charleston Mercury*, August 25, 1826; *Daily National Journal*, September 2, 1826.

23. Roberts, "Memoirs," 76; *New-York Daily Advertiser*, October 20, 1826.

24. Roberts, "Memoirs," 76.

25. Jackson to Wilson, January 4, 1827, in *AJP*, 6:253.

26. Editorial notes, Robert Butler to Jackson, September 15, 1826, Jackson to John Coffee, September 25, 1826, Jackson to Wilson, January 4, 1827, in *AJP*, 6:197, 210, 211, 216; *Nashville Republican*, October 21, 1826.

27. Southard's account, 1827, Samuel Southard Papers, LOC; Michael Birkner, "The General, the Secretary, and the President: An Episode in the Presidential Campaign of 1828," *THQ* 42 (1983): 244.

28. Birkner, "General, the Secretary, and the President," 245; editorial note, in *AJP*, 6:227.

29. Jackson to Houston, October 23, 1826, November 22, 1826, in *AJP*, 6:228–230, 235.

30. Houston to Jackson, December 13, 1826, in *AJP*, 6:241.

31. Jackson to Houston, December 15, 1826, in *AJP*, 6:243.

32. Birkner, "General, the Secretary, and the President," 246; Jackson to Livingston, January 30, 1826, Houston to Jackson, January 13, 1827, in *AJP*, 6:135, 262.

33. Jackson to Houston, January 5, 1827, in *AJP*, 6:254.

34. Jackson to Southard, January 5, 1827, Eaton to Jackson, January 27, 1827, in *AJP*, 6:255, 267–268.

35. Birkner, "General, the Secretary, and the President," 245–246; Southard to Jackson, February 9, 1827, Jackson to Southard, March 6, 1827, in *AJP*, 6:288–289, 296–299; Houston to Jackson, February 15, 1827, in Jackson, *Correspondence*, 6:494; Southard to Jackson, February 27, 1827, Southard Papers, LOC.

36. *United States Telegraph*, June 29, 1827; *Daily National Journal*, July 9, 1827.

37. John Taliaferro to Southard, May 5, 1827, Southard Papers; Birkner, "General, the Secretary, and the President," 246.

Chapter 12: Ink

1. Parsons, *Birth of Modern Politics*, 135; Andrew Jackson Donelson to Edward G. W. Butler, Butler Family Papers, HNOC; Macon to Bartlett Yancey, January 29, 1826, Yancey Papers.

2. Smith, *Press, Politics, and Patronage*, 75; John Eaton to Andrew Jackson, May 5, 1826, in *AJP*, 6:168–169; Donald B. Cole, *Vindicating Andrew Jackson: The 1828 Election and the Rise of the Two-Party System* (Lawrence: University Press of Kansas, 2009), 49; Henry Eckford to Henry Clay, May 29, 1827, Joseph Durham Learned to Henry Clay, September 27, 1827, Joseph M. Street to Henry Clay, October 16, 1827, in Clay, *Papers*, 6:606–607, 1079, 1153–1154.

3. Peterson, *Great Triumvirate*, 146; Henry Clay to James Brown, March 27, 1827, in Clay, *Papers*, 6:361; Edward L. Mayo, "Republicanism, Antipartyism, and Jacksonian Party Politics: A View from the Nation's Capital," *American Quarterly* 31 (Spring 1979): 8.

4. Amos Kendall, *Autobiography of Amos Kendall*, ed. William Stickney (New York: Peter Smith, 1949), 115.

5. James D. Daniels, "Amos Kendall: Kentucky Journalist, 1815–1829," *FCHQ* 52 (January 1978): 50–51; Richard B. Latner, "A New Look at Jacksonian Politics," *JAH* 61 (March 1975): 944; Kendall to Clay, January 21, 1825, Kendall to Clay, February 19,

1825, Kendall to Clay, March 23, 1825, in Clay, *Papers*, 4:35, 77, 136; Kendall, *Autobiography*, 265; Elbert B. Smith, *Francis Preston Blair* (New York: Free Press, 1980), 30.

6. Kendall to Clay, April 28, 1825, October 4, 1825, in Clay, *Papers*, 4:305–306, 718–720; Heidler and Heidler, *Henry Clay*, 203.

7. Donald B. Cole, *Martin Van Buren and the American Political System* (Princeton, NJ: Princeton University Press, 1984), 156; Donald B. Cole, *A Jackson Man: Amos Kendall and the Rise of American Democracy* (Baton Rouge: Louisiana State University Press, 2004), 93–97; Johnson to Jackson, October 27, 1826, Johnson to Martin Van Buren, September 22, 1827, in James A. Padgett, ed., "The Letters of Colonel Richard M. Johnson of Kentucky," *RKHS* 39 (July 1941): 265, 268.

8. Kirwan, *Crittenden*, 76; Kendall to F. G. Flügel, April 4, 1839, Kendall Papers; Kendall to Clay, September 26, 1827, October 10, 1827, in Clay, *Papers*, 6:1071–1072, 1031–1032; Cole, *Amos Kendall*, 101, 107.

9. Clay to Blair, January 8, 1825, in Clay, *Papers*, 4:9.

10. Frank F. Mathias, "Henry Clay and His Kentucky Power Base," *RKHS* 78 (Spring 1980): 130; Heidler and Heidler, *Henry Clay*, 204–205.

11. Kendall to Clay, February 6, 1828, May 28, 1828, Charles S. Todd to Clay, February 18, 1828, Clay to Francis Brooke, June 5, 1828, in Clay, *Papers*, 7:81, 104, 306–307, 326; Albany *Argus*, March 14, 1828.

12. Frederic Hudson, *Journalism in the United States, 1690–1872* (New York: Harper, 1873), 246.

13. Allen Walker Read, "Could Andrew Jackson Spell?" *American Speech* 38 (October 1963): 188–194; *United States Telegraph*, March 25, 1828.

14. Albany *Argus*, June 6, 1828; Charles Hammond to Henry Clay, November 5, 1827, in Clay, *Papers*, 6:1232–1233; Jill LePore, *A Is for American: Letters and Other Characters in the Newly United States* (New York: Knopf, 2002), 112.

15. W. Stephen Belko, *The Invincible Duff Green: Whig of the West* (Columbia: University of Missouri Press, 2006), 128; Smith, *Press, Politics, and Patronage*, 62–63; Eric Eriksson, "Official Newspaper Organs and the Campaign of 1828," *THQ* 8 (January 1925): 240; Smith, *First Forty Years*, 212; Florence Weston, *The Election of 1828* (Washington, DC: Ruddick, 1938), 157.

16. Green to Jackson, July 8, 1827, in *AJP*, 6:354–355.

17. Green to Buchanan, October 12, 1826, in Buchanan, *Works*, 1:217.

18. Buchanan to Green, October 16, 1826, in Buchanan, *Works*, 1:218–219.

19. Buchanan to Jackson, May 29, 1825, Jackson to Buchanan, June 25, 1825, in Buchanan, *Works*, 1:138–140; Jackson to Buchanan, April 8, 1826, Buchanan to Jackson, September 21, 1826, Jackson to Buchanan, January 29, 1827, in *AJP*, 6:162–163, 212–213, 271–272.

20. Baltimore *American Farmer*, July 12, 1822; Catherine Clinton, *The Plantation Mistress: Women's World in the Old South* (New York: Pantheon, 1982), 41–42; *Daily National Intelligencer*, July 7, 12, 1825.

21. *National Journal*, June 19, 1827; Alexandria *Gazette*, November 24, 1827.

22. Buchanan to Ingham, July 12, 1827, Buchanan to *Lancaster Journal*, August 8, 1827, in Buchanan, *Works*, 1:260, 263–267; editorial note, Jackson to Beverley, June 5, 1827, Jackson to Buchanan, July 15, 1827, Jackson to the Public, July 18, 1827, Buchanan to Jackson, August 10, 1827, in *AJP*, 6:329–330, 359–366, 373–374.

23. Clay "To the Public," July 4, 1827, Clay to Southard, July 9, 1827, in Clay, *Papers*, 6:728–730, 755.

24. New York *American*, August 14, 1827; *Charleston City Gazette*, September 13, 1827; Clay to James Erwin, August 4, 1827, Joseph F. Caldwell to Clay, August 8, 1827, Daniel Webster to Clay, August 22, 1827, Clay to Gales and Seaton, August 6, 1827, in Clay, *Papers*, 6:850, 852–853, 863, 949; Robert V. Remini, *The Election of Jackson* (Philadelphia: J. B. Lippincott, 1963), 65.

25. Edward Ingersoll to Henry Clay, August 11, 1827, Clay to Charles Hammond, October 30, 1827, in Clay, *Papers*, 6:888, 1204; New York *American*, August 14, 1827; B. McLaughlin to William K. Ruffin, August 20, 1827, in J. G. deR. Hamilton, ed., *The Papers of Thomas Ruffin* (Raleigh, NC: Edwards and Broughton, 1928–1920), 1:402; Benjamin Estill to James Barbour, August 26, 1827, Tyler Family Scrapbook, W&M.

26. Jackson to Amos Kendall, September 4, 1827, in *AJP*, 6:388; Belko, *Duff Green*, 121–122.

27. Jackson to William B. Lewis, September 1, 1827, article "General Jackson," c. September 4, 1827, in *AJP*, 6:387, 391; John C. Calhoun to John McLean, September 3, 1827, in Calhoun, *Papers*, 10:306.

28. Jackson to John Coffee, September 29, 1827, in *AJP*, 6:394.

29. *NWR*, October 6, 1827. See William B. Lewis to Andrew Jackson, February 17, 1845, Lewis Letters.

30. Richard B. Maury to Henry Clay, August 14, 1827, in Clay, *Papers*, 6:902; William B. Lewis to Andrew Jackson, February 17, 1845, Lewis Letters.

31. Daniel Webster to William Gaston, May 31, 1826, Gaston Papers, SHC; Halperin, "Pro-Jackson Sentiment," 226.

32. *Argus of Western America*, August 8, 1827.

33. Jabez D. Hammond to Clay, August 29, 1827, editorial note, in Clay, *Papers*, 6:974.

34. Lynn W. Turner, *William Plumer of New Hampshire, 1759–1850* (Chapel Hill: University of North Carolina Press, 1962), 325–327; Claude G. Bowers, *The Party Battles of the Jackson Period* (Chautauqua, NY: Chautauqua Press, 1923), 32.

35. Isaac Hill, *Brief Sketch of the Life, Character, and Services of Major General Andrew Jackson* (Concord, NH: Mann, Hoag, 1828), note 6; *Daily National Intelligencer*, January 22, 1828; Donald B. Cole, *Jacksonian Democracy in New Hampshire, 1800–1851* (Cambridge, MA: Harvard University Press, 1970), 75; Pasley, "Tyranny of Printers," 355–356.

36. An Old Republican Soldier (Abel Parker) to Isaac Hill, January 8, 1828, Joel Parker Papers, 1685–1939, MHS.

37. Simon Newton Dexter North, *History and Present Condition of the Newspaper and Periodical Press of the United States: With a Catalogue of the Publications of the Census Year* (Washington, DC: Government Printing Office, 1884), 47; Daniel Webster to Henry Clay, March 25, 1827, Clay to Webster, October 25, 1827, in Clay, *Papers*, 6:354–355, 1187; Remini, *Election of Jackson*, 77, 81.

38. William Ellery Channing, *The Works of William Ellery Channing, D.D.* (Boston: American Unitarian Association, 1875), 139; New York *American*, November 9, 1827; Smith, *Press, Politics, and Patronage*, chaps. 5–6; Hudson, *Journalism in the United States*; John Tebbel and Sarah Miles Watts, *The Press and the Presidency: From George Washington to Ronald Reagan* (New York: Oxford University Press, 1985), 63–73; John Nerone, *The Culture of the Press in the Early Republic* (New York: Garland, 1989); Richard B. Kielbowicz, *News in the Mail: The Press, Post Office, and Public Information, 1700–1860s* (New York: Greenwood, 1989), chap. 4; Carol Sue Humphrey, *The Press of the Young Republic, 1783–1833* (Westport, CT: Greenwood, 1996), chap. 8.

Chapter 13: Magician

1. Van Buren, *Autobiography*, 109.

2. William C. Yates, *Joseph C. Yates: First Mayor of Schenectady, Seventh Governor of New York* (n.p., 1936; Microform ed., Salt Lake City: Genealogical Society of Utah, 1941); George Rogers Howell and John H. Munsell, *History of Schenectady New York from 1662 to 1886* (New York: Munsell and Co., 1886), 79–80.

3. Van Buren, *Autobiography*, 113–114.

4. David Crockett, *A Narrative of the Life of David Crockett* (Philadelphia: Carey and Hart, 1834), 85–86.

5. Van Buren, *Autobiography*, 28.

6. Silbey, *Van Buren*, xiii.

7. Silbey, *Van Buren*, 39; Peterson, *State Constitutional Conventions of the 1820s*, 126; Cheathem, *Jackson and the Rise of the Democrats*, 95; Michael Wallace, "Changing Concepts of Party in the United States: New York, 1815–1828," *AHR* 74 (1968): 454.

8. Silbey, *Van Buren*, 43.

9. Remini, *Van Buren and the Making of the Democratic Party*, 85–86; George Erving to William H. Crawford, May 23, 1823, Crawford Papers, Duke.

10. Van Buren, *Autobiography*, 157; Silbey, *Van Buren*, 48.

11. Weston, *Election of 1828*, 86; Silbey, *Van Buren*, 47–48; Remini, *Election of Jackson*, 39.

12. Lewis Williams to Newton Cannon, March 13, 1824, Cannon Papers; C. T. Mercer to William Gaston, May 6, 1824, Gaston Papers; Calhoun to Jackson, June 4, 1826, in *AJP*, 6:177–178.

13. Jackson to Calhoun, July 18, 1826, in *AJP*, 6:187–188.

14. Forbes, *Missouri Compromise*, 205; Cole, *1828 Election*, 46.

15. Richard R. John, *Spreading the News: The American Postal System from Franklin to Morse* (Cambridge, MA: Harvard University Press, 1995), 66, 81; Calhoun to McLean, May 29, 1827, in Calhoun, *Papers*, 10:290; John Bailey to John B. Davis, January 3, 1827, February 17, 1827, Davis Letters; Niven, *Calhoun*, 124–125; Gretchen Garst Ewing, "Duff Green, John C. Calhoun, and the Election of 1828," *SCHM*, 79 (April 1978): 130–131.

16. Memorandum of loan to Duff Green, May 20, 1826, in Jackson, *Correspondence*, 3:301; Smith, *Press, Politics, and Patronage*, 64–65; Belko, *Duff Green*, 121; Lowe, "John H. Eaton," 131–132; Eriksson, "Official Newspaper Organs," 233; Green to Calhoun, September 5, 1827, in Calhoun, *Papers*, 10:308; *New-York Daily Advertiser*, January 26, 1827.

17. John Niven, *Martin Van Buren: The Romantic Age of Politics* (New York: Oxford University Press, 1983), 168, 170, 177–178; Houston to Jackson, January 13, 1827, in *AJP*, 6:262; *Scioto Gazette*, April 26, 1827; James Brown to Henry Clay, May 12, 1827, in Clay, *Papers*, 6:544; Remini, *Election of Jackson*, 56, 58–59.

18. Lowe, "John H. Eaton," 135; Van Buren to Jackson, November 4, 1827, in *AJP*, 6:399; Remini, *Election of Jackson*, 61.

19. William B. Lewis to Lewis Cass, February 28, 1842, Lewis Letters. Among the members of the Nashville Central Committee were John Overton (chairman), Felix Grundy, George Washington Campbell, William L. Brown, William Berkeley Lewis, Edward Ward, and Alfred Balch. Also see Cole, *1828 Election*, 73; Clifton, "Life of John Overton," 56–57; Cheathem, *Jackson and the Rise of the Democrats*, 98.

20. Wilentz, *American Democracy*, 242.

21. Remini, *Van Buren and the Making of the Democratic Party*, 59–63.

22. Richmond *Enquirer*, February 21, 26, 1824. Also see Charles H. Ambler, *Thomas Ritchie: A Study in Virginia Politics* (Richmond, VA: Bell Book & Stationary, 1913), 93; Earle, *Jacksonian Antislavery*, 50; Forbes, *Missouri Compromise*, 213–214.

23. Van Buren to Ritchie, January 13, 1827, Van Buren Papers, LOC.

24. Matthew Mason, *Slavery and Politics in the Early American Republic* (Chapel Hill: University of North Carolina Press, 2006), 214.

25. James Hamilton Jr. to Mrs. dePetit, March 21, 1827, James Hamilton Jr. Papers, SHC; Niven, *Van Buren*, 182; Hamilton to Jackson, February 16, 1827, in Jackson, *Correspondence*, 3:344; *New-York Daily Advertiser*, January 26, 1827.

26. Parson, *Election of 1828*, 129–130; Nathaniel Macon to Bartlett Yancey, December 24, 1826, Yancey Papers.

27. Crawford to Bartlett Yancey, December 2, 1827, Lewis Williams to Yancey, December 11, 1827, Yancey Papers; New York *American*, January 15, 1828; Crawford to Van Buren, August 15, 1827, in William Henry Williams, ed., "Ten Letters from William Harris Crawford to Martin Van Buren," *GHQ* 49 (March 1965): 70; Crawford to Hugh Lawson White, May 27, 1827, in Jackson, *Correspondence*, 3:365.

28. Hoffman, *Jackson and North Carolina*, 12–13; Forbes, *Missouri Compromise*, 227.

29. Pasley, *"Tyranny of Printers,"* 390–391; Smith, *Press, Politics, and Patronage*, 65.

30. William G. Shade, *Democratizing the Old Dominion: Virginia and the Second Party System, 1824–1861* (Charlottesville: University Press of Virginia, 1996), 87; Ambler, *Ritchie*, 109–110.

31. James Hamilton Jr. to Andrew Jackson, February 16, 1827, in Jackson, *Correspondence*, 3:344; Tobias Watkins to John B. Davis, June 13, 1827, Davis Letters; Forbes, *Missouri Compromise*, 227–228; Remini, *Election of Jackson*, 81–86; *United States Telegraph*, October 29, 1828.

32. Shade, *Democratizing the Old Dominion*, 87; Harry Ammon, "The Richmond Junto, 1800–1824," *VMHB* 61 (October 1953): 395–418; Rigali, "Election of 1824," 239.

33. James K. Polk to Alfred Flournoy, December 6, 1827, in Polk, *Correspondence*, 1:101; Augustine H. Shepherd to Bartlett Yancey, December 13, 1827, Yancey Papers; Cole, *1828 Election*, 135–136; Edward Pessen, *Jacksonian America: Society, Personality, and Politics* (Homewood, IL: Dorsey Press, 1979), 173; Lowe, "John H. Eaton," 133; Albany *Argus*, September 19, 1828.

34. Van Buren to Thomas Ritchie, January 13, 1827, Van Buren Papers.

35. James S. Chase, *Emergence of the Presidential Nominating Convention, 1789–1932* (Urbana: University of Illinois Press, 1973), 100, 107.

36. *New-York Daily Advertiser*, January 26, 1827.

37. Note of John Thompson Brown, September 25, 1827, Brown, Coulter, Tucker Papers, W&M; William B. Rochester to Henry Clay, August 1, 1827, in Clay, *Papers*, 6:837.

38. Van Buren to Jackson, September 14, 1827, in *AJP*, 6:392–393; Niven, *Van Buren*, 191–192; "Jefferson's Ten Rules" (Brooklyn, NY: Brooklyn Eagle Book, 1900).

39. Van Buren, *Autobiography*, 243.

Chapter 14: Mud

1. Jackson to Coffee, June 20, 1828, in *AJP*, 6:469.

2. Tregle, *Louisiana in the Age of Jackson*, 208; Henry Johnson to Jackson, March 31, 1827, Jackson to Johnson, April 18, 1827, in *AJP*, 6:307, 312; Joseph G. Tregle Jr.,

"Andrew Jackson and the Continuing Battle of New Orleans," *JER* 1 (Winter 1981): 384.

3. Alfred Balch to Jackson, November 26, 1827, in *AJP*, 6:401; Jackson to John Coffee, November 27, 1827, Coffee Family Papers; James A. Hamilton, *Reminiscences of James A. Hamilton; or, Men and Events, at Home and Abroad, during Three Quarters of a Century* (New York: Charles Scribner, 1869), 67–69.

4. Livermore, *Twilight of Federalism*, 127.

5. Alvin Kass, *Politics in New York State, 1800–1830* (New York: Syracuse University Press, 1965), 124; Remini, *Election of Jackson*, 107; Hamilton to Timothy Pickering, July 3, 1828, in Hamilton, *Reminiscences*, 77; Harry L. Watson, *Jacksonian Politics and Community Conflict: The Emergence of the Second Party System in Cumberland County North Carolina* (Baton Rouge: Louisiana State University Press, 1981), 118–119; Remini, *Election of Jackson*, 106; Niven, *Van Buren*, 212; Albany *Argus*, September 30, 1828; Bertram Wyatt-Brown, "Prelude to Abolitionism: Sabbatarian Politics and the Rise of the Second Party System," *JAH* 58 (September 1971): 326.

6. Tregle, "Jackson and the Continuing Battle of New Orleans," 386; Cole, *1828 Election*, 157.

7. Editorial note, in *AJP*, 6:407; Hayne to Jackson, December 27, 1827, in Jackson, *Correspondence*, 3:386.

8. Hamilton, *Reminiscences*, 68–70.

9. Editorial note, in *AJP*, 6:407; Leonard P. Curry, "Election Year—Kentucky, 1828," *RKHS* 55 (1957): 200; Robert Tinkler, *James Hamilton of South Carolina* (Baton Rouge: Louisiana State University Press, 2004), 74; Tregle, "Jackson and the Continuing Battle of New Orleans," 210, 386, 388; Philip Yost Jr. to Henry Clay, January 8, 1828, in Clay, *Papers*, 7:26; Read, "Could Andrew Jackson Spell?" 188.

10. Ronald P. Formisano and Kathleen Smith Kutolowski, "Antimasonry and Masonry: The Genesis of Protest, 1826–1827," *American Quarterly* 29 (1977): 159; Robert V. Remini, "Martin Van Buren and the Tariff of Abominations," *AHR* 63 (July 1958): 904.

11. Ilisevich, "Baldwin and Jackson," 45–46; Eaton to Jackson, March 4, 1828, in *AJP*, 6:428.

12. Charles Hammond to Henry Clay, August 10, 1827, in Clay, *Papers*, 6:877; Klein, *Pennsylvania Politics*, 245.

13. Silbey, *Van Buren*, 52–53; Henry Clay to John J. Crittenden, February 14, 1828, in Clay, *Papers*, 7:95; Weston, *Election of 1828*, 131; Albany *Argus*, May 6, 1828; John Bailey to John B. Davis, March 8, 1828, May 10, 1828, Davis Letters; Remini, "Tariff of Abominations," 909–915.

14. Remini, "Tariff of Abominations," 916; Weston, *Election of 1828*, 131.

15. Richmond *Enquirer*, July 18, 1828; Ambler, *Ritchie*, 114.

16. John Carter to Robert Y. Hayne, October 22, 1828, Hamilton Papers; Albany *Argus*, August 1, 1828; Arthur P. Hayne to Jackson, September 20, 1828, in *AJP*, 6:506–507; Robert Y. Hayne to Jackson, September 3, 1828, in Jackson, *Correspondence*, 3:432–434; Maartje Janse, "'Anti Societies Are Now All the Rage': Jokes, Criticism, and Violence in Response to the Transformation of American Reform, 1825–1835," *JER* 36 (Summer 2016): 260.

17. Albany *Argus*, June 6, 1828, August 8, 1828, September 19, 1828, November 8, 1828; *United States Telegraph*, March 25, 1828; Leonard, *Invention of Party Politics*, 76–77; Weston, *Election of 1828*, 79; Parsons, *Birth of Modern Politics*, 160.

18. Joel H. Silbey, ed., *The American Party Battle: Election Campaign Pamphlets, 1828–1876* (Cambridge, MA: Harvard University Press, 1999), 1:55–82; Roger Fischer, *Tippecanoe and Trinkets Too: The Material Culture of American Presidential Campaigns, 1828–1984* (Urbana: University of Illinois Press, 1988), 1, 9, 15–17; Remini, *Election of Jackson*, 108; Earl to Longacre, May 9, 1828, Ralph E. W. Earl Papers, TSLA; Georgia Brady Bumgardner, "Political Portraiture: Two Prints of Andrew Jackson," *American Art Journal* 18 (Autumn 1986): 86–89.

19. Clay to Thurlow Weed, February 27, 1828, Peter Porter to Clay, March 15, 1828, Clay to Adam Beatty, June 20, 1828, in Clay, *Papers*, 7:124, 164, 357.

20. Adams, *Memoirs*, 7:232; Remini, *Election of 1828*, 45; Francis P. Weisenburger, *The Life of John McLean, a Politician on the United States Supreme Court* (Columbus: Ohio State University Press, 1937), 52–53.

21. Charles H. Bell, *The Bench and Bar of New Hampshire* (Boston: Houghton Mifflin, 1894), 459; Benjamin Perley Poore, *Perley's Reminiscences of Sixty Years* (New York: W. A. Houghton, 1886), 1:28–29; Hannah Cordis Statement, April 29, 1828, Russell Jarvis Papers, LOC.

22. Fred Kaplan, *John Quincy Adams, American Visionary* (New York: Harper, 2014), 427; Jonathan Porter to Russell Jarvis, April 30, 1828, Jarvis Papers, LOC; Report of the Committee, House of Representatives, May 26, 1828, *Register of Debates*, 20th Cong., 1 Sess., 2715–2723.

23. Gideon Morgan Jr. to Clay, April 7, 1827, Clay to Peter Porter, March 20, 1828, Porter to Clay, March 26, 1828, Porter to Clay, April 6, 1828, Clay to Porter, April 12, 1828, in Clay, *Papers*, 6:409, 7:175, 190, 216, 225; Harlan, "Career of Lewis," 25; Jackson to Nathaniel W. Williams, February 23, 1828, Williams to Jackson, February 27, 1828, Jackson to Felix Grundy, in *AJP*, 6:421–424, 495.

24. John Overton to John Coffee, August 16, 1828, John Coffee Papers, TLSA; Affidavit of William B. Lewis, April 3, 1828, Campbell Papers, TLSA; John Eaton to Aaron Ogden Dayton, August 1828, John Henry Eaton Letter, FHS; *United States Telegraph*, October 20, 1828; Jackson to William B. Lewis, July 16, 1828, Jackson to Lewis, August 19, 1828, in *AJP*, 6:482, 500; Eaton to Jackson, August 21, 1828, in Jackson, *Correspondence*, 3:428–429.

25. *Scioto Gazette*, July 12, 1827.

26. Columbus (Ohio) *Monitor*, December 22, 1827; New York *American*, January 15, 1828; Louis McLane to Catherine McLane, May 15, 1824, McLane Papers; Jackson to Richard Keith Call, March 20, 1828, Jackson to John Eaton, March 28, 1828, in *AJP*, 6:433, 441; New York *Evening Post*, January 21, 1828; Susan Decatur to Jackson, January 22, 1828, *Daily Cincinnati Republican*, September 5, 1828.

27. Eaton to Carey, March 11, 1828, Cook War of 1812 in the South Collection, HNOC.

28. Steubenville *Herald*, June 23, 1827.

29. Livermore, *Twilight of Federalism*, 160; Binns to Clay, February 27, 1825, in Clay, *Papers*, 4:84–85; Smith, *Press, Politics, and Patronage*, 74; John Binns, *Recollections of the Life of John Binns* (Philadelphia: Parry and McMillan, 1854), 250, 259; Albany *Argus*, June 6, 1828.

30. "The Friend of Reform and Corruption's Adversary," June 23, 1828, Cook War of 1812 in the South Collection, HNOC; Smith, *Press, Politics, and Patronage*, 71; Albany *Argus*, June 6, 1828, June 24, 1828, August 1, 1828; Coffin Handbill Rebuttal, Dallam Papers, MDHS; Cole, *Jacksonian Democracy*, 75.

31. "Supplemental account of some of the bloody deeds of General Jackson, being a supplement to the 'Coffin handbill.' Cuts of 6 coffins . . . John Taliaferro. Member of Congress from Northern Neck, Va. 1828. Northern Neck, 1828," LOC. The provenance is evident only in a penciled notation that reads, "Published at the offices of the U.S. Telegraph." The image is available online at https://www.loc.gov/item/rbpe.18601400/.

32. *United States Telegraph*, March 25, 1828; *Truth's Advocate*, June 1828, September 1828; Bill of Sale, November 17, 1788, records of land and slave acquisitions, in *AJP*, 1:15, 432–437, editorial note, in *AJP*, 6:468, 486.

33. Jackson to Rachel Jackson, December 17, 1811, editorial notes, in *AJP*, 2:261, 273, 290, 6:469; *United States Telegraph*, March 25, 1828.

34. Thomas E. Waggaman to unknown, November 29, 1828, Tyler Family Scrapbook; editorial notes, in *AJP*, 6:469, 486; *United States Telegraph*, October 29, 1828.

35. Jackson to Andrew Jackson Jr., July 4, 1829, in Jackson, *Correspondence*, 4:49–50; Larry McKee, "The Archaeological Study of Slavery and Plantation Life in Tennessee," *THQ* 59 (Fall 2000): 197.

36. Jackson to Wilson Lumpkin, February 15, 1828, in *AJP*, 6:418.

37. A short narrative of Lyncoya for Major Lee by Andrew Jackson, Charles Carter Lee and Lee Family Papers, UVA.

38. Short Narrative of Lyncoya, Lee Family Papers; New York *Evening Post*, July 3, 1828; *United States Telegraph*, July 3, 1828.

39. *Truth's Advocate*, January 1828, February 1828, March 1828, April 1828, June 1828, September 1828; Hammond to Clay, March 28, 1827; Clay to Daniel Webster, August 19, 1827; Webster to Clay, September 27, 1827, in Clay, *Papers*, 6:369, 921, 1084–1085.

40. William Henry Smith, "Charles Hammond and His Relations to Henry Clay and John Quincy Adams, or Constitutional Limitations and the Contest for Freedom of Speech and the Press," an address delivered before the Chicago Historical Society, May 20, 1884 (Chicago: Chicago Historical Society, 1885) and Jeffrey P. Brown, "The Ohio Federalists, 1803–1815," *JER* 2 (Autumn 1982): 266, 278; Hammond to Clay, April 1824, in Clay, *Papers*, 3:730.

41. Hammond to Clay, October 29, 1827, in Clay, *Papers*, 6:1199; Smith, "Charles Hammond," 47.

42. Hammond to unknown, July 7, 1828, Tobias Watkins to William Gaston, July 15, 1828, Gaston Papers; Pasley, *"Tyranny of Printers,"* 392; James H. Witherspoon to Jackson, April 16, 1825, Affidavit of Thomas Stephenson, July 30, 1828, Certificate of Samuel Mays, July 31, 1828, Statement of Nathaniel Stephenson, August 1, 1828, in Jackson, *Correspondence*, 3:282–283, 416–417; Lewis to Coffee, July 27, 1828, Dyas Collection of John Coffee Papers, TSLA.

43. Clay to Hammond, December 23, 1826, Henry Clay Papers, Duke; Jackson to William B. Lewis, December 12, 1826, Eaton to Jackson, December 22, 1826, in *AJP*, 6:240, 245.

44. Sworn Statement of Elizabeth Craighead, December 2, 1826, Sworn Statement of Sally Smith, December 10, 1826, in Jackson, *Correspondence*, 3:319–323; *Knoxville Register*, June 25, 1827.

45. Norma Basch, "Marriage, Morals, and Politics in the Election of 1828," *JAH* 80 (December 1993): 896–897; Klein, *Pennsylvania Politics*, 249.

46. *United States Telegraph*, July 7, 1827; Jackson to Peter Force et al., June 1827, Green to Jackson, July 8, 1827, Jackson to Green, August 13, 1827, in *AJP*, 6:351, 354–355, 375; Hammond to Clay, March 28, 1827, in Clay, *Papers*, 6:369.

47. Clifton, "Overton as Jackson's Friend," 31–32; Basch, "Marriage, Morals, and Politics," 908–912; Rachel Jackson to Elizabeth Courts Love Watson, July 18, 1827, in *AJP*, 6:367.

Chapter 15: Triumph

1. Ralph Ketcham, *Presidents Above Party: The First American Presidency, 1789–1829* (Chapel Hill: University of North Carolina Press, 1984), 154.

2. Van Buren to Hamilton, August 8, 1828, in Hamilton, *Reminiscences*, 78; Cole, *1828 Election*, 179; Parsons, *Birth of Modern Politics*, 180, 184; G. Sweeny to John Hooe, October 29, 1828, Papers of John Hooe, UVA.

3. Lewis to Van Buren, August 8, 1828, Van Buren Papers; Cole, *Van Buren*, 173–174; Niven, *Van Buren*, 213–214; Richard M. Johnson to Van Buren, September 25, 1828, in Padgett, "Letters of Colonel Richard M. Johnson," 273; Weston, *Election of 1828*, 173–174.

4. Clay to Sloane, November 12, 1828, Clay to Adam Beatty, November 13, 1828, Clay to Francis Brooke, November 18, 1828, in Clay, *Papers*, 7:535–536, 541.

5. Jackson to John Coffee, November 24, 1828, in Jackson, *Correspondence*, 3:447; James K. Polk to Jackson, December 5, 1828, in Polk, *Correspondence*, 1:213; Samuel Smith et al. to Jackson, December 4, 1828, in *AJP*, 6:538.

6. Rachel Jackson to Louise Moreau Davezac de Lassy Livingston, December 1, 1828, John Eaton to Rachel Jackson, December 7, 1828, in *AJP*, 6:536–537, 543.

Epilogue

1. Robert V. Remini, *Andrew Jackson and the Course of American Freedom, 1822–1832* (New York: Harper & Row, 1981), 153–154; Horn, *The Hermitage*, 134; Charles Havens Hunt, *Life of Edward Livingston* (New York: D. Appleton and Company, 1864), 319.

2. Rachel Jackson to Elizabeth Courts Love Watson, July 18, 1827, in *AJP*, 6:368.

3. *Nashville Republican*, December 26, 1828. The obituary notice that contains this description was most likely written by John Overton; Jackson to Jean Baptiste Plauche, December 27, 1828, in *AJP*, 6:547.

4. Jackson to Francis Preston Blair, December 18, 1828, Jackson to Richard Keith Call, December 22, 1828, in *AJP*, 6:546.

5. Remini, *Jackson and the Course of American Freedom*, 153–154; Horn, *The Hermitage*, 134.

6. Van Buren, *Autobiography*, 231.

7. Ibid.

8. Ibid., 232.

9. David S. Heidler and Jeanne T. Heidler, "'Not a Ragged Mob': The Inauguration of 1829," *White House History* 15 (Fall 2004): 14–23.

10. Van Buren, *Autobiography*, 232.

11. John Overton to Ralph E. W. Earl, September 1, 1829, quoted in Frances Clifton, "The Life of John Overton," 57.

INDEX

JEANNE T. HEIDLER is professor emerita of
history at the United States Air Force Academy.
She and her husband, DAVID S. HEIDLER, have
collaborated on numerous books, including the
critically acclaimed *Henry Clay: The Essential
American* and the award-winning *Washington's
Circle: The Creation of the President*. They live in
Colorado Springs, Colorado.